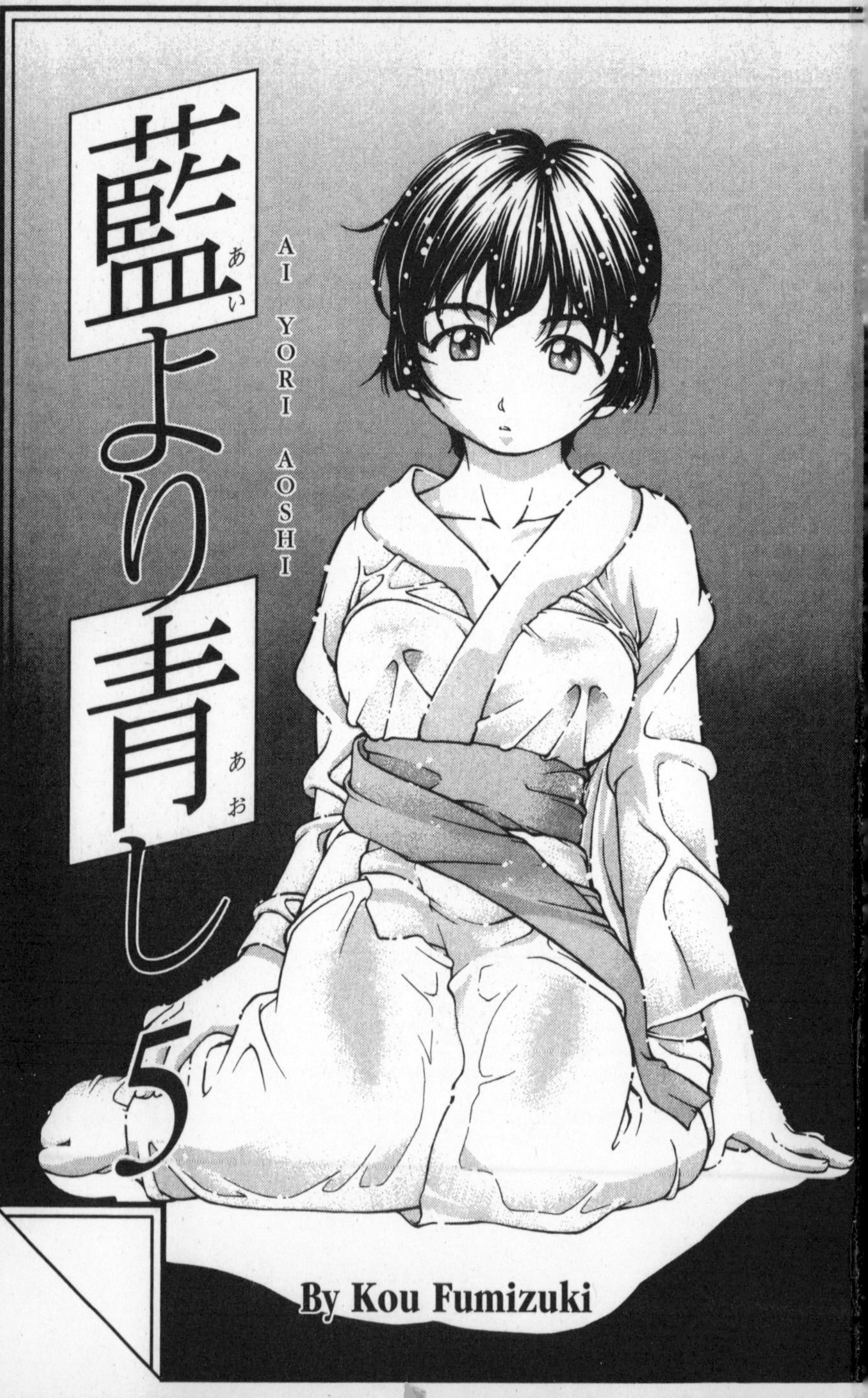
藍より青し 5
あい
あお
AI YORI AOSHI
By Kou Fumizuki

Ai Yori Aoshi Vol. 5
written by Kou Fumizuki
illustrated by Kou Fumizuki

Translation - Alethea Nibley & Athena Nibley
Copy Editor - Kathy Schilling
English Adaptation - Jamie Rich
Retouch and Lettering - Patrick Tran
Graphic Designer - James Dashiell
Production Artist - Yoohae Yang
Cover Design - Gary Shum

Editor - Jake Forbes
Digital Imaging Manager - Chris Buford
Pre-Press Manager - Antonio DePietro
Production Managers - Jennifer Miller and Mutsumi Miyazaki
Art Director - Matt Alford
Managing Editor - Jill Freshney
VP of Production - Ron Klamert
President and C.O.O. - John Parker
Publisher and C.E.O. - Stuart Levy

A **TOKYOPOP**® Manga

TOKYOPOP Inc.
5900 Wilshire Blvd. Suite 2000
Los Angeles, CA 90036

E-mail: info@TOKYOPOP.com
Come visit us online at www.TOKYOPOP.com

ISBN: 1-59182-649-7

First TOKYOPOP printing: September 2004
10 9 8 7 6 5 4 3 2 1
Printed in the USA

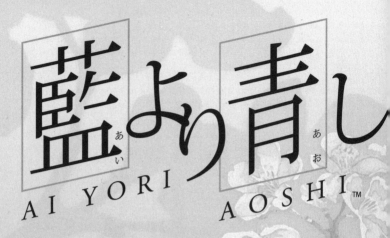

AI YORI AOSHI™

VOLUME 5

STORY & ART
BY
KOU FUMIZUKI

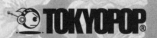

TOKYOPOP®

HAMBURG // LONDON // LOS ANGELES // TOKYO

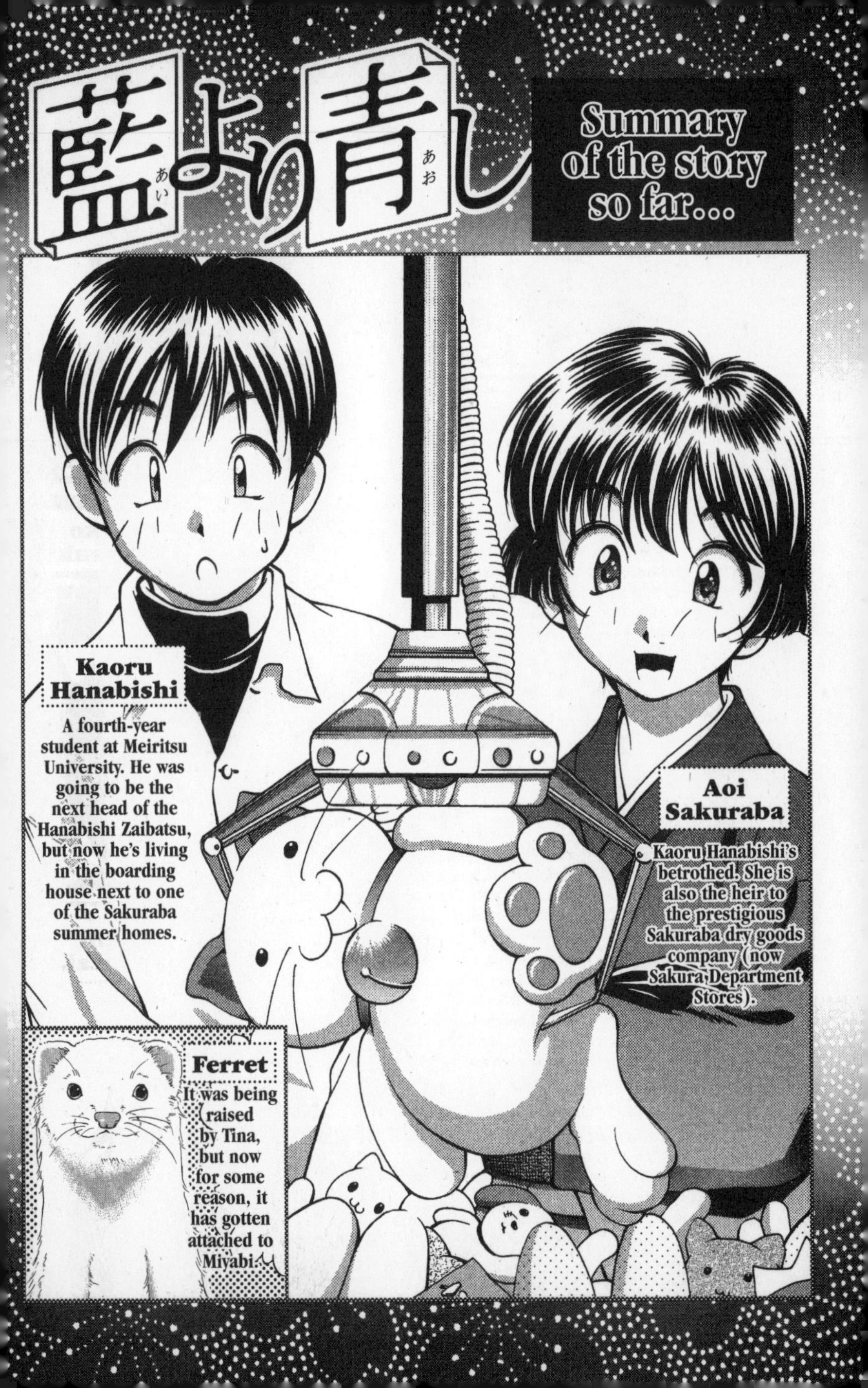

藍より青し
Summary of the story so far...
Kaoru Hanabishi
A fourth-year student at Meiritsu University. He was going to be the next head of the Hanabishi Zaibatsu, but now he's living in the boarding house next to one of the Sakuraba summer homes.
Aoi Sakuraba
Kaoru Hanabishi's betrothed. She is also the heir to the prestigious Sakuraba dry goods company (now Sakura Department Stores).
Ferret
It was being raised by Tina, but now for some reason, it has gotten attached to Miyabi.

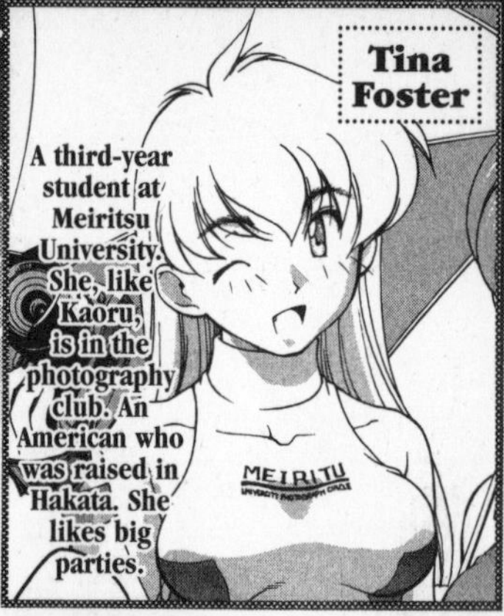
Tina Foster
A third-year student at Meiritsu University. She, like Kaoru, is in the photography club. An American who was raised in Hakata. She likes big parties.
MEIRITU

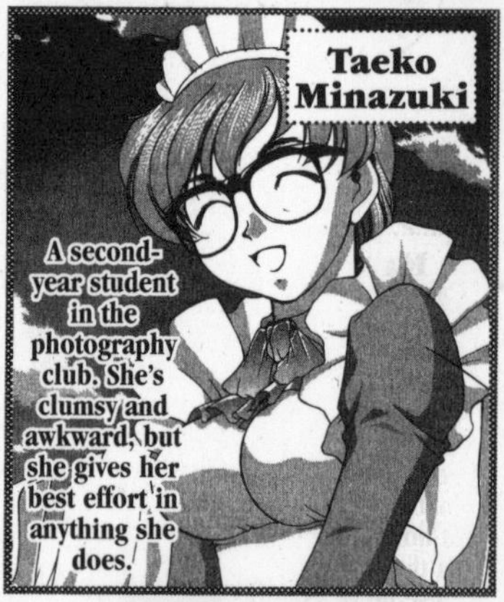
Taeko Minazuki
A second-year student in the photography club. She's clumsy and awkward, but she gives her best effort in anything she does.

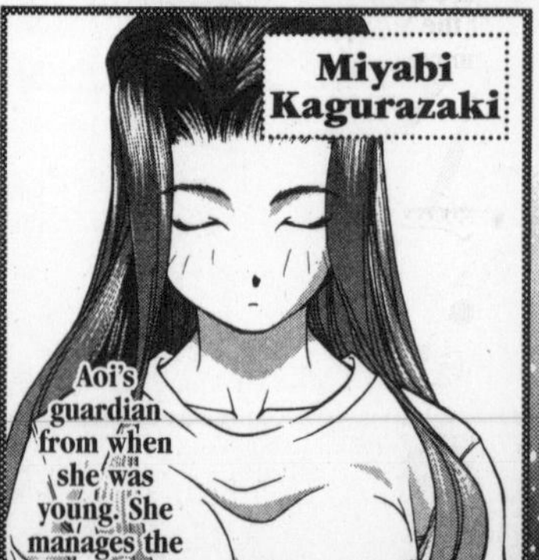
Miyabi Kagurazaki
Aoi's guardian from when she was young. She manages the lives of Aoi and Kaoru.

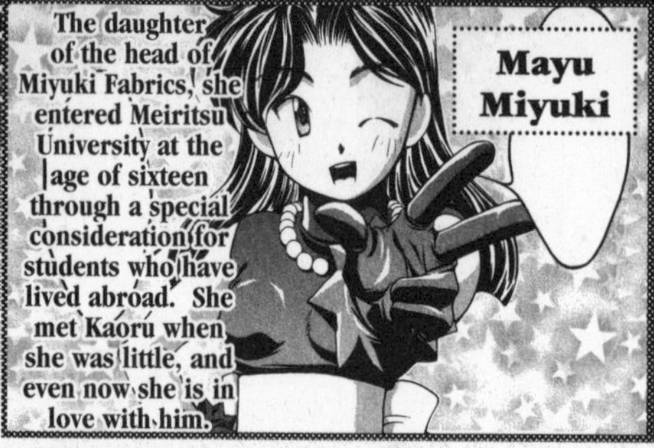
Mayu Miyuki
The daughter of the head of Miyuki Fabrics, she entered Meiritsu University at the age of sixteen through a special consideration for students who have lived abroad. She met Kaoru when she was little, and even now she is in love with him.

Kaoru Hanabishi was torn away from his mother when he was very young and raised as the heir of the Hanabishi Zaibatsu; however, he found he was unable to endure the harsh responsibilities placed on him, and he ran away from home to live by himself. He continued life in this fashion right up until the arrival of Aoi Sakuraba, who had been his betrothed and who loved him for eighteen years. Kaoru was blown away by her devotion, but her request for him to go back to the Hanabishi was the one thing he could not do. Aoi recognized the pain this caused Kaoru, so she decided to leave her own family, the Sakuraba, instead. Rather than lose her daughter, Aoi's mother conceded to allow the two of them to live together.

The couple moved to a western-style house that had previously been one of the Sakuraba's summer homes, and they now share the estate with Aoi's guardian, Miyabi Kagurazaki. There is a catch, though--while Aoi and Miyabi live in the main house, Kaoru has to live in the boarding house adjacent to it.

Shortly after, Tina Foster and Taeko Minazuki, members of Kaoru's photography club, moved into the boarding house, as well. Tina, a native speaker of the Hakata dialect (having been raised in Hakata since she was five), moved in when she saw a fake flyer that Miyabi had posted to make people believe they were running a boarding house for real, as opposed to the two lovers living there illegitimately; Taeko, having been fired from her previous job as a housekeeper, joined the household to be its housekeeper. In order to avoid creating a scandal for the Sakuraba family, Aoi must keep up the pretense that she is Kaoru's landlady, and not his fiancée.

More than a year has passed since they moved onto that estate, and Kaoru has become a college senior. Also, Mayu Miyuki has returned to Japan from England. She had met Kaoru when she was young. He was a high school student at the time, and ever since, she secretly held a faint love for him in her heart. This fact is having more than a small effect on the relationship between Kaoru and Aoi.

藍より青し 5

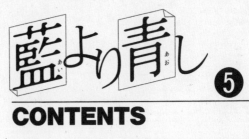

CONTENTS

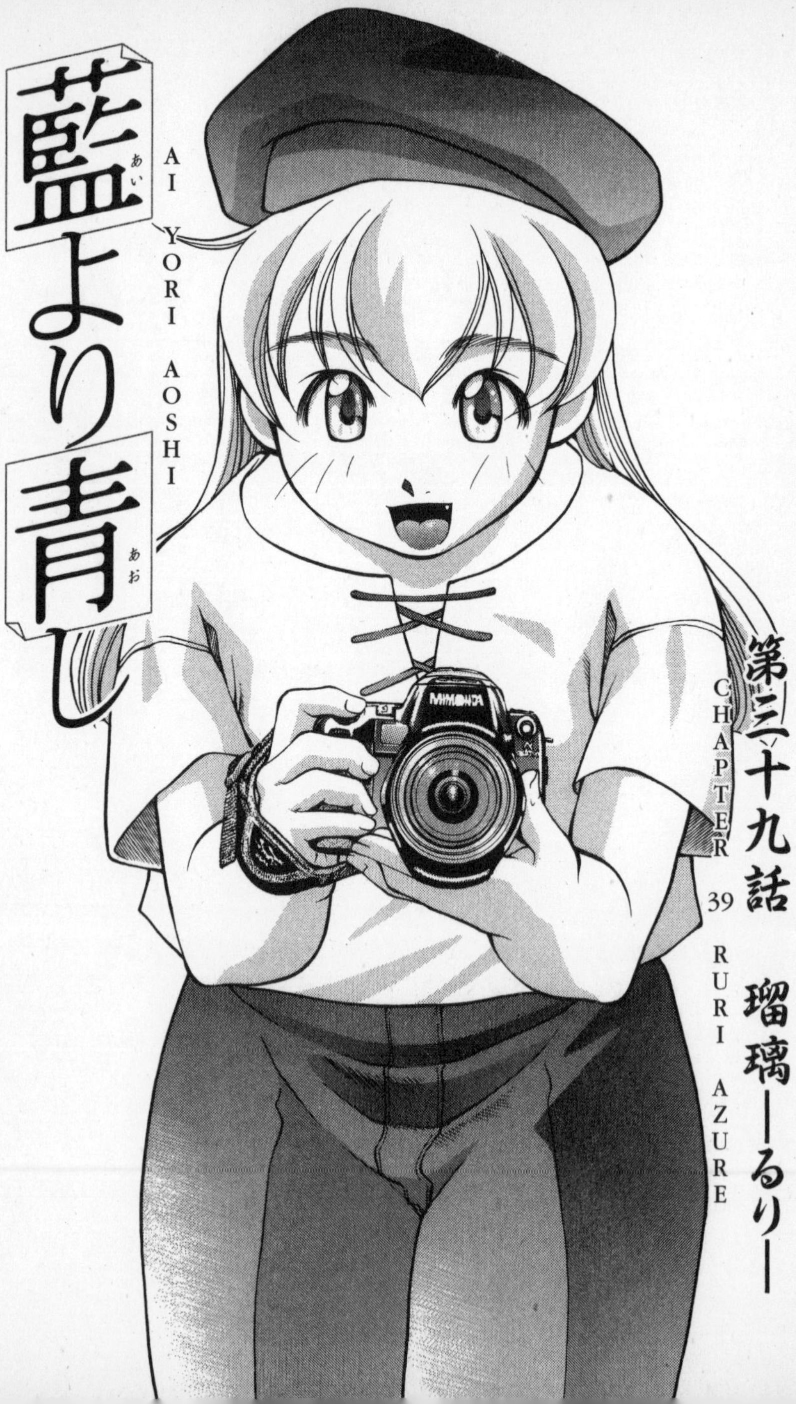
藍より青し
AI YORI AOSHI
第三十九話
CHAPTER 39
瑠璃—るり—
RURI AZURE

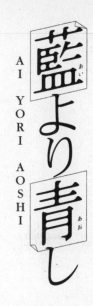

藍より青し

AI
YORI
AOSHI

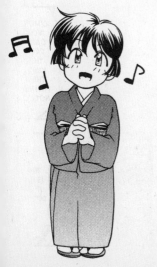

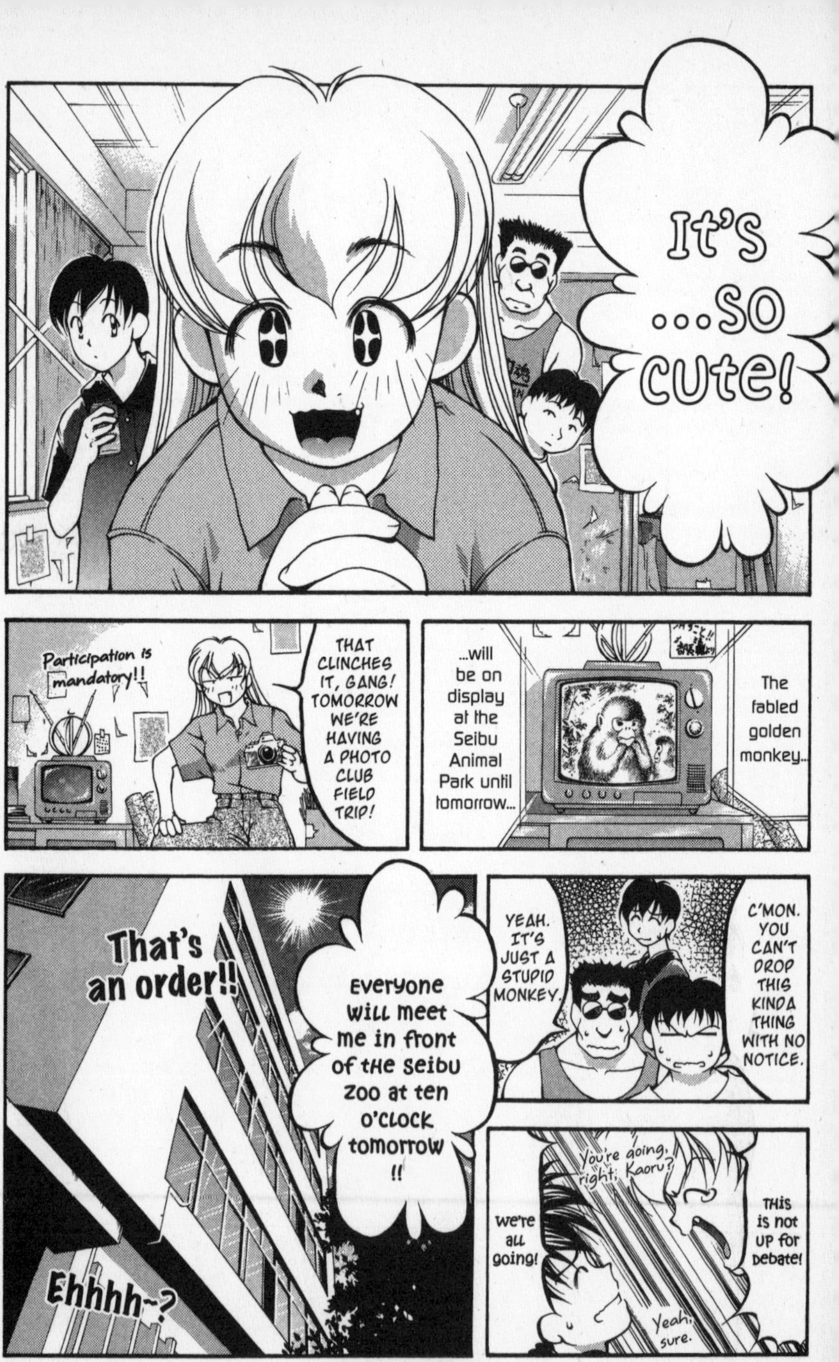
It's ...so cute!
The fabled golden monkey...
...will be on display at the Seibu Animal Park until tomorrow...
THAT CLINCHES IT, GANG! TOMORROW WE'RE HAVING A PHOTO CLUB FIELD TRIP!
Participation is mandatory!!
C'MON. YOU CAN'T DROP THIS KINDA THING WITH NO NOTICE.
YEAH. IT'S JUST A STUPID MONKEY.
THIS is not UP for Debate!
You're going, right, Kaoru?
We're all going!
Yeah, sure.
Everyone will meet me in front of the Seibu zoo at ten o'clock tomorrow !!
That's an order!!
Ehhhh~?

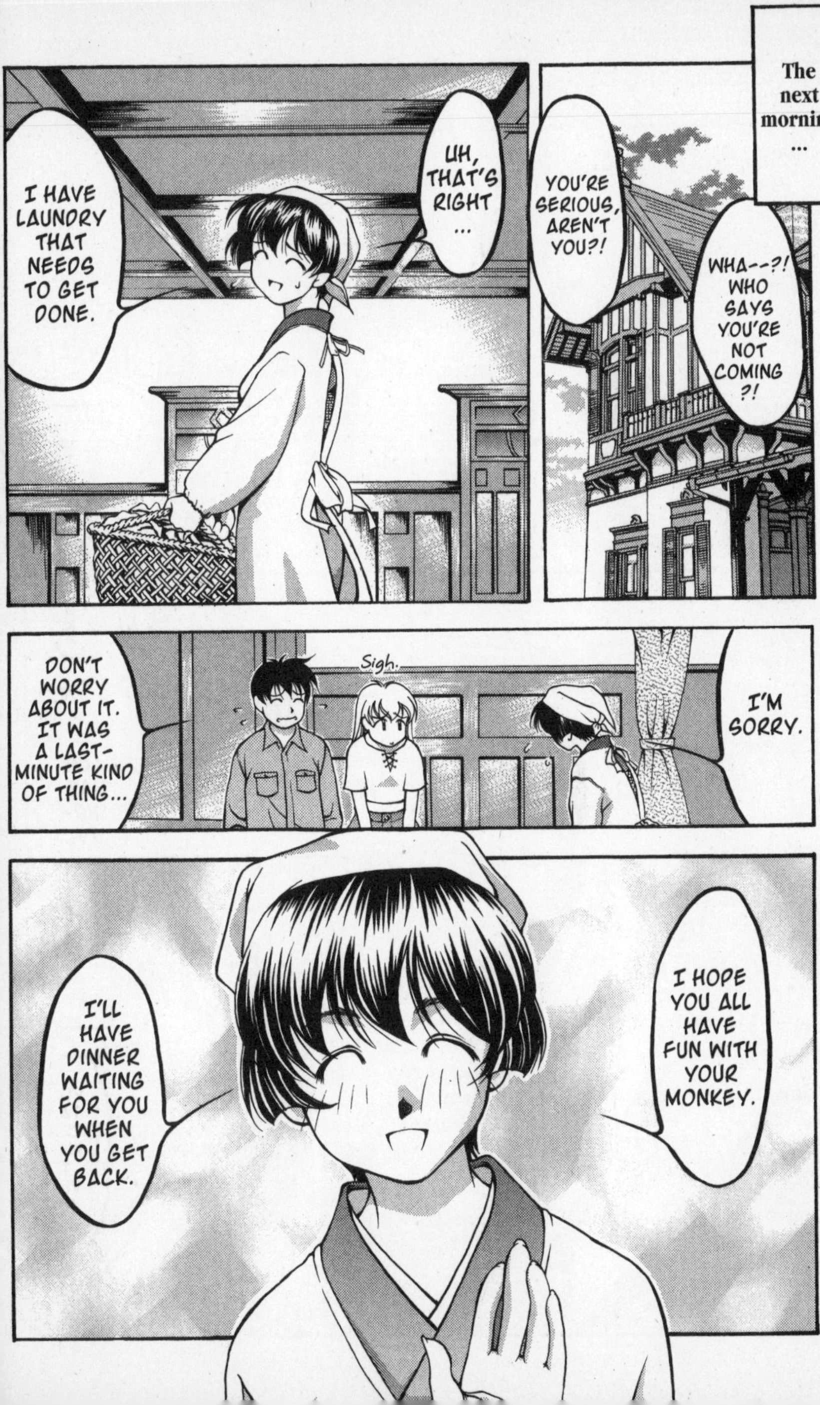
The next morning ...
WHA--?! WHO SAYS YOU'RE NOT COMING ?!
YOU'RE SERIOUS, AREN'T YOU?!
UH, THAT'S RIGHT ...
I HAVE LAUNDRY THAT NEEDS TO GET DONE.
I'M SORRY.
Sigh.
DON'T WORRY ABOUT IT. IT WAS A LAST-MINUTE KIND OF THING...
I HOPE YOU ALL HAVE FUN WITH YOUR MONKEY.
I'LL HAVE DINNER WAITING FOR YOU WHEN YOU GET BACK.

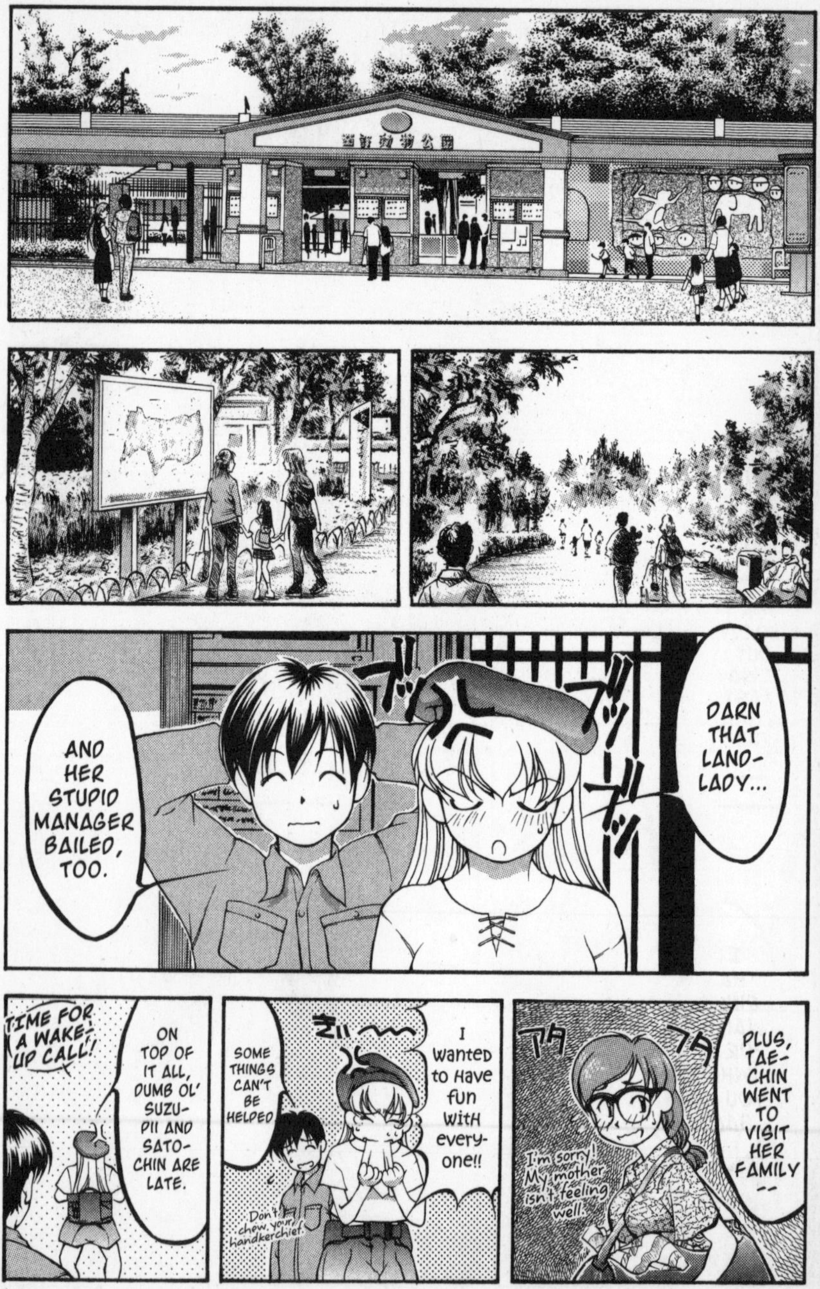
DARN THAT LAND-LADY...
AND HER STUPID MANAGER BAILED, TOO.
アタ フタ
PLUS, TAE-CHIN WENT TO VISIT HER FAMILY --
I'm sorry! My mother isn't feeling well.
I wanted to have fun with every-one!!
SOME THINGS CAN'T BE HELPED
Don't chew your handkerchief.
ON TOP OF IT ALL, DUMB OL' SUZU-PII AND SATO-CHIN ARE LATE.
TIME FOR A WAKE-UP CALL!

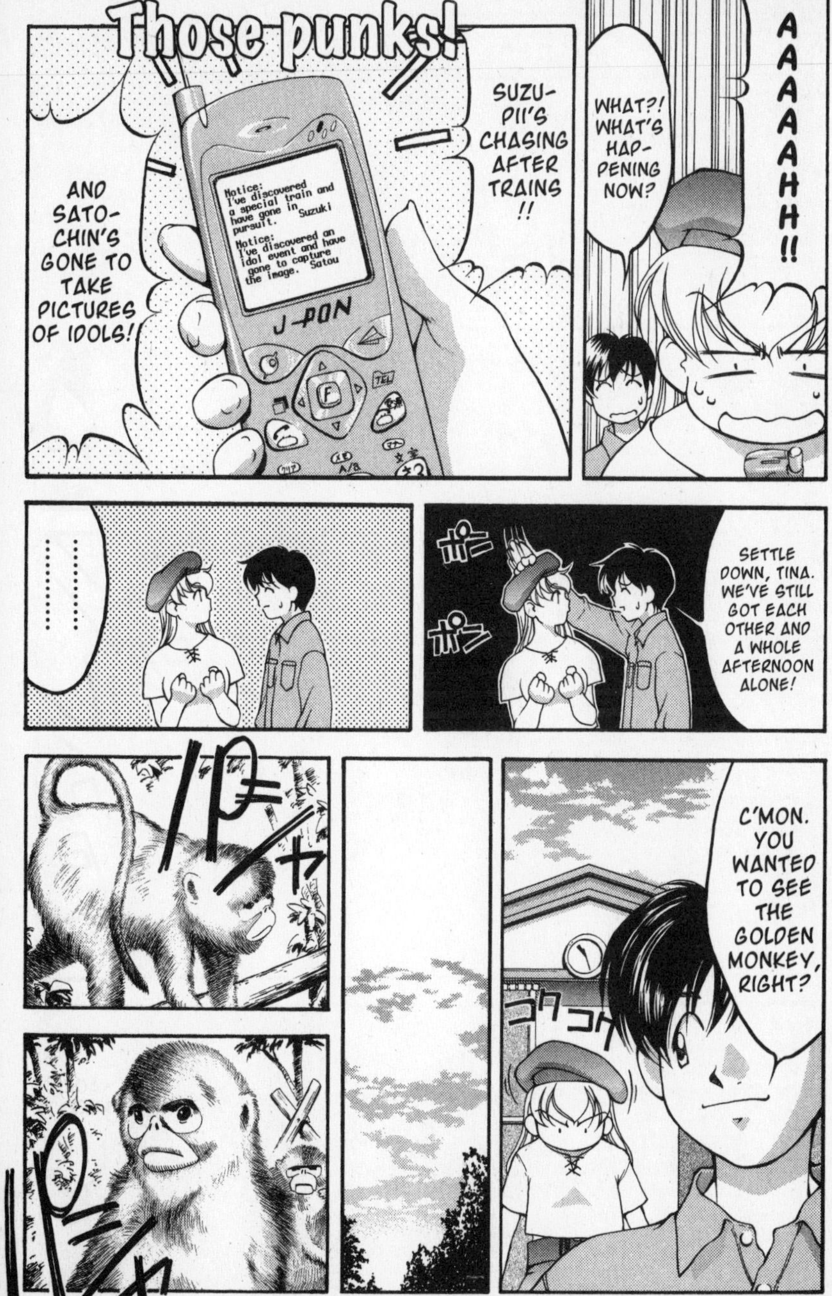
AAAAAAAHH!!
WHAT?! WHAT'S HAPPENING NOW?
Those punks!
SUZU-PII'S CHASING AFTER TRAINS!!
Notice: I've discovered a special train and have gone in pursuit. Suzuki
Notice: I've discovered an idol event and have gone to capture the image. Satou
J-PON
AND SATO-CHIN'S GONE TO TAKE PICTURES OF IDOLS!
SETTLE DOWN, TINA. WE'VE STILL GOT EACH OTHER AND A WHOLE AFTERNOON ALONE!
ポン
ポン
......
C'MON. YOU WANTED TO SEE THE GOLDEN MONKEY, RIGHT?

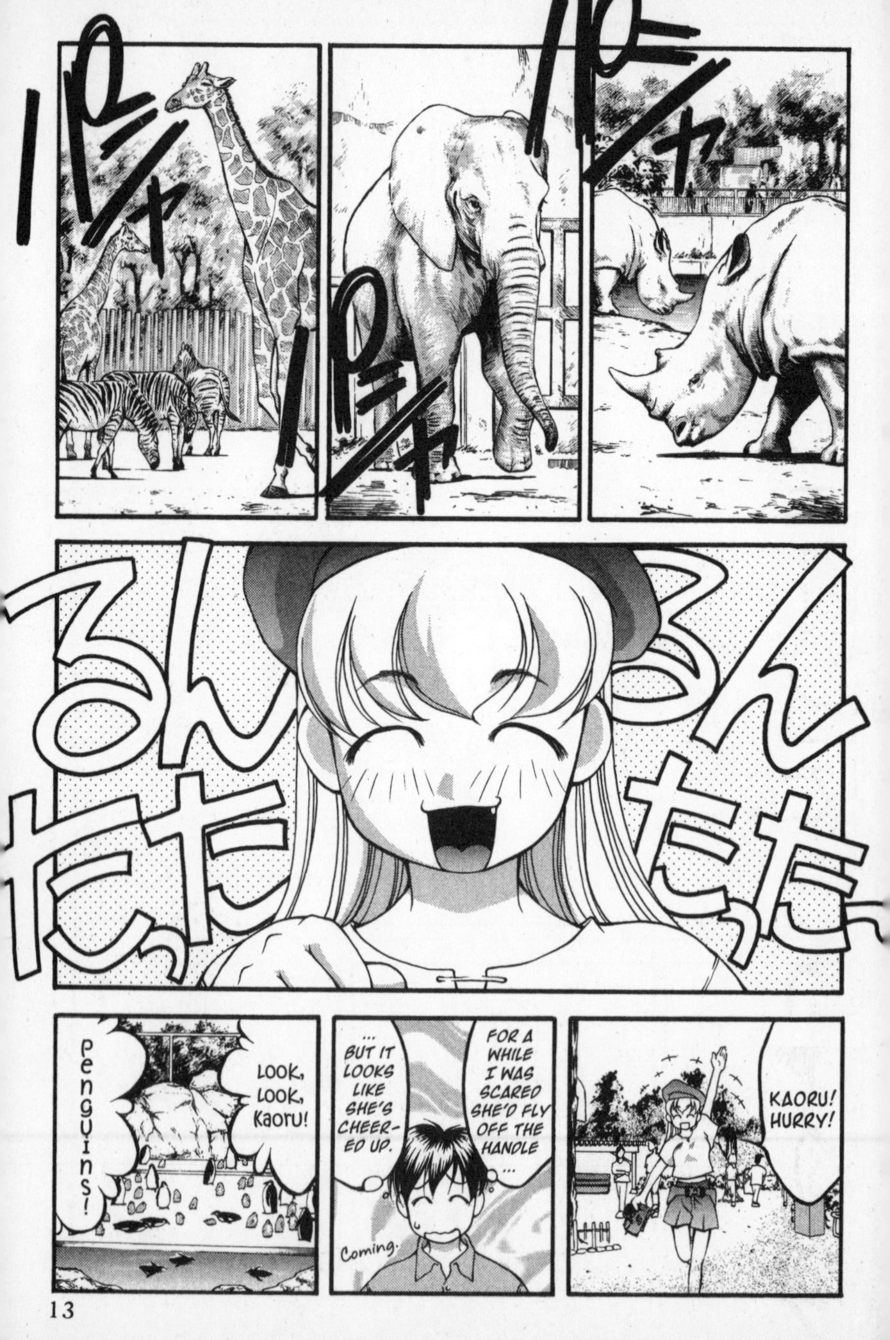
パシャ
パシャ
パシャ
るんるん たったー
るんるん たった
KAORU! HURRY!
FOR A WHILE I WAS SCARED SHE'D FLY OFF THE HANDLE ...
... BUT IT LOOKS LIKE SHE'S CHEER-ED UP.
Coming.
LOOK, LOOK, Kaoru!
Penguins!

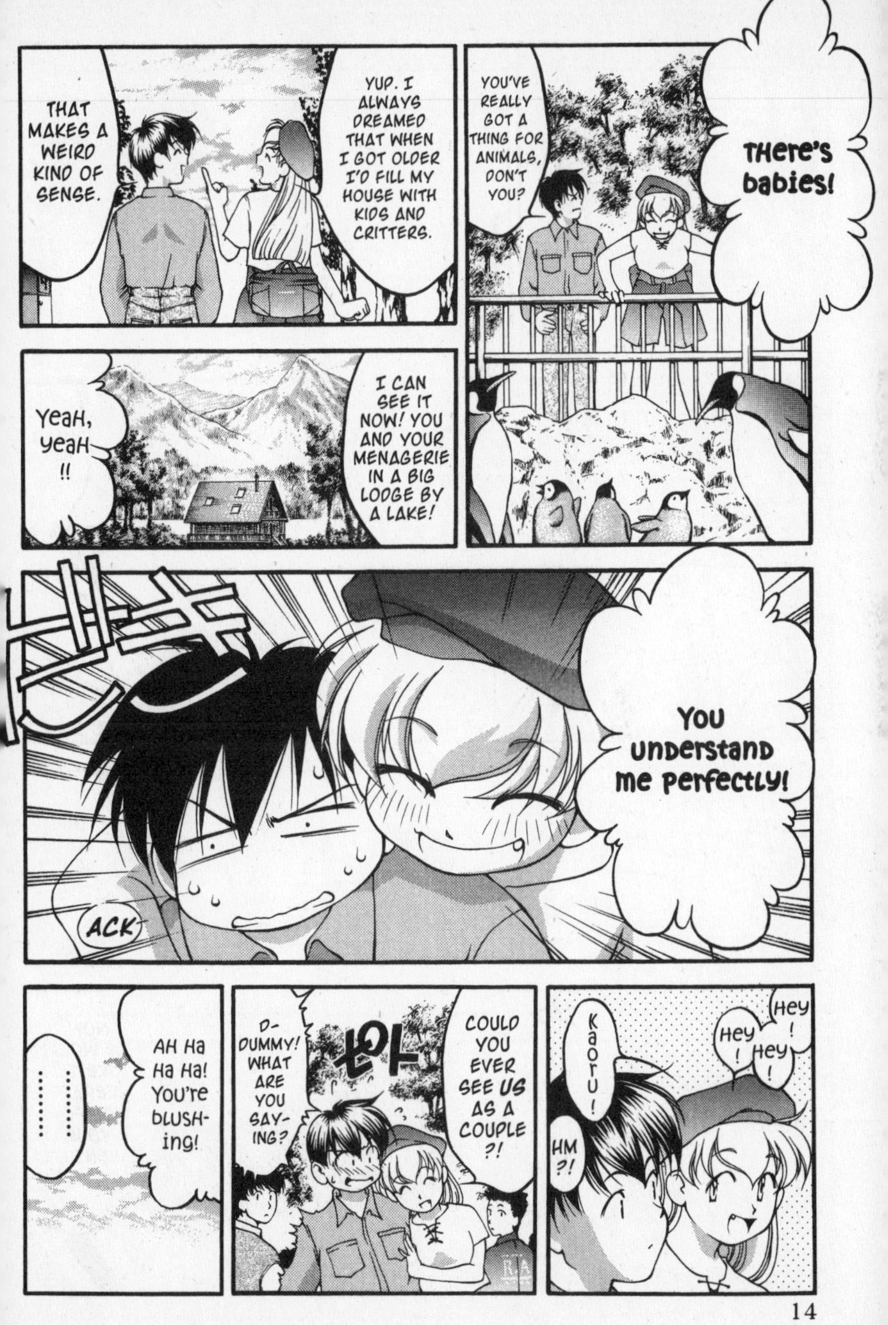
There's babies!
You've really got a thing for animals, don't you?
Yup. I always dreamed that when I got older I'd fill my house with kids and critters.
That makes a weird kind of sense.
I can see it now! You and your menagerie in a big lodge by a lake!
Yeah, yeah!!
You understand me perfectly!
ACK
Hey! Hey! Hey!
Kaoru!
HM?!
Could you ever see us as a couple?!
D-dummy! What are you saying?
Ah ha ha ha! You're blush-ing!
......

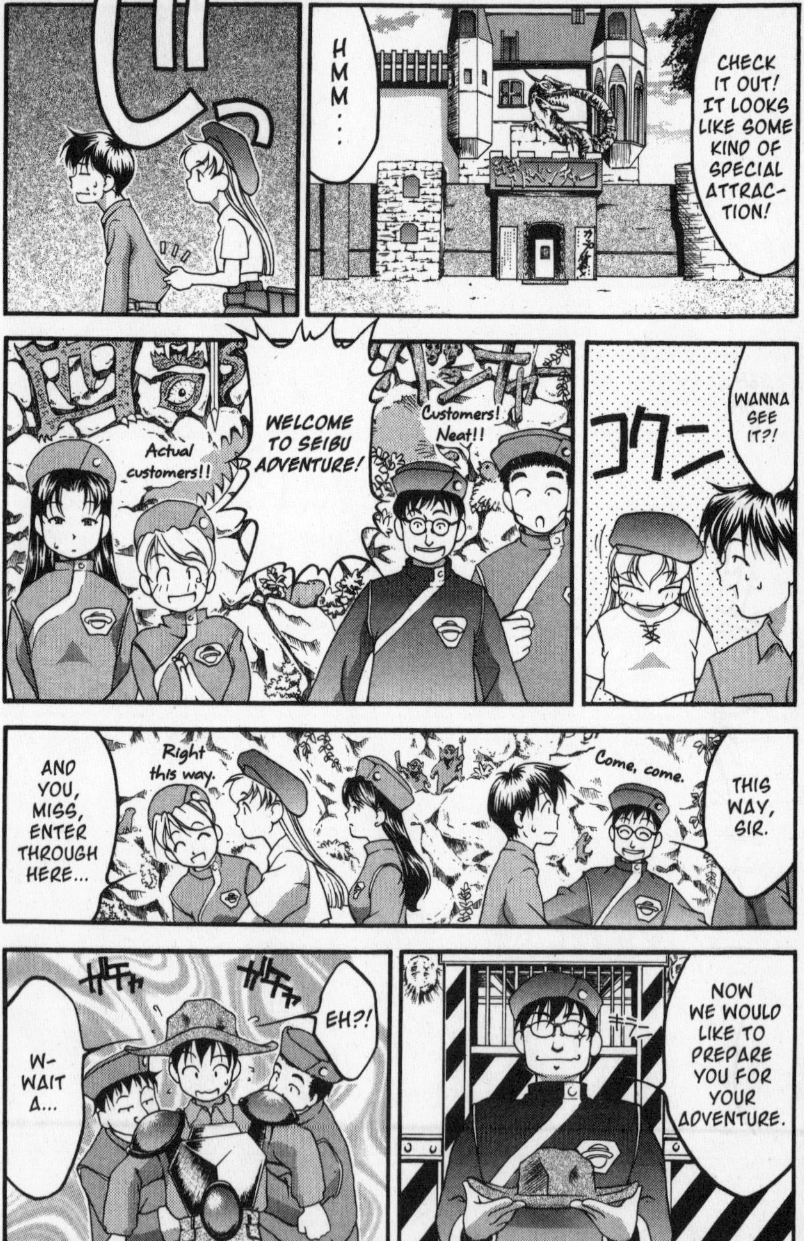

CHECK IT OUT! IT LOOKS LIKE SOME KIND OF SPECIAL ATTRACTION!
HMM...
じっ
WANNA SEE IT?!
コクン
Customers! Neat!!
WELCOME TO SEIBU ADVENTURE!
Actual customers!!
THIS WAY, SIR.
Come, come.
Right this way.
AND YOU, MISS, ENTER THROUGH HERE...
NOW WE WOULD LIKE TO PREPARE YOU FOR YOUR ADVENTURE.
EH?!
W-WAIT A...

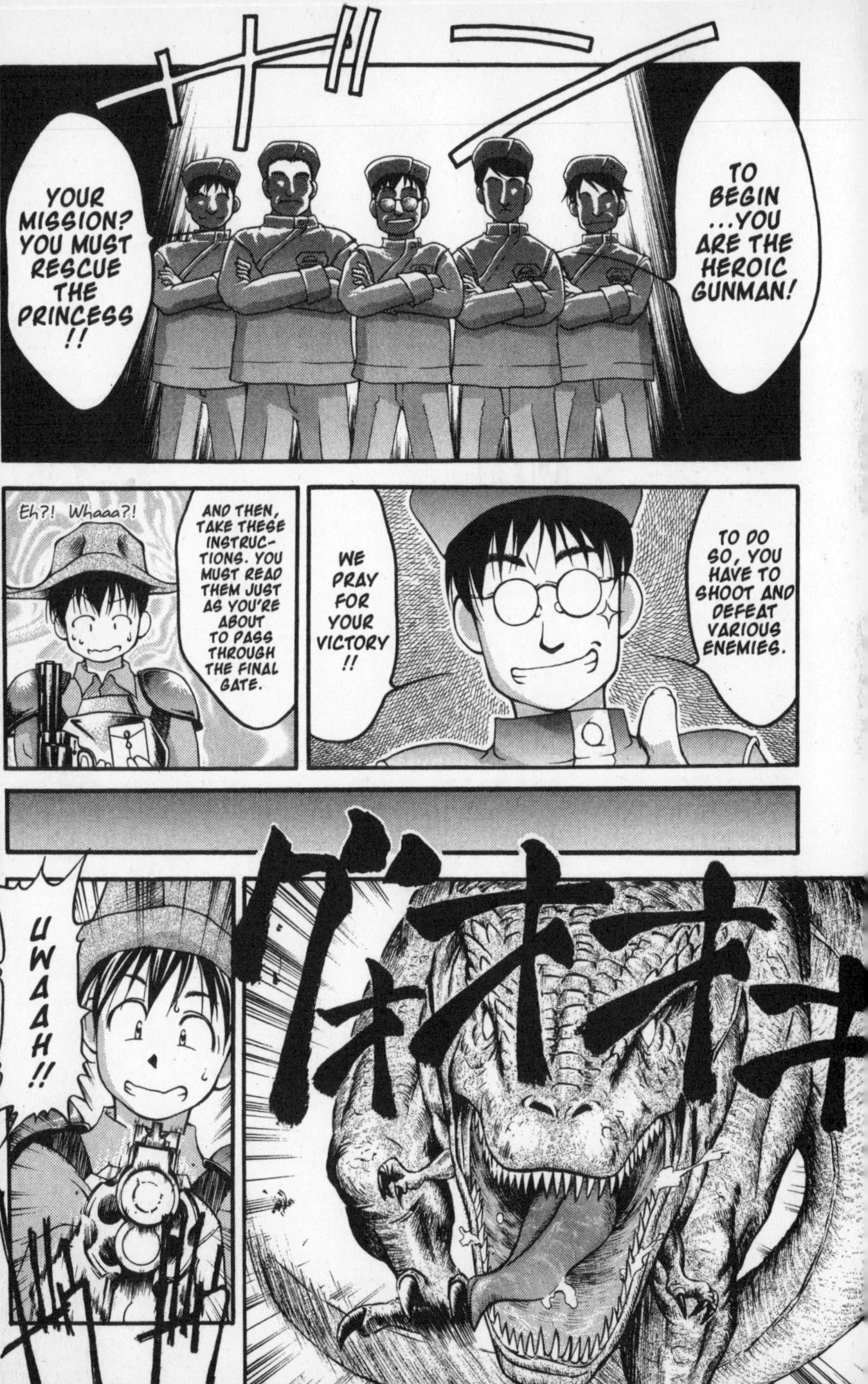
TO BEGIN ...YOU ARE THE HEROIC GUNMAN!
YOUR MISSION? YOU MUST RESCUE THE PRINCESS!!
TO DO SO, YOU HAVE TO SHOOT AND DEFEAT VARIOUS ENEMIES.
WE PRAY FOR YOUR VICTORY!!
AND THEN, TAKE THESE INSTRUC-TIONS. YOU MUST READ THEM JUST AS YOU'RE ABOUT TO PASS THROUGH THE FINAL GATE.
Eh?! Whaaa?!
UWAAAH!!

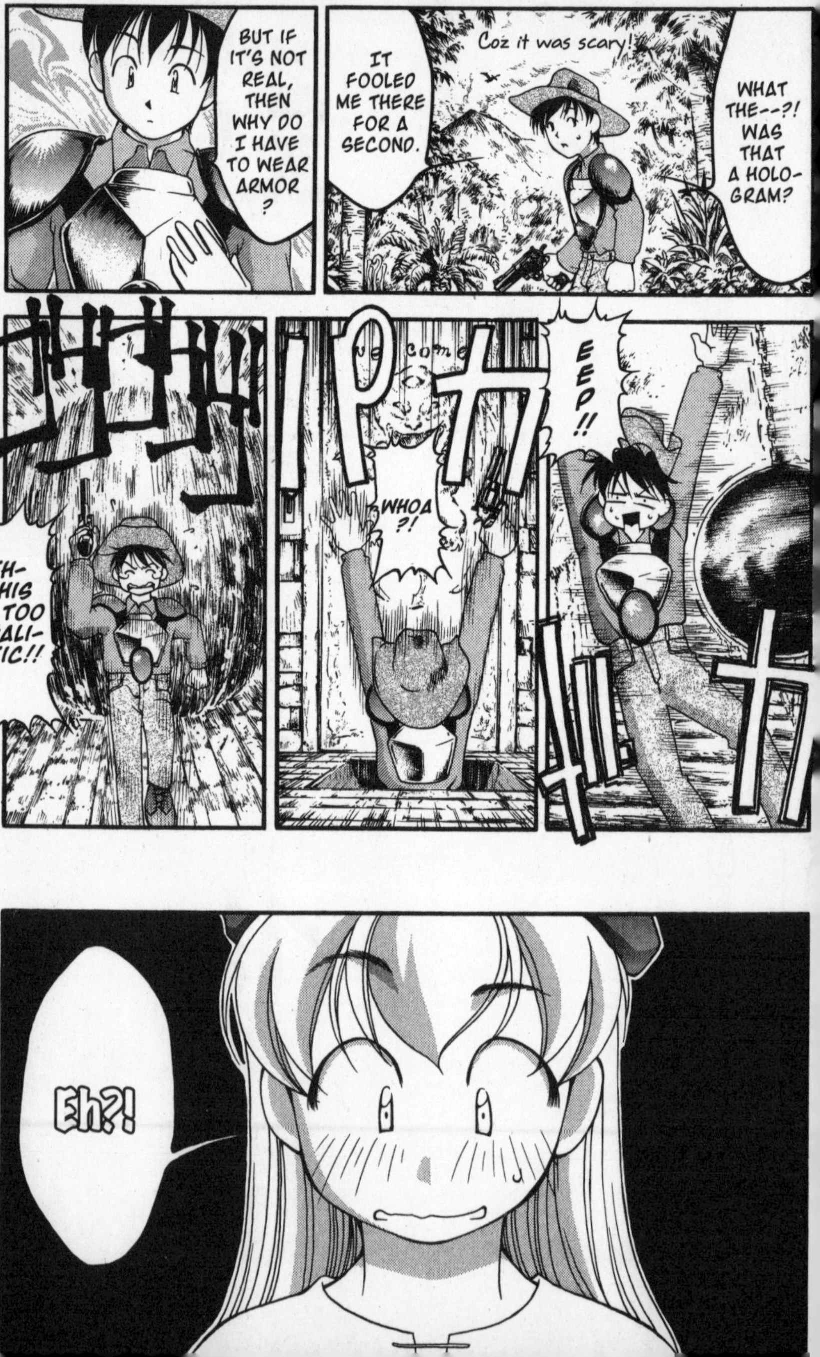
WHAT THE--?! WAS THAT A HOLOGRAM?
Coz it was scary!
IT FOOLED ME THERE FOR A SECOND.
BUT IF IT'S NOT REAL, THEN WHY DO I HAVE TO WEAR ARMOR?
EEP!!
パカ
WHOA?!
TH-THIS IS TOO REALISTIC!!
Eh?!

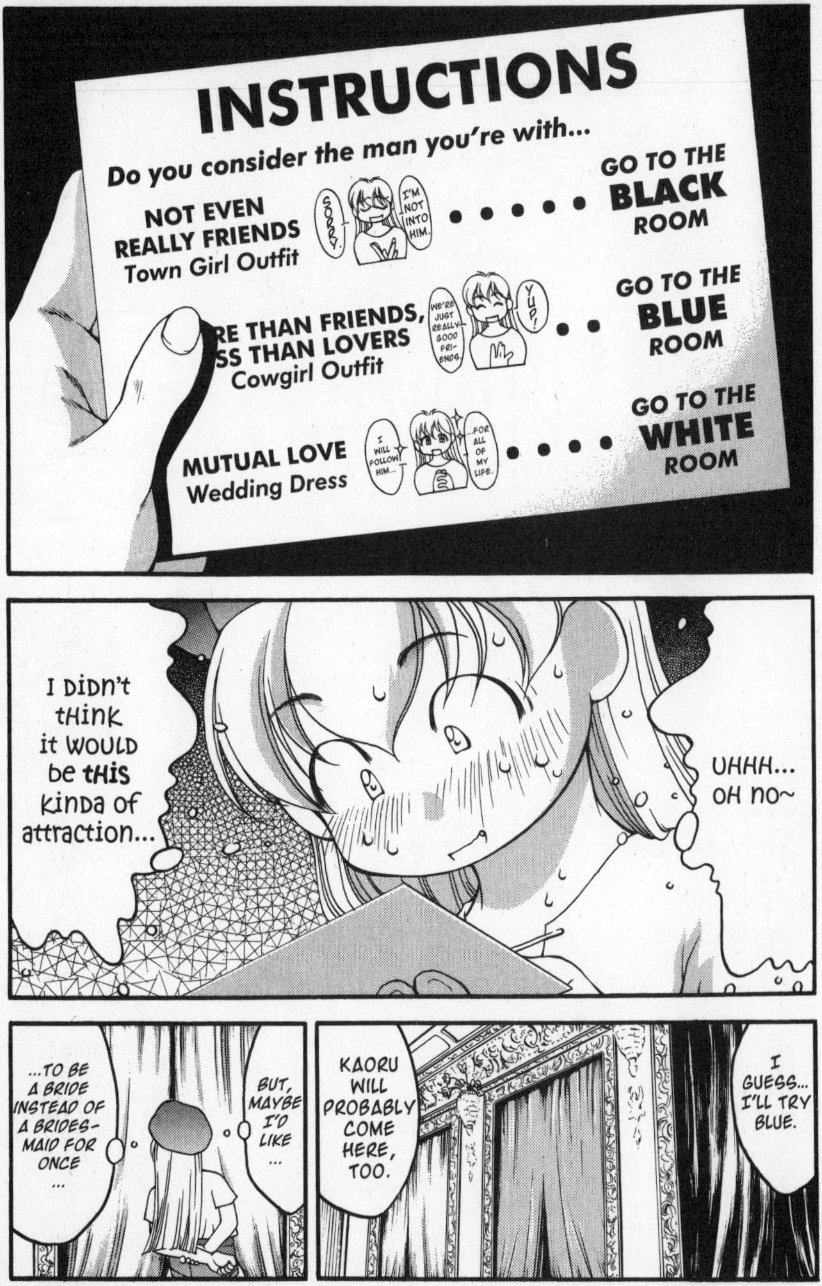
INSTRUCTIONS
Do you consider the man you're with...
NOT EVEN REALLY FRIENDS
Town Girl Outfit
SORRY.
I'M NOT INTO HIM.
GO TO THE BLACK ROOM
RE THAN FRIENDS,
SS THAN LOVERS
Cowgirl Outfit
YUP!
WE'RE JUST REALLY GOOD FRI-ENDS.
GO TO THE BLUE ROOM
MUTUAL LOVE
Wedding Dress
...FOR ALL OF MY LIFE.
I WILL FOLLOW HIM...
GO TO THE WHITE ROOM
UHHH... OH no~
I DIDN'T think it WOULD be tHIS kinda of attraction...
I GUESS... I'LL TRY BLUE.
KAORU WILL PROBABLY COME HERE, TOO.
BUT, MAYBE I'D LIKE ...
...TO BE A BRIDE INSTEAD OF A BRIDES-MAID FOR ONCE ...

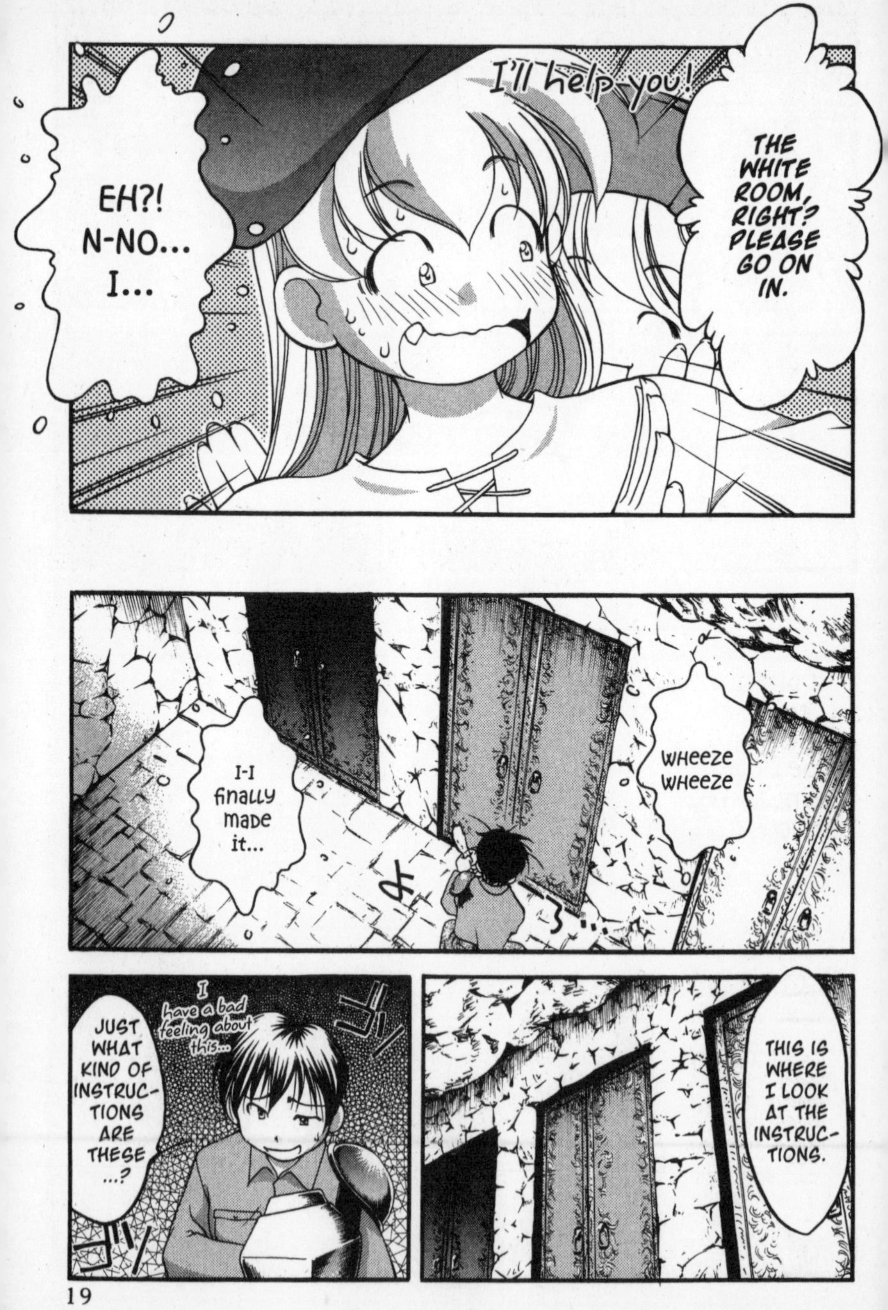
THE WHITE ROOM, RIGHT? PLEASE GO ON IN.
I'll help you!
EH?! N-NO... I...
WHEEZE WHEEZE
I-I finally made it...
THIS IS WHERE I LOOK AT THE INSTRUCTIONS.
I have a bad feeling about this...
JUST WHAT KIND OF INSTRUC-TIONS ARE THESE ...?

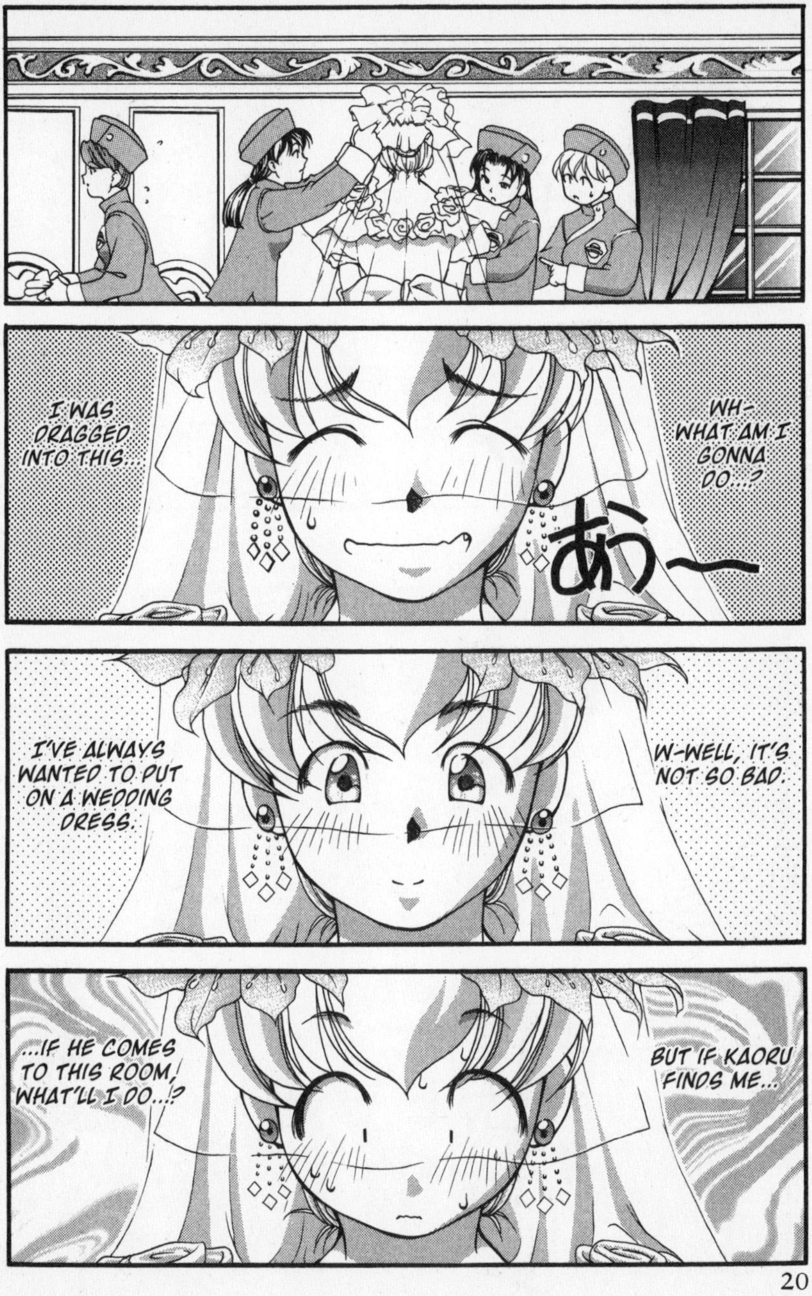
WH- WHAT AM I GONNA DO...?
あう〜〜
I WAS DRAGGED INTO THIS...
W-WELL, IT'S NOT SO BAD.
I'VE ALWAYS WANTED TO PUT ON A WEDDING DRESS.
BUT IF KAORU FINDS ME...
...IF HE COMES TO THIS ROOM, WHAT'LL I DO...?

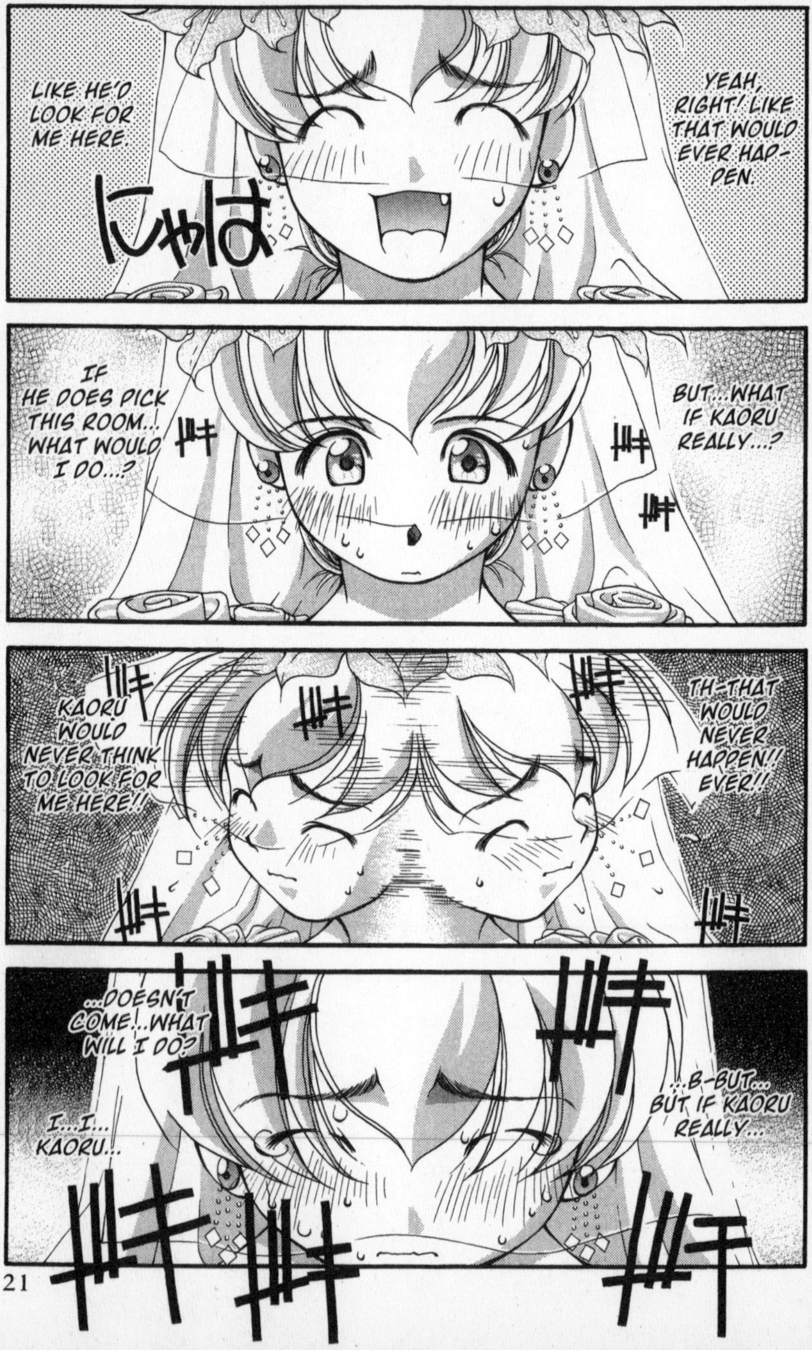
YEAH, RIGHT! LIKE THAT WOULD EVER HAP-PEN.
LIKE HE'D LOOK FOR ME HERE.
にゃは
BUT...WHAT IF KAORU REALLY...?
IF HE DOES PICK THIS ROOM... WHAT WOULD I DO...?
TH-THAT WOULD NEVER HAPPEN!! EVER!!
KAORU WOULD NEVER THINK TO LOOK FOR ME HERE!!
...B-BUT... BUT IF KAORU REALLY...
...DOESN'T COME!..WHAT WILL I DO?
I...I... KAORU...

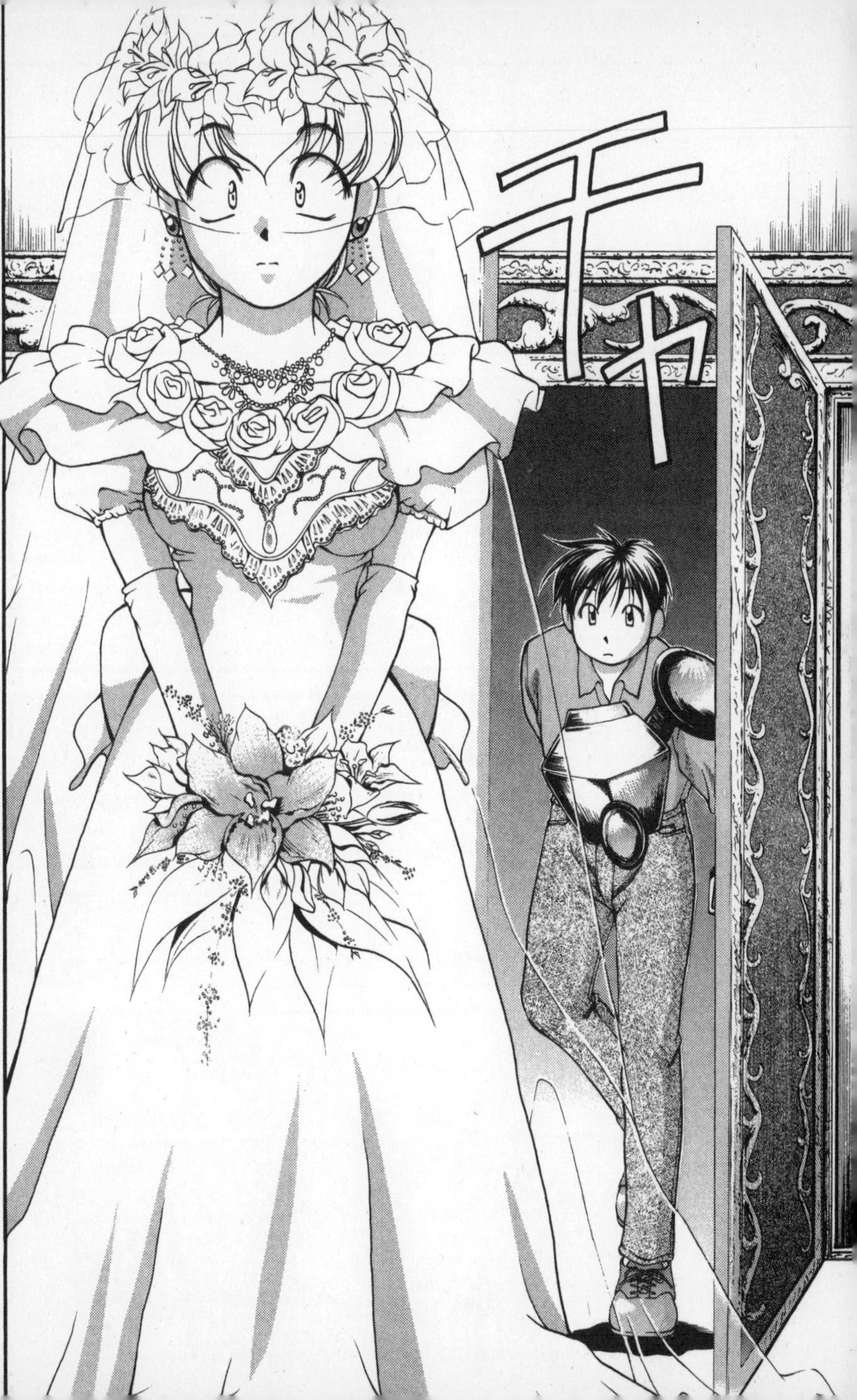
ガチャ

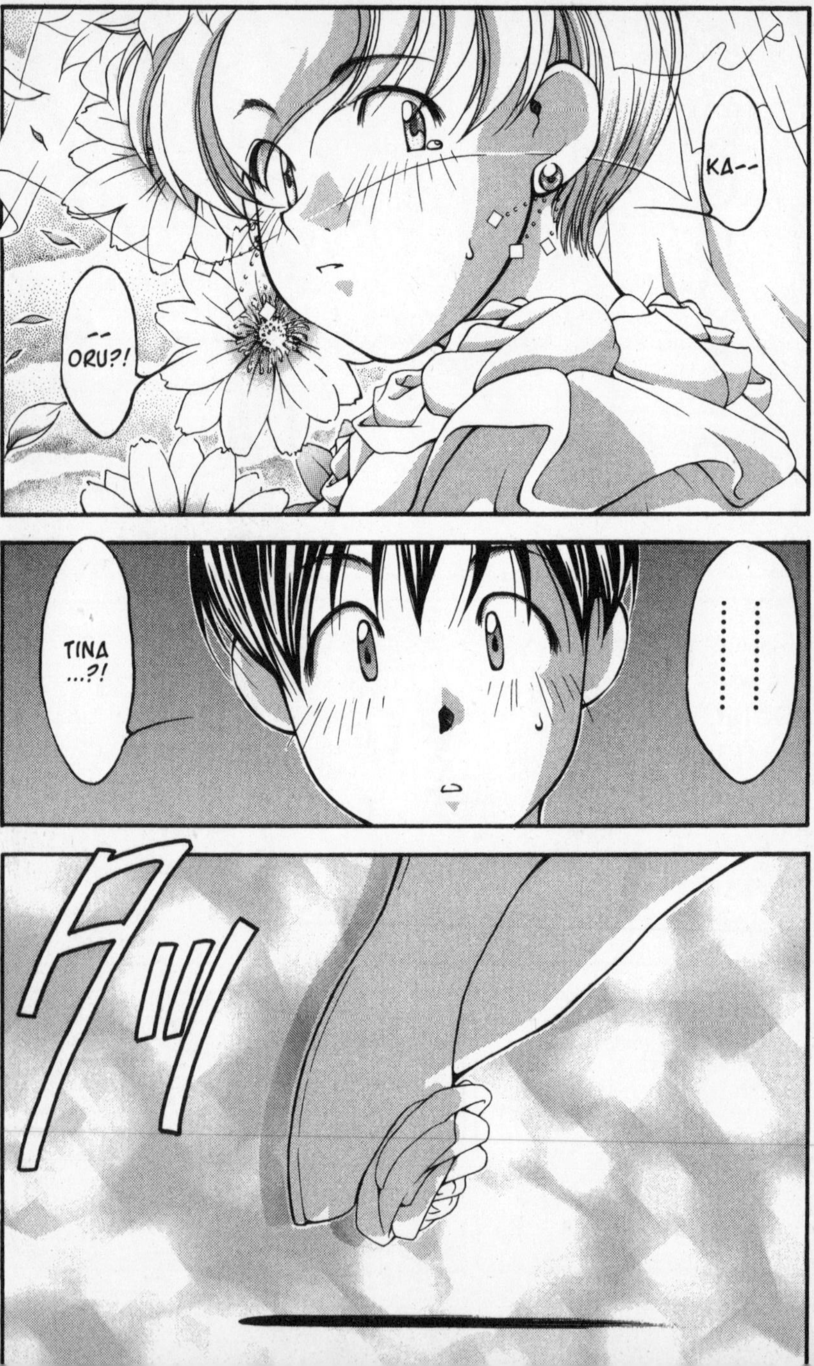
KA--
--ORU?!
......
TINA ...?!
タッ

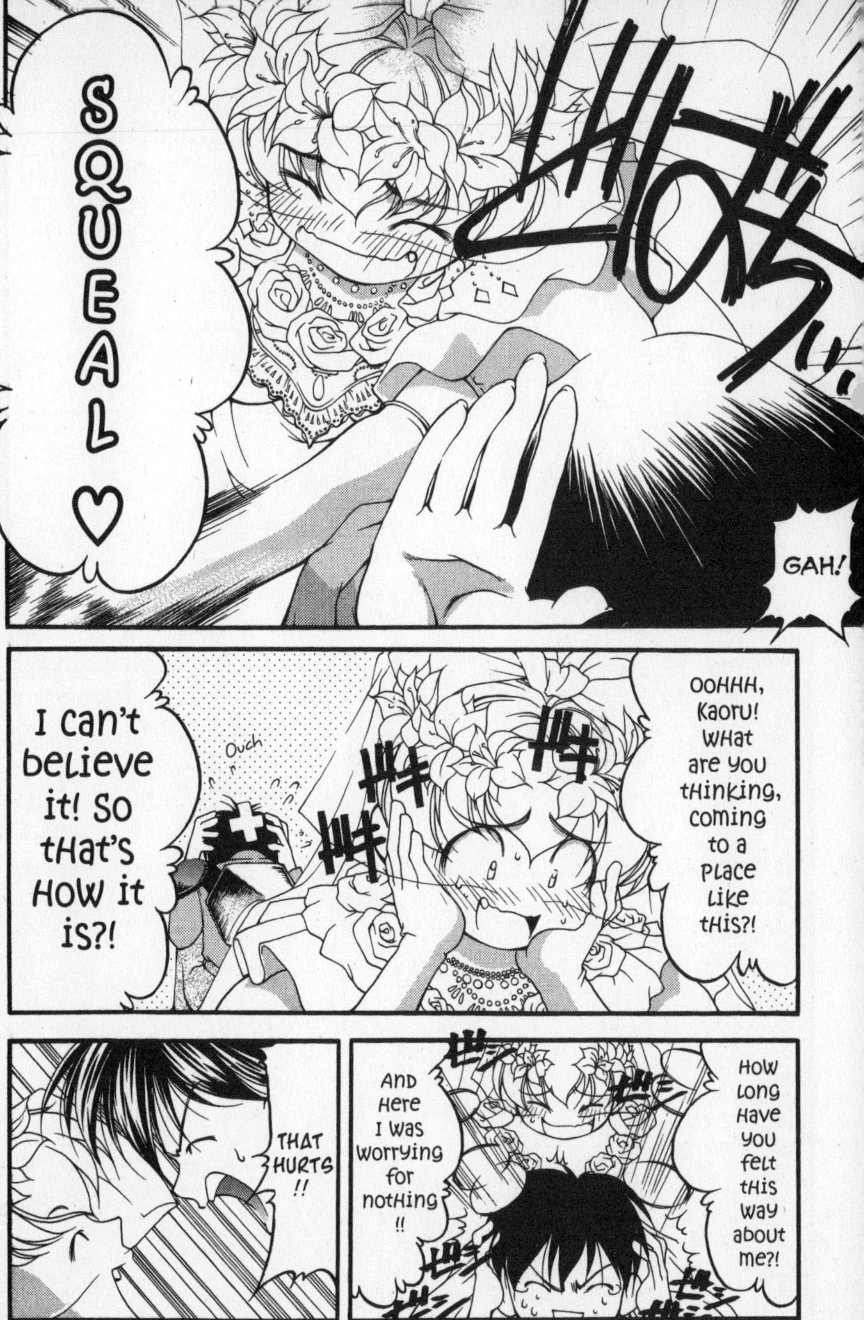
GAH!
SQUEAL ♡
OOHHH, Kaoru! What are you thinking, coming to a place like this?!
Ouch
I can't believe it! So that's how it is?!
How long have you felt this way about me?!
And here I was worrying for nothing!!
THAT HURTS!!

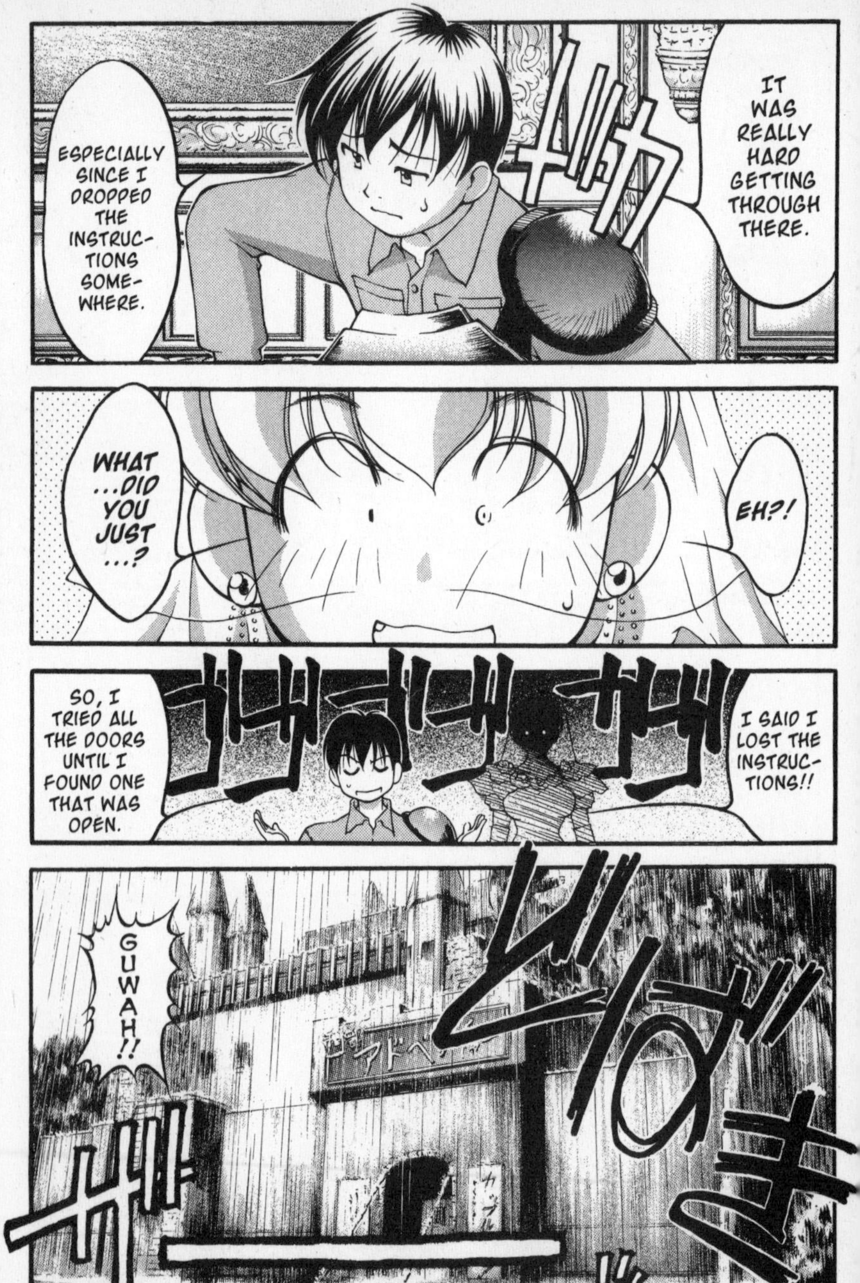
IT WAS REALLY HARD GETTING THROUGH THERE.
ESPECIALLY SINCE I DROPPED THE INSTRUC-TIONS SOME-WHERE.
EH?!
WHAT ...DID YOU JUST ...?
I SAID I LOST THE INSTRUC-TIONS!!
SO, I TRIED ALL THE DOORS UNTIL I FOUND ONE THAT WAS OPEN.
GUWAH!!

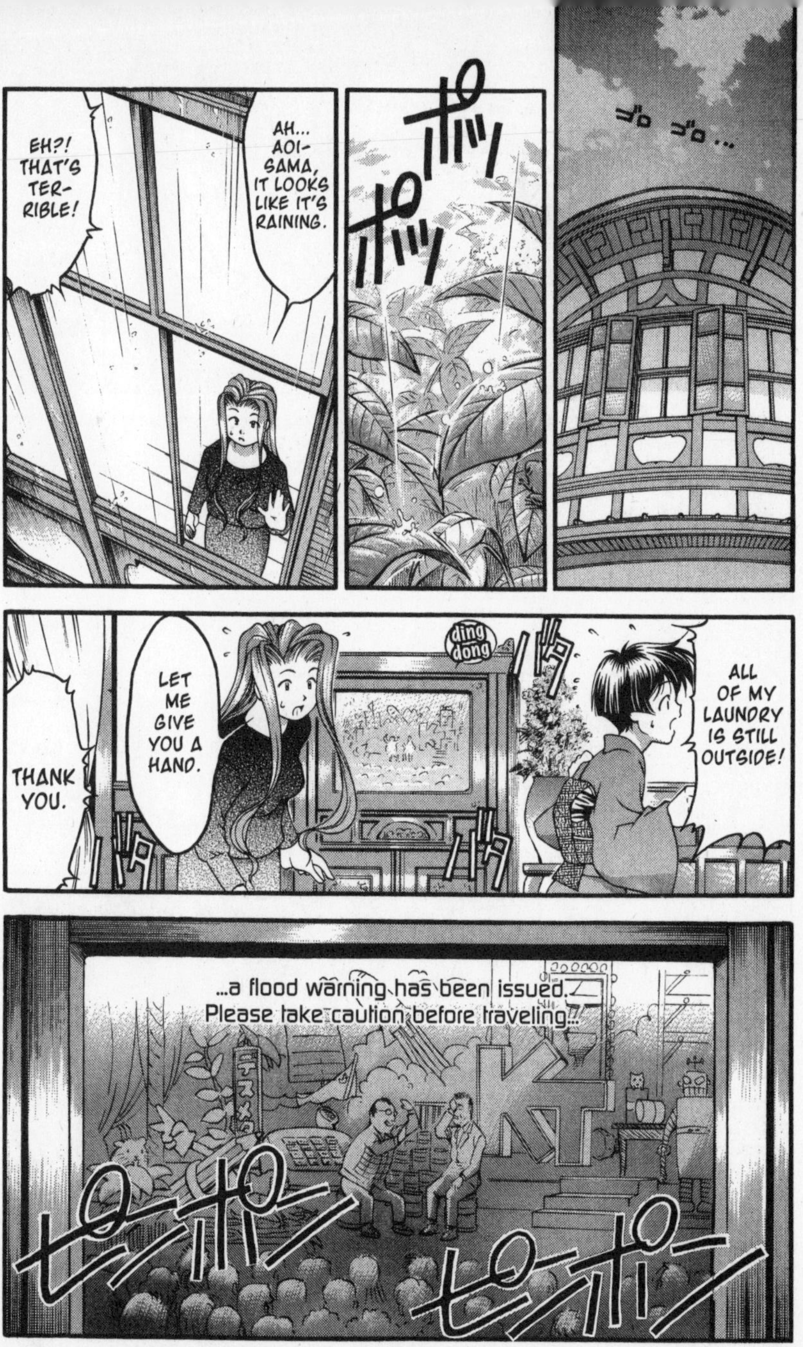
ゴロ ゴロ...
ポツ ポツ
AH... AOI-SAMA, IT LOOKS LIKE IT'S RAINING.
EH?! THAT'S TER-RIBLE!
ALL OF MY LAUNDRY IS STILL OUTSIDE!
ding dong
バタ
LET ME GIVE YOU A HAND.
THANK YOU.
バタ
バタ
...a flood warning has been issued.
Please take caution before traveling...
ピンポン
ピンポン

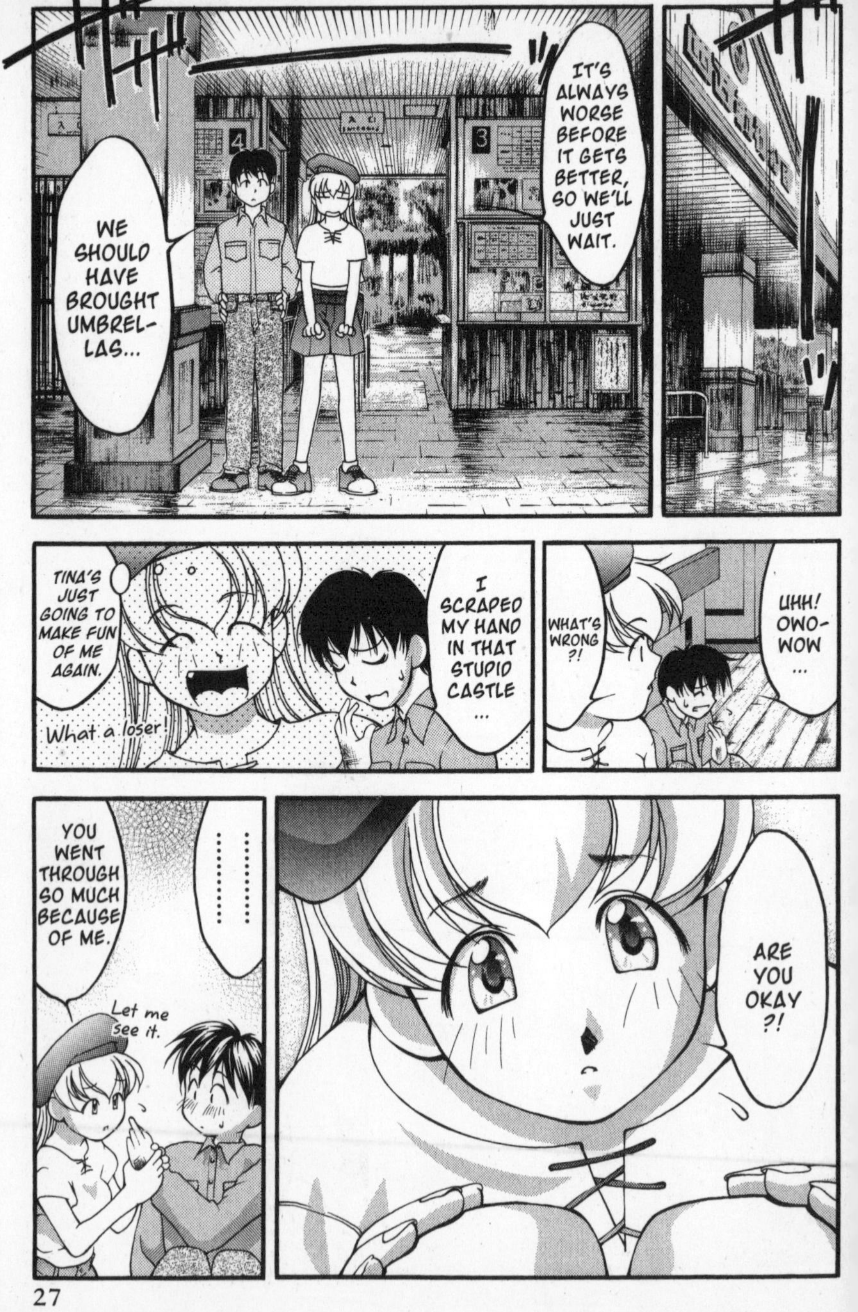
IT'S ALWAYS WORSE BEFORE IT GETS BETTER, SO WE'LL JUST WAIT.
WE SHOULD HAVE BROUGHT UMBREL-LAS...
UHH! OWO-WOW ...
WHAT'S WRONG ?!
I SCRAPED MY HAND IN THAT STUPID CASTLE ...
TINA'S JUST GOING TO MAKE FUN OF ME AGAIN.
What a loser!
ARE YOU OKAY ?!
......
YOU WENT THROUGH SO MUCH BECAUSE OF ME.
Let me see it.

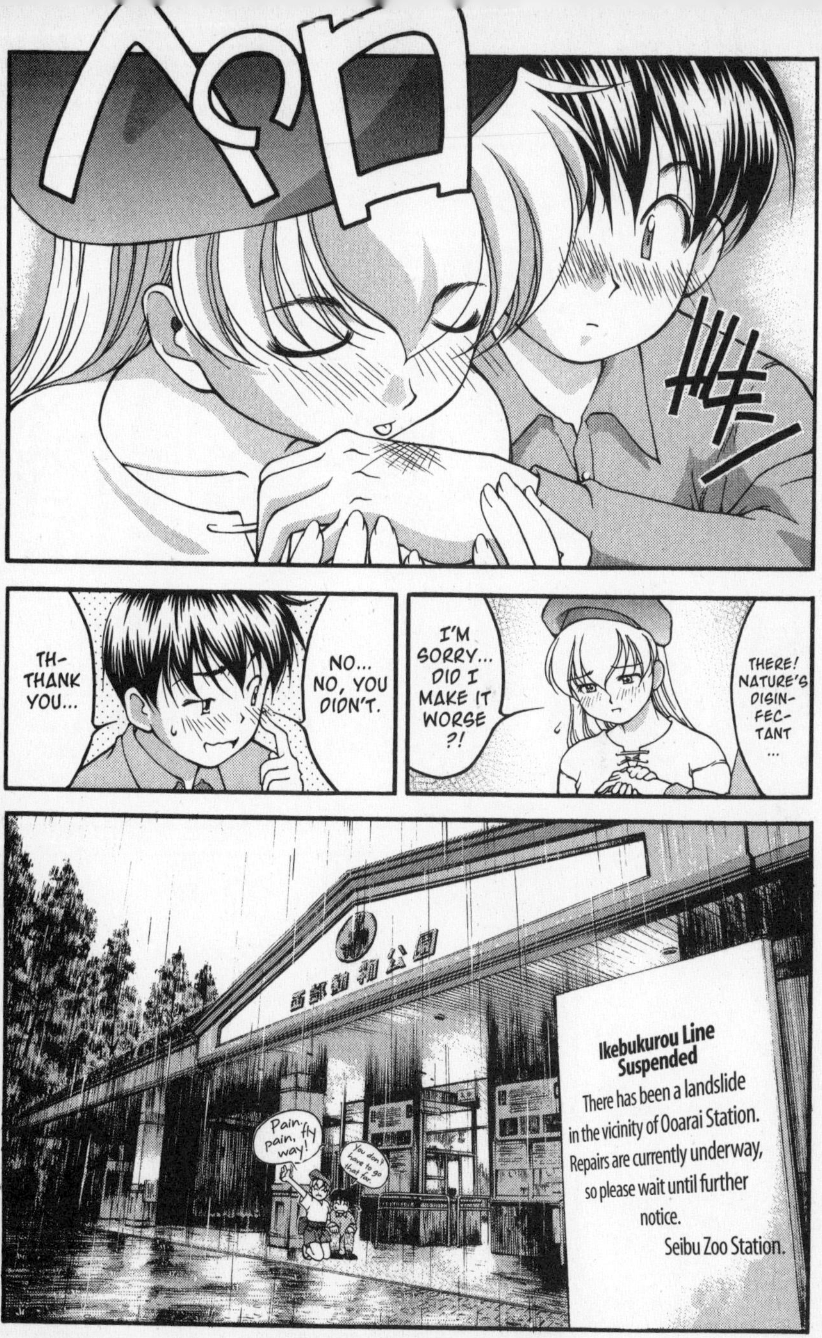
THERE! NATURE'S DISIN-FECTANT ...
I'M SORRY... DID I MAKE IT WORSE ?!
NO... NO, YOU DIDN'T.
TH-THANK YOU...
Ikebukurou Line Suspended
There has been a landslide in the vicinity of Ooarai Station. Repairs are currently underway, so please wait until further notice.
Seibu Zoo Station.
You don't have to go that far.
Pain, pain, fly way!

藍(あい)より青(あお)し

AI YORI AOSHI

第四十話 CHAPTER 40

相聞歌―そうもんか― SOUMONKA SERENADE

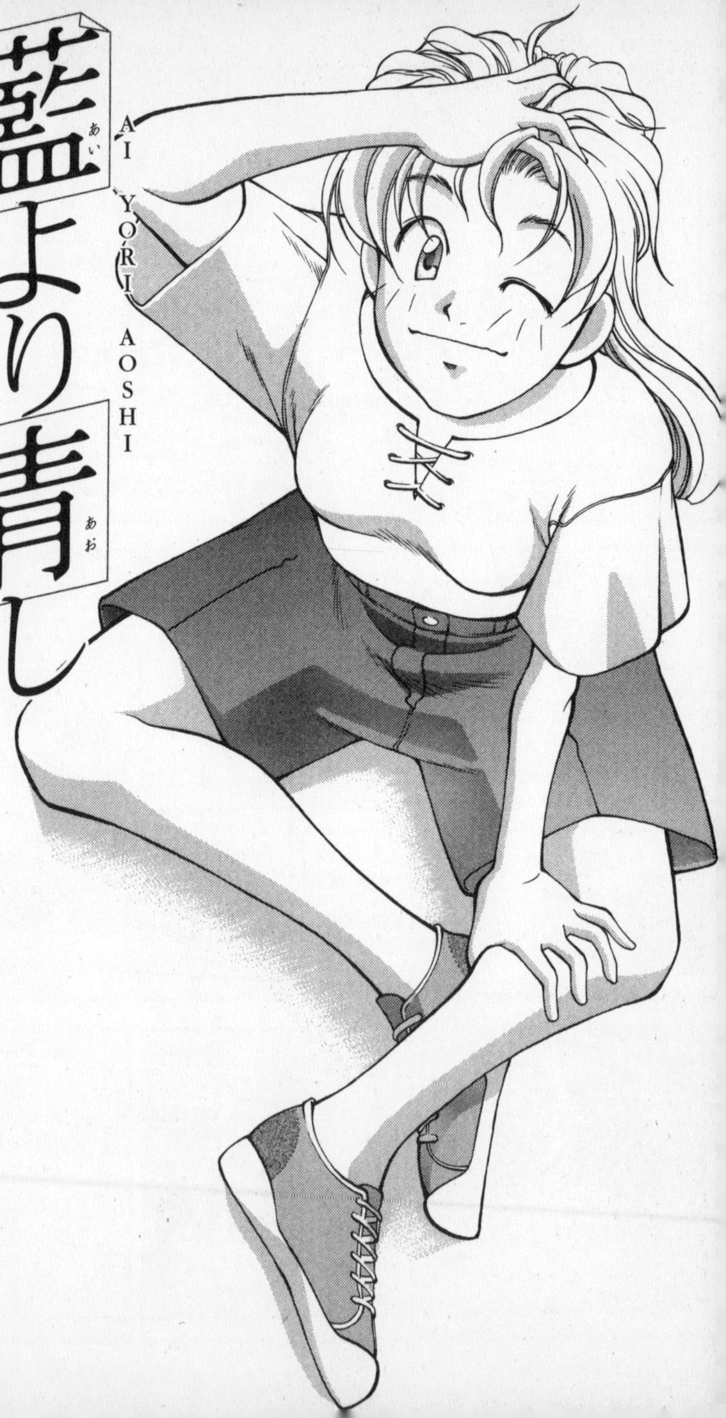

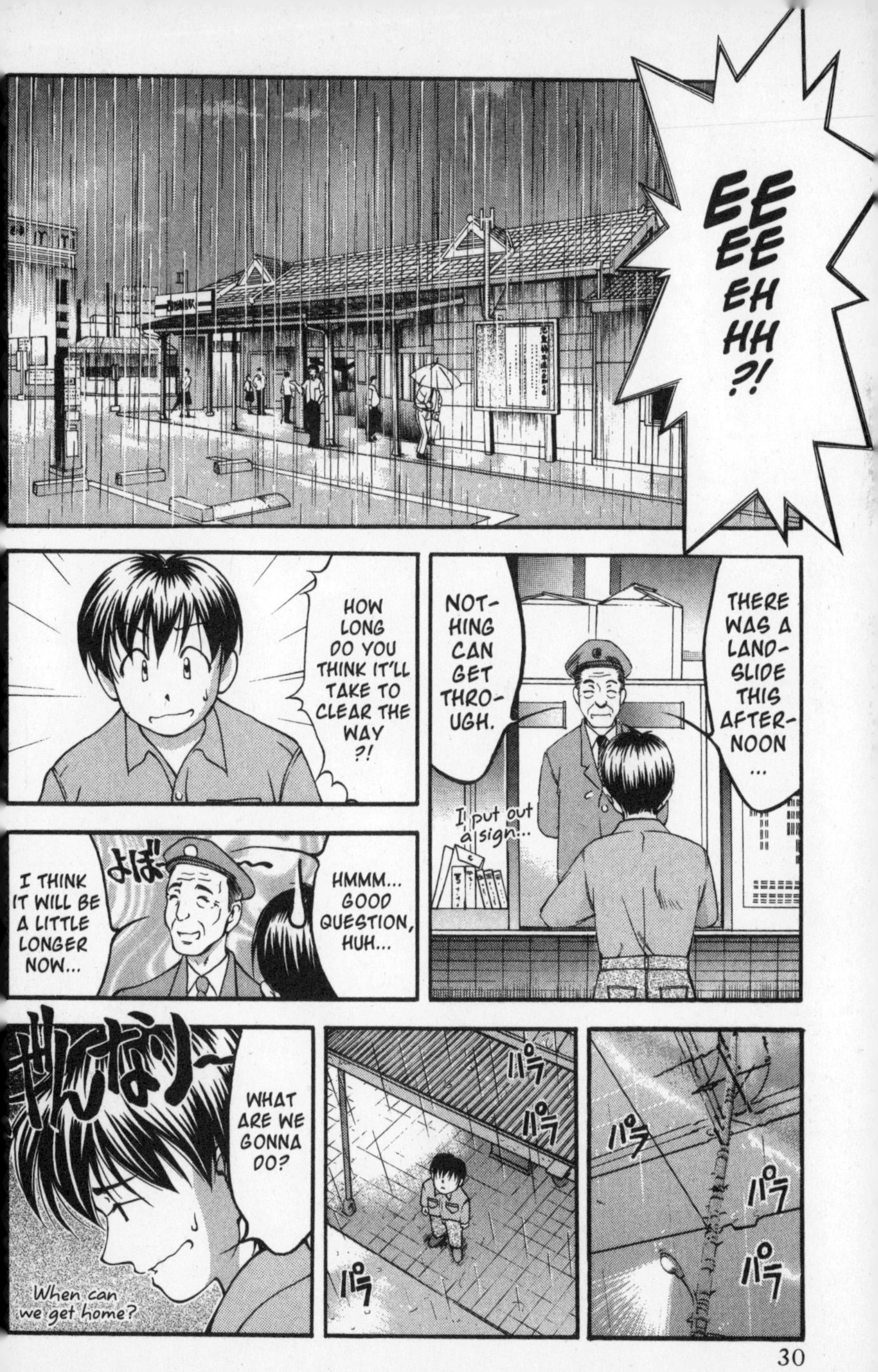
EEEEEEHHH?!
THERE WAS A LANDSLIDE THIS AFTERNOON...
NOTHING CAN GET THROUGH.
I put out a sign...
HOW LONG DO YOU THINK IT'LL TAKE TO CLEAR THE WAY?!
HMMM... GOOD QUESTION, HUH...
よぼー
I THINK IT WILL BE A LITTLE LONGER NOW...
パラ
パラ
パラ
パラ
パラ
パラ
パラ
WHAT ARE WE GONNA DO?
When can we get home?

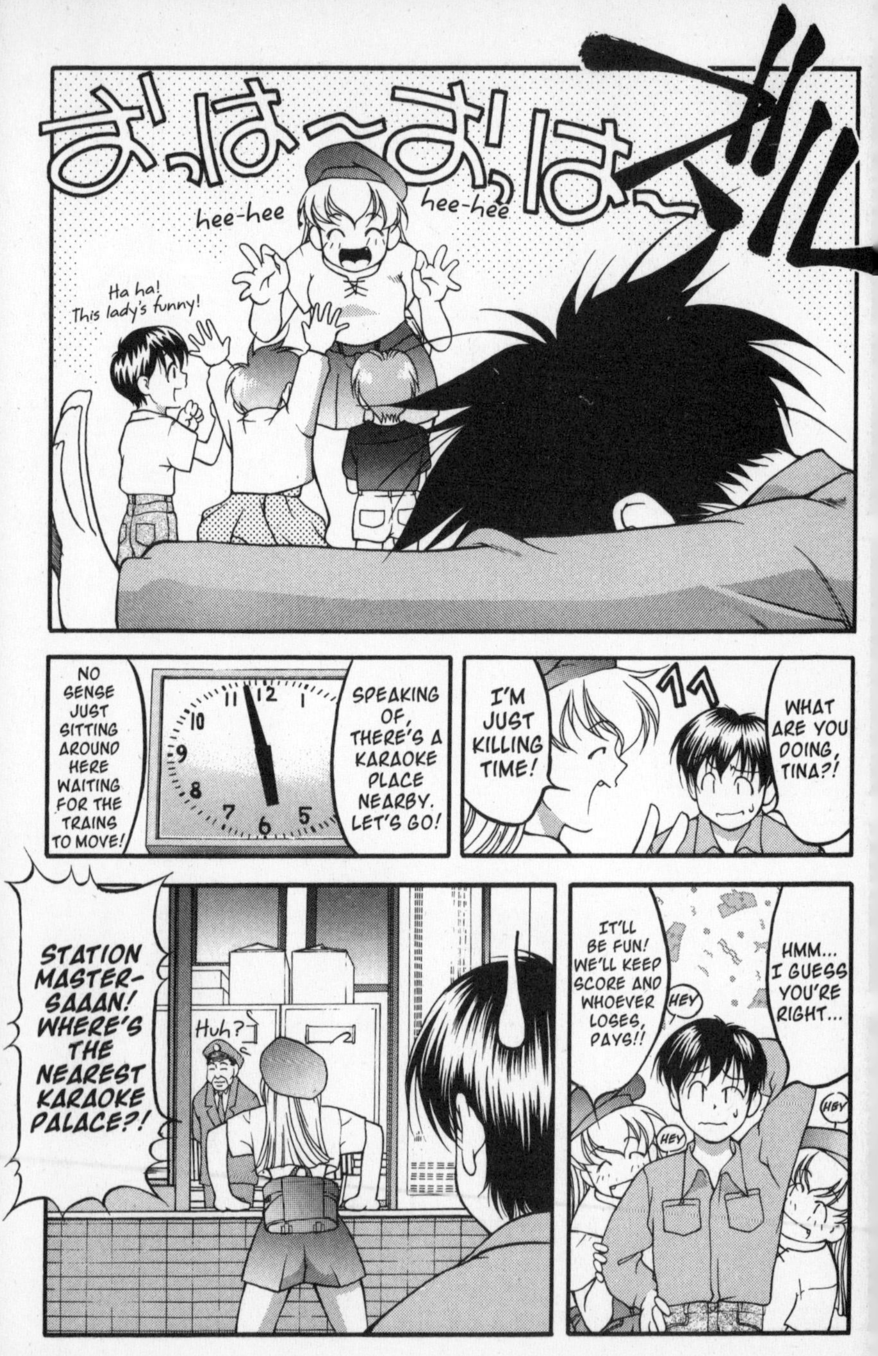
おっは〜おっは〜
hee-hee
hee-hee
Ha ha! This lady's funny!
WHAT ARE YOU DOING, TINA?!
I'M JUST KILLING TIME!
SPEAKING OF, THERE'S A KARAOKE PLACE NEARBY. LET'S GO!
NO SENSE JUST SITTING AROUND HERE WAITING FOR THE TRAINS TO MOVE!
HMM... I GUESS YOU'RE RIGHT...
IT'LL BE FUN! WE'LL KEEP SCORE AND WHOEVER LOSES, PAYS!!
HEY
HEY
HEY
STATION MASTER-SAAAN! WHERE'S THE NEAREST KARAOKE PALACE?!
Huh?

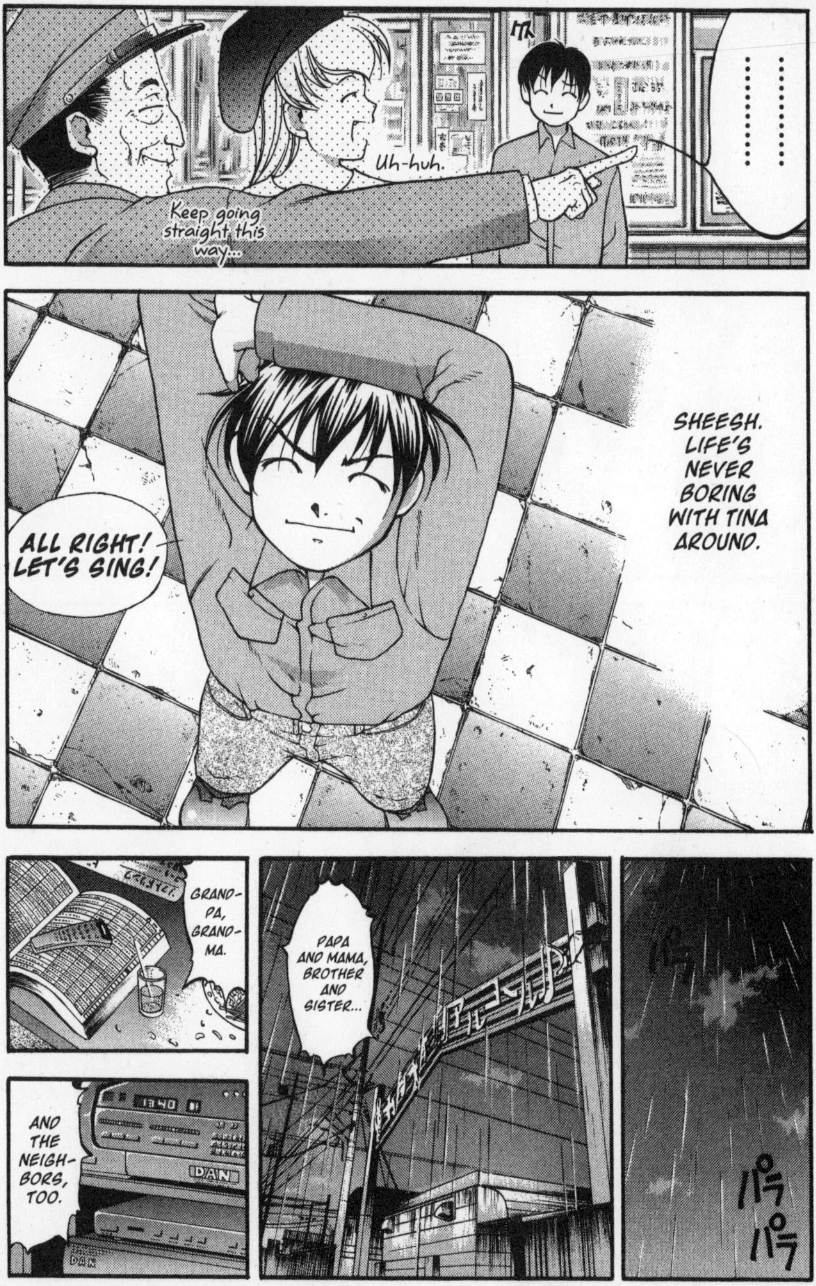
......
Uh-huh.
Keep going straight this way...
SHEESH. LIFE'S NEVER BORING WITH TINA AROUND.
ALL RIGHT! LET'S SING!
パラ パラ
PAPA AND MAMA, BROTHER AND SISTER...
GRANDPA, GRANDMA.
AND THE NEIGHBORS, TOO.
DAN

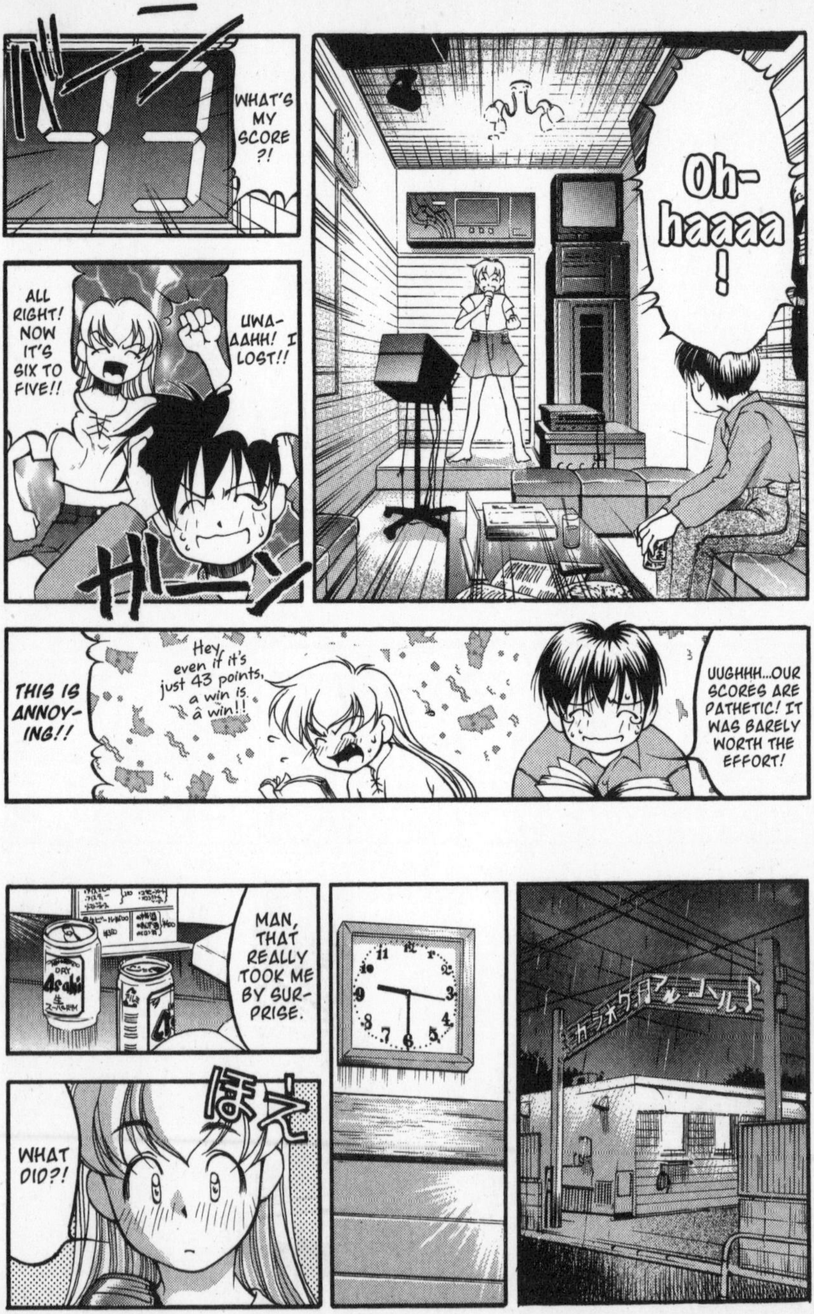

Oh-haaaa!
WHAT'S MY SCORE ?!
UWA-AAHH! I LOST!!
ALL RIGHT! NOW IT'S SIX TO FIVE!!
ガーン
UUGHHH...OUR SCORES ARE PATHETIC! IT WAS BARELY WORTH THE EFFORT!
Hey, even if it's just 43 points, a win is a win!!
THIS IS ANNOY-ING!!
MAN, THAT REALLY TOOK ME BY SUR-PRISE.
ほえ
WHAT DID?!

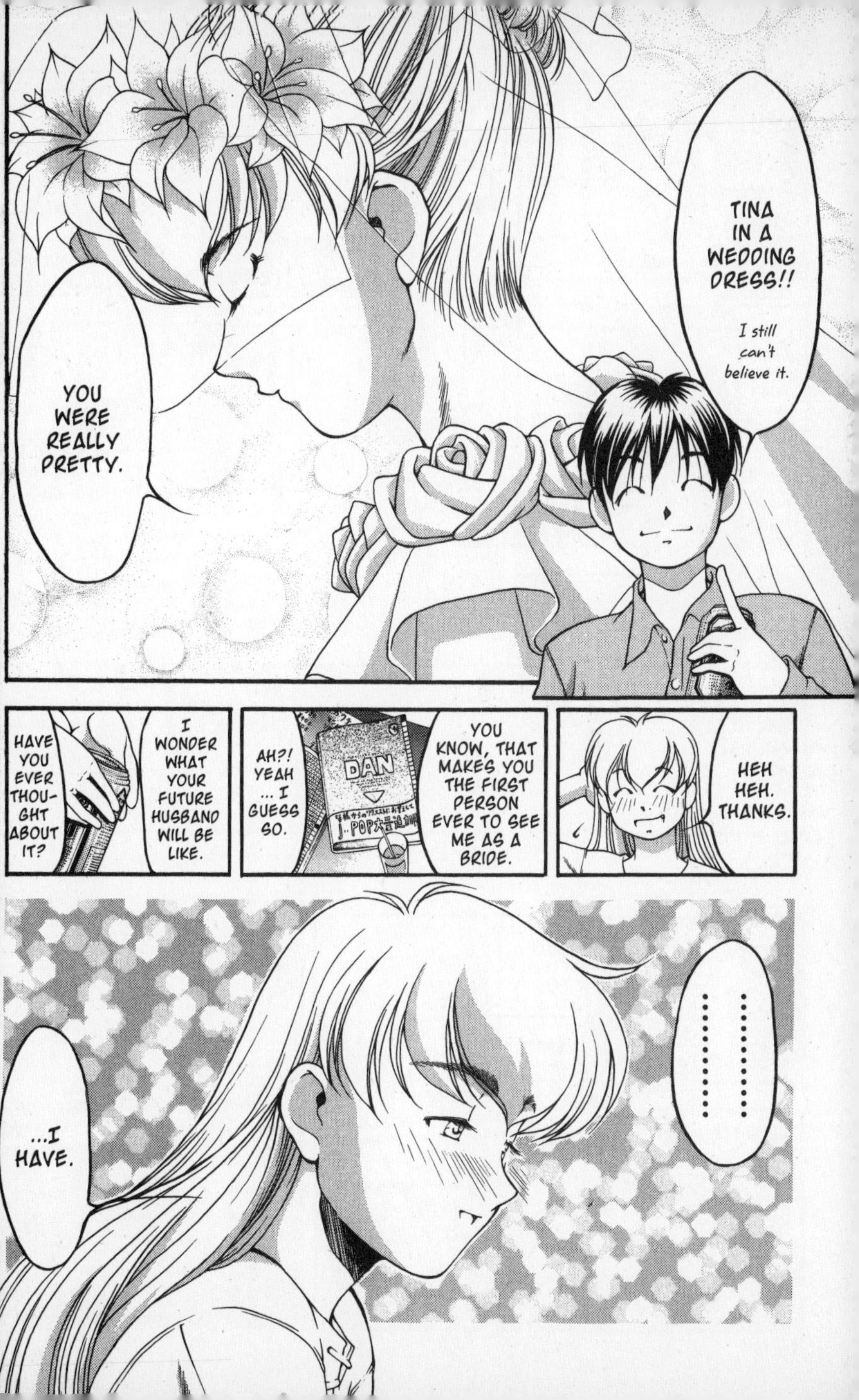
TINA IN A WEDDING DRESS!!
I still can't believe it.
YOU WERE REALLY PRETTY.
HEH HEH. THANKS.
YOU KNOW, THAT MAKES YOU THE FIRST PERSON EVER TO SEE ME AS A BRIDE.
DAN
AH?! YEAH ... I GUESS SO.
I WONDER WHAT YOUR FUTURE HUSBAND WILL BE LIKE.
HAVE YOU EVER THOUGHT ABOUT IT?
......
...I HAVE.

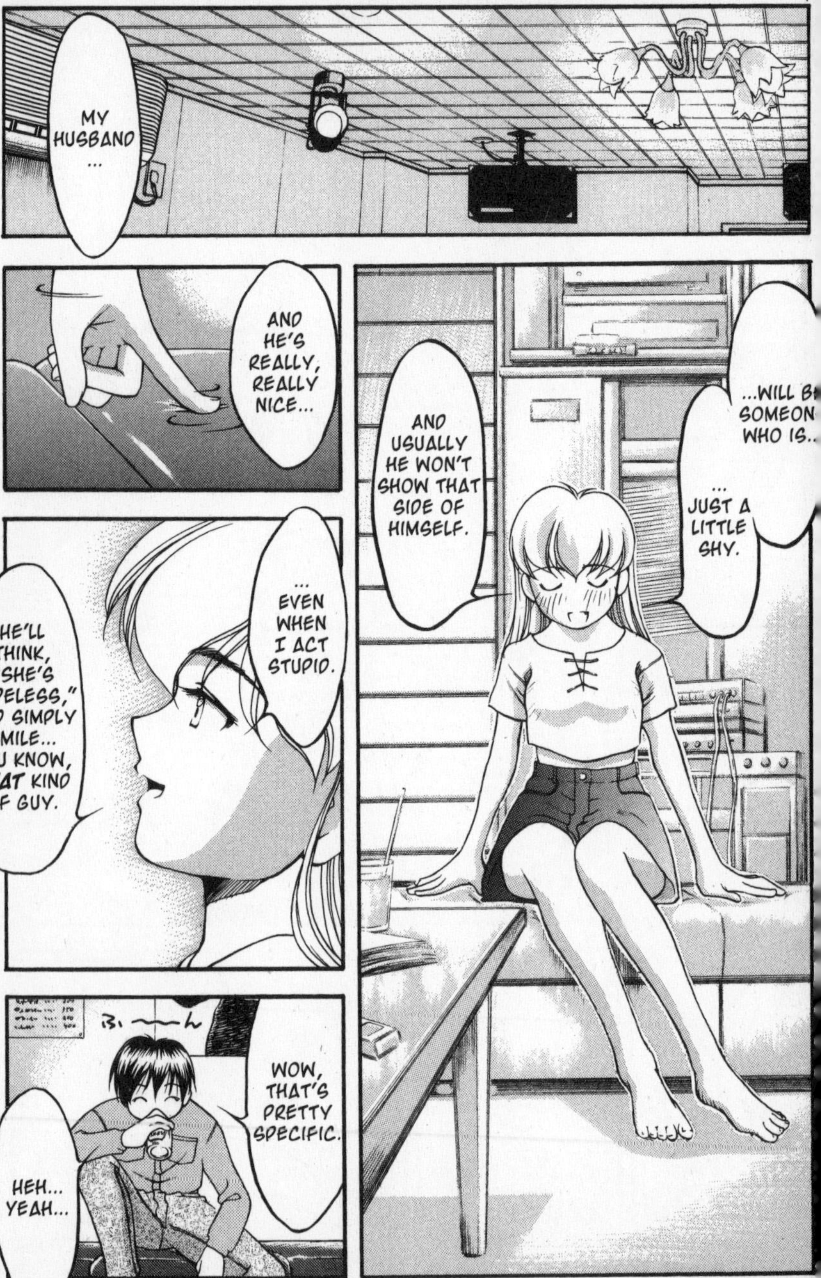
MY HUSBAND ...
...WILL B SOMEON WHO IS..
... JUST A LITTLE SHY.
AND USUALLY HE WON'T SHOW THAT SIDE OF HIMSELF.
AND HE'S REALLY, REALLY NICE...
... EVEN WHEN I ACT STUPID.
HE'LL THINK, "SHE'S HOPELESS," AND SIMPLY SMILE... YOU KNOW, **THAT** KIND OF GUY.
ぶ〜〜ん
WOW, THAT'S PRETTY SPECIFIC.
HEH... YEAH...

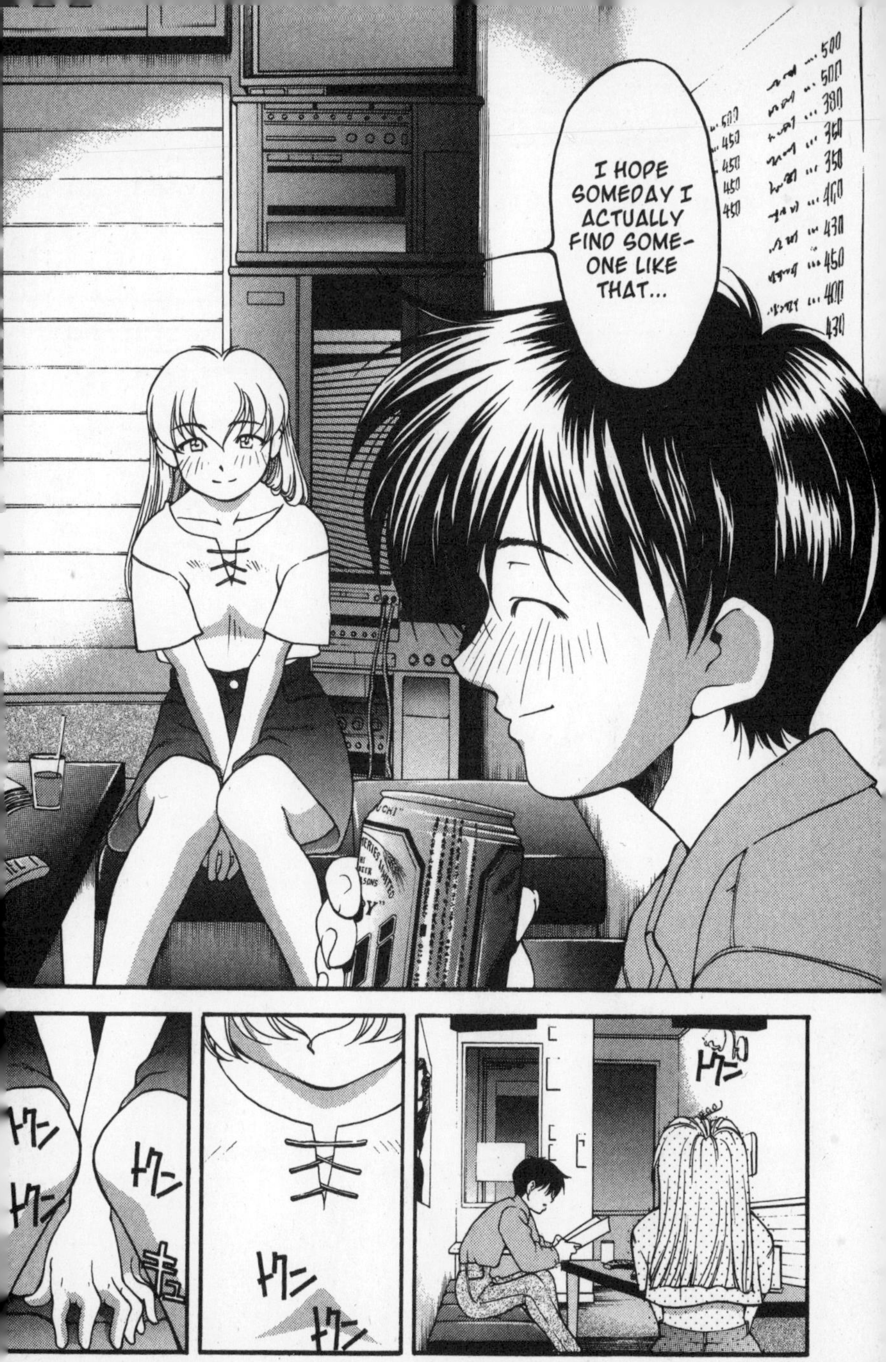
I HOPE SOMEDAY I ACTUALLY FIND SOME-ONE LIKE THAT...

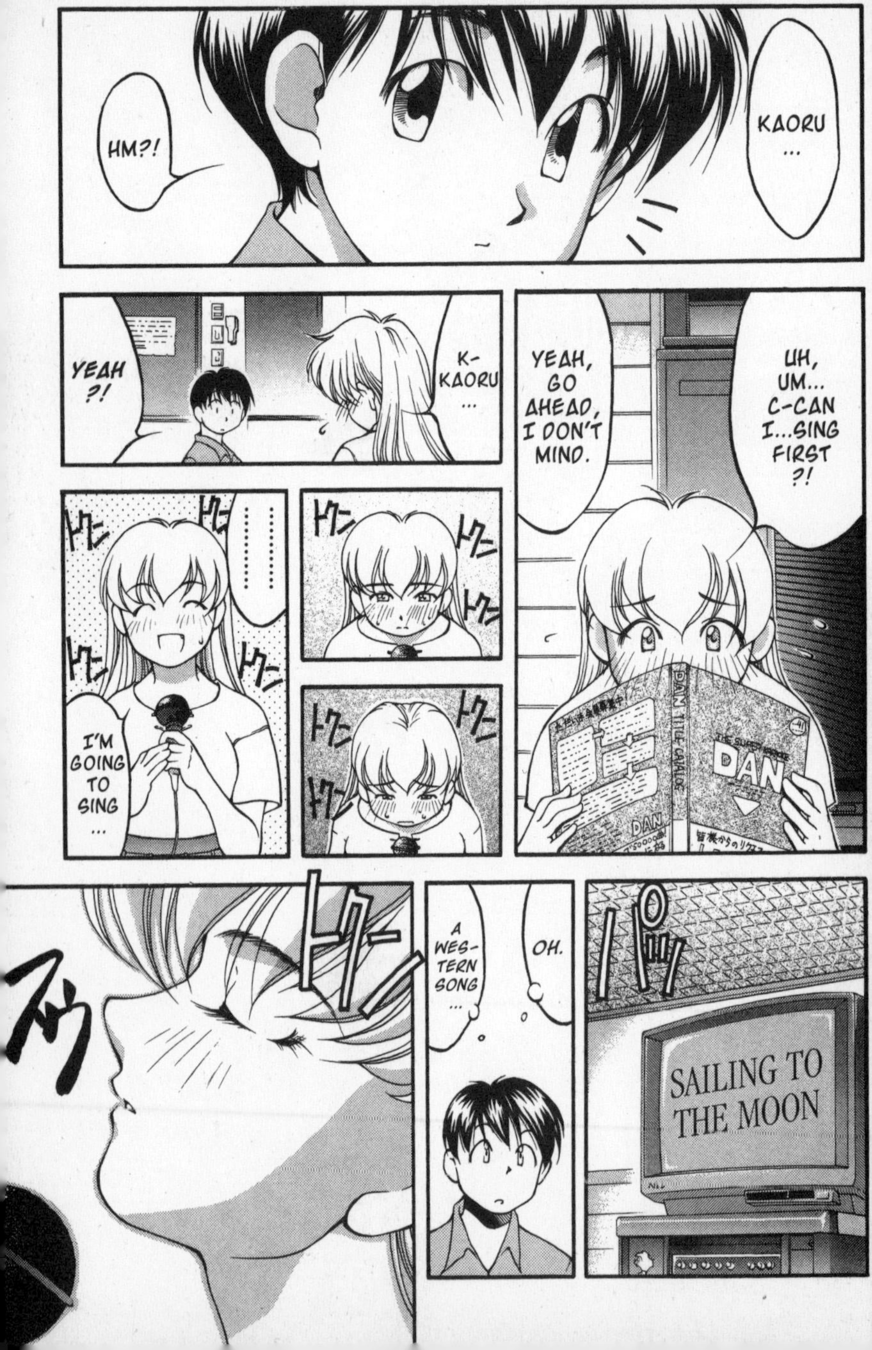
KAORU ...
HM?!
UH, UM... C-CAN I...SING FIRST ?!
YEAH, GO AHEAD, I DON'T MIND.
K-KAORU ...
YEAH ?!
トクン
トクン
......
I'M GOING TO SING ...
パッ
SAILING TO THE MOON
OH.
A WES-TERN SONG ...
トクーン

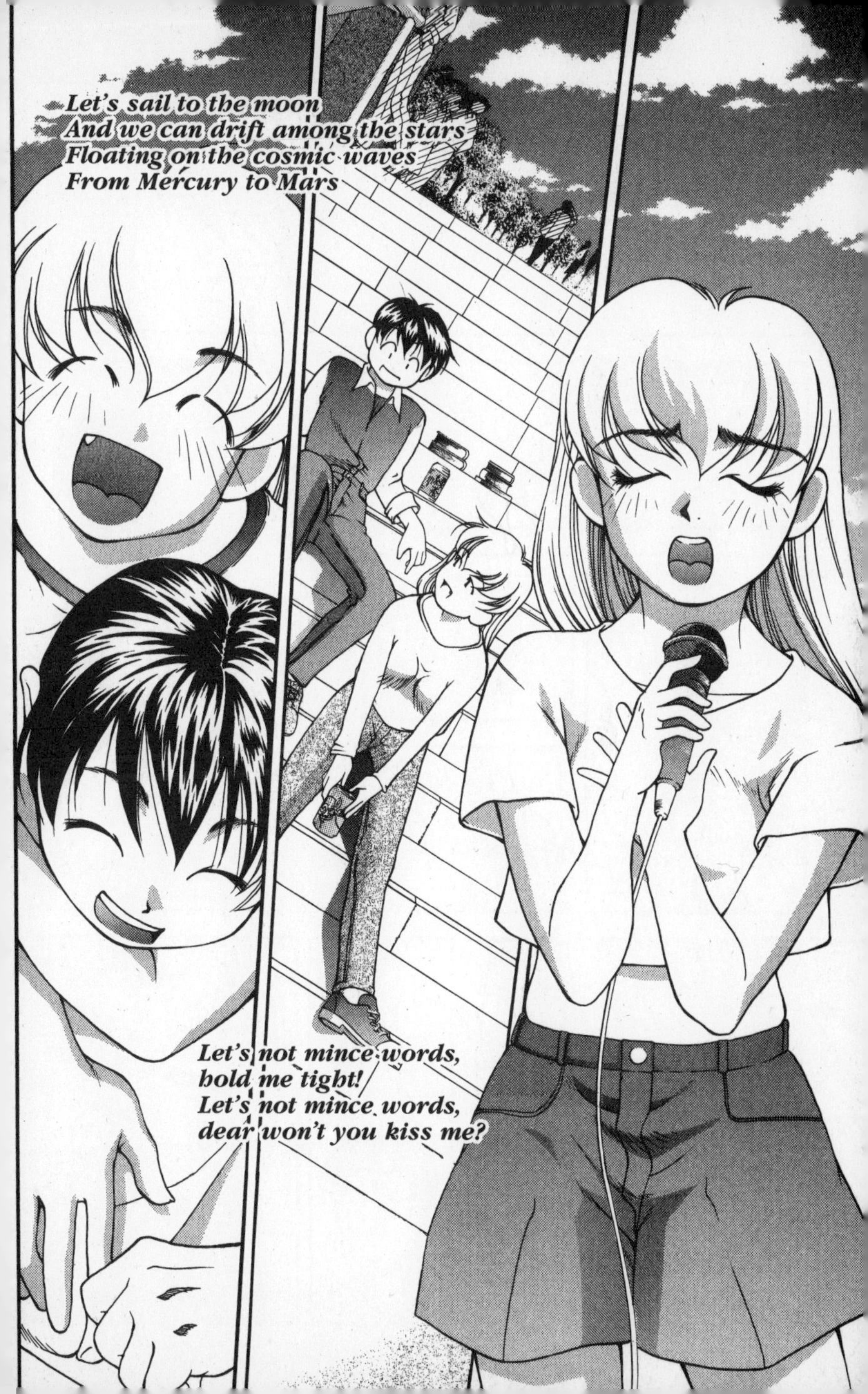
Let's sail to the moon
And we can drift among the stars
Floating on the cosmic waves
From Mercury to Mars
Let's not mince words, hold me tight!
Let's not mince words, dear won't you kiss me?

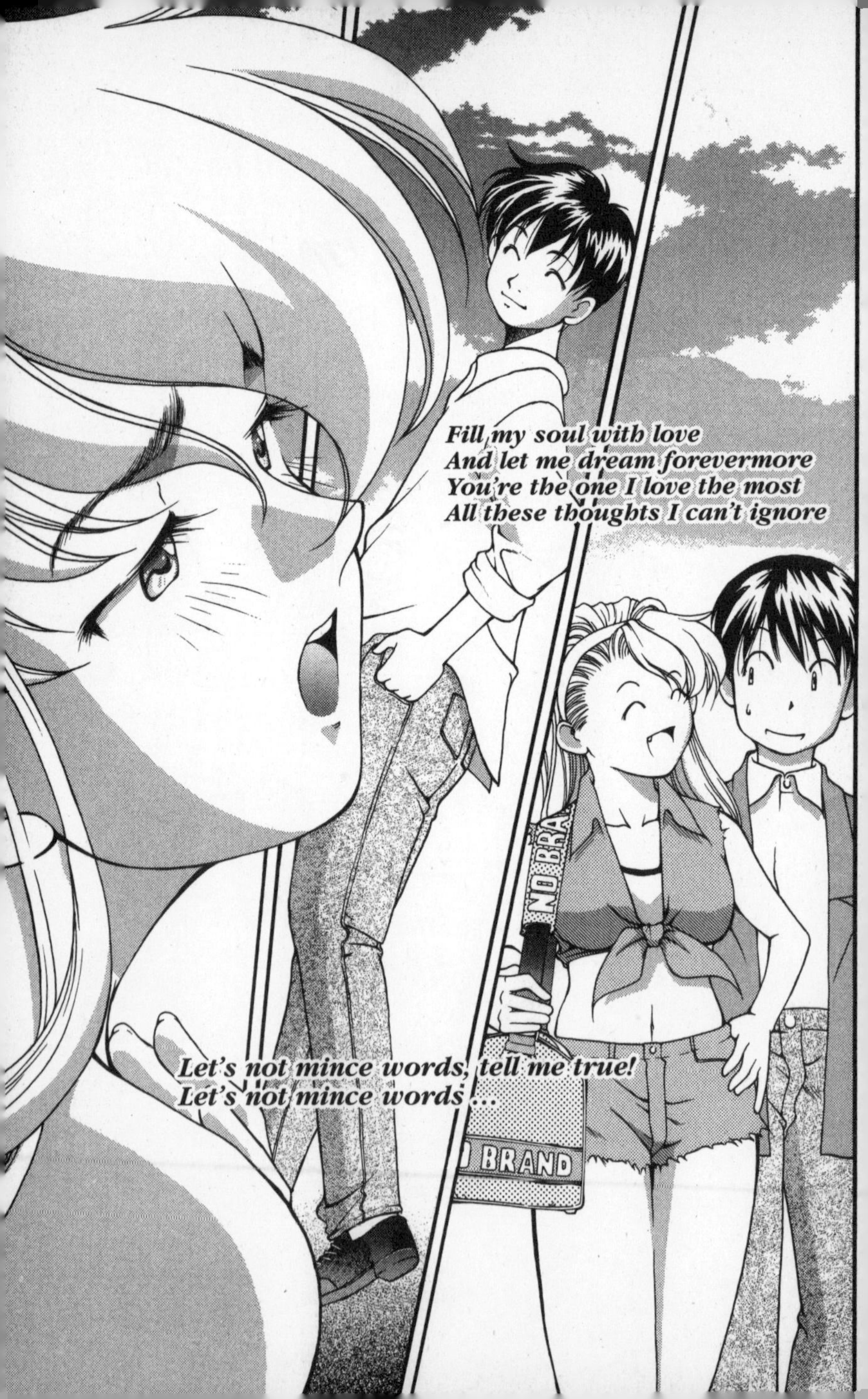
Fill my soul with love
And let me dream forevermore
You're the one I love the most
All these thoughts I can't ignore
NO BRAND
BRAND
Let's not mince words, tell me true!
Let's not mince words ...

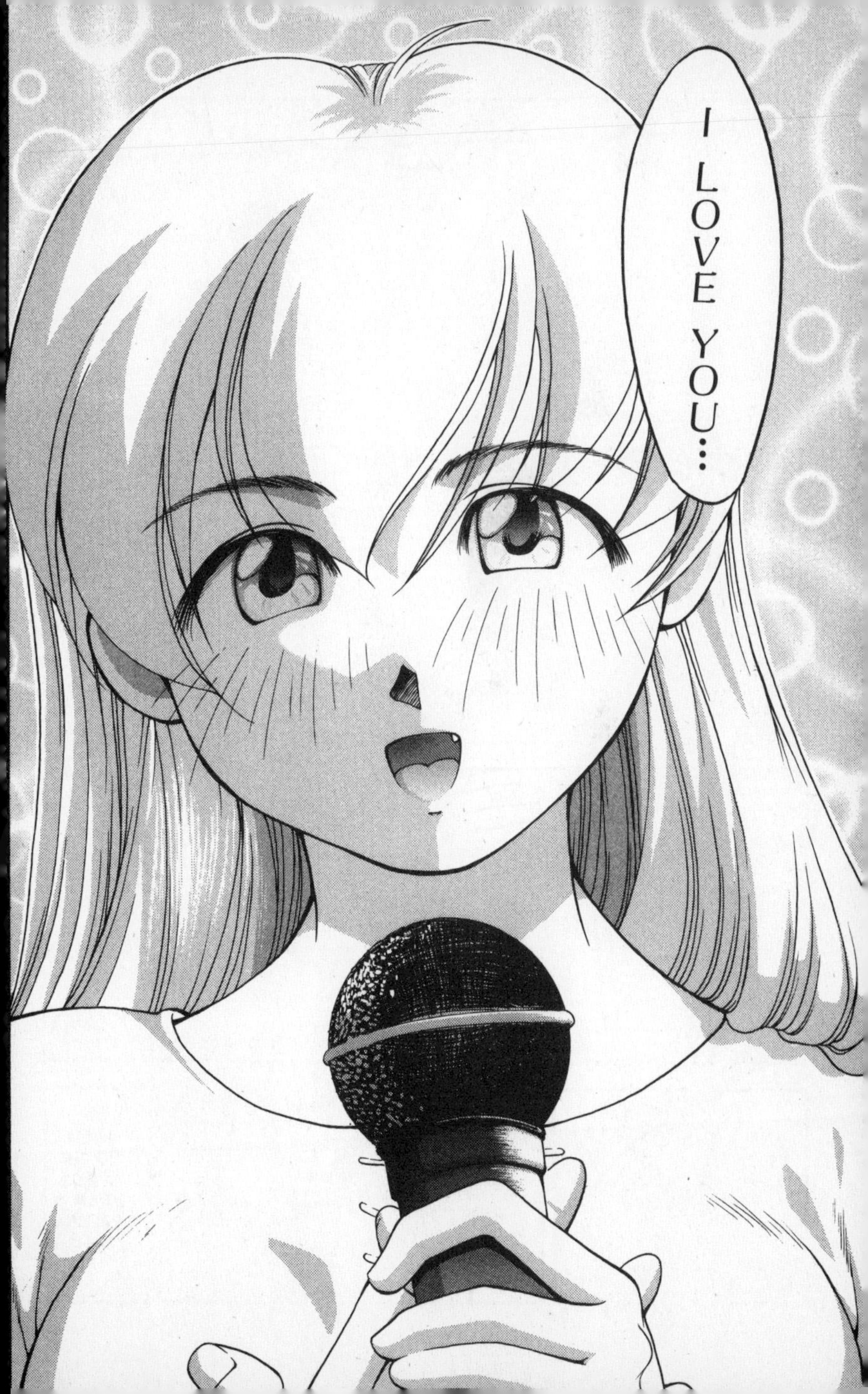
I LOVE YOU...

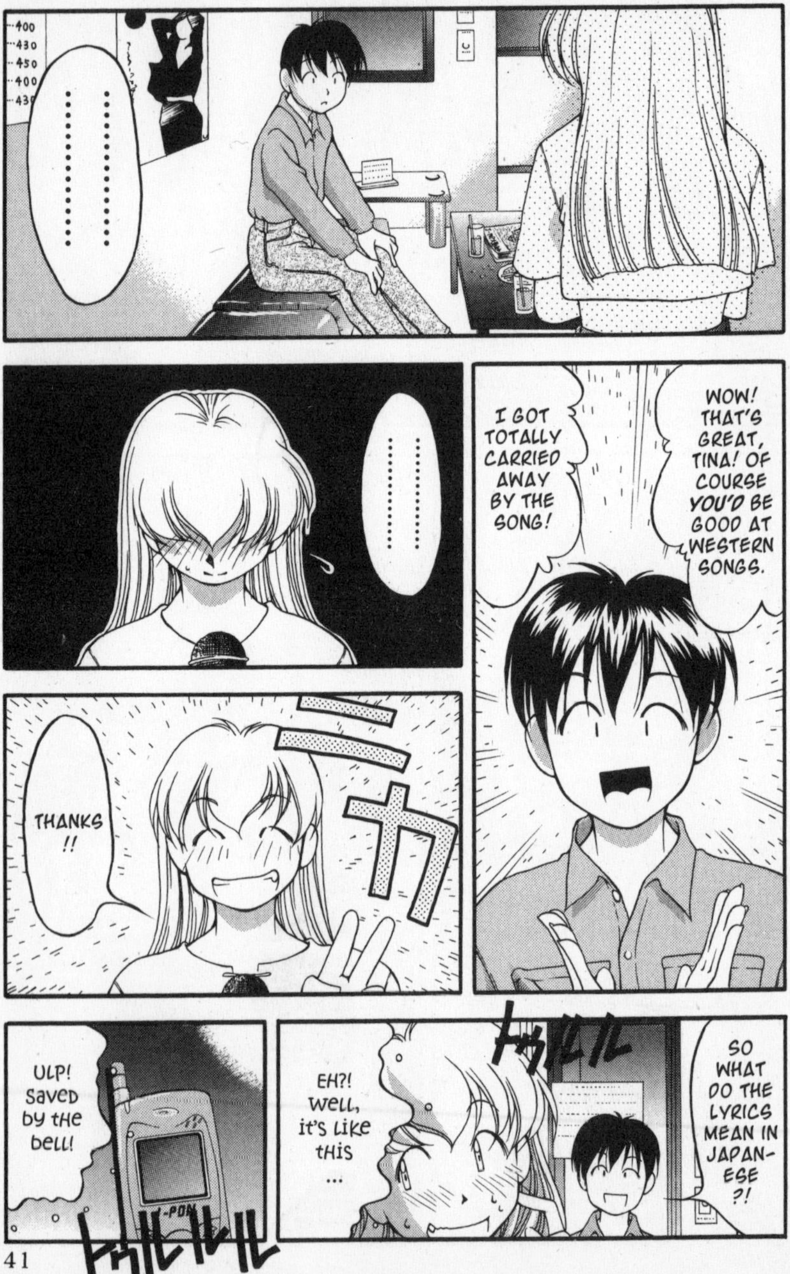
....
....
WOW! THAT'S GREAT, TINA! OF COURSE YOU'D BE GOOD AT WESTERN SONGS.
I GOT TOTALLY CARRIED AWAY BY THE SONG!
....
ニカ
THANKS!!
SO WHAT DO THE LYRICS MEAN IN JAPAN-ESE?!
EH?! Well, it's like this ...
ULP! Saved by the bell!

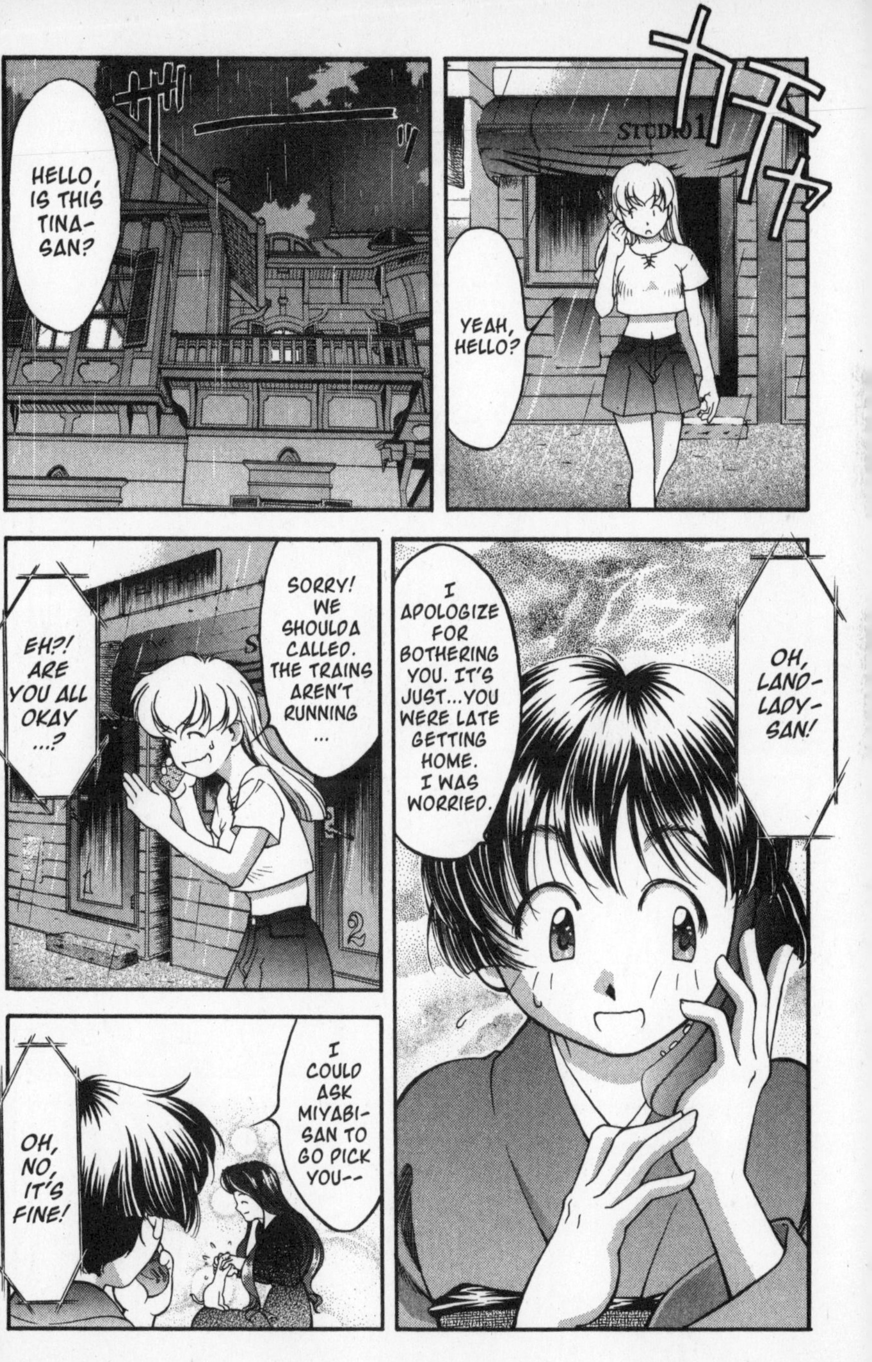
カチャ
STUDIO 1
YEAH, HELLO?
ザー
HELLO, IS THIS TINA-SAN?
OH, LANDLADY-SAN!
I APOLOGIZE FOR BOTHERING YOU. IT'S JUST...YOU WERE LATE GETTING HOME. I WAS WORRIED.
SORRY! WE SHOULDA CALLED. THE TRAINS AREN'T RUNNING ...
EH?! ARE YOU ALL OKAY ...?
I COULD ASK MIYABI-SAN TO GO PICK YOU--
OH, NO, IT'S FINE!

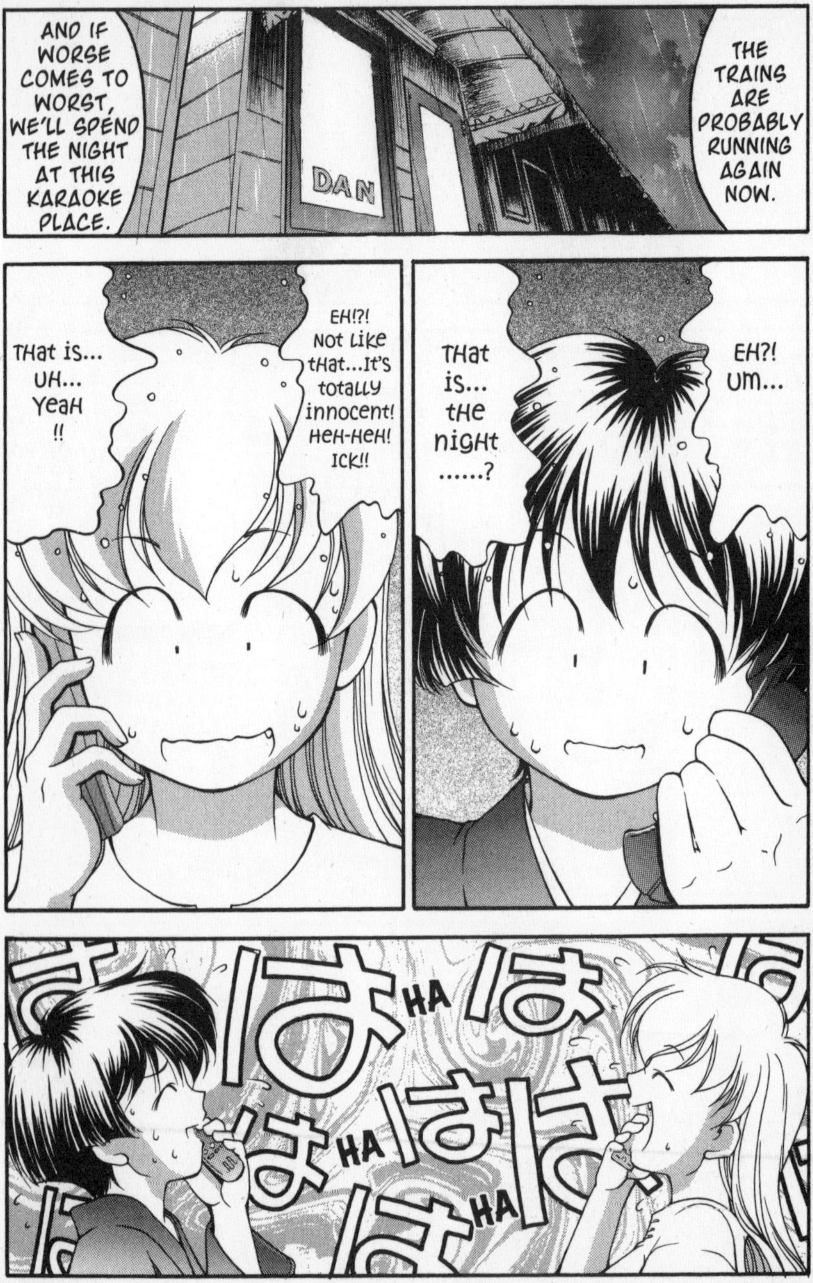
THE TRAINS ARE PROBABLY RUNNING AGAIN NOW.
AND IF WORSE COMES TO WORST, WE'LL SPEND THE NIGHT AT THIS KARAOKE PLACE.
DAN
EH?! UM...
THAt is... tHE night ......?
EH!?! Not Like tHat...It's totaLLy innocent! HEH-HEH! ICK!!
THat is... UH... YeaH !!
HA
HA
HA

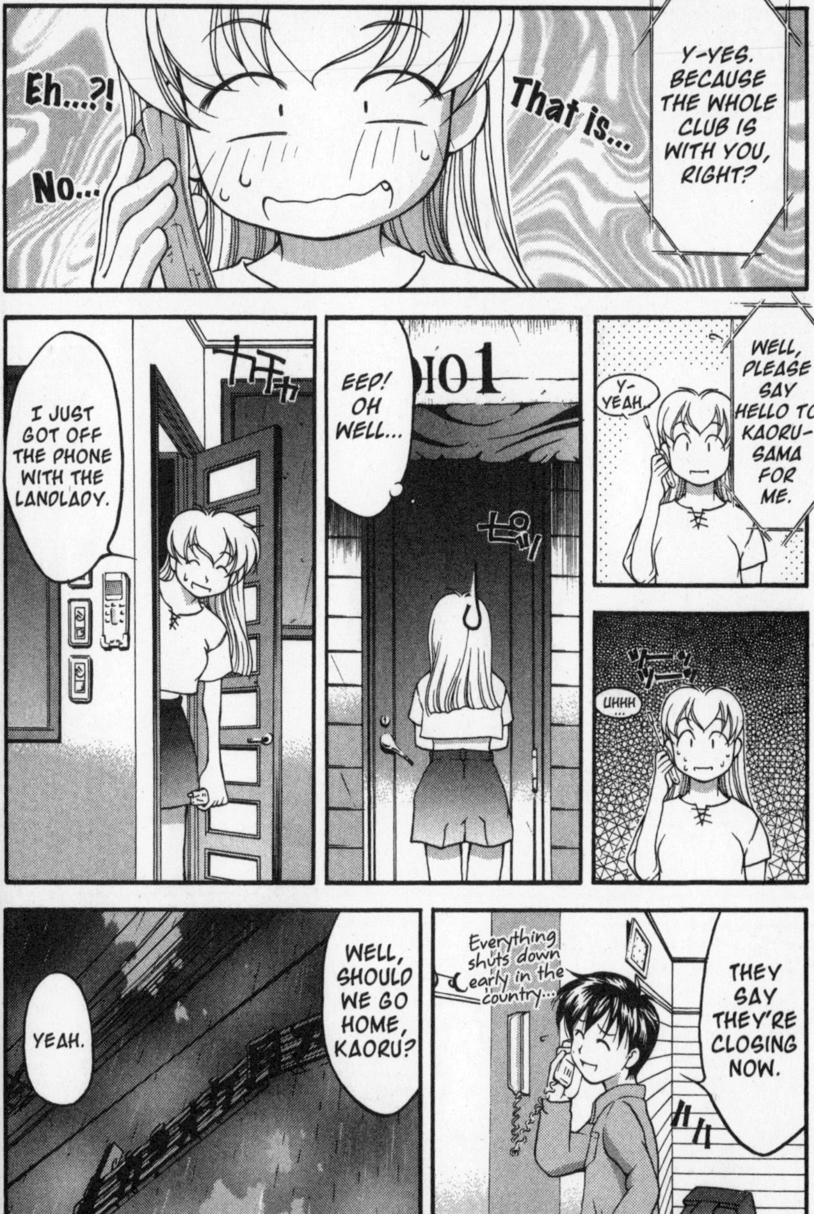
Y-YES. BECAUSE THE WHOLE CLUB IS WITH YOU, RIGHT?
That is...
Eh...?!
No...
WELL, PLEASE SAY HELLO TO KAORU-SAMA FOR ME.
Y-YEAH.
UHHH...
EEP! OH WELL...
I JUST GOT OFF THE PHONE WITH THE LANDLADY.
THEY SAY THEY'RE CLOSING NOW.
Everything shuts down early in the country...
WELL, SHOULD WE GO HOME, KAORU?
YEAH.

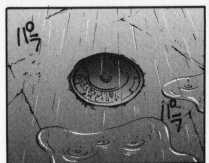

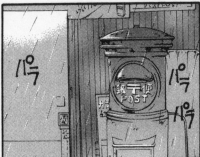

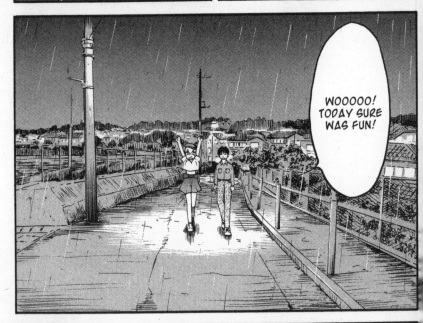

WOOOOO! TODAY SURE WAS FUN!

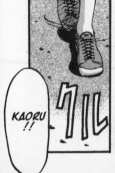

KAORU!!

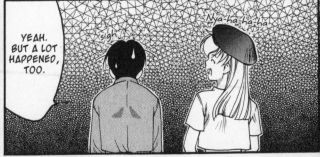

YEAH. BUT A LOT HAPPENED, TOO.

sigh

Nya-ha-ha-ha

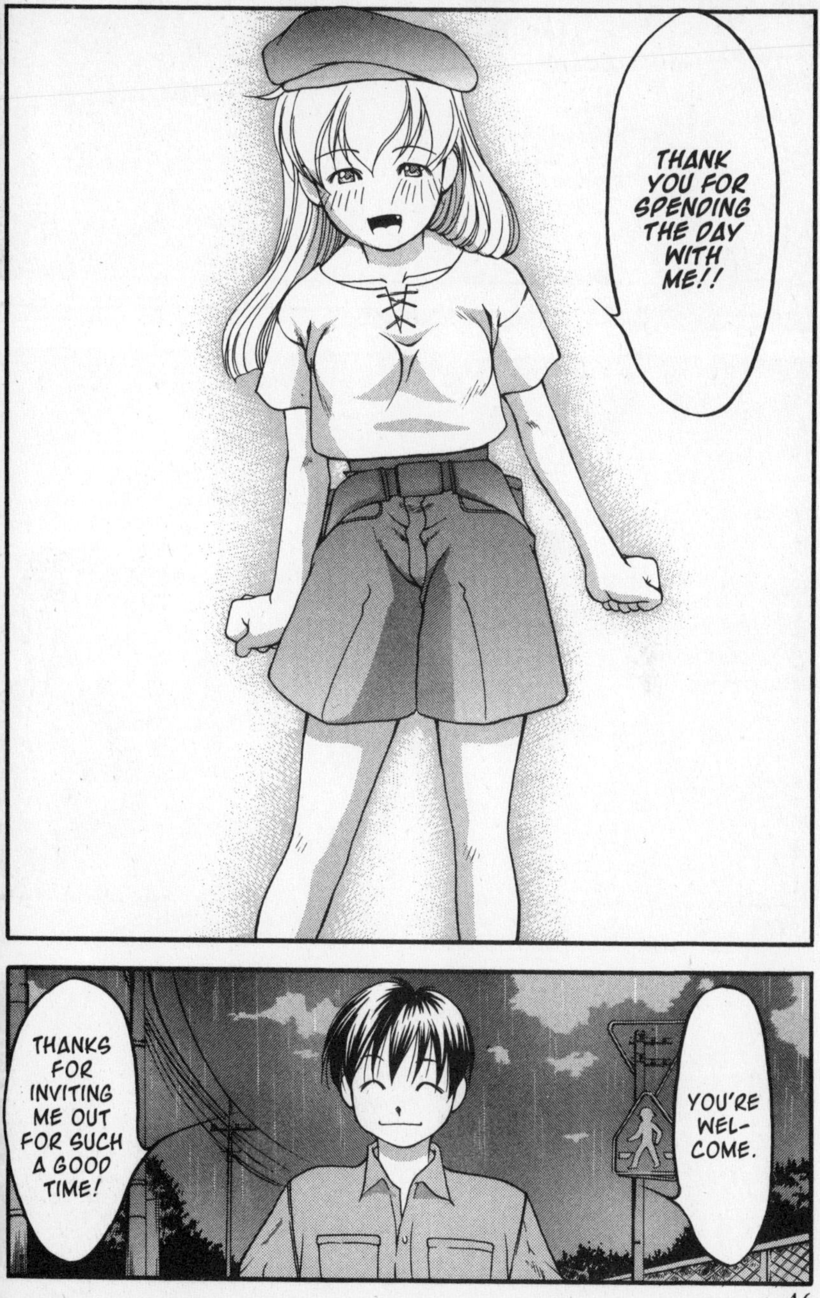
THANK YOU FOR SPENDING THE DAY WITH ME!!
YOU'RE WEL-COME.
THANKS FOR INVITING ME OUT FOR SUCH A GOOD TIME!

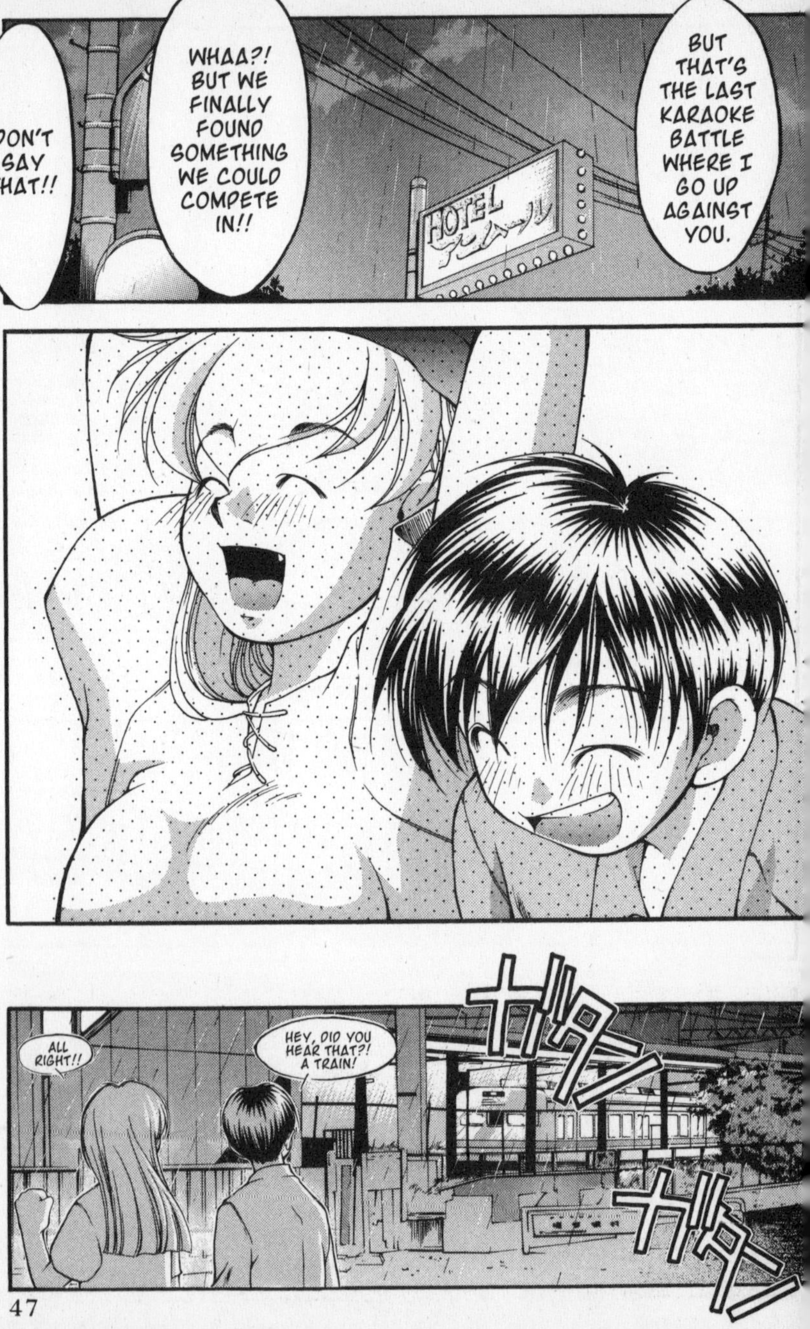
BUT THAT'S THE LAST KARAOKE BATTLE WHERE I GO UP AGAINST YOU.
HOTEL
WHAA?! BUT WE FINALLY FOUND SOMETHING WE COULD COMPETE IN!!
DON'T SAY THAT!!
ガタン
ガタン
HEY, DID YOU HEAR THAT?! A TRAIN!
ALL RIGHT!!

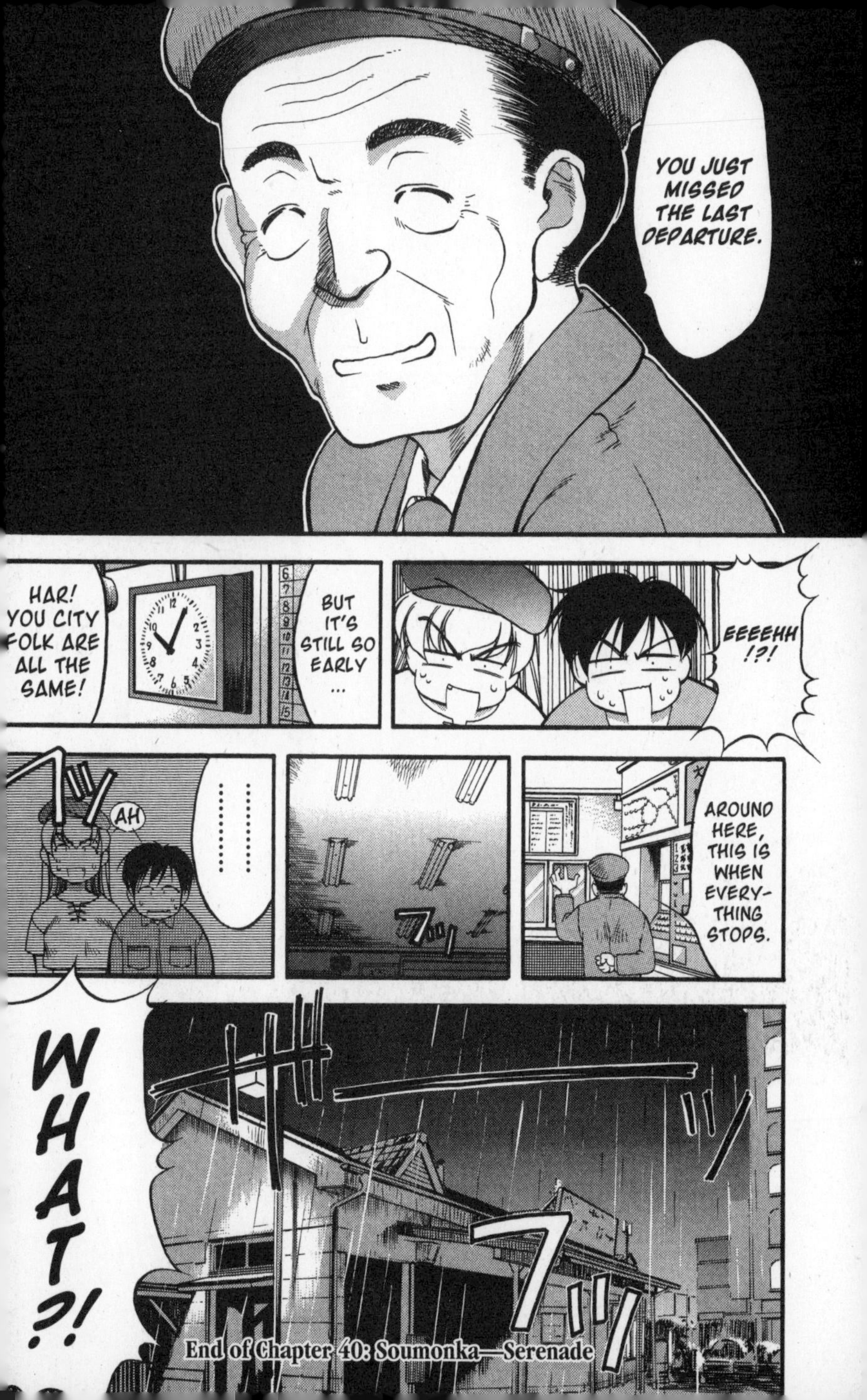

YOU JUST MISSED THE LAST DEPARTURE.
EEEEHH !?!
BUT IT'S STILL SO EARLY ...
HAR! YOU CITY FOLK ARE ALL THE SAME!
AROUND HERE, THIS IS WHEN EVERY-THING STOPS.
......
AH
WHAT?!
End of Chapter 40: Soumonka—Serenade

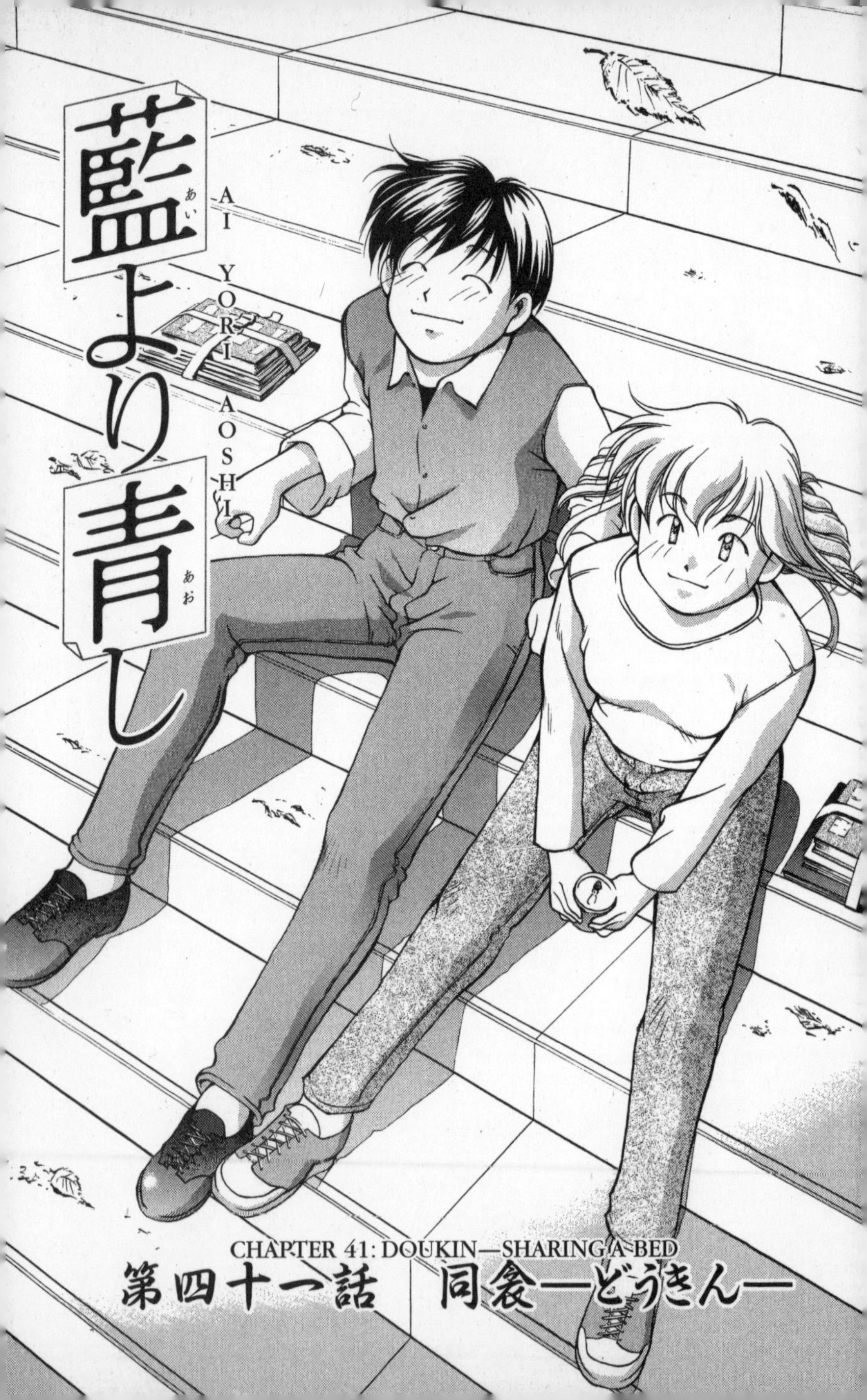
藍(あい)より青(あお)し
AI YORI AOSHI
CHAPTER 41: DOUKIN—SHARING A BED
第四十一話　同衾—どうきん—

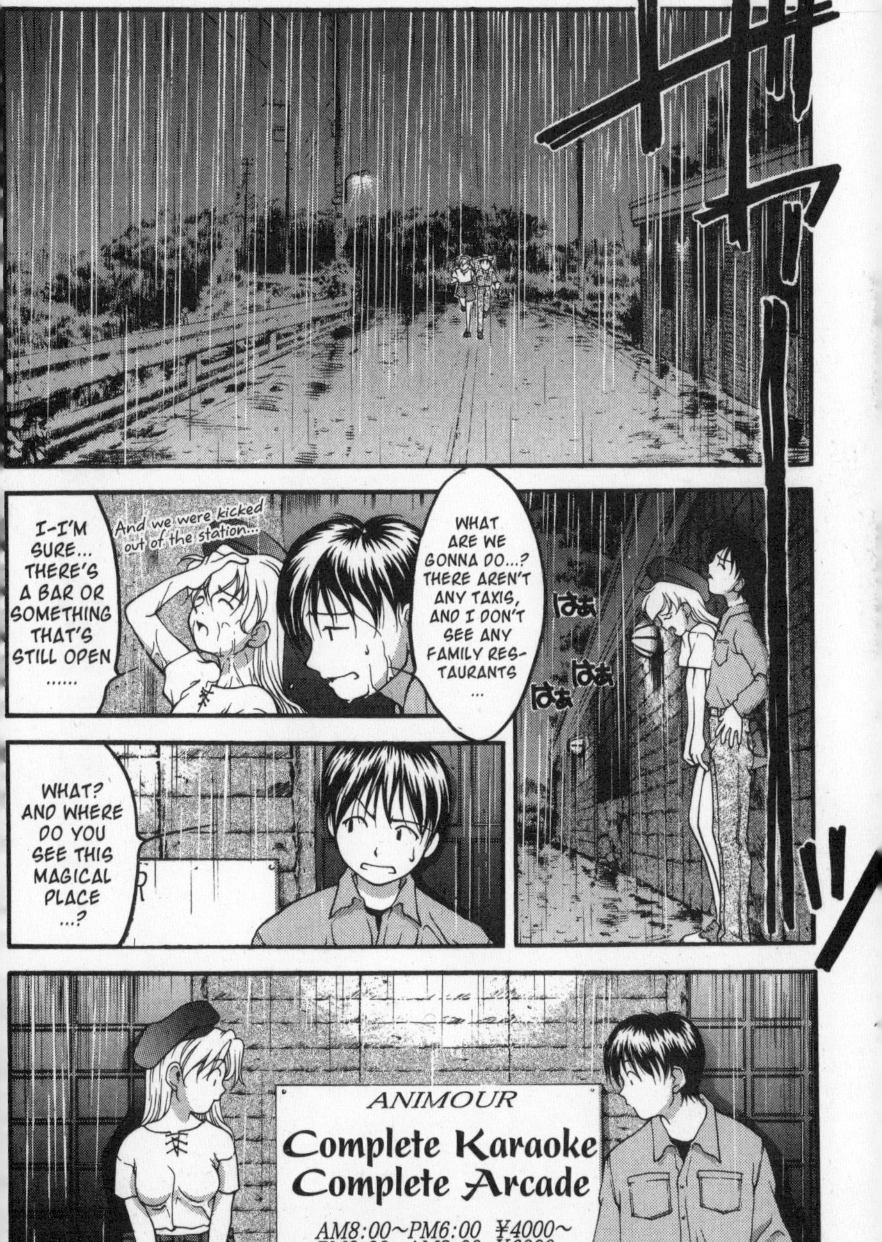
はぁ
はぁ
はぁ
WHAT ARE WE GONNA DO...? THERE AREN'T ANY TAXIS, AND I DON'T SEE ANY FAMILY RES-TAURANTS ...
And we were kicked out of the station...
I-I'M SURE... THERE'S A BAR OR SOMETHING THAT'S STILL OPEN ......
WHAT? AND WHERE DO YOU SEE THIS MAGICAL PLACE ...?
ANIMOUR
Complete Karaoke
Complete Arcade
AM8:00~PM6:00 ¥4000~
PM6:00~AM8:00 ¥6000~

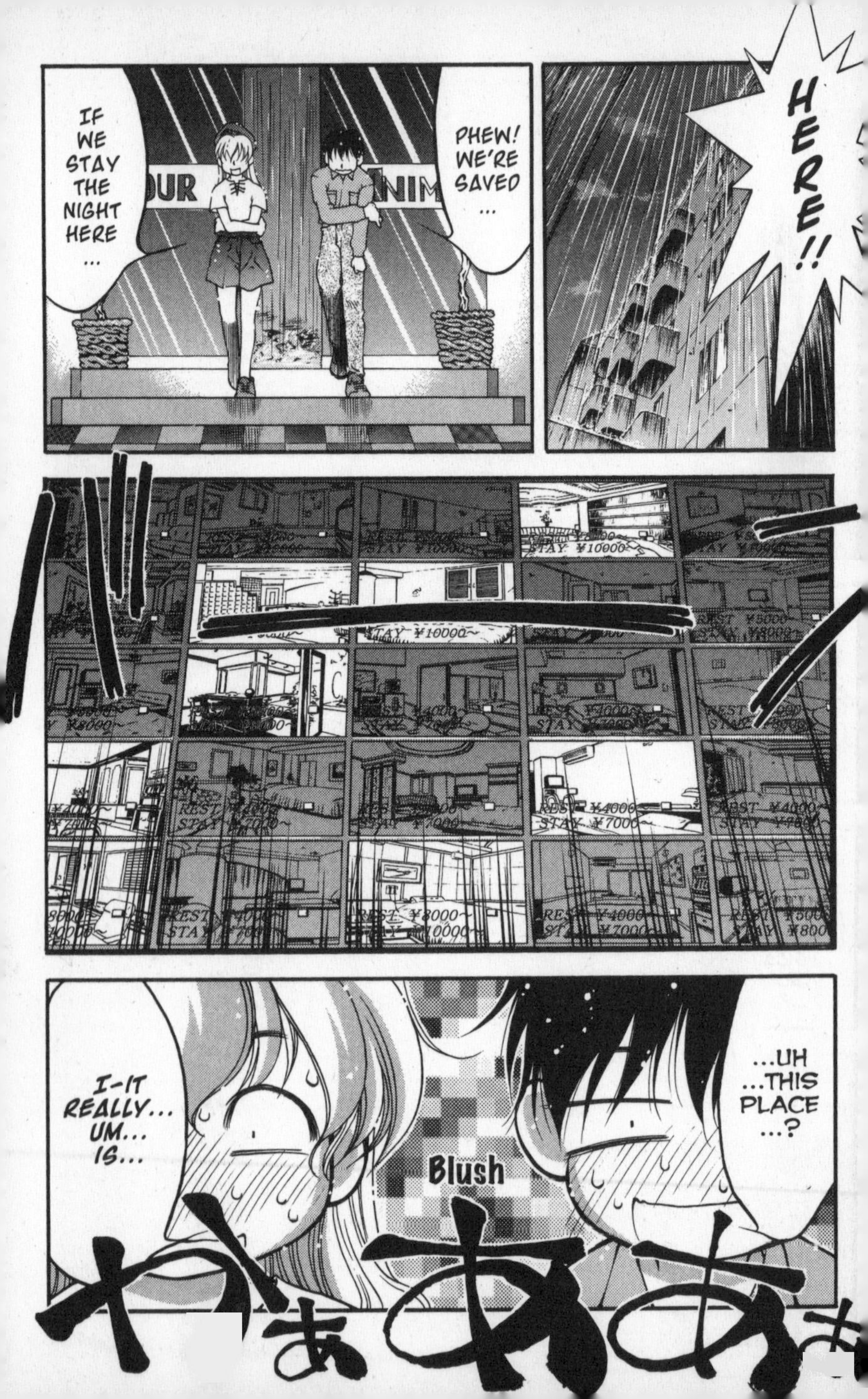
HERE!!
PHEW! WE'RE SAVED ...
IF WE STAY THE NIGHT HERE ...
...UH ...THIS PLACE ...?
Blush
I-IT REALLY... UM... IS...

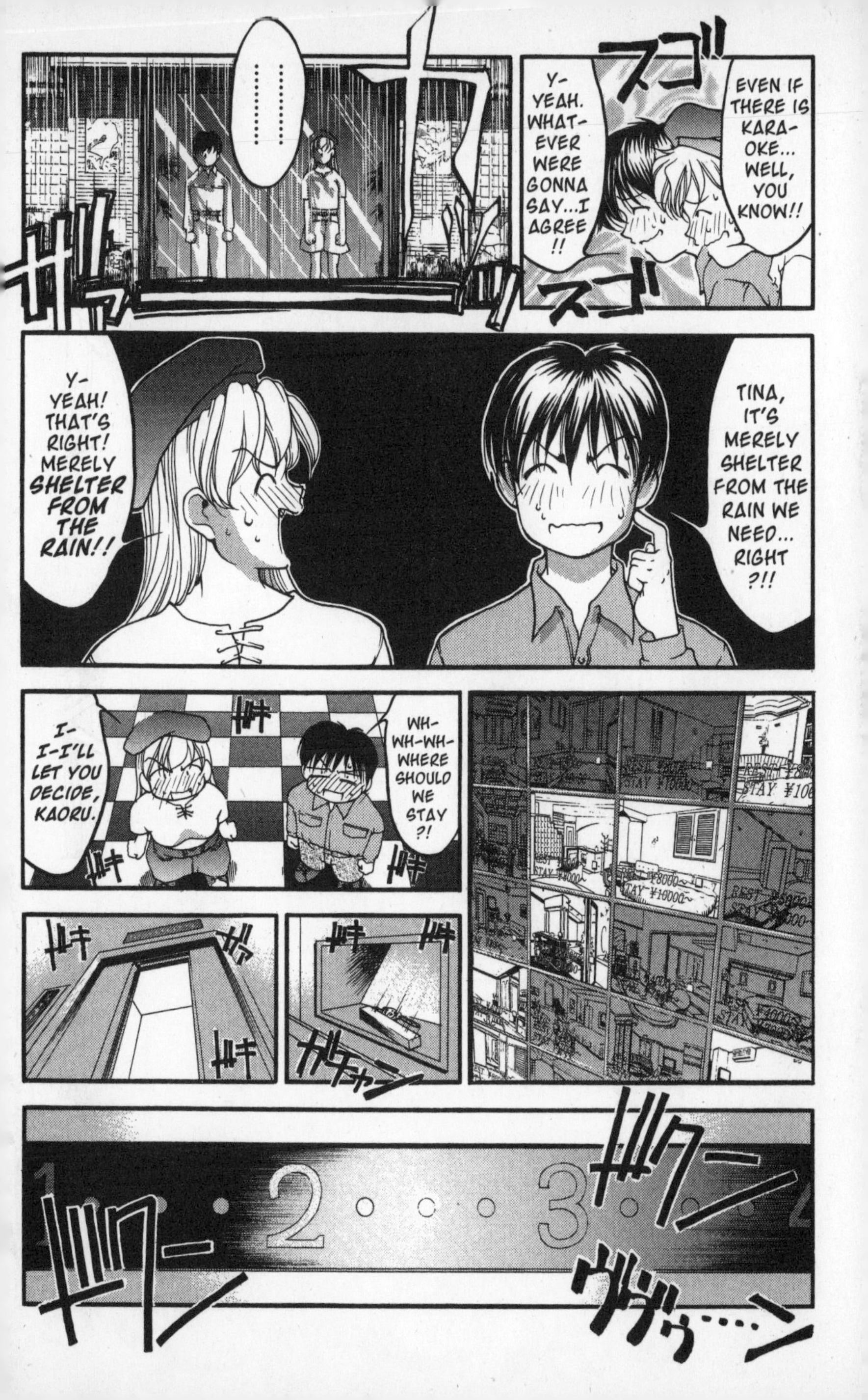
EVEN IF THERE IS KARA-OKE... WELL, YOU KNOW!!
Y-YEAH. WHAT-EVER WERE GONNA SAY...I AGREE!!
......
TINA, IT'S MERELY SHELTER FROM THE RAIN WE NEED... RIGHT?!!
Y-YEAH! THAT'S RIGHT! MERELY SHELTER FROM THE RAIN!!
WH-WH-WH-WHERE SHOULD WE STAY?!
I-I-I'LL LET YOU DECIDE, KAORU.
1 2 3 4

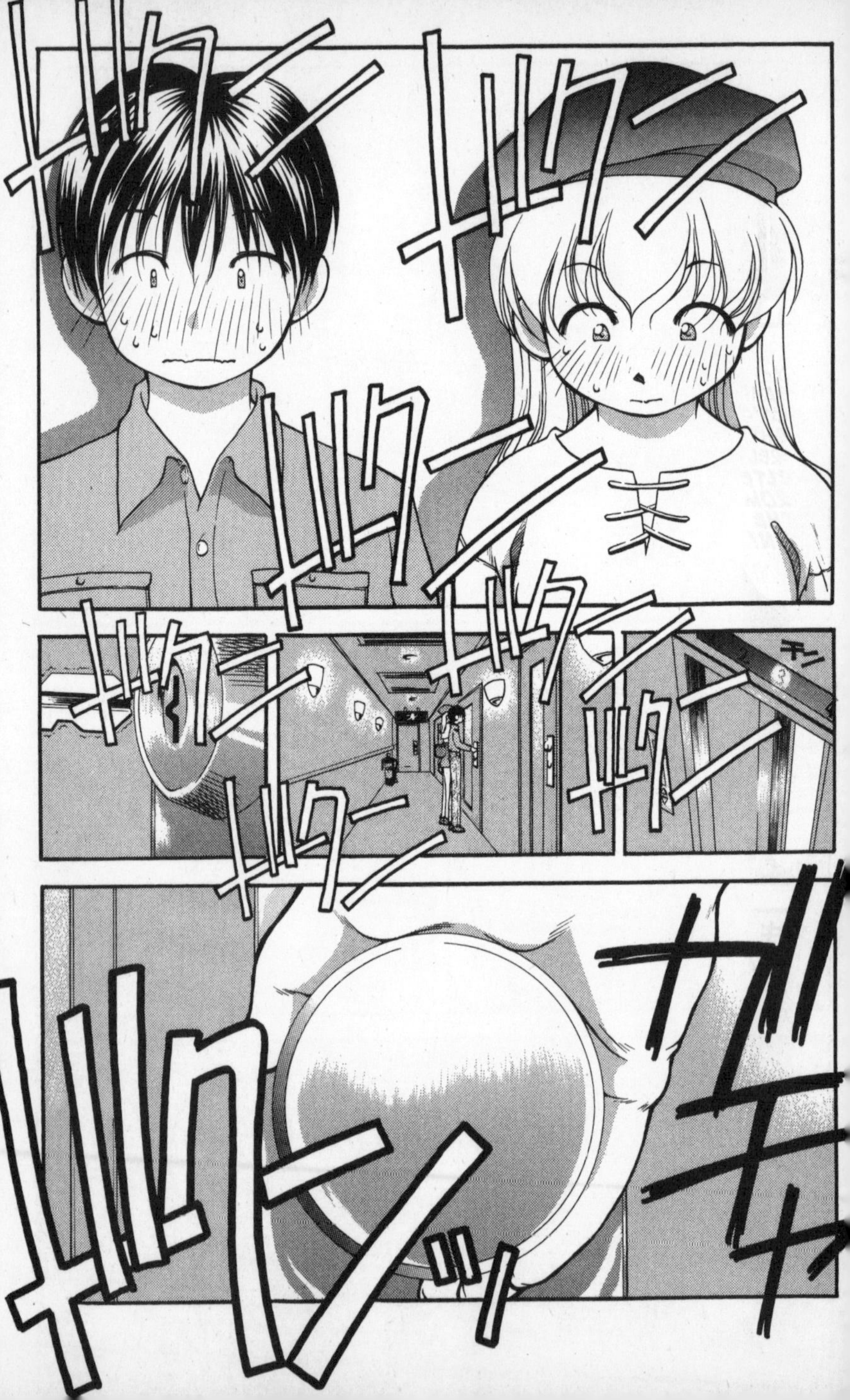
ドックン
ドックン
ドックン
チン
ドックン
ドックン
ドックン
ドックン
ガチャ
ドックン

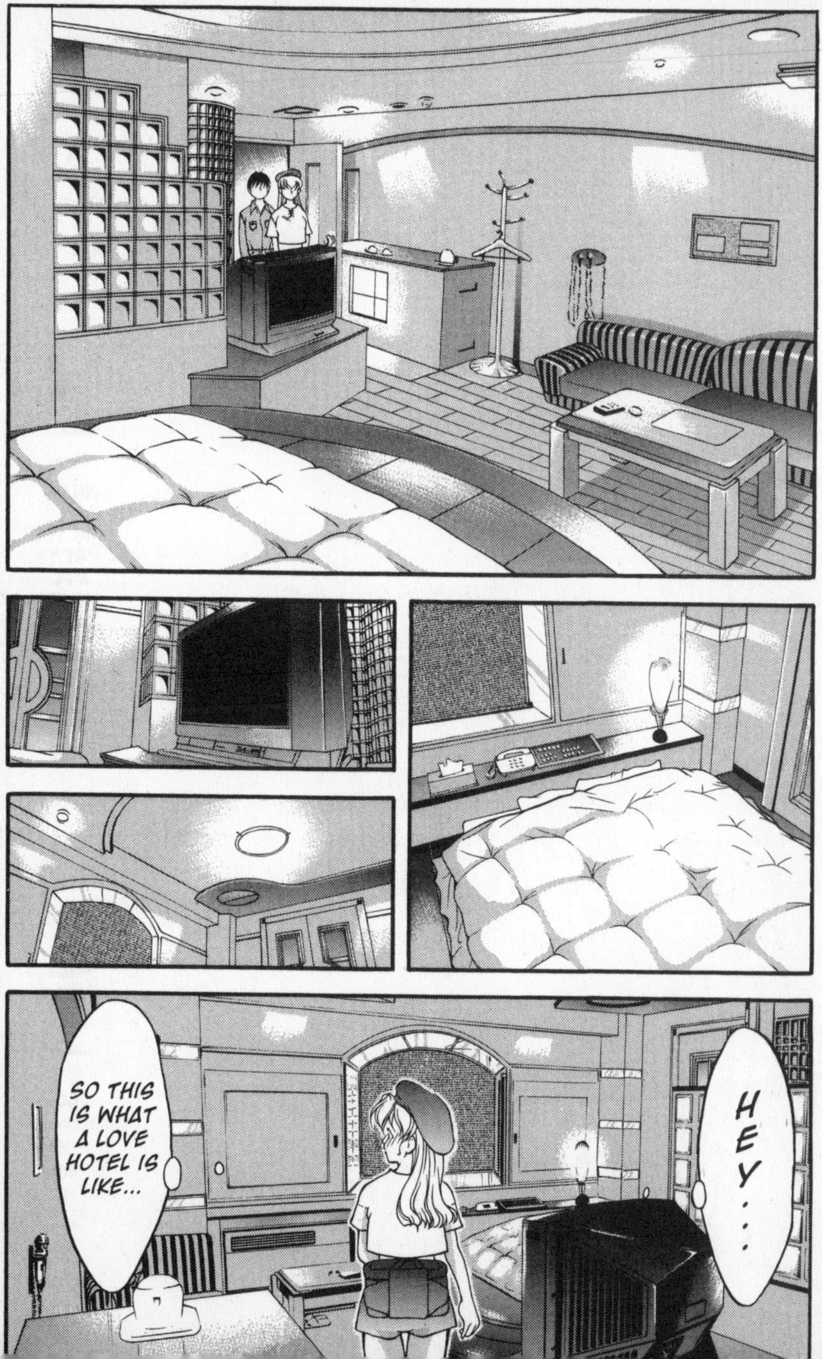
HEY...
SO THIS IS WHAT A LOVE HOTEL IS LIKE...

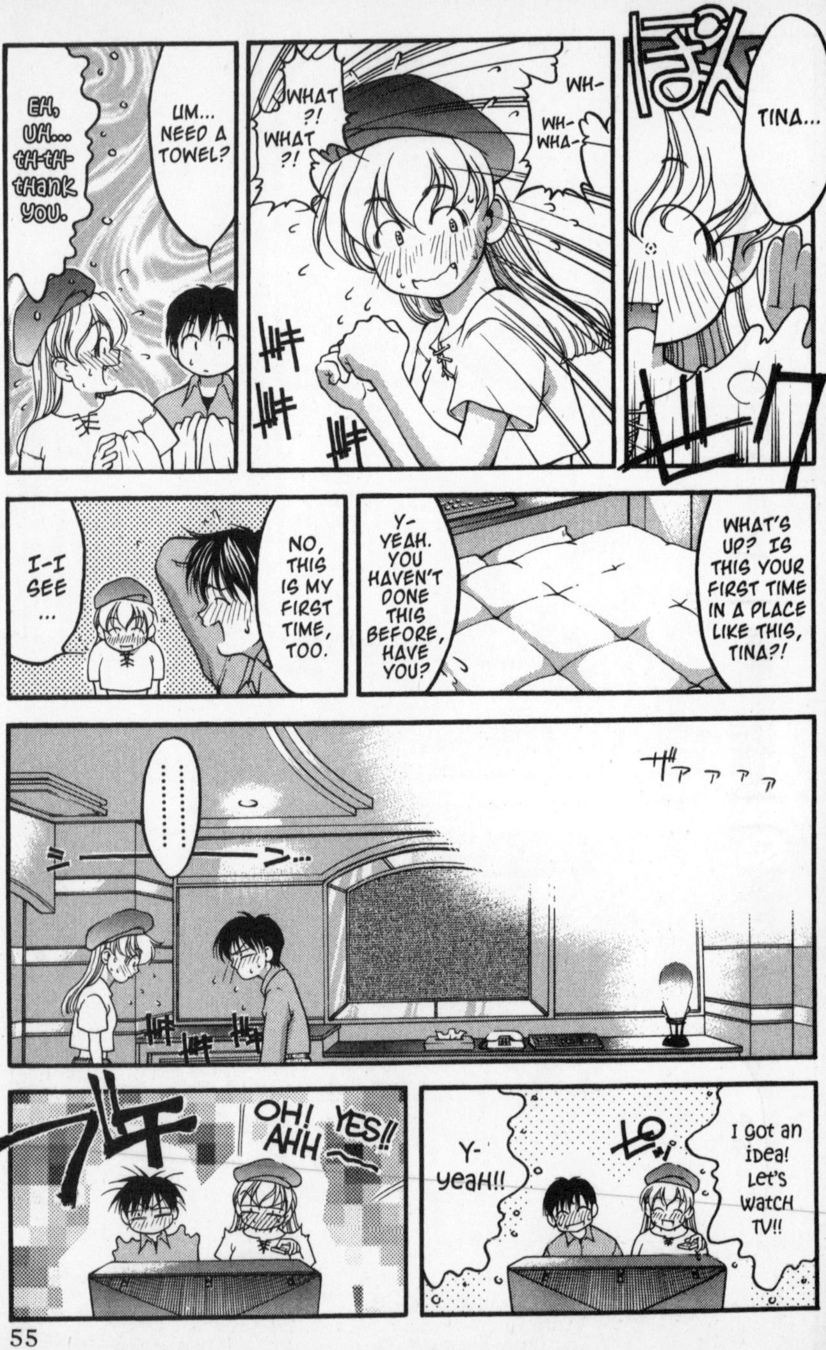
ぽん
TINA...
ビク
WH-
WH-WHA-
WHAT?!
WHAT?!
UM... NEED A TOWEL?
EH, UH... TH-TH-THANK YOU.
WHAT'S UP? IS THIS YOUR FIRST TIME IN A PLACE LIKE THIS, TINA?!
Y-YEAH. YOU HAVEN'T DONE THIS BEFORE, HAVE YOU?
NO, THIS IS MY FIRST TIME, TOO.
I-I SEE ...
ザァァァァ
......
シーーーン...
I got an idea! Let's watch TV!!
ピッ
Y-yeah!!
OH! AHH~ YES!!
ブチ

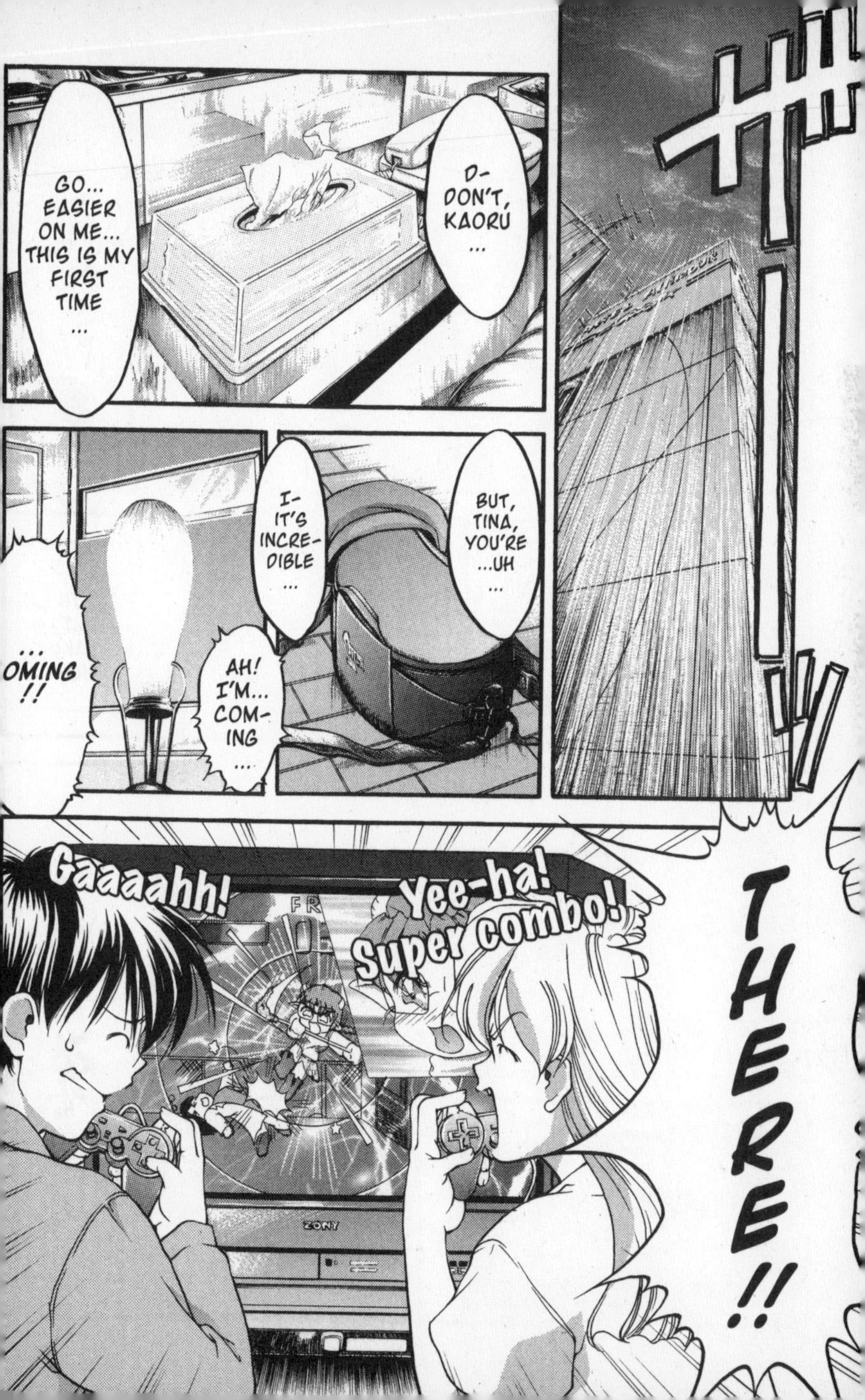
D-DON'T, KAORU ...
GO... EASIER ON ME... THIS IS MY FIRST TIME ...
BUT, TINA, YOU'RE ...UH ...
I-IT'S INCREDIBLE ...
AH! I'M... COMING ...
...OMING !!
THERE!!
Yee-ha! Super combo!
Gaaaaahh!
ZONY

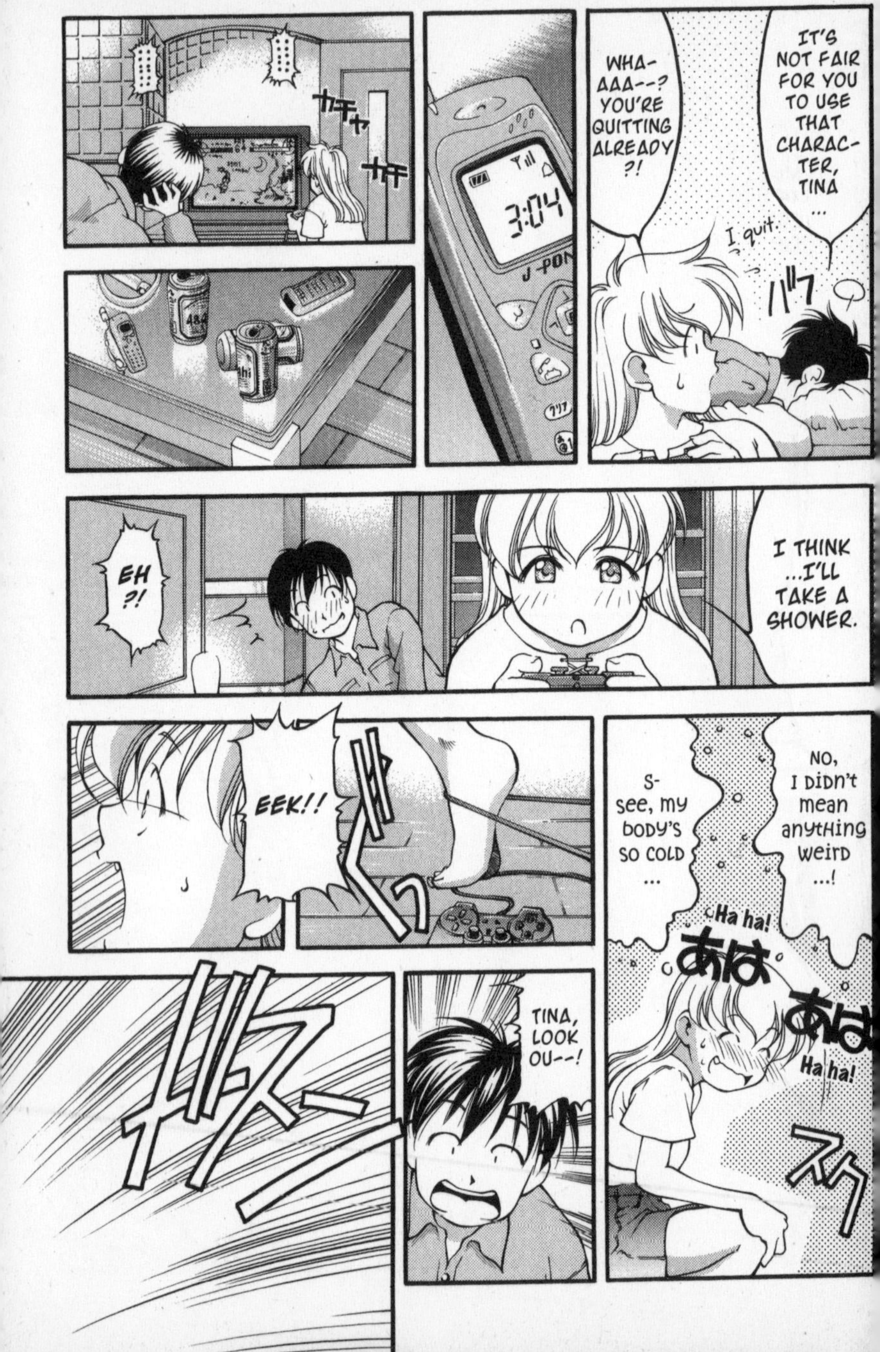

IT'S NOT FAIR FOR YOU TO USE THAT CHARACTER, TINA ...
WHA-AAA--? YOU'RE QUITTING ALREADY ?!
I quit.
3:04
I THINK ...I'LL TAKE A SHOWER.
EH ?!
NO, I DIDN'T mean anything weird ...!
S- see, my body's so cold ...
Ha ha!
あは
あは
Ha ha!
EEK!!
TINA, LOOK OU--!

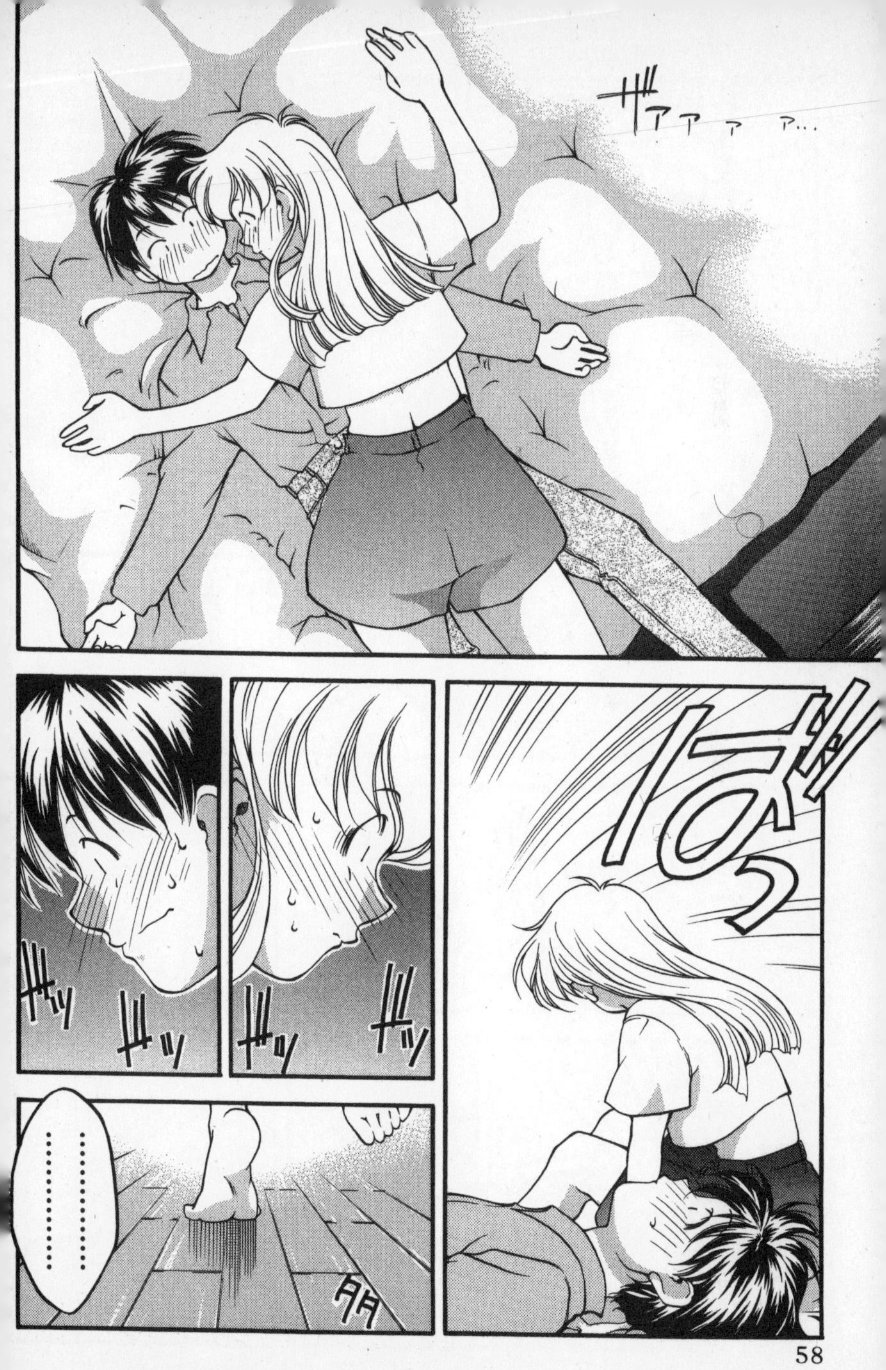
ザァァァァ…
ばっ
ギッ
ギッ
ギッ
ギッ
…………

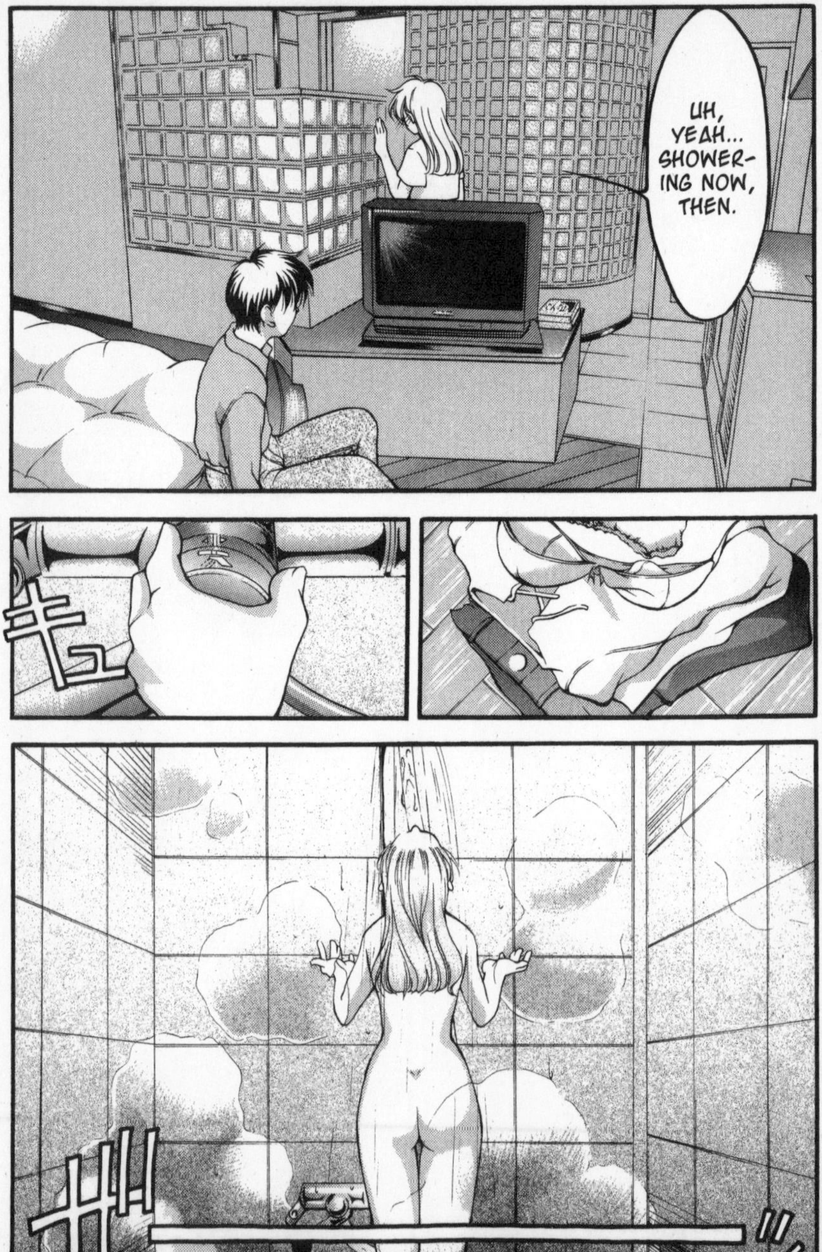
UH, YEAH... SHOWERING NOW, THEN.
キュ
ザー

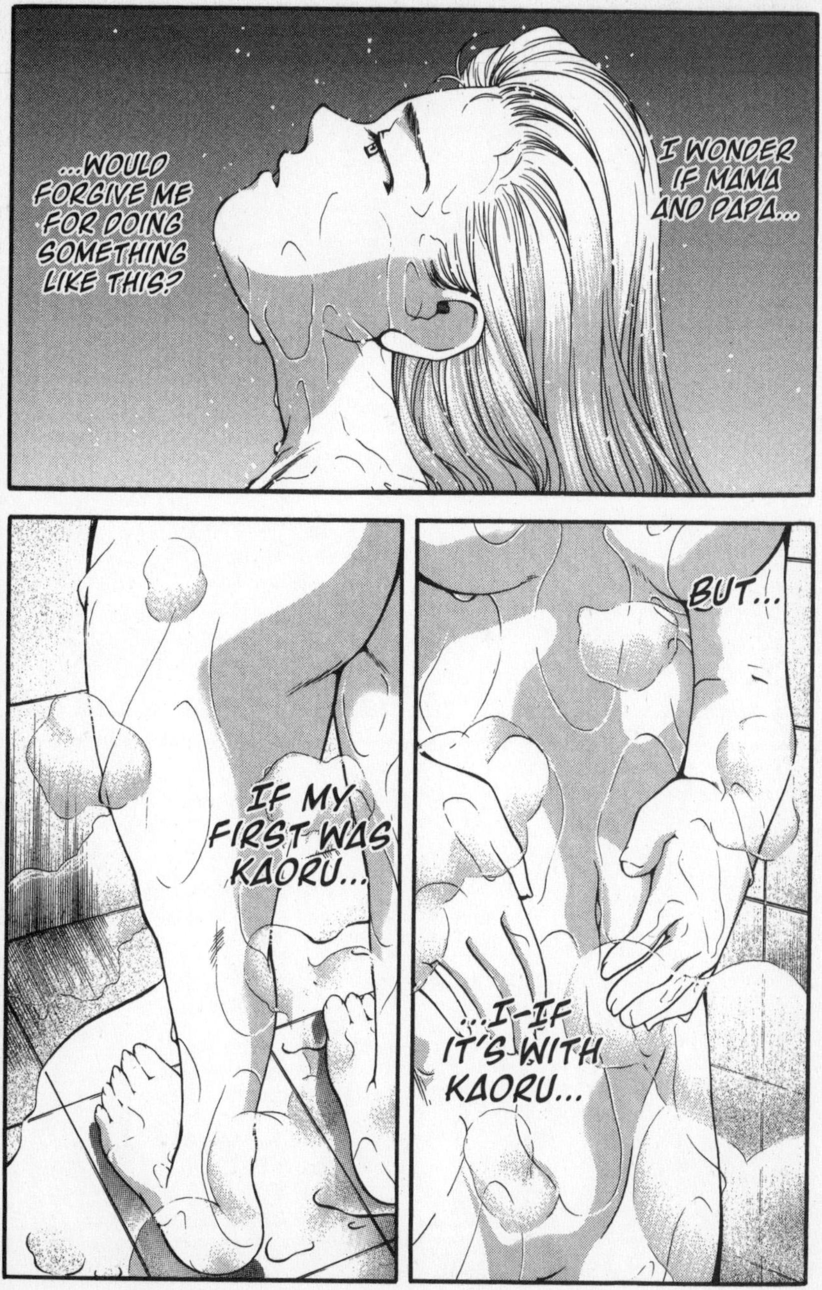
I WONDER IF MAMA AND PAPA...
...WOULD FORGIVE ME FOR DOING SOMETHING LIKE THIS?
BUT...
...I-IF IT'S WITH KAORU...
IF MY FIRST WAS KAORU...

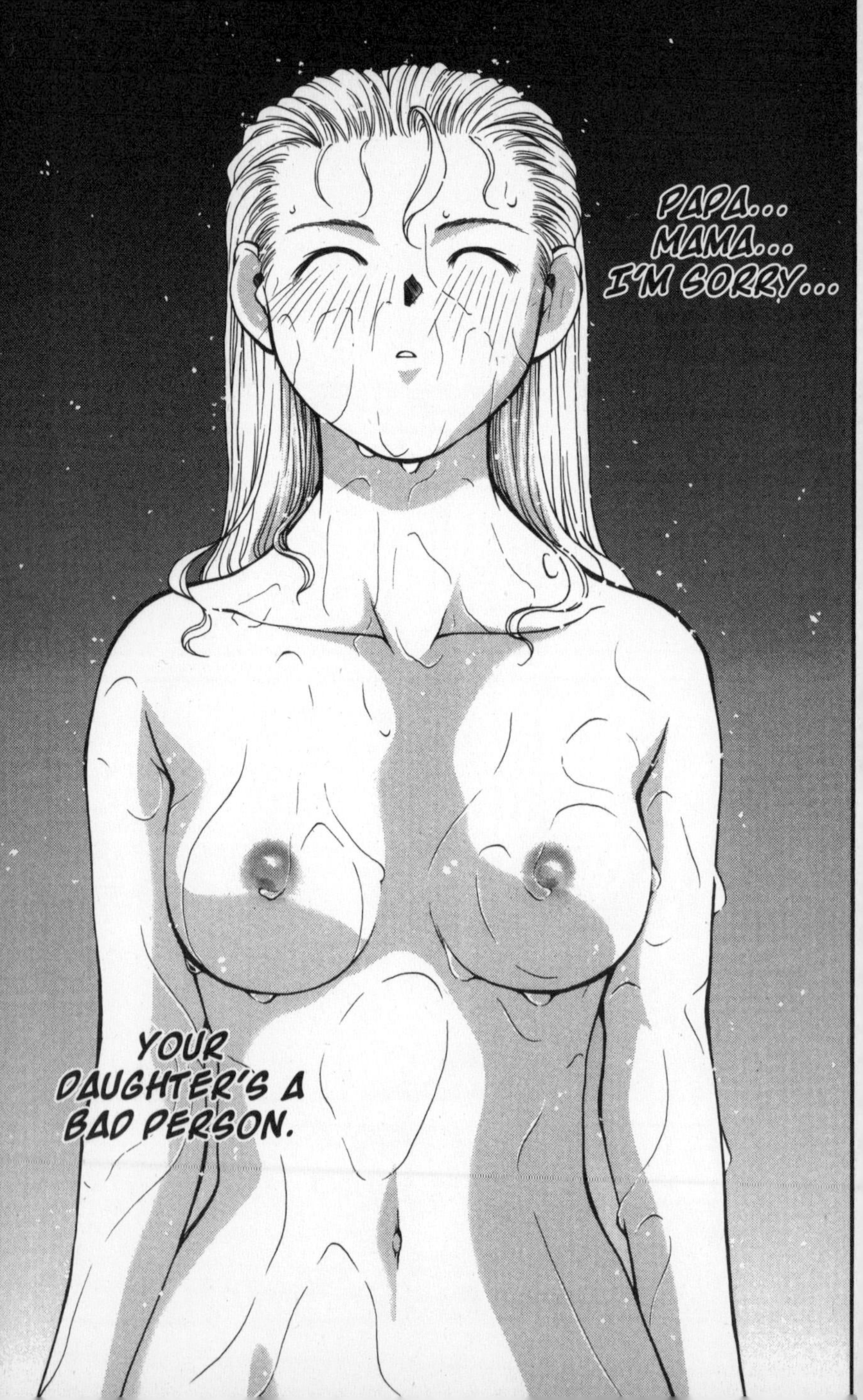
PAPA... MAMA... I'M SORRY...
YOUR DAUGHTER'S A BAD PERSON.

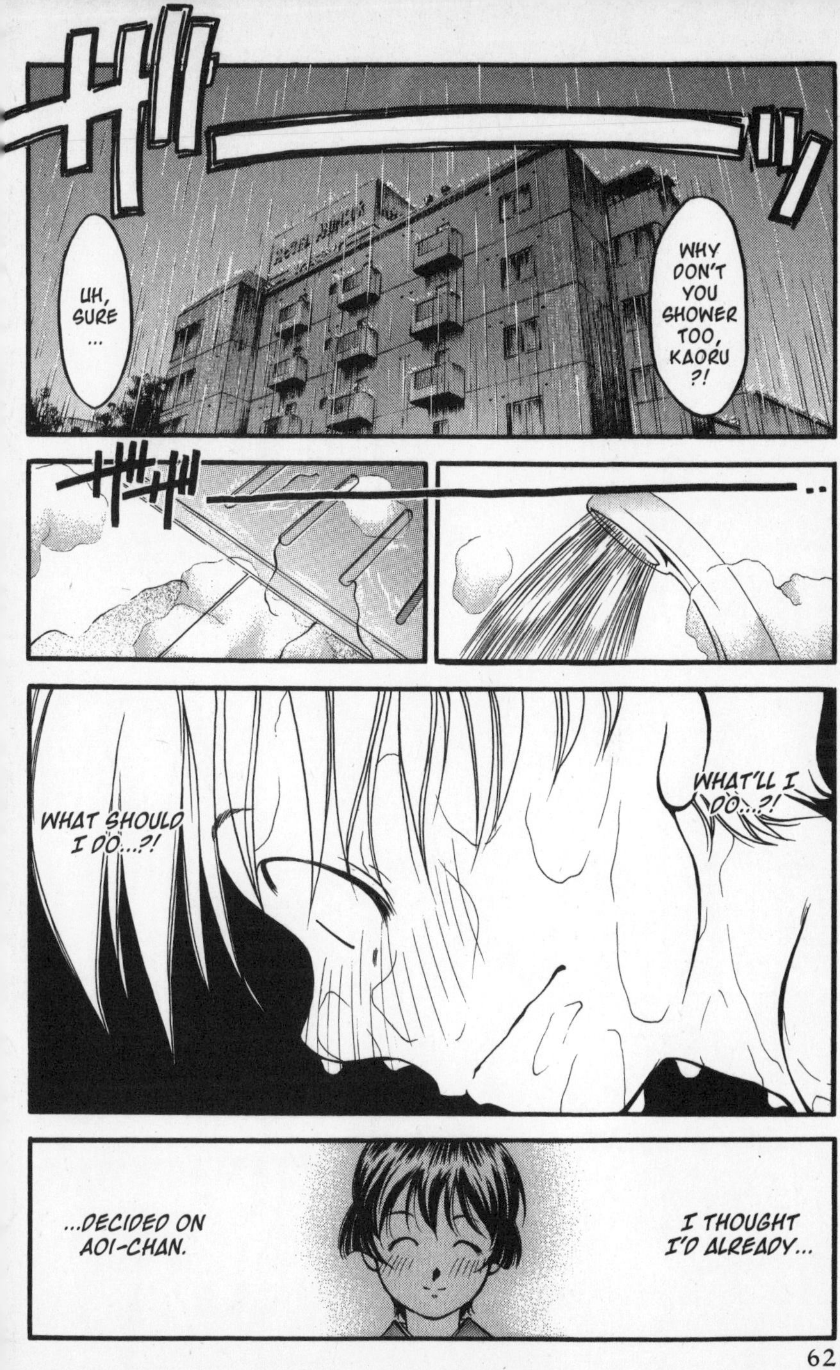
WHY DON'T YOU SHOWER TOO, KAORU ?!
UH, SURE ...
WHAT'LL I DO...?!
WHAT SHOULD I DO...?!
I THOUGHT I'D ALREADY...
...DECIDED ON AOI-CHAN.

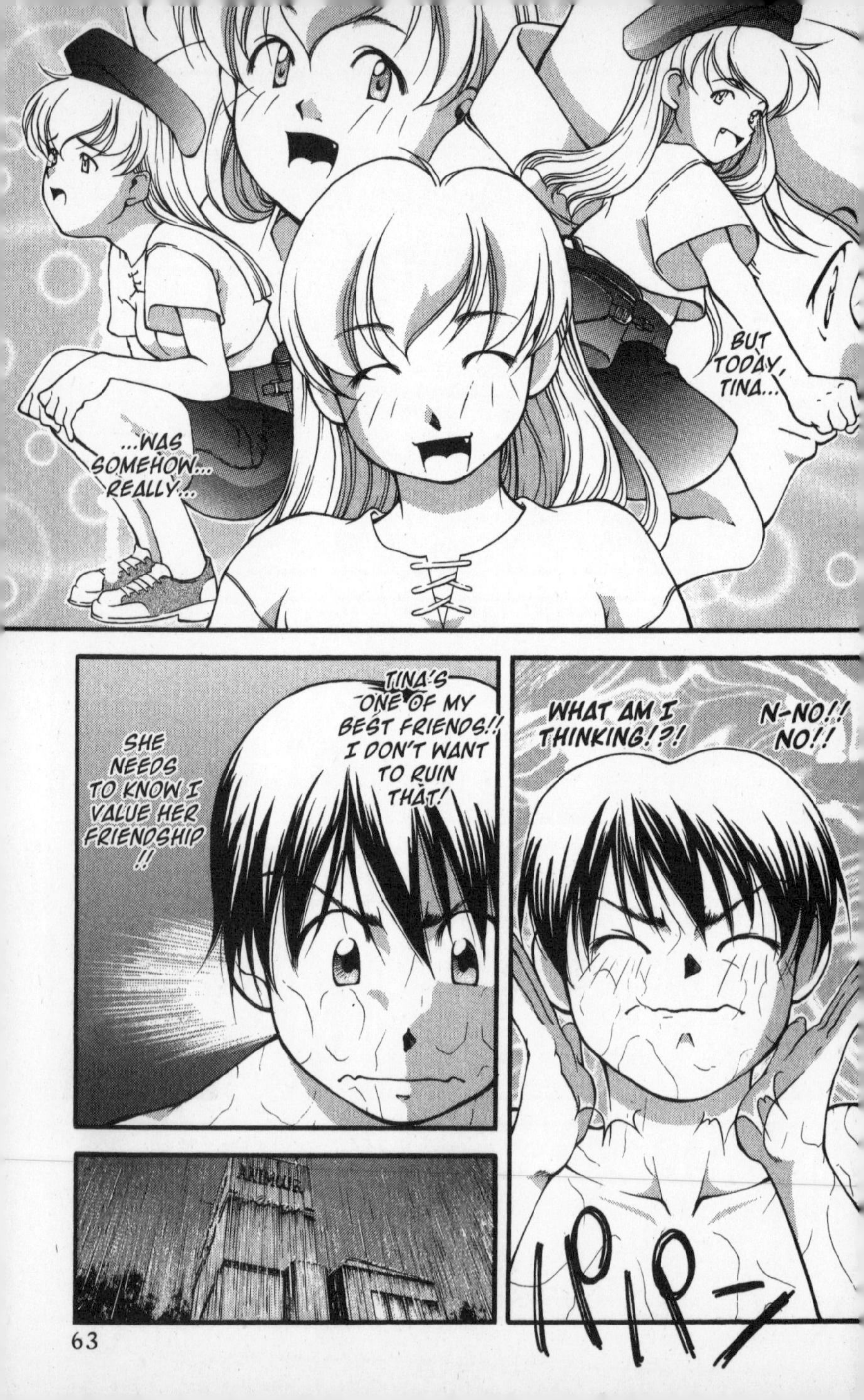
BUT TODAY, TINA...
...WAS SOMEHOW... REALLY...
N-NO!! NO!!
WHAT AM I THINKING!?!
TINA'S ONE OF MY BEST FRIENDS!! I DON'T WANT TO RUIN THAT!
SHE NEEDS TO KNOW I VALUE HER FRIENDSHIP!!

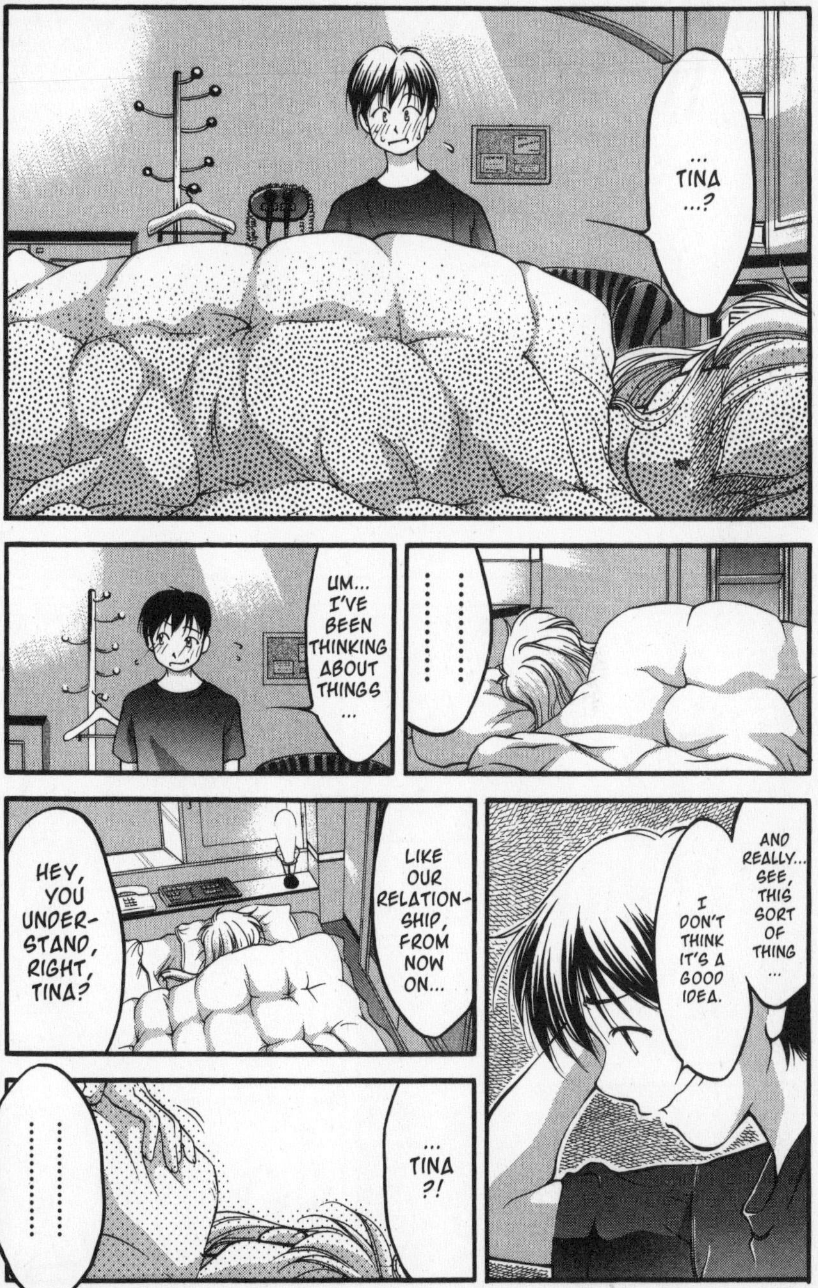
... TINA ...?
....
UM... I'VE BEEN THINKING ABOUT THINGS ...
AND REALLY... SEE, THIS SORT OF THING ...
I DON'T THINK IT'S A GOOD IDEA.
LIKE OUR RELATION-SHIP, FROM NOW ON...
HEY, YOU UNDER-STAND, RIGHT, TINA?
... TINA ?!
....

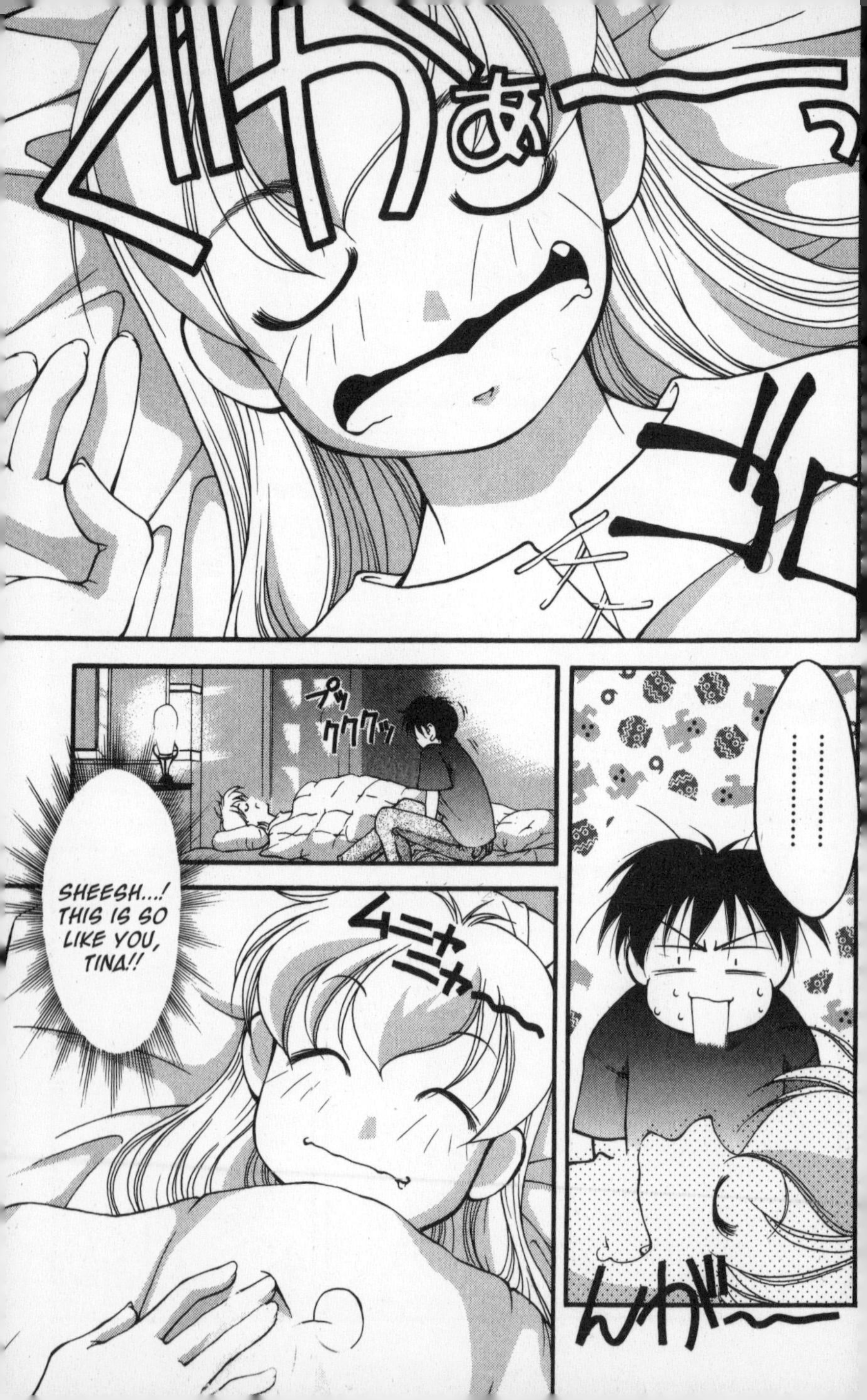
……
んがー〜
プッ
ククッ
SHEESH…! THIS IS SO LIKE YOU, TINA!!
ムニャニャ〜

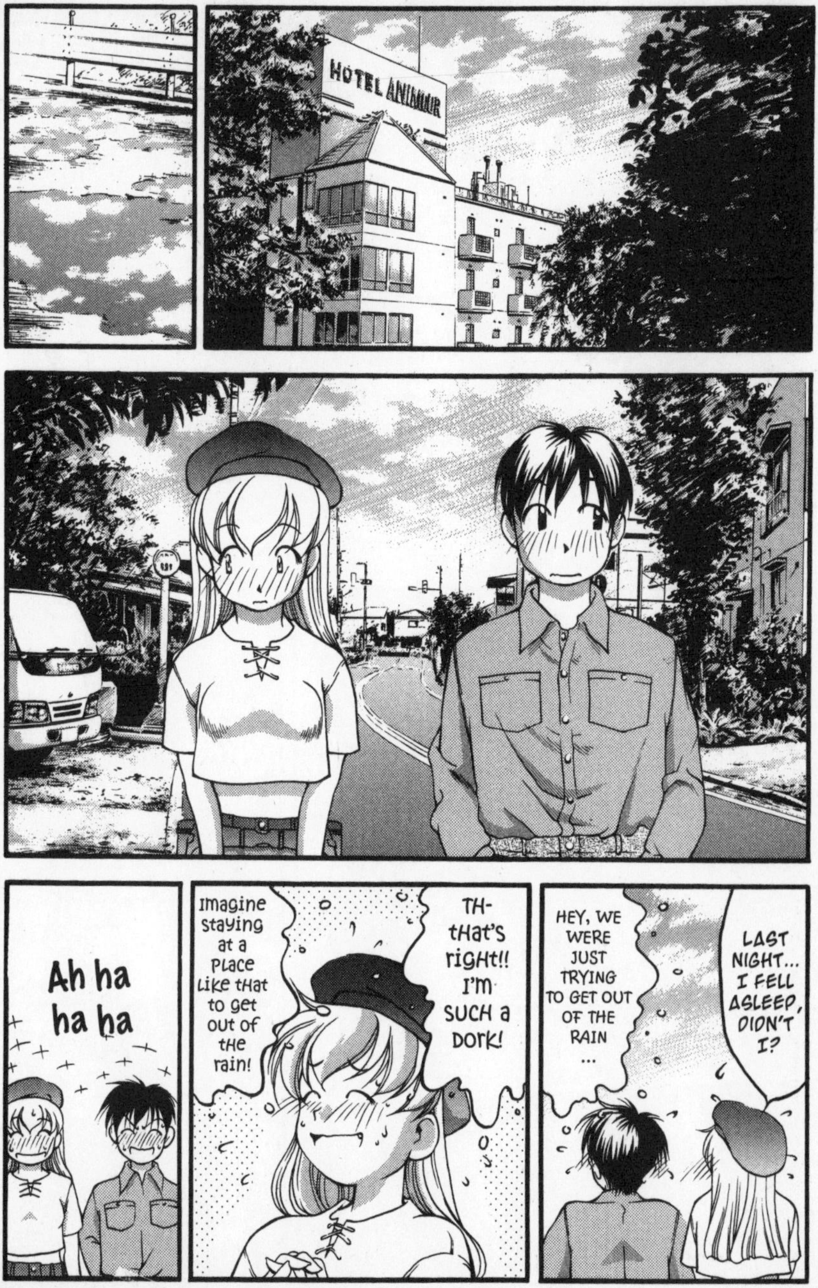
HOTEL
LAST NIGHT... I FELL ASLEEP, DIDN'T I?
HEY, WE WERE JUST TRYING TO GET OUT OF THE RAIN ...
TH-that's right!! I'm SUCH a DORK!
Imagine staying at a place like that to get out of the rain!
Ah ha ha ha

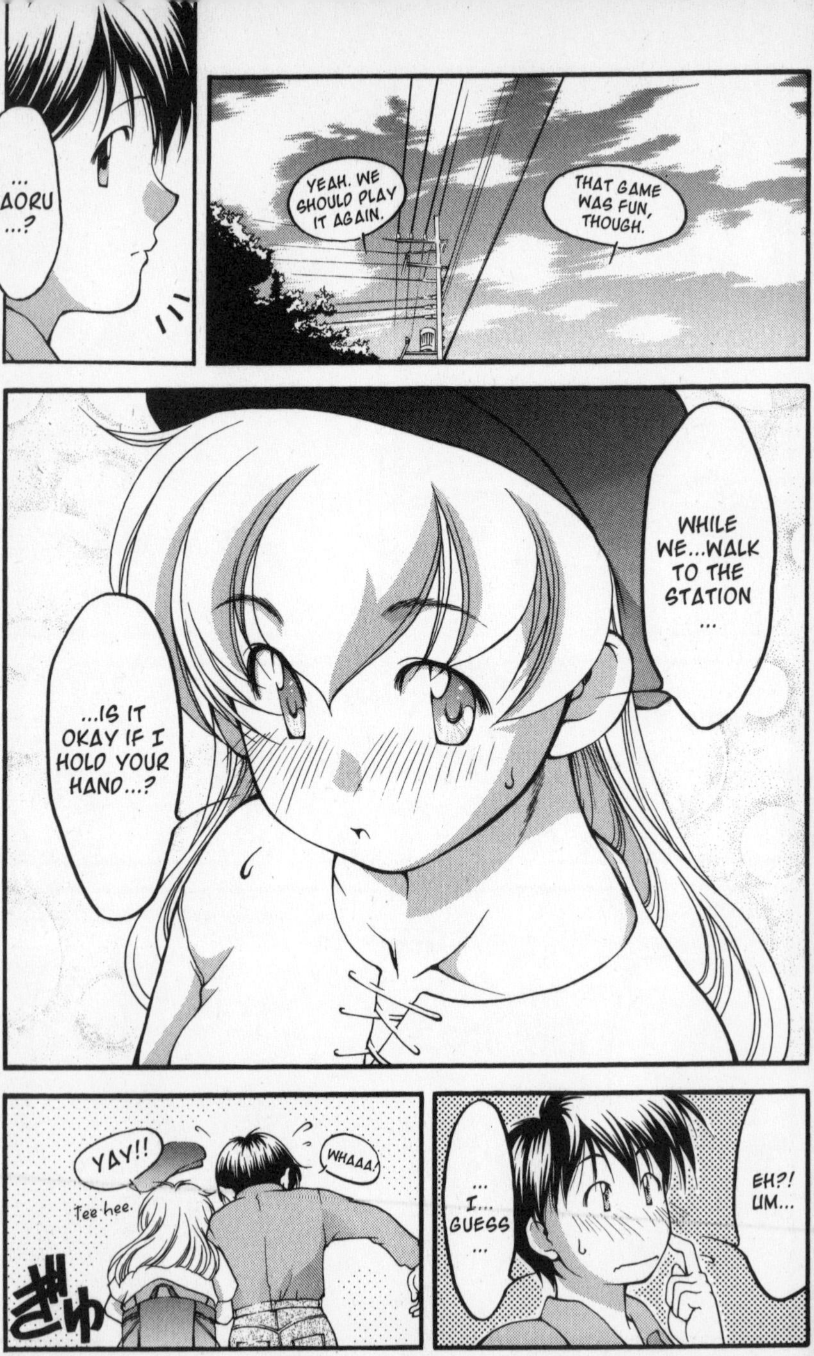
THAT GAME WAS FUN, THOUGH.
YEAH. WE SHOULD PLAY IT AGAIN.
... KAORU ...?
WHILE WE...WALK TO THE STATION ...
...IS IT OKAY IF I HOLD YOUR HAND...?
EH?! UM...
... I... GUESS ...
WHAAA!
YAY!!
Tee hee.
ぎゅ

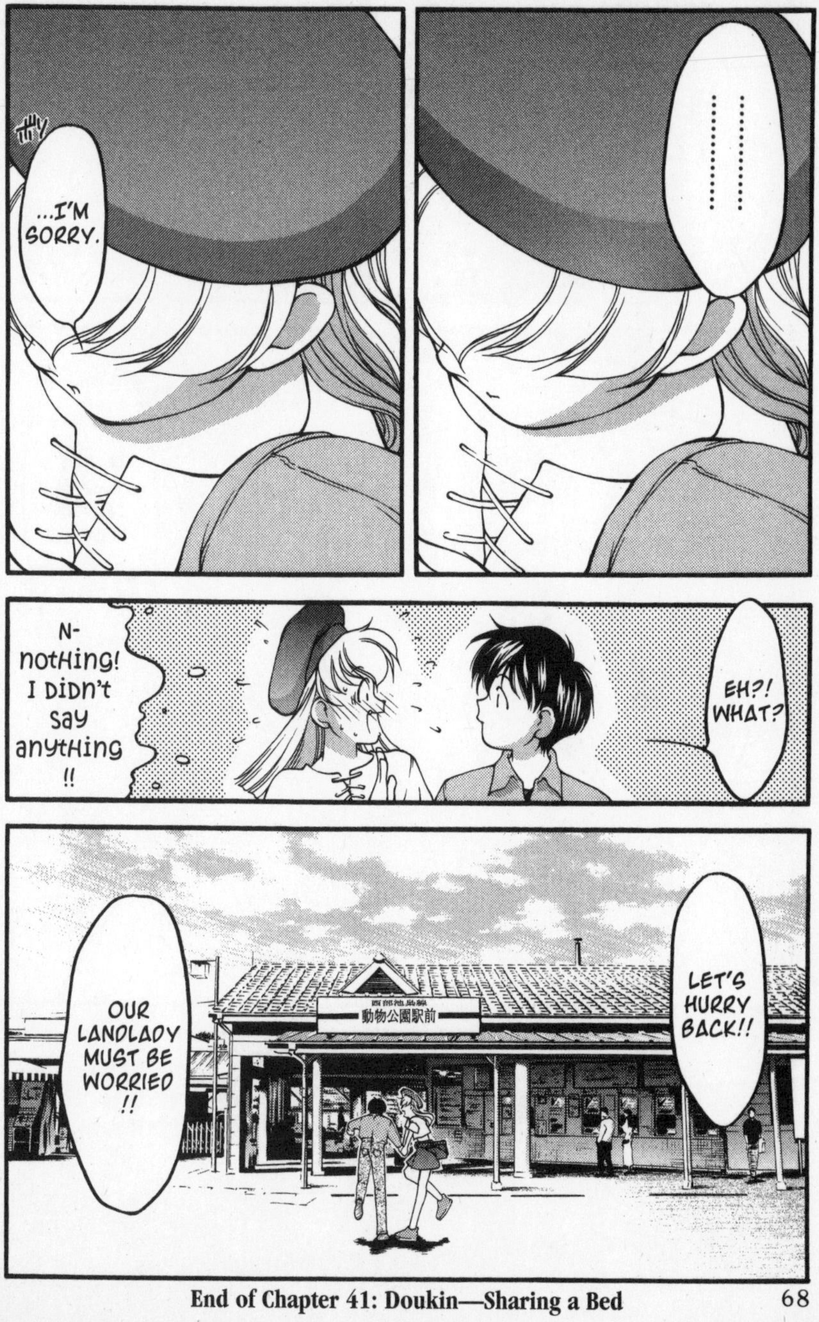
......
...I'M SORRY.
EH?! WHAT?
N-nothing! I didn't say anything!!
LET'S HURRY BACK!!
動物公園駅前
OUR LANDLADY MUST BE WORRIED!!

End of Chapter 41: Doukin—Sharing a Bed

藍より青し

AI YORI AOSHI

SPECIAL CHAPTER AMATERASU SUN GODDESS

特別編 天照―あまてらす―

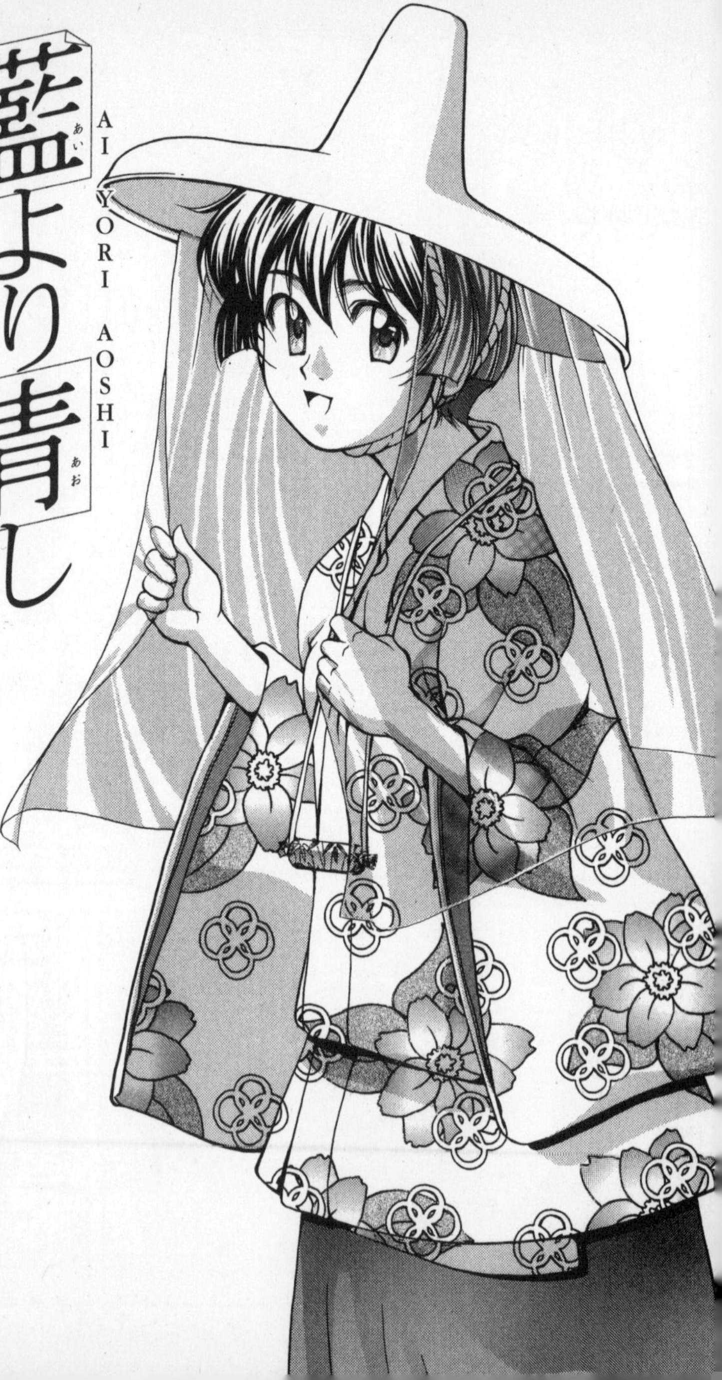

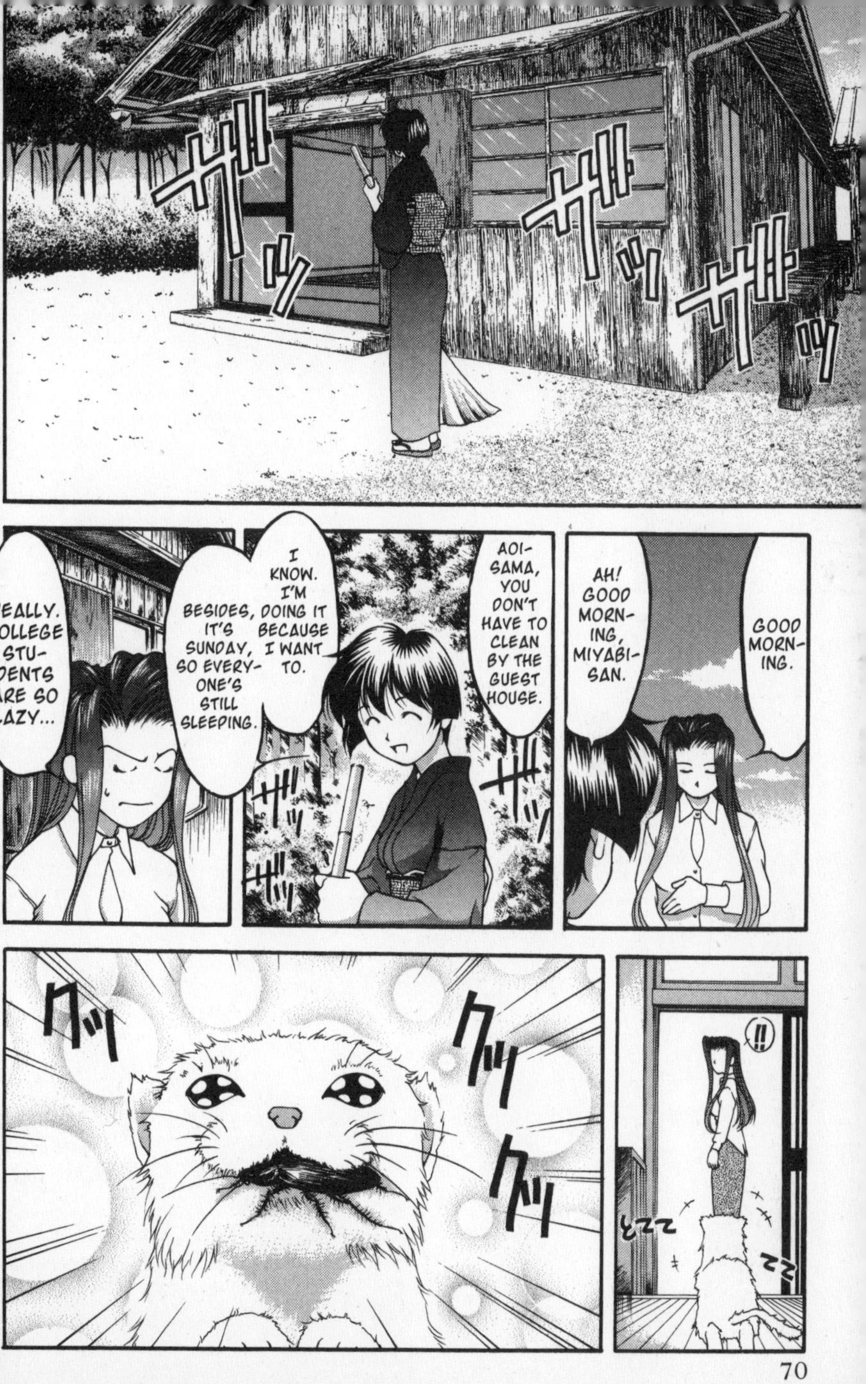
GOOD MORNING.
AH! GOOD MORNING, MIYABI-SAN.
AOI-SAMA, YOU DON'T HAVE TO CLEAN BY THE GUEST HOUSE.
I KNOW. I'M DOING IT BECAUSE I WANT TO.
BESIDES, IT'S SUNDAY, SO EVERYONE'S STILL SLEEPING.
REALLY. COLLEGE STUDENTS ARE SO LAZY...
!!
ZZZ
ZZ

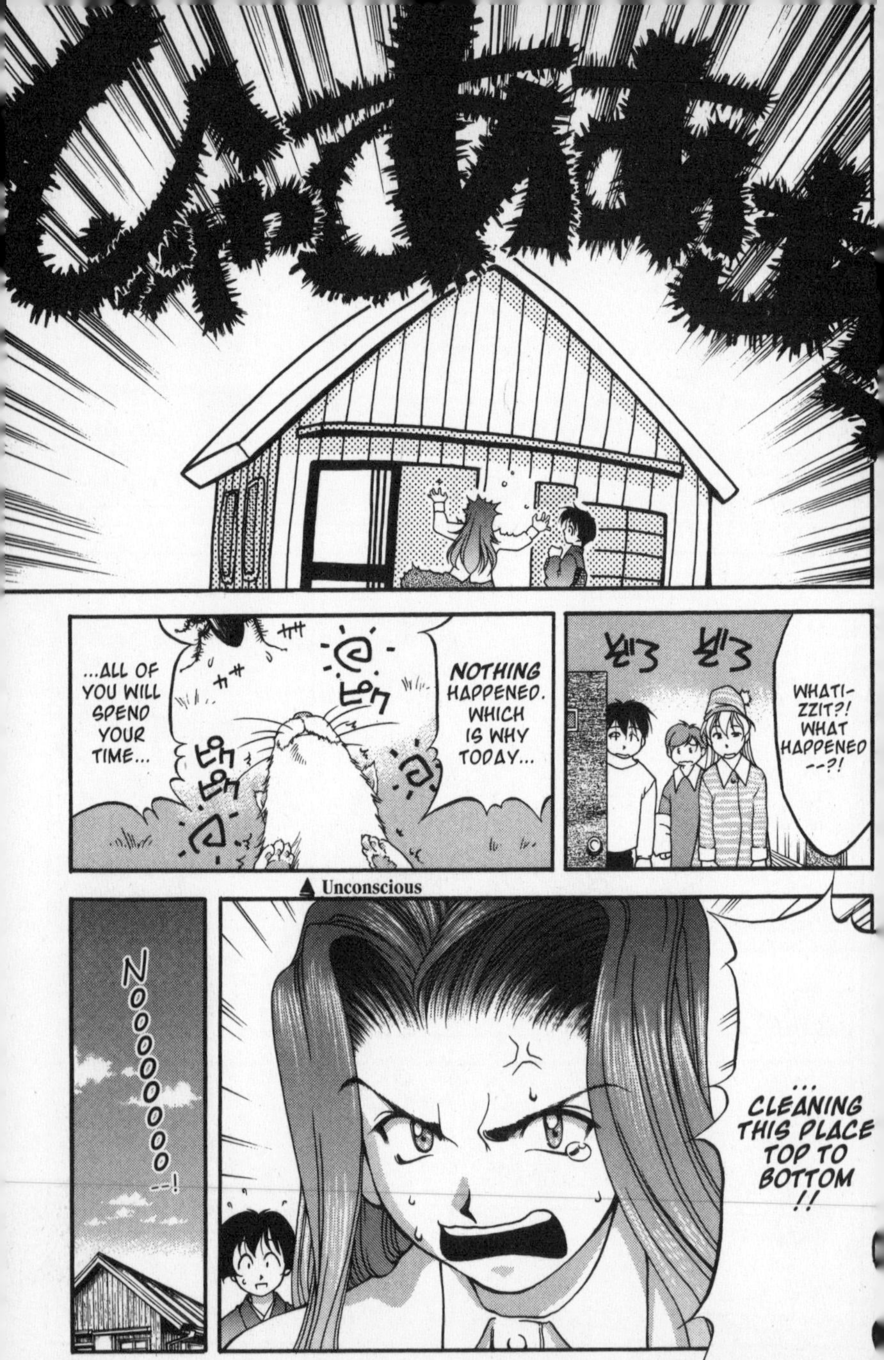
WHATI-ZZIT?! WHAT HAPPENED--?!
NOTHING HAPPENED. WHICH IS WHY TODAY...
...ALL OF YOU WILL SPEND YOUR TIME...
▲Unconscious
...CLEANING THIS PLACE TOP TO BOTTOM!!
Noooooooooo--!

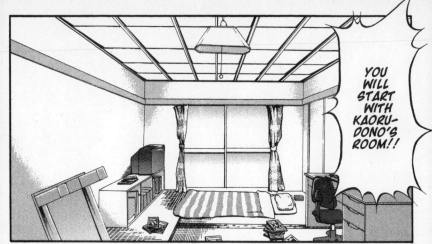

YOU WILL START WITH KAORU-DONO'S ROOM!!

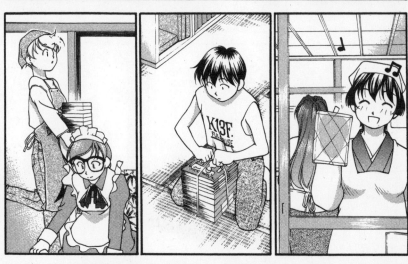

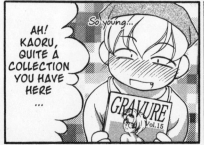

AH! KAORU, QUITE A COLLECTION YOU HAVE HERE ...

So, young...

GRAVURE Vol.15

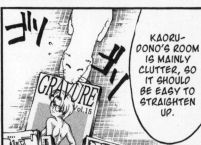

KAORU-DONO'S ROOM IS MAINLY CLUTTER, SO IT SHOULD BE EASY TO STRAIGHTEN UP.

GRAVURE Vol.15

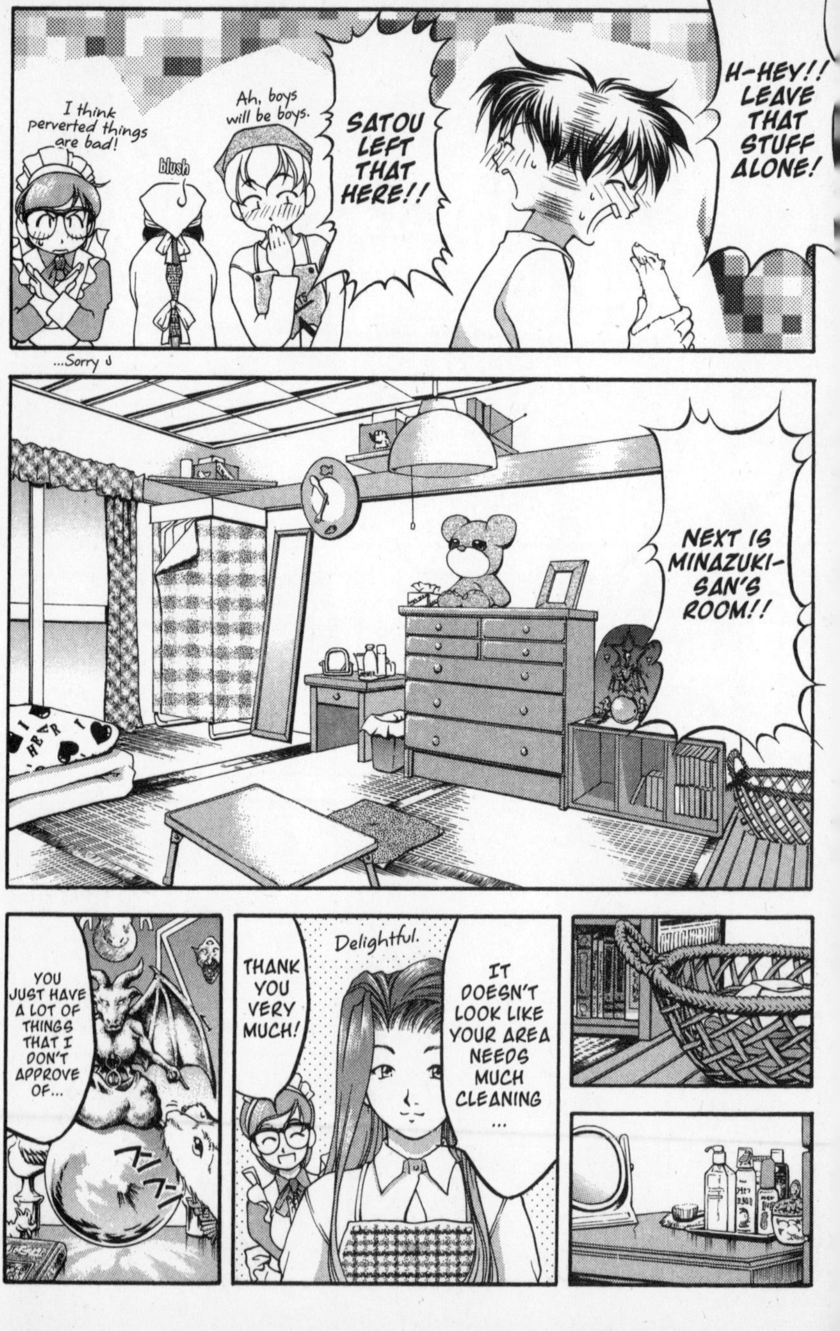
H-HEY!! LEAVE THAT STUFF ALONE!
SATOU LEFT THAT HERE!!
Ah, boys will be boys.
blush
I think perverted things are bad!
...Sorry
NEXT IS MINAZUKI-SAN'S ROOM!!
IT DOESN'T LOOK LIKE YOUR AREA NEEDS MUCH CLEANING ...
Delightful.
THANK YOU VERY MUCH!
YOU JUST HAVE A LOT OF THINGS THAT I DON'T APPROVE OF...

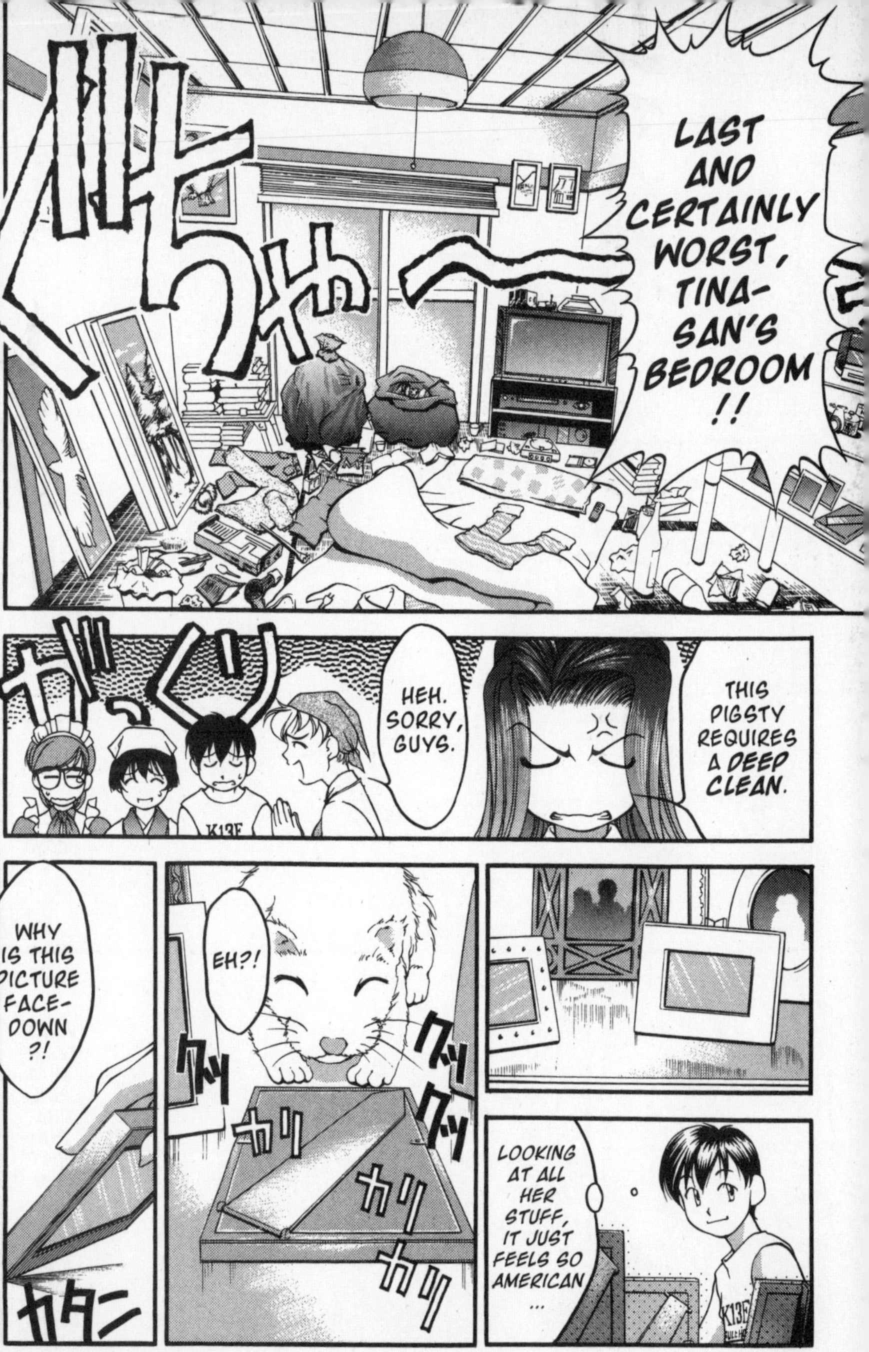
LAST AND CERTAINLY WORST, TINA-SAN'S BEDROOM !!
THIS PIGSTY REQUIRES A DEEP CLEAN.
HEH. SORRY, GUYS.
LOOKING AT ALL HER STUFF, IT JUST FEELS SO AMERICAN ...
EH?!
WHY IS THIS PICTURE FACE-DOWN ?!

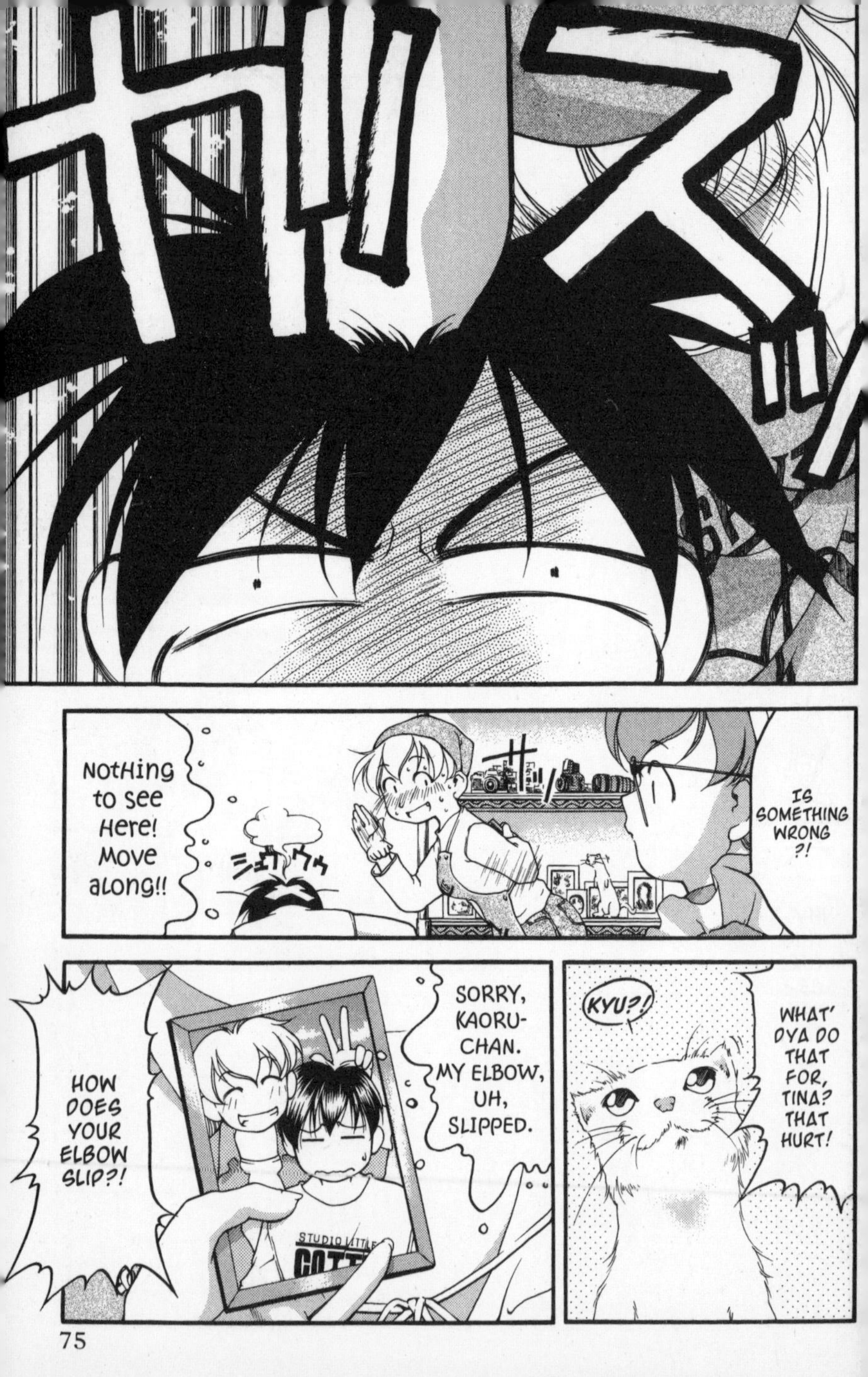
IS SOMETHING WRONG ?!
Nothing to see Here! Move along!!
WHAT'DYA DO THAT FOR, TINA? THAT HURT!
KYU?!
SORRY, KAORU-CHAN. MY ELBOW, UH, SLIPPED.
HOW DOES YOUR ELBOW SLIP?!

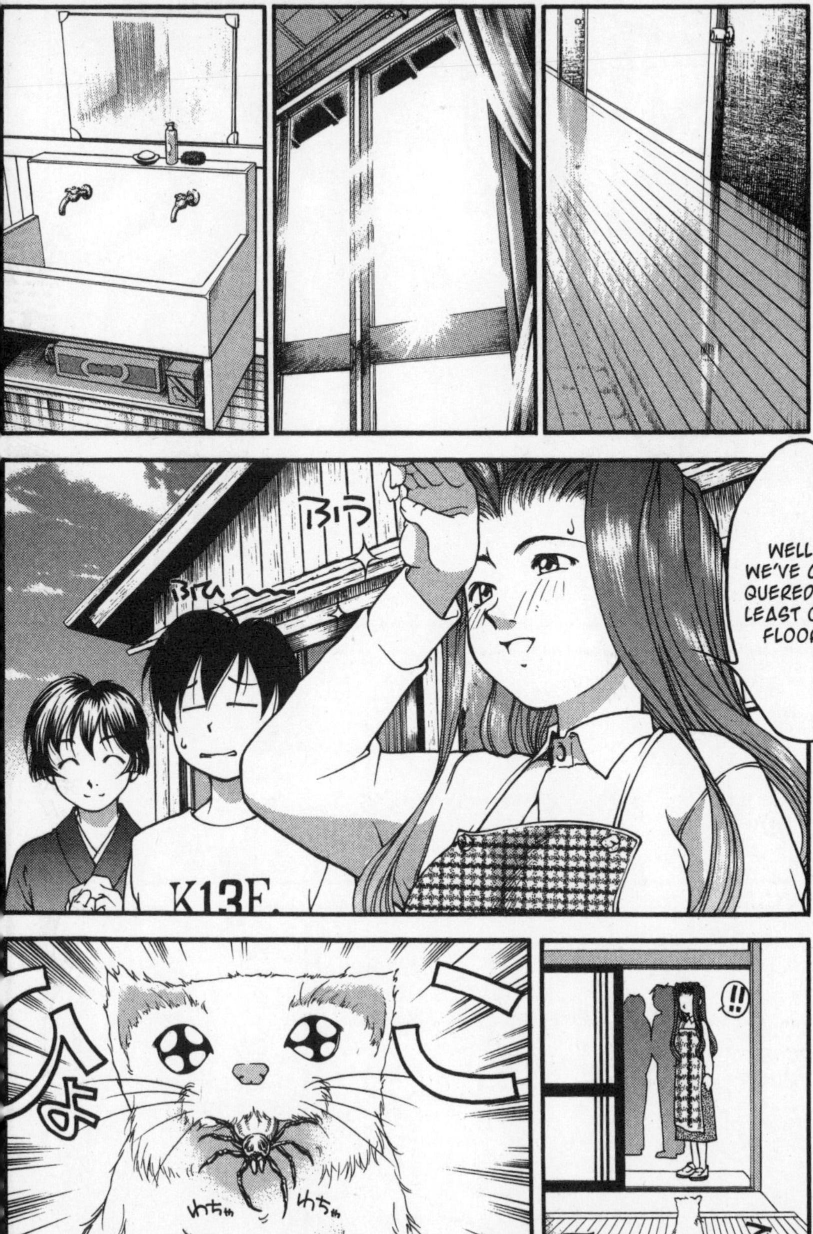
WELL, WE'VE CON-QUERED AT LEAST ONE FLOOR.
!!

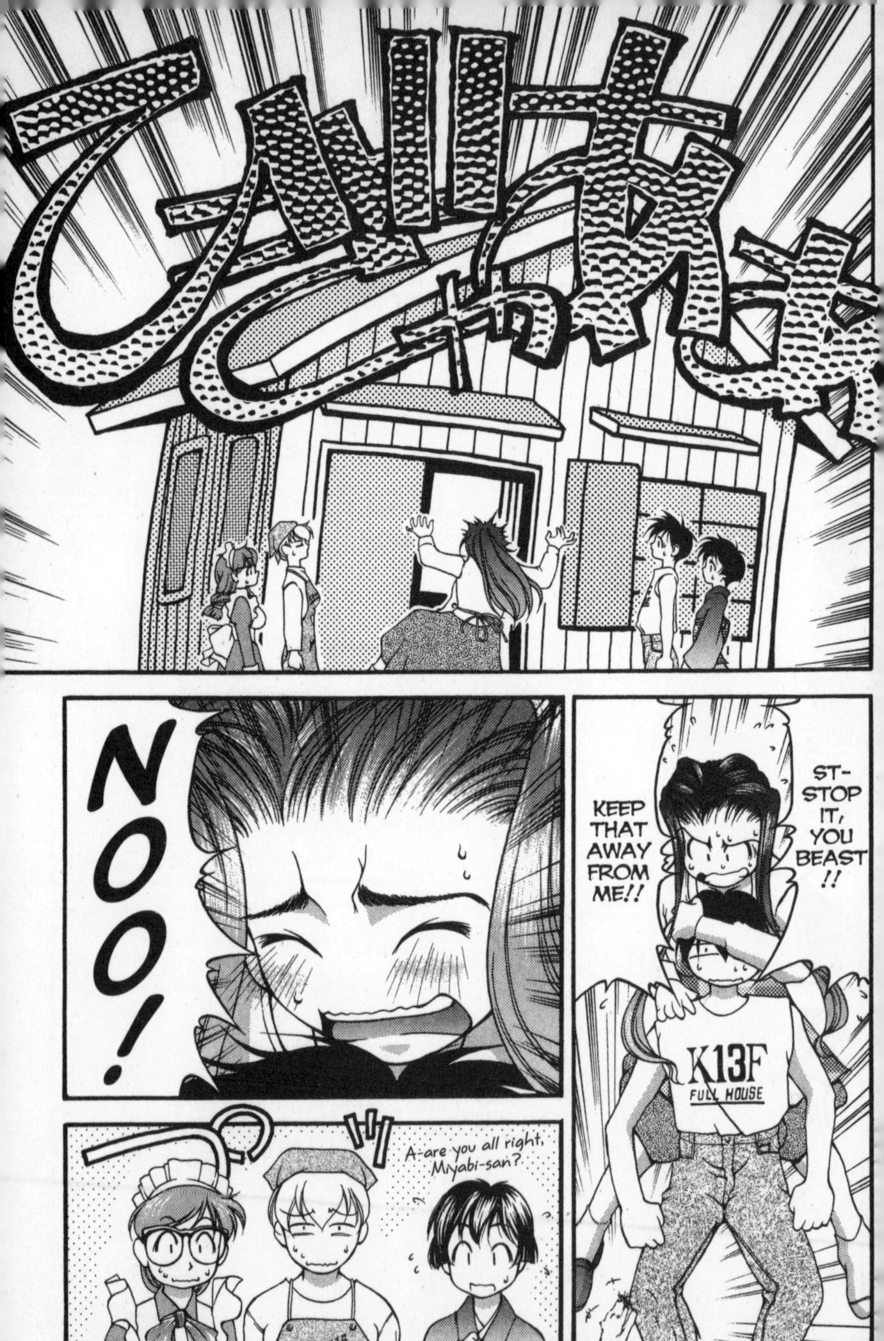
ST-STOP IT, YOU BEAST!!
KEEP THAT AWAY FROM ME!!
K13F
FULL HOUSE
NOO!
A-are you all right, Miyabi-san?

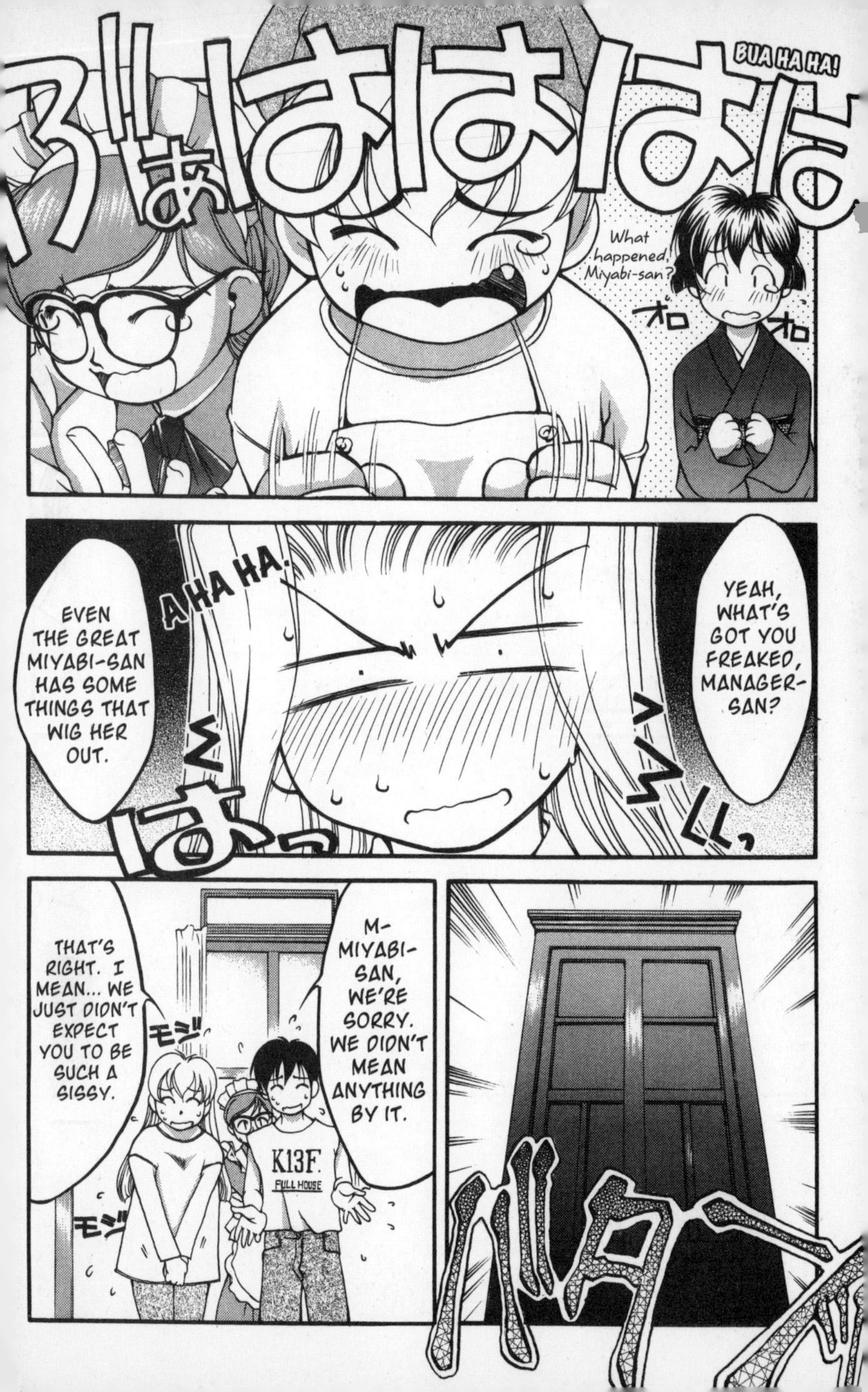
BUA HA HA!
What happened, Miyabi-san?
オロ オロ
YEAH, WHAT'S GOT YOU FREAKED, MANAGER-SAN?
A HA HA.
EVEN THE GREAT MIYABI-SAN HAS SOME THINGS THAT WIG HER OUT.
M-MIYABI-SAN, WE'RE SORRY. WE DIDN'T MEAN ANYTHING BY IT.
THAT'S RIGHT. I MEAN... WE JUST DIDN'T EXPECT YOU TO BE SUCH A SISSY.
モジ
モジ
K13F.
FULL HOUSE

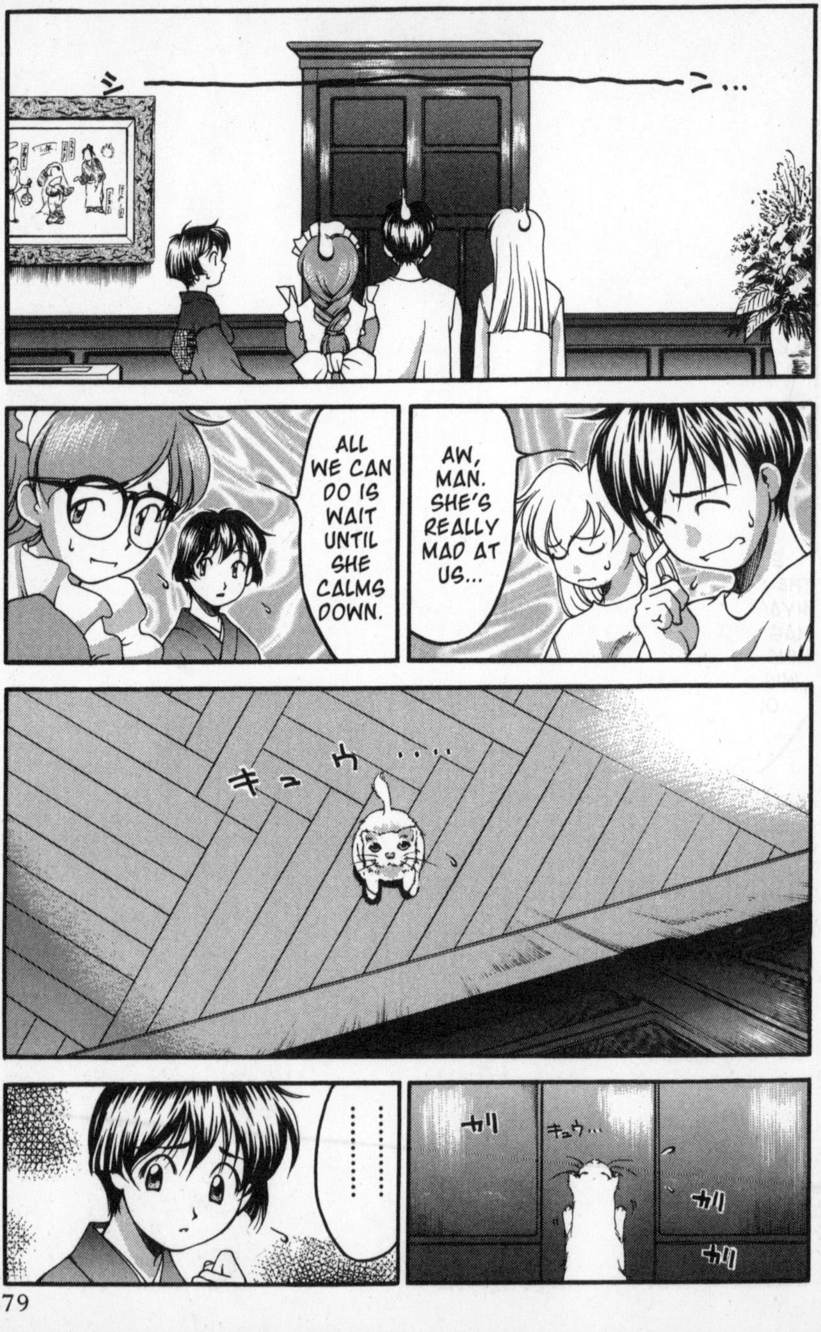
シ――ン…
AW, MAN. SHE'S REALLY MAD AT US...
ALL WE CAN DO IS WAIT UNTIL SHE CALMS DOWN.
キュウ…
カリ
キュウ…
カリ
カリ
......

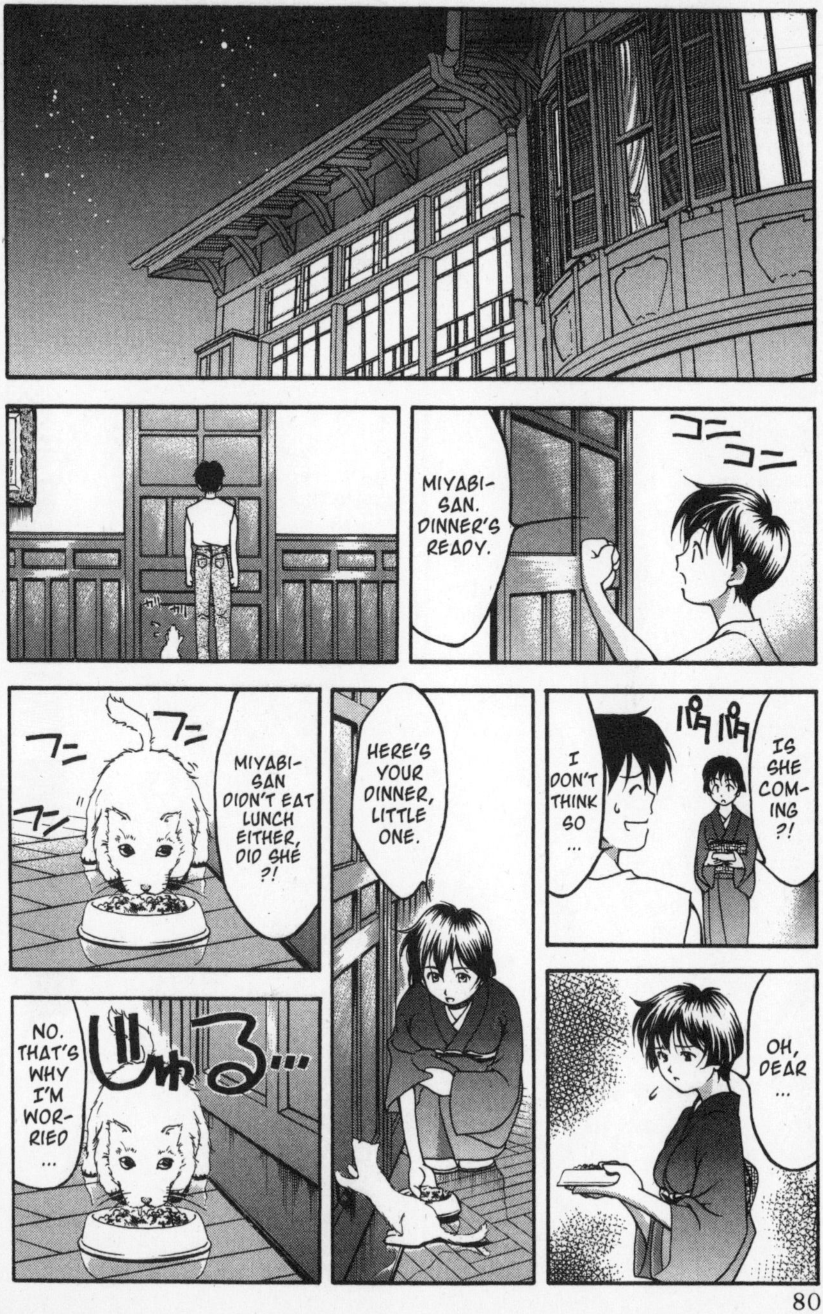
コンコン
MIYABI-SAN. DINNER'S READY.
パタパタ
IS SHE COMING?!
I DON'T THINK SO ...
OH, DEAR ...
HERE'S YOUR DINNER, LITTLE ONE.
フンフン
MIYABI-SAN DIDN'T EAT LUNCH EITHER, DID SHE?!
じゅる...
NO. THAT'S WHY I'M WORRIED ...

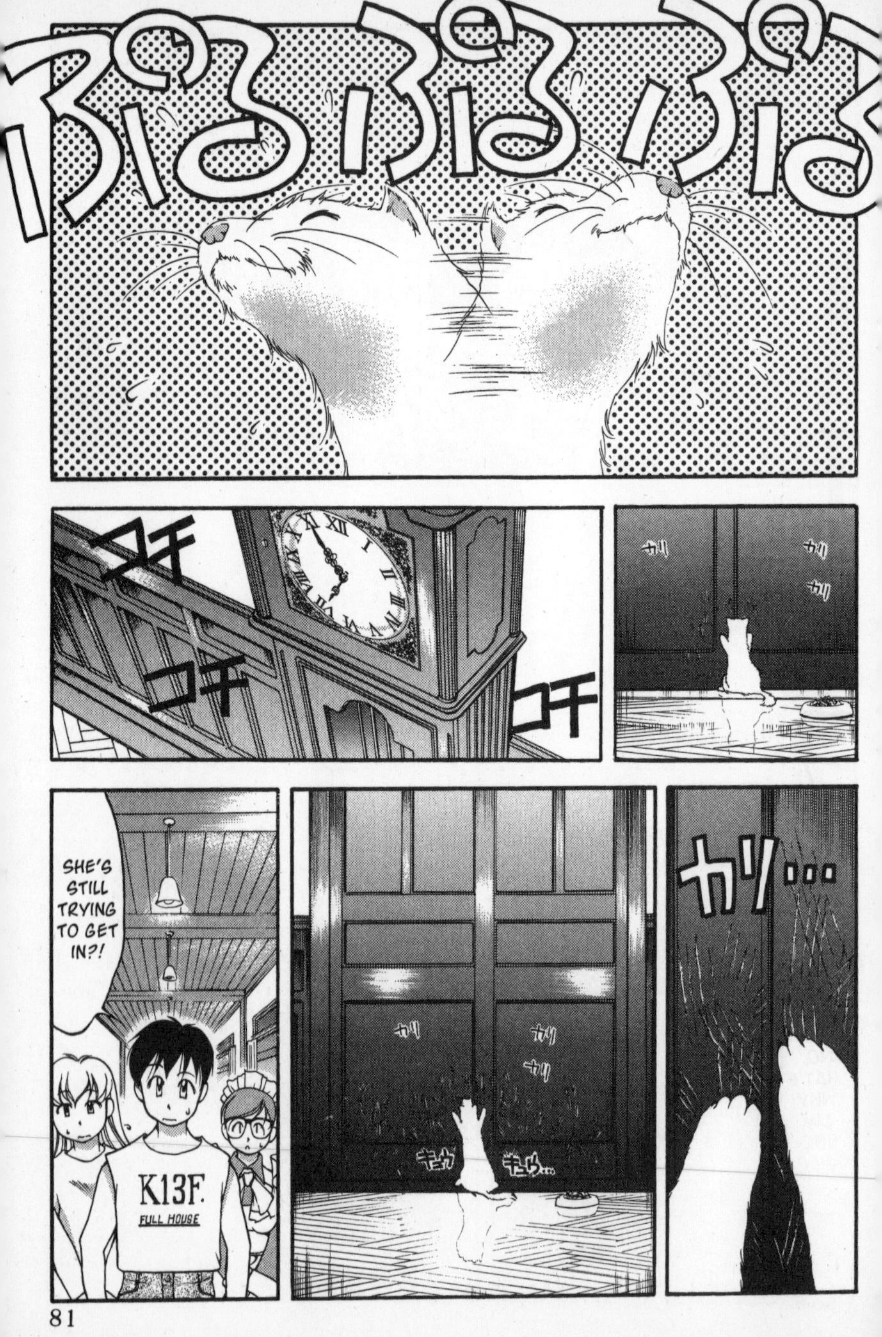
ぷるぷるぷる
カリ
カリ
カリ
コチ
コチ
コチ
カリ…
カリ
カリ
カリ
ギュウ
ギュウ…
SHE'S STILL TRYING TO GET IN?!

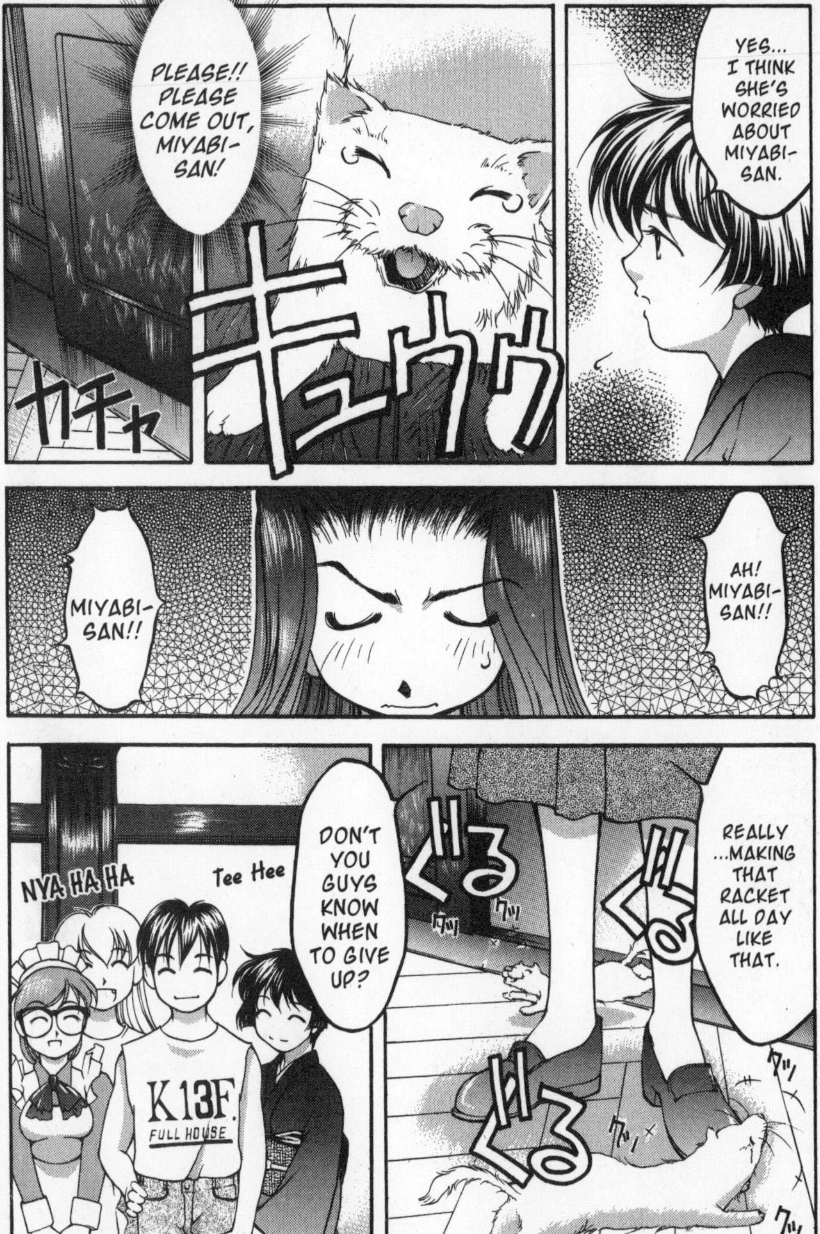
YES... I THINK SHE'S WORRIED ABOUT MIYABI-SAN.
PLEASE!! PLEASE COME OUT, MIYABI-SAN!
キュウウ
カチャ
AH! MIYABI-SAN!!
MIYABI-SAN!!
REALLY ...MAKING THAT RACKET ALL DAY LIKE THAT.
DON'T YOU GUYS KNOW WHEN TO GIVE UP?
ぐる
ぐる
Tee Hee
NYA HA HA
K13F.
FULL HOUSE

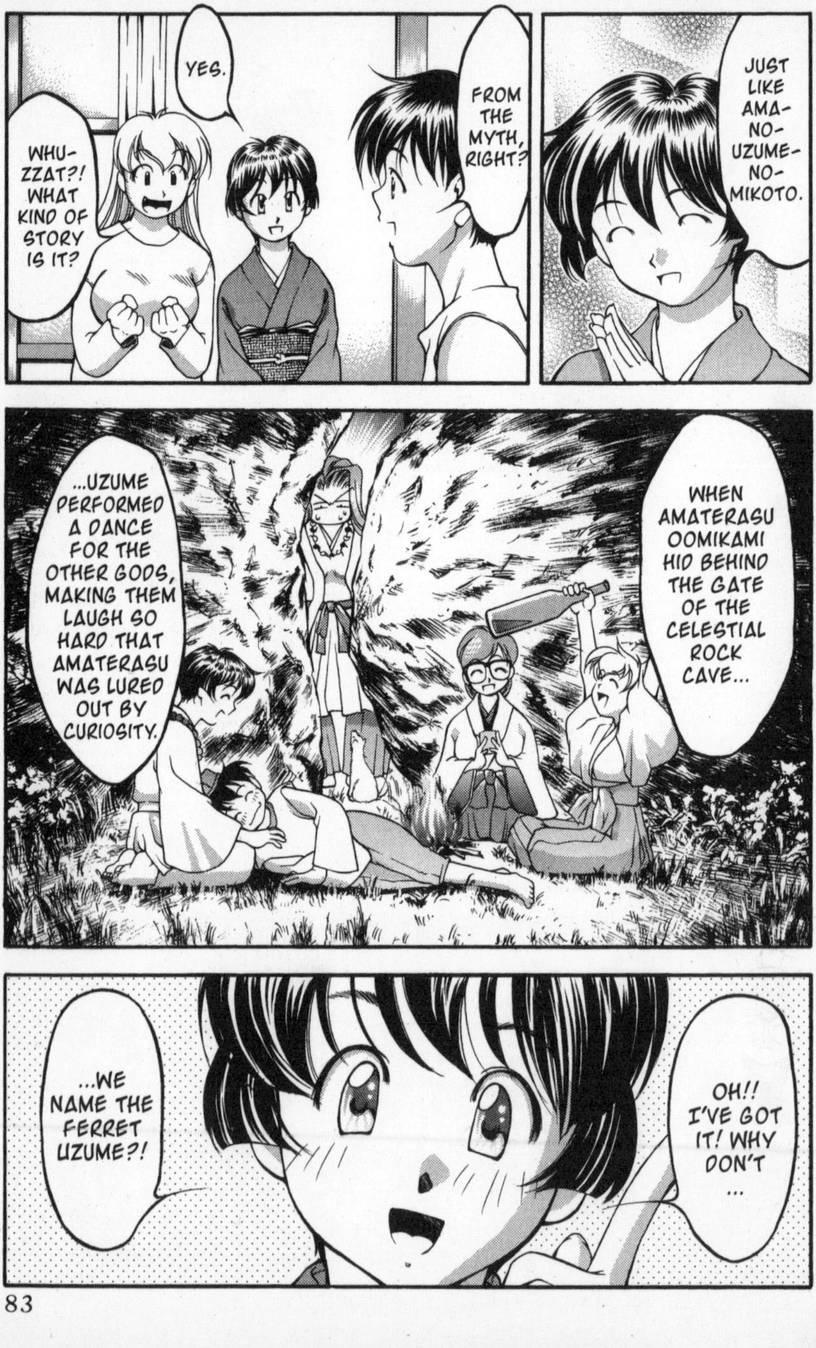
JUST LIKE AMA-NO-UZUME-NO-MIKOTO.
FROM THE MYTH, RIGHT?
YES.
WHUZZAT?! WHAT KIND OF STORY IS IT?
WHEN AMATERASU OOMIKAMI HID BEHIND THE GATE OF THE CELESTIAL ROCK CAVE...
...UZUME PERFORMED A DANCE FOR THE OTHER GODS, MAKING THEM LAUGH SO HARD THAT AMATERASU WAS LURED OUT BY CURIOSITY.
OH!! I'VE GOT IT! WHY DON'T ...
...WE NAME THE FERRET UZUME?!

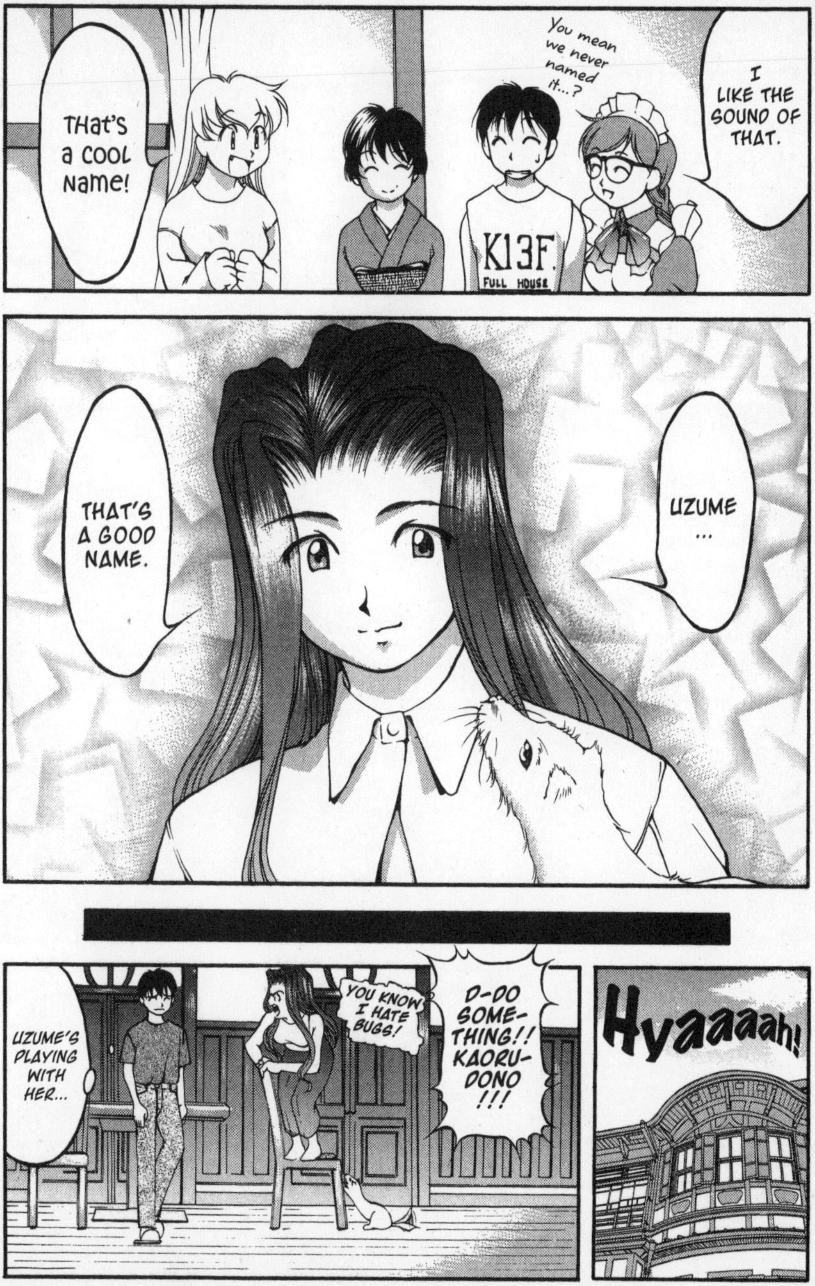
I LIKE THE SOUND OF THAT.
You mean we never named it...?
That's a cool name!
UZUME ...
THAT'S A GOOD NAME.
Hyaaaaah!
D-DO SOMETHING!! KAORU-DONO !!!
YOU KNOW I HATE BUGS!
UZUME'S PLAYING WITH HER...
K13F. FULL HOUSE

End of Special Chapter: Amaterasu—Sun Goddess

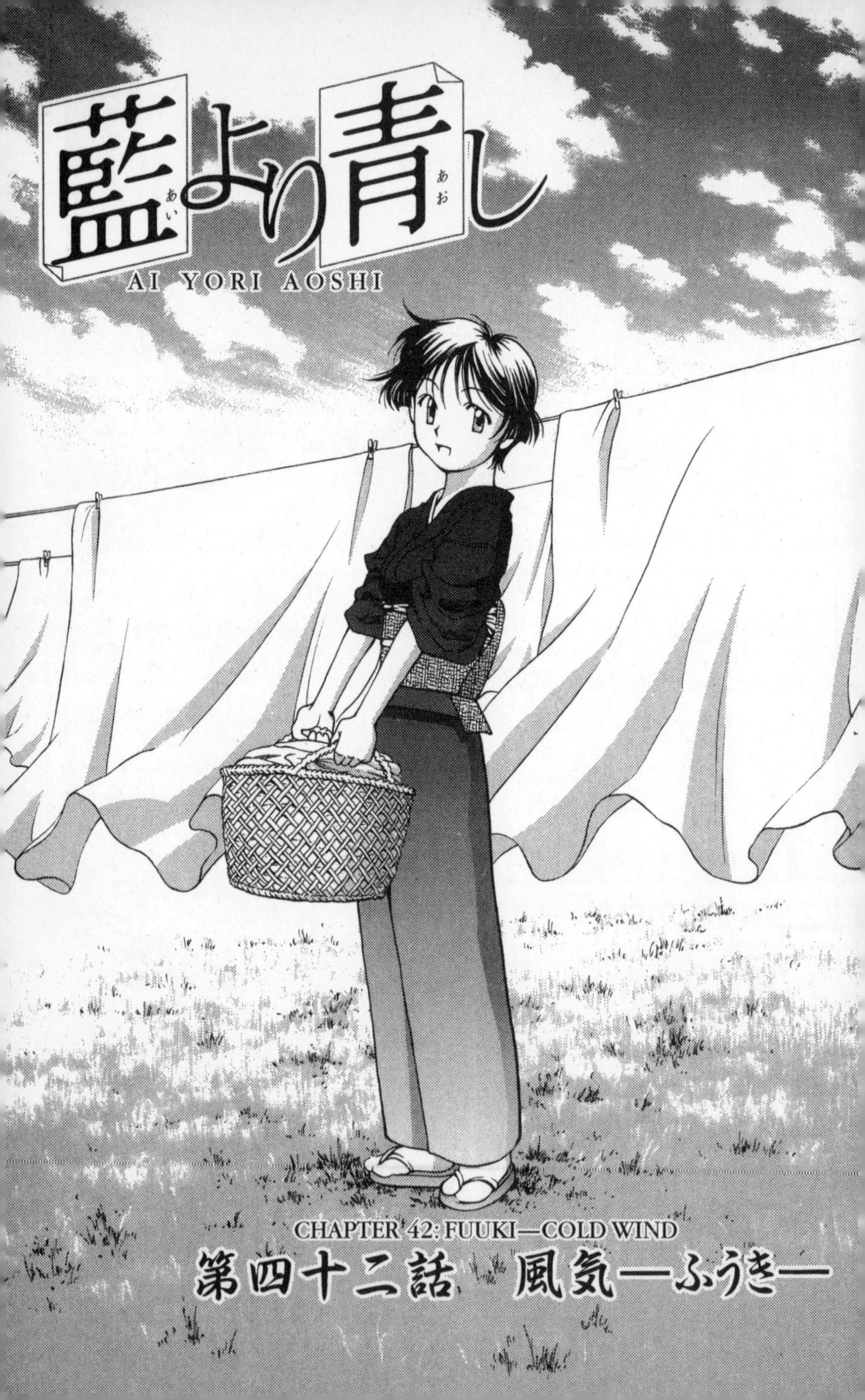
藍(あい)より青(あお)し
AI YORI AOSHI
CHAPTER 42: FUUKI—COLD WIND
第四十二話　風気—ふうき—

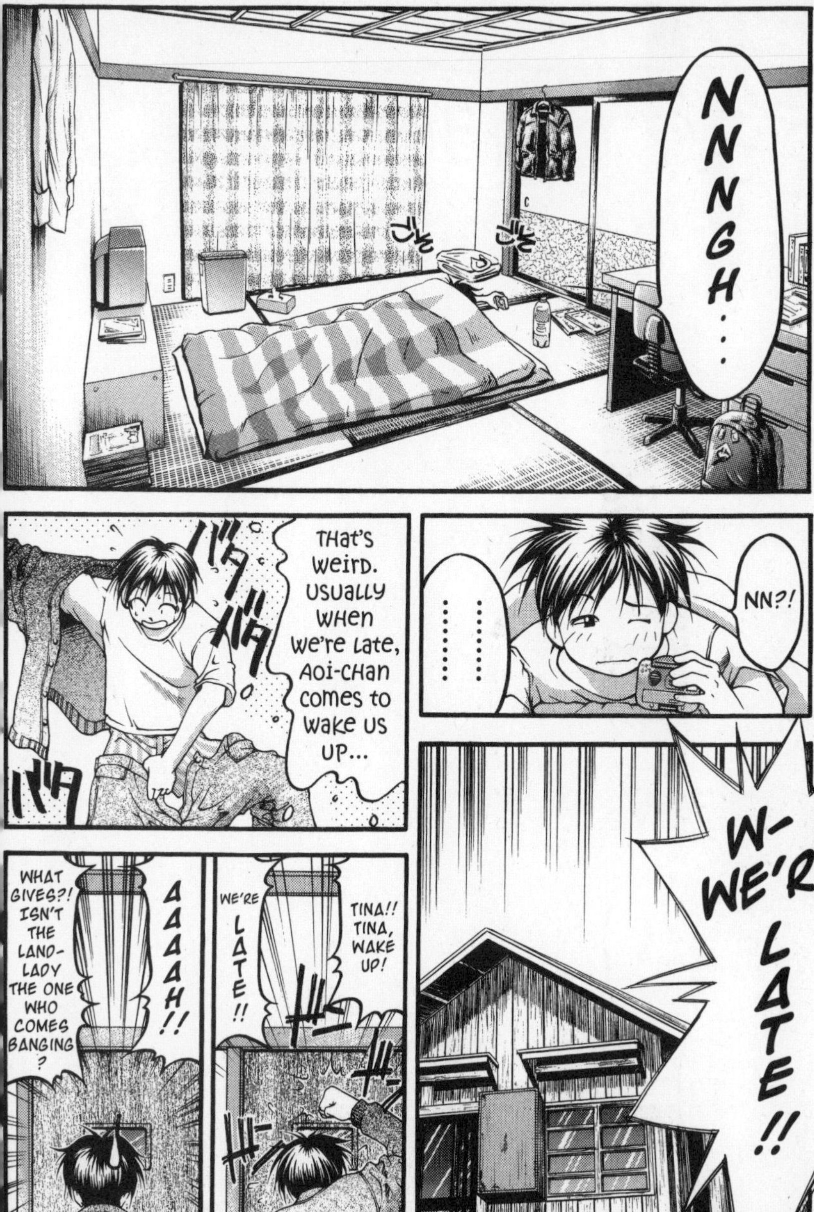
NNNGH...
NN?!
......
That's weird. Usually when we're late, Aoi-chan comes to wake us up...
W-WE'RE LATE!!
TINA!! TINA, WAKE UP!
WE'RE LATE!!
AAAAAH!!
WHAT GIVES?! ISN'T THE LANDLADY THE ONE WHO COMES BANGING?

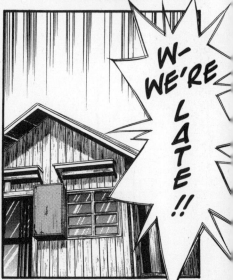

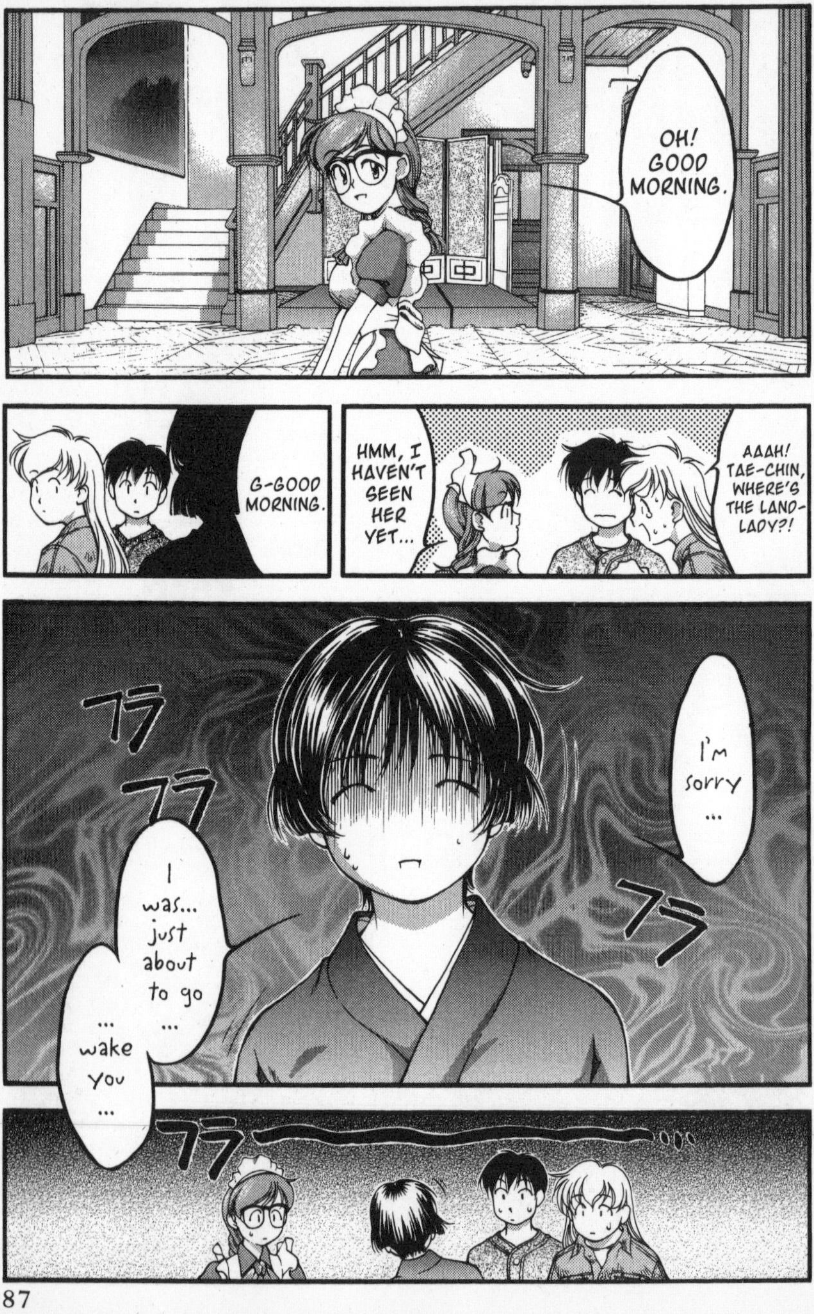
OH! GOOD MORNING.
AAAH! TAE-CHIN, WHERE'S THE LAND-LADY?!
HMM, I HAVEN'T SEEN HER YET...
G-GOOD MORNING.
フラ
フラ
I'm sorry ...
フラ
I was... just about to go ... ... wake you ...
フラ——————…

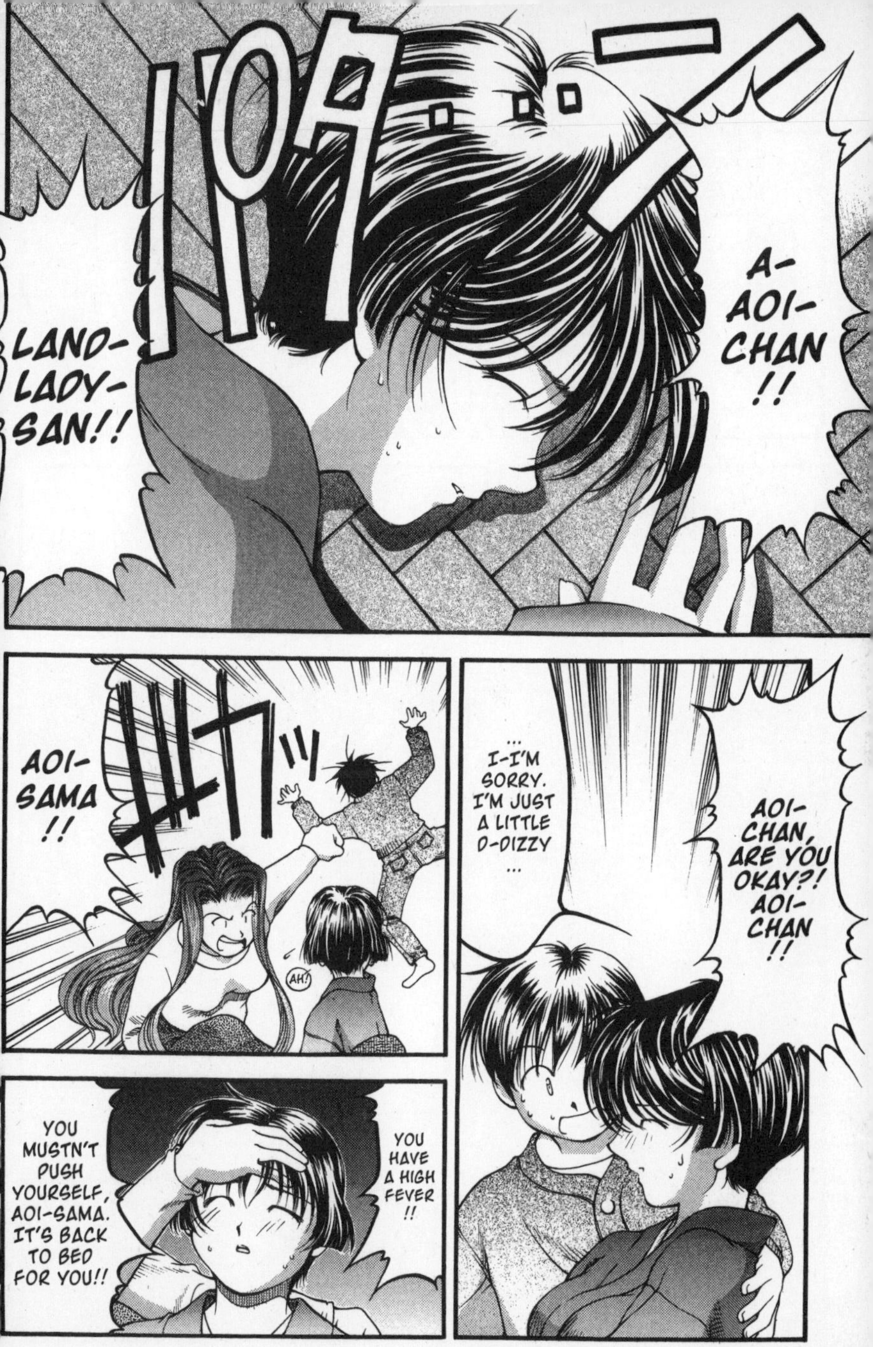
A-
AOI-CHAN!!
LAND-LADY-SAN!!
AOI-CHAN, ARE YOU OKAY?! AOI-CHAN!!
... I-I'M SORRY. I'M JUST A LITTLE D-DIZZY ...
AOI-SAMA!!
AH!
YOU HAVE A HIGH FEVER!!
YOU MUSTN'T PUSH YOURSELF, AOI-SAMA. IT'S BACK TO BED FOR YOU!!

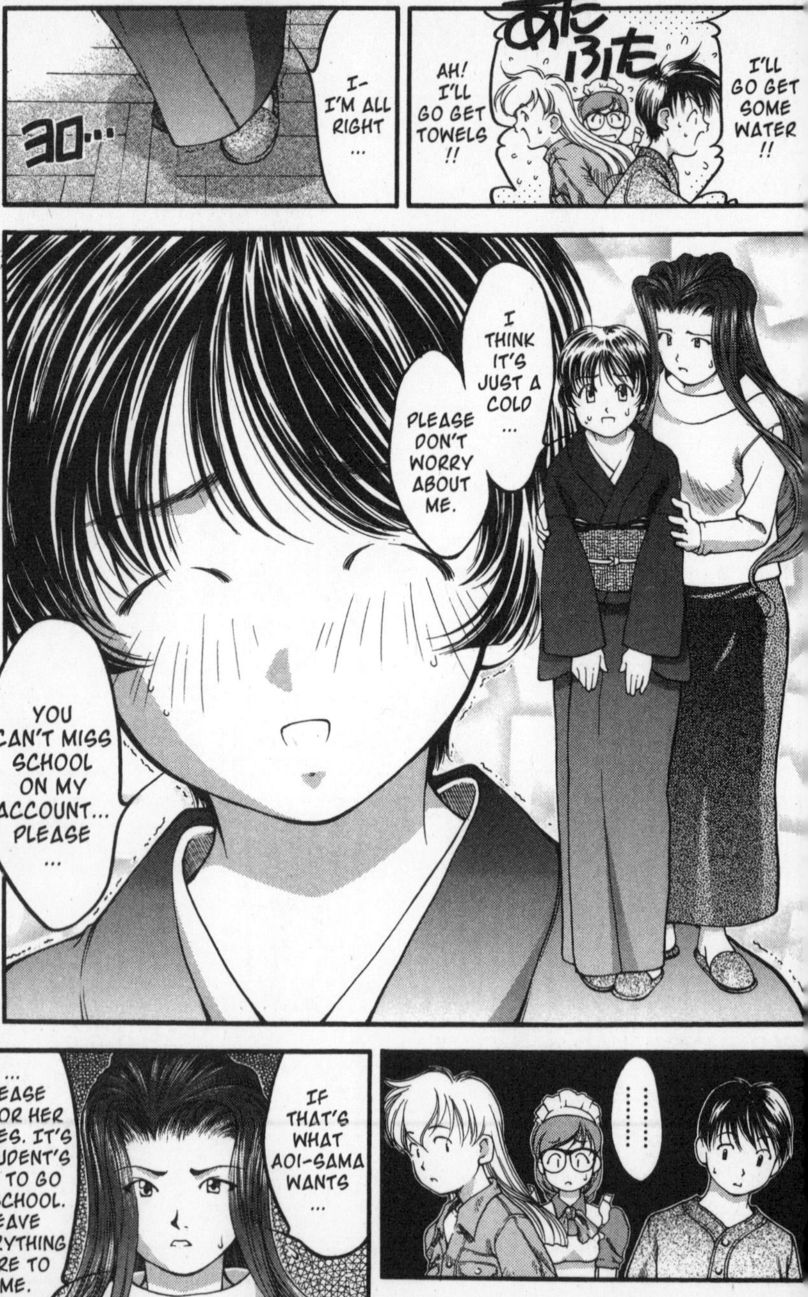
I'LL GO GET SOME WATER!!
あたふた
AH! I'LL GO GET TOWELS!!
I-I'M ALL RIGHT...
ヨロ...
I THINK IT'S JUST A COLD... PLEASE DON'T WORRY ABOUT ME.
YOU CAN'T MISS SCHOOL ON MY ACCOUNT... PLEASE...
......
IF THAT'S WHAT AOI-SAMA WANTS...
...PLEASE HONOR HER WISHES. IT'S A STUDENT'S JOB TO GO TO SCHOOL. LEAVE EVERYTHING HERE TO ME.

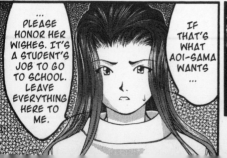

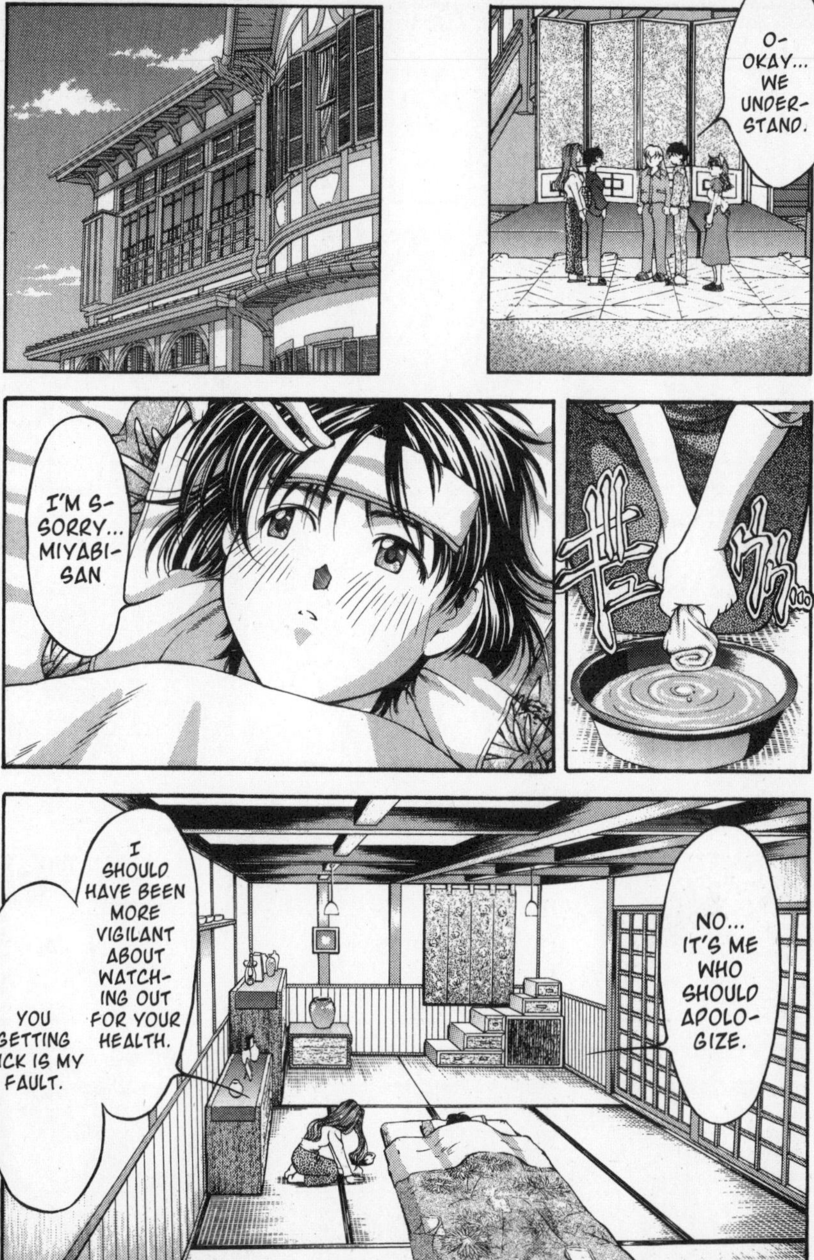
O-OKAY... WE UNDERSTAND.
ギュウ...
I'M S-SORRY... MIYABI-SAN
NO... IT'S ME WHO SHOULD APOLOGIZE.
I SHOULD HAVE BEEN MORE VIGILANT ABOUT WATCHING OUT FOR YOUR HEALTH.
YOU GETTING SICK IS MY FAULT.

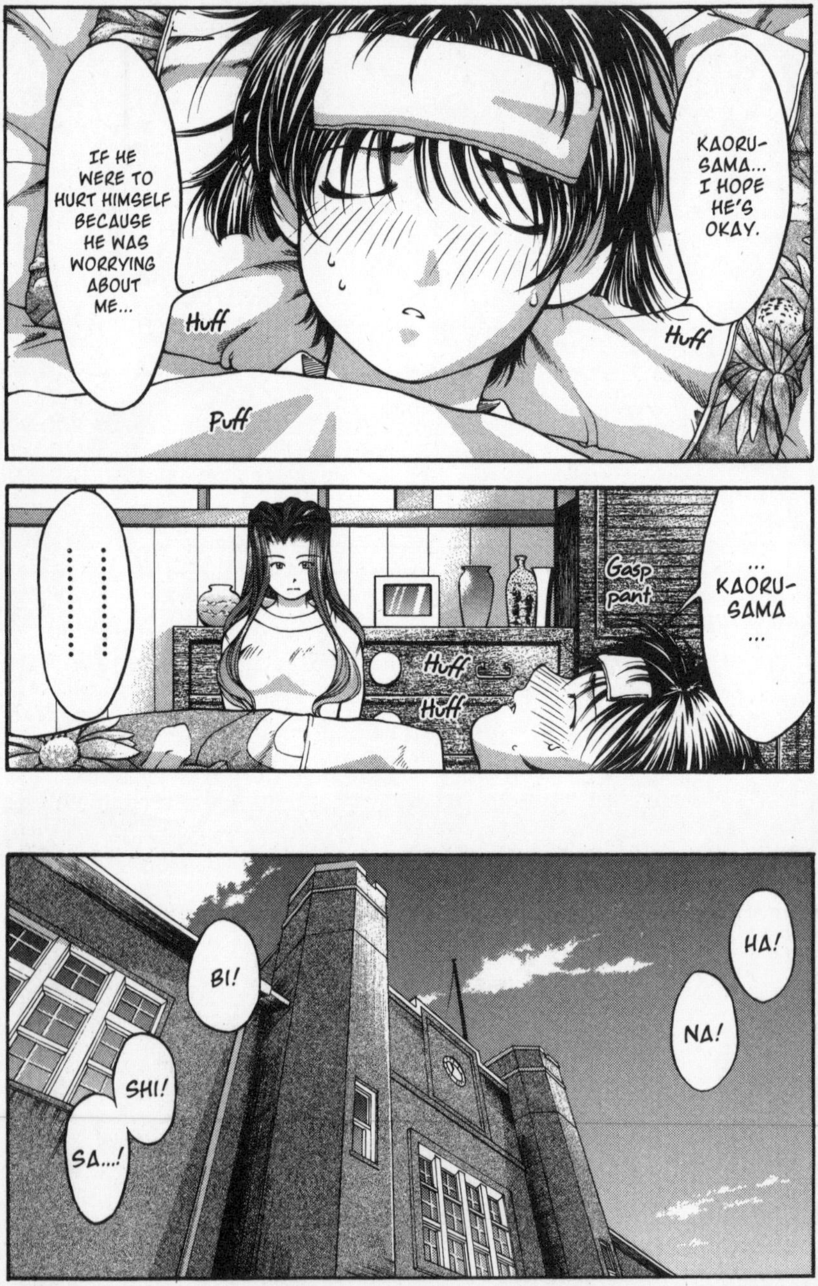
KAORU-SAMA... I HOPE HE'S OKAY.
Huff
IF HE WERE TO HURT HIMSELF BECAUSE HE WAS WORRYING ABOUT ME...
Huff
Puff
... KAORU-SAMA ...
Gasp pant
Huff
Huff
......
HA!
NA!
BI!
SHI!
SA...!

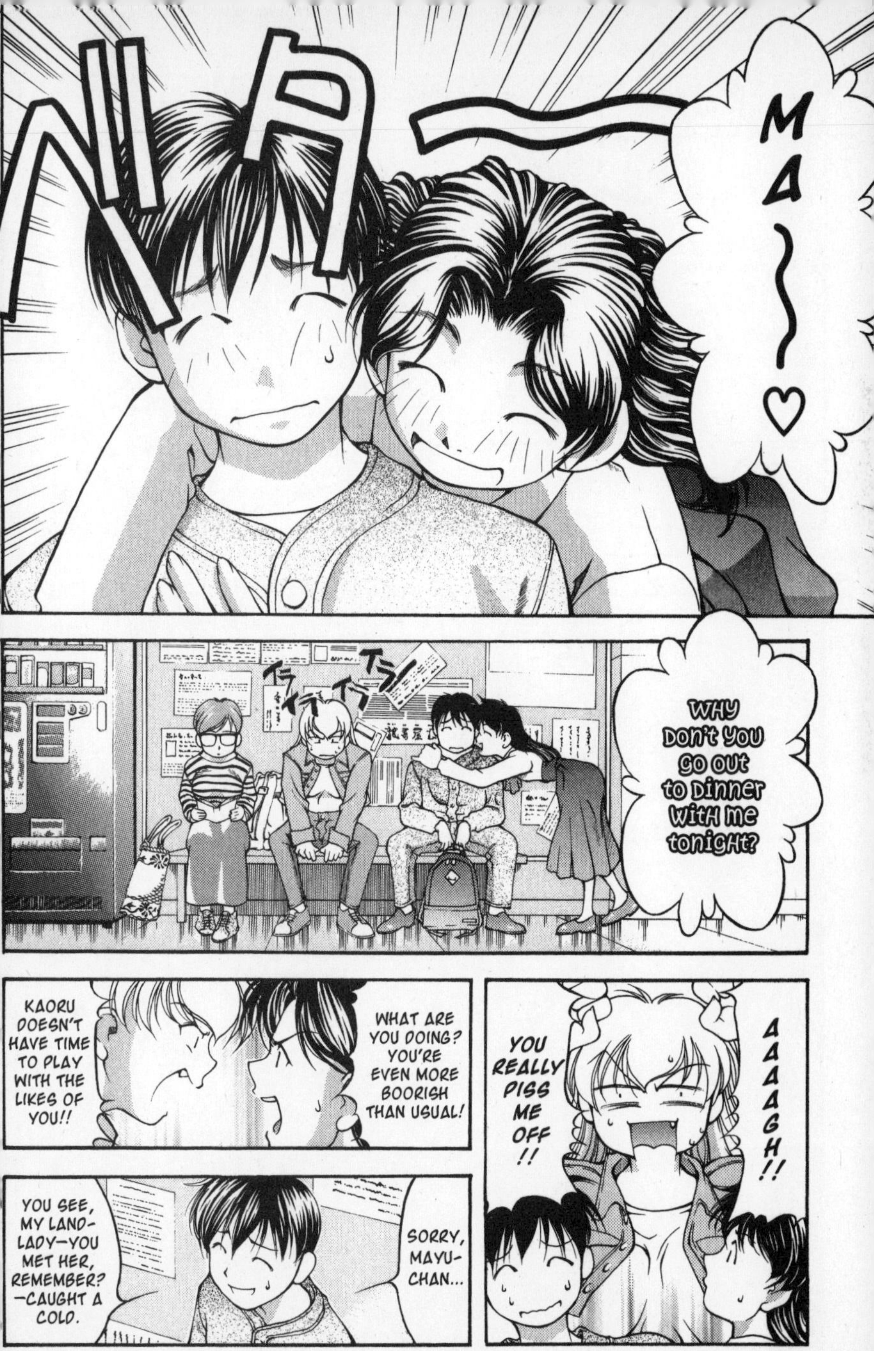

ベタ〜
MA~~~♡
イラ イラ イラ イラ
WHY DON'T YOU GO OUT TO DINNER WITH ME TONIGHT?
AAAAAGH!!
YOU REALLY PISS ME OFF!!
WHAT ARE YOU DOING? YOU'RE EVEN MORE BOORISH THAN USUAL!
KAORU DOESN'T HAVE TIME TO PLAY WITH THE LIKES OF YOU!!
SORRY, MAYU-CHAN...
YOU SEE, MY LAND-LADY—YOU MET HER, REMEMBER? —CAUGHT A COLD.

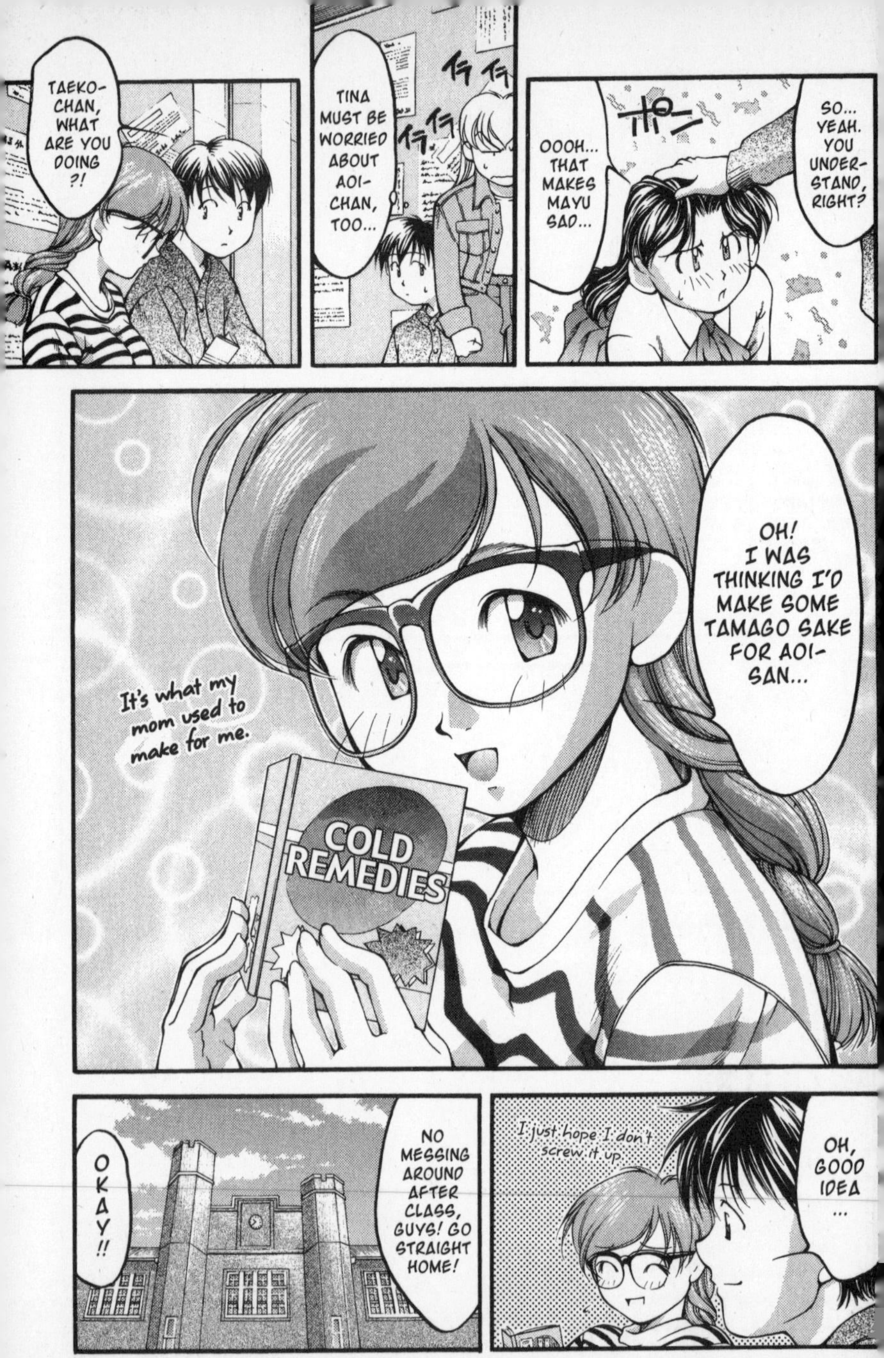
SO... YEAH. YOU UNDERSTAND, RIGHT?
OOOH... THAT MAKES MAYU SAD...
TINA MUST BE WORRIED ABOUT AOI-CHAN, TOO...
TAEKO-CHAN, WHAT ARE YOU DOING?!
OH! I WAS THINKING I'D MAKE SOME TAMAGO SAKE FOR AOI-SAN...
It's what my mom used to make for me.
COLD REMEDIES
OH, GOOD IDEA ...
I just hope I don't screw it up.
NO MESSING AROUND AFTER CLASS, GUYS! GO STRAIGHT HOME!
OKAY!!

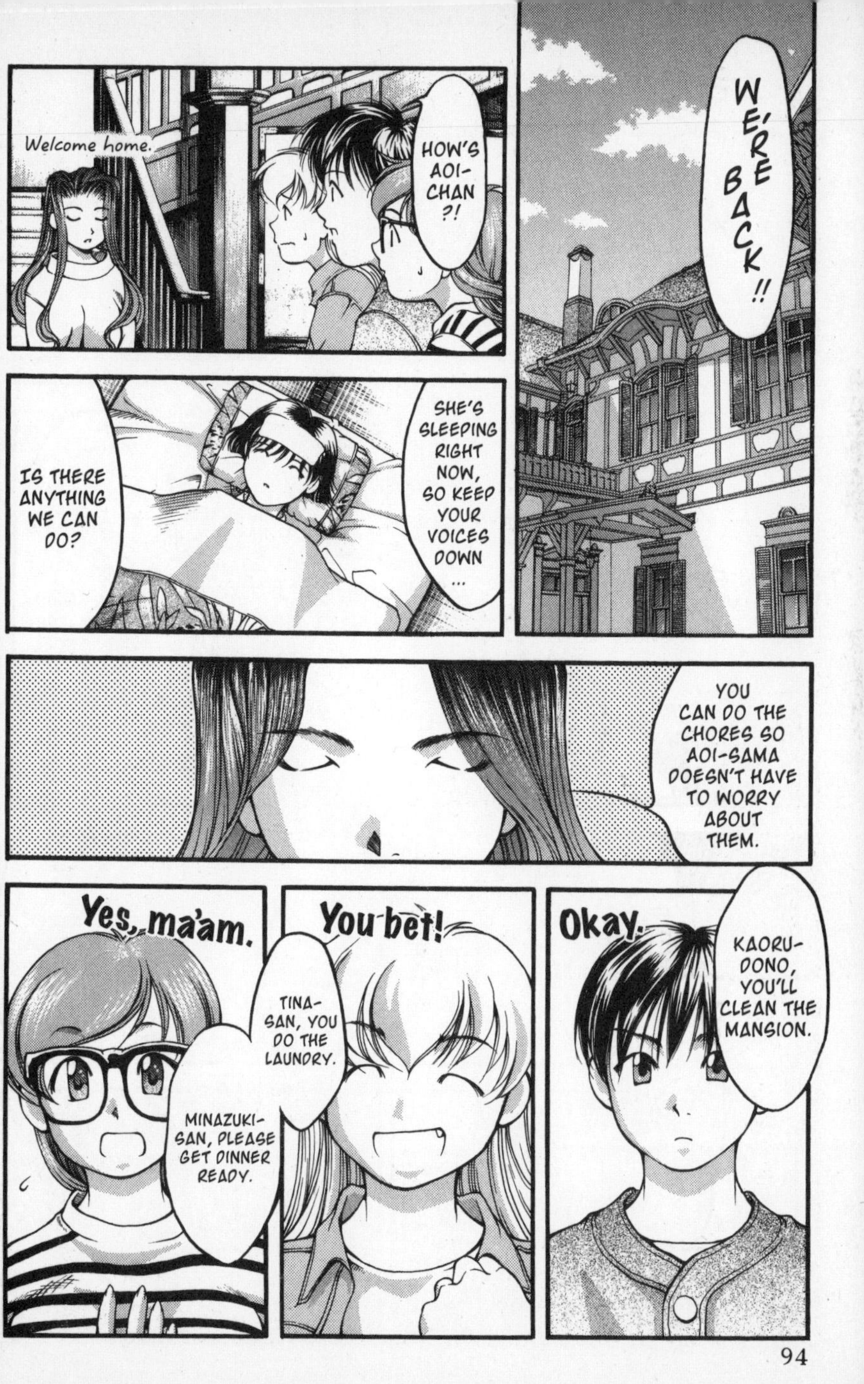
WE'RE BACK!!
HOW'S AOI-CHAN?!
Welcome home.
SHE'S SLEEPING RIGHT NOW, SO KEEP YOUR VOICES DOWN...
IS THERE ANYTHING WE CAN DO?
YOU CAN DO THE CHORES SO AOI-SAMA DOESN'T HAVE TO WORRY ABOUT THEM.
KAORU-DONO, YOU'LL CLEAN THE MANSION.
Okay.
TINA-SAN, YOU DO THE LAUNDRY.
You bet!
MINAZUKI-SAN, PLEASE GET DINNER READY.
Yes, ma'am.

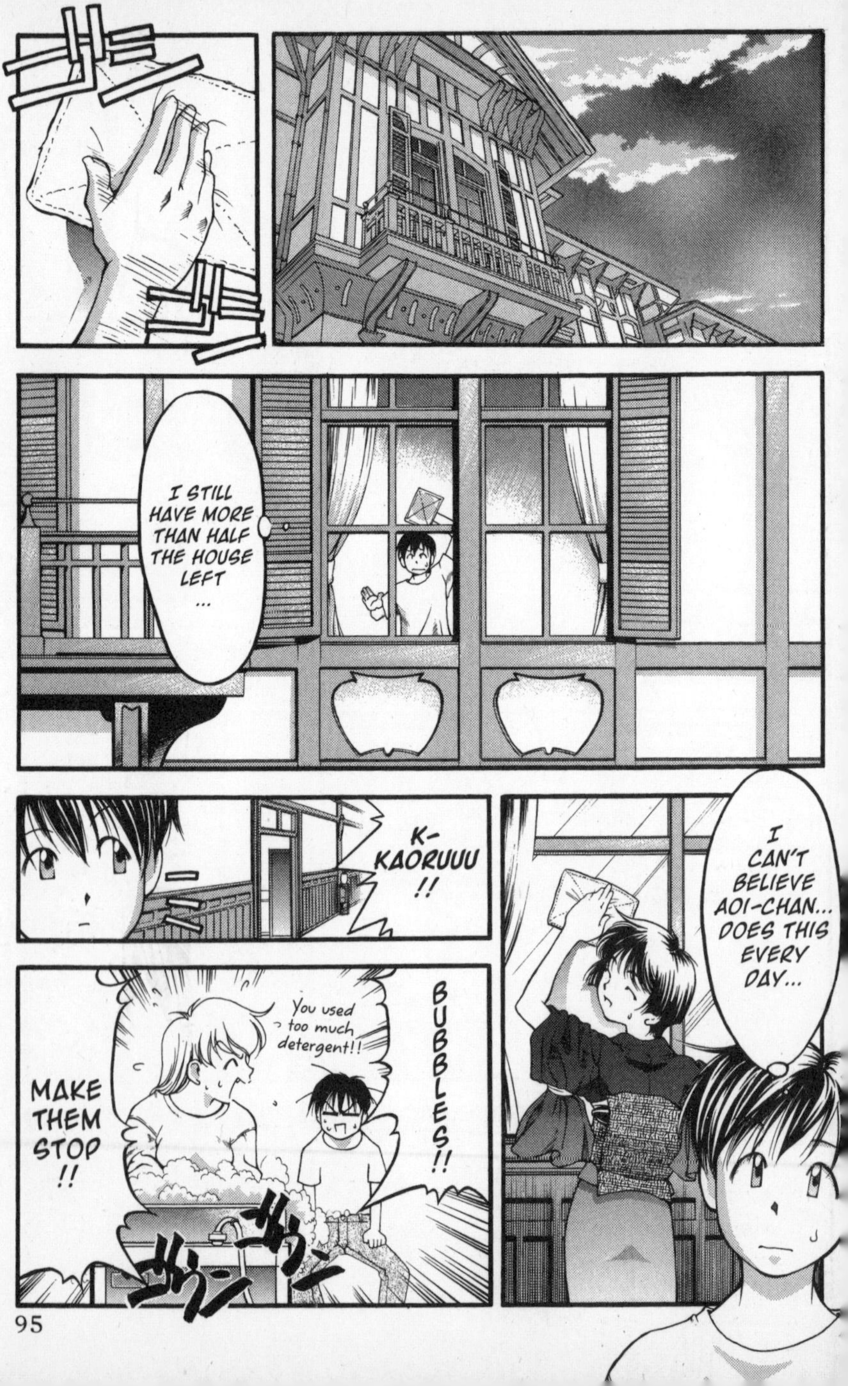
I STILL HAVE MORE THAN HALF THE HOUSE LEFT ...
I CAN'T BELIEVE AOI-CHAN... DOES THIS EVERY DAY...
K-KAORUUU !!
BUBBLES!!
You used too much detergent!!
MAKE THEM STOP !!

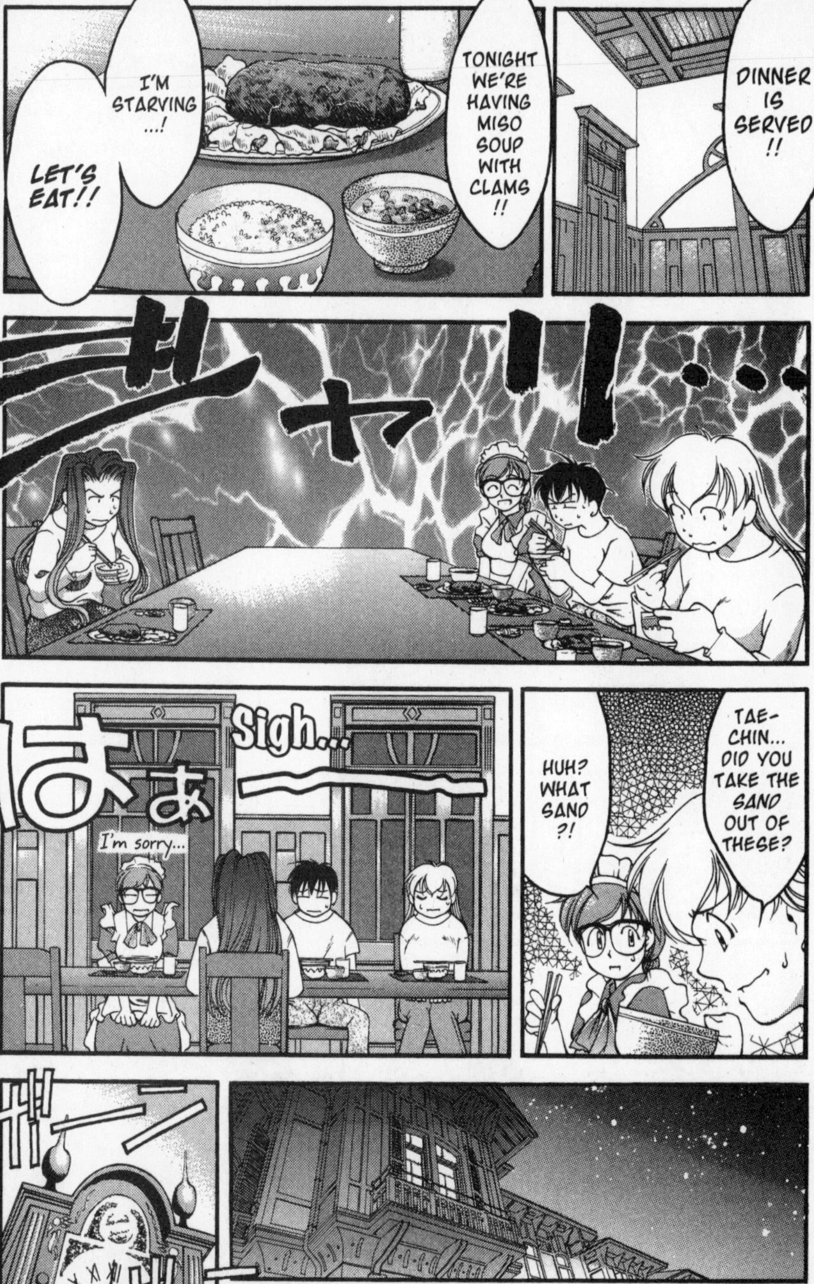
DINNER IS SERVED!!
TONIGHT WE'RE HAVING MISO SOUP WITH CLAMS!!
I'M STARVING...!
LET'S EAT!!
TAE-CHIN... DID YOU TAKE THE SAND OUT OF THESE?
HUH? WHAT SAND?!
Sigh...
I'm sorry...

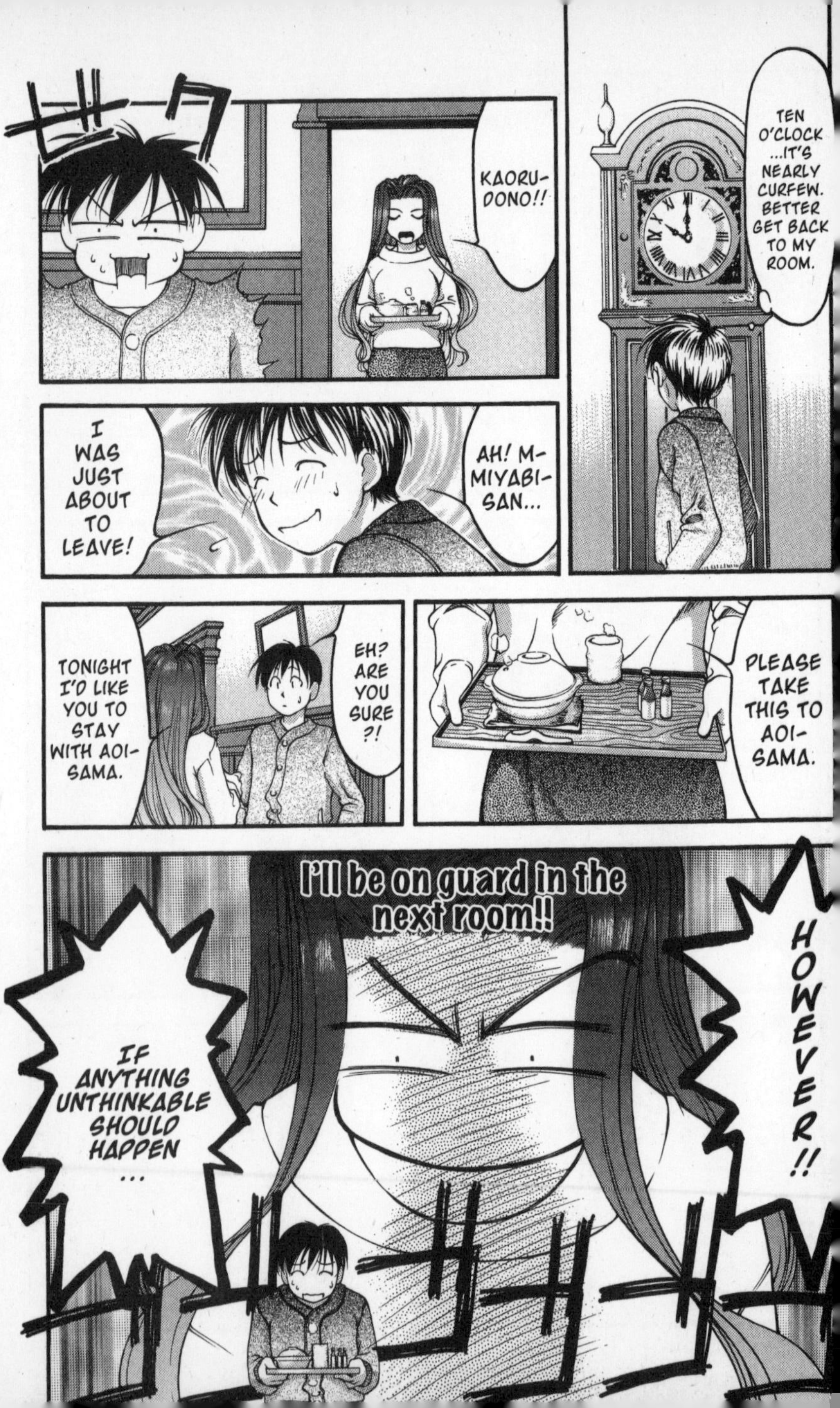
TEN O'CLOCK ...IT'S NEARLY CURFEW. BETTER GET BACK TO MY ROOM.
KAORU-DONO!!
AH! M-MIYABI-SAN...
I WAS JUST ABOUT TO LEAVE!
PLEASE TAKE THIS TO AOI-SAMA.
TONIGHT I'D LIKE YOU TO STAY WITH AOI-SAMA.
EH? ARE YOU SURE?!
HOWEVER!!
I'll be on guard in the next room!!
IF ANYTHING UNTHINKABLE SHOULD HAPPEN...

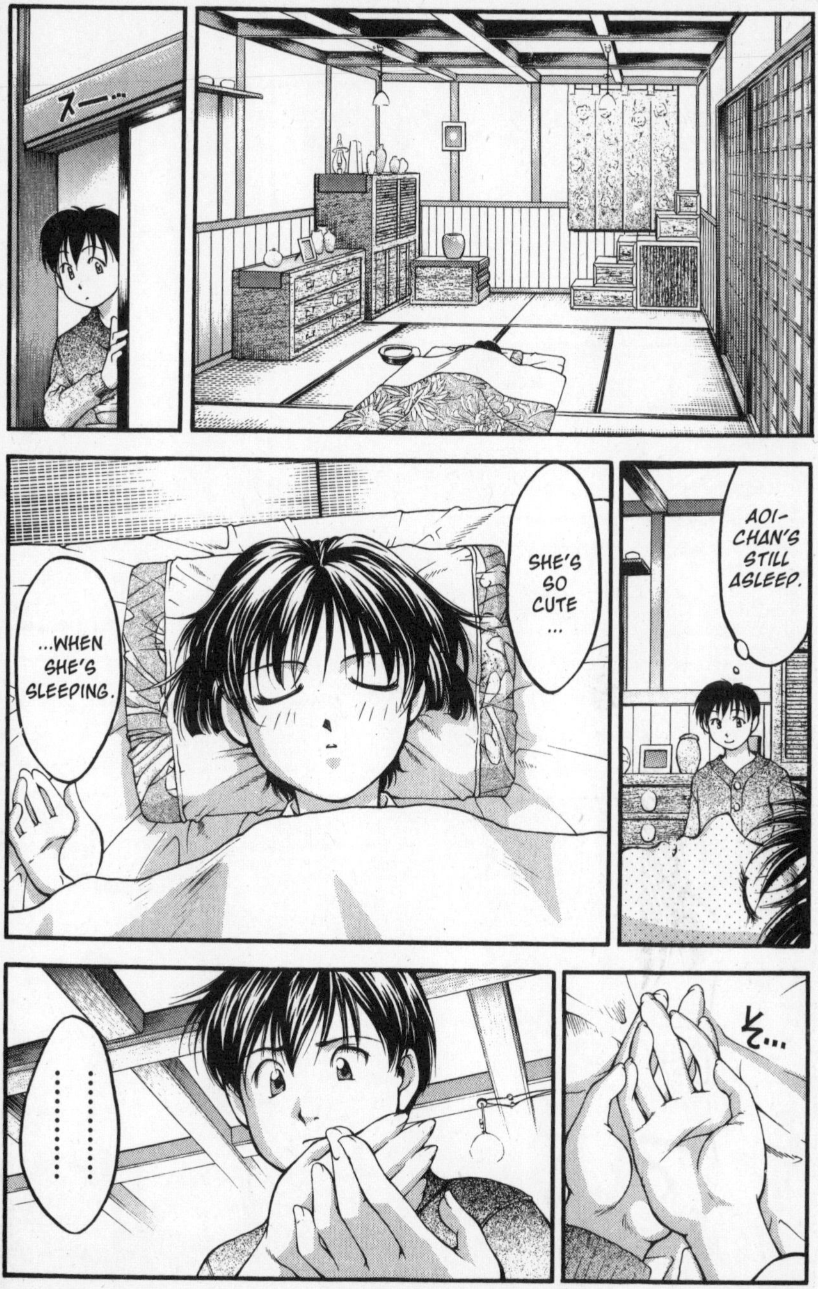
スー…
AOI-CHAN'S STILL ASLEEP.
SHE'S SO CUTE ...
...WHEN SHE'S SLEEPING.
ピく...
....

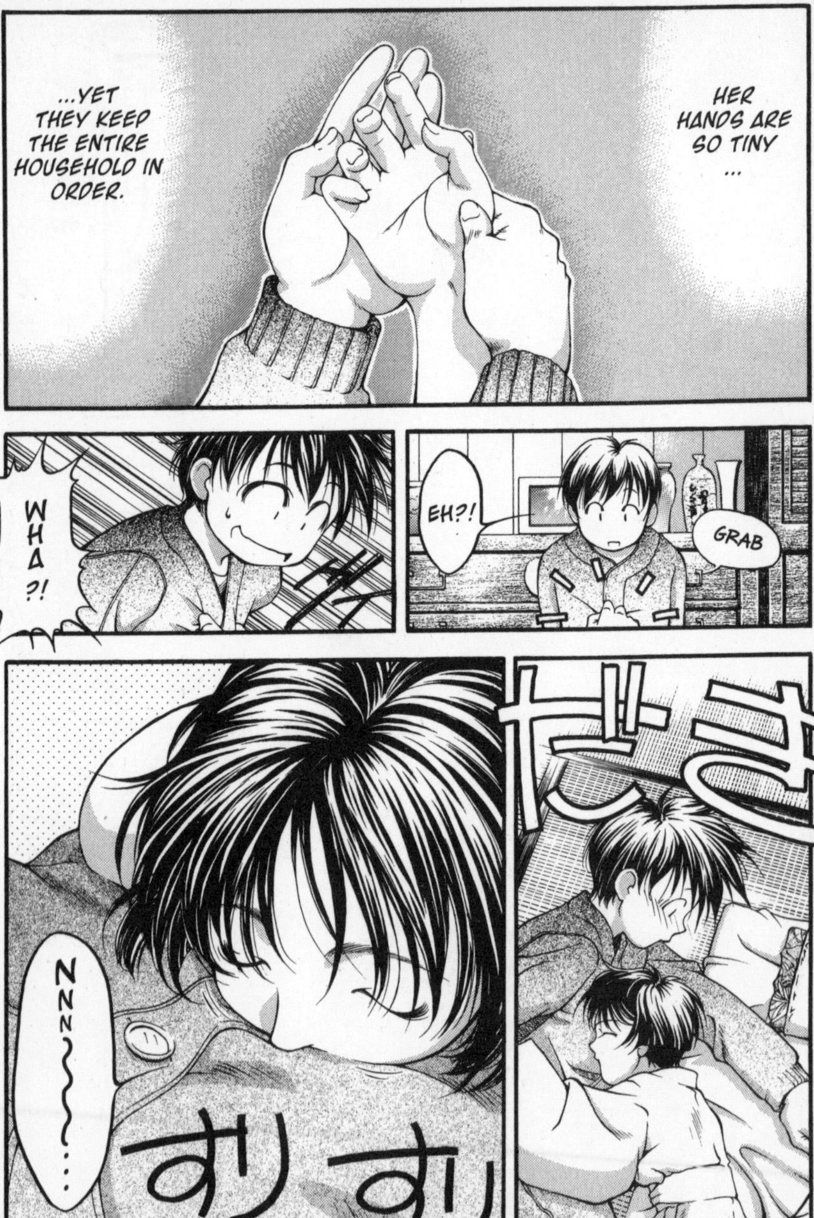
HER HANDS ARE SO TINY ...
...YET THEY KEEP THE ENTIRE HOUSEHOLD IN ORDER.
GRAB
EH?!
WHA?!
だき
NNN~~...
すりすり

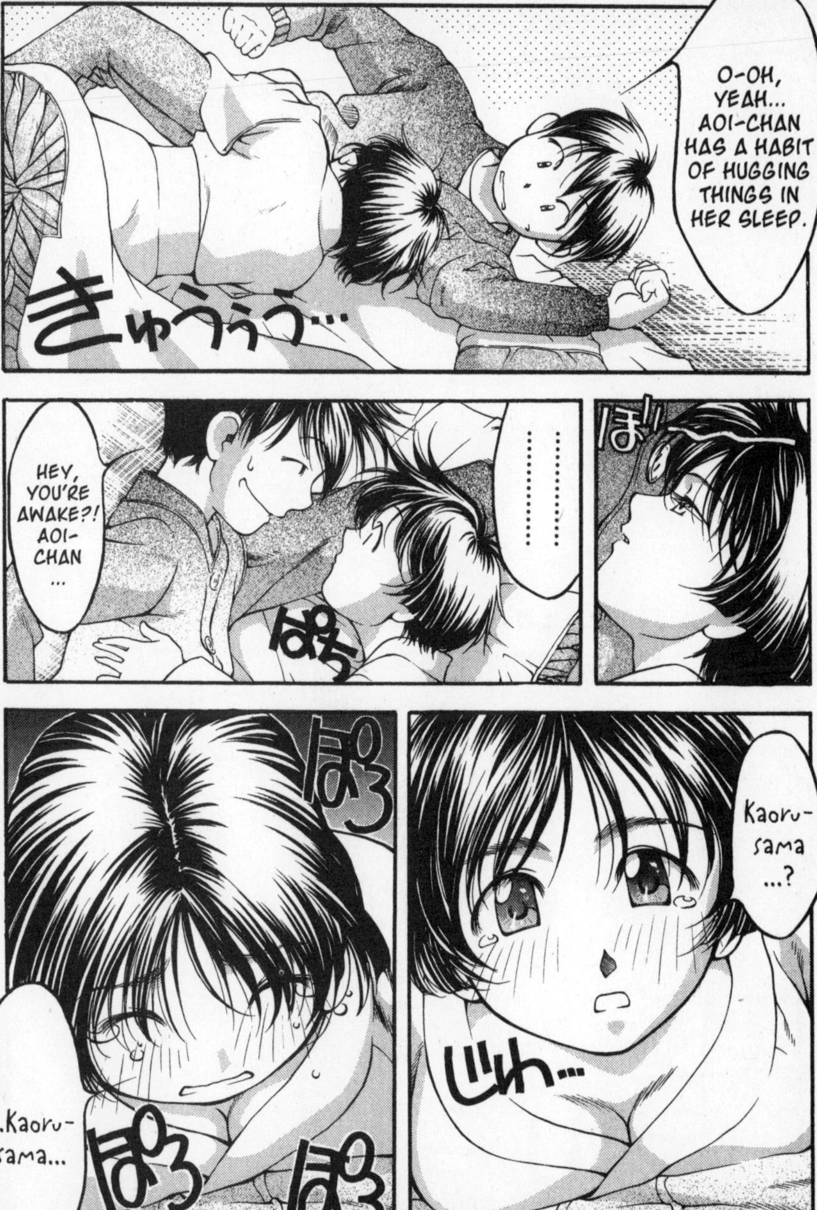
O-OH, YEAH... AOI-CHAN HAS A HABIT OF HUGGING THINGS IN HER SLEEP.
......
HEY, YOU'RE AWAKE?! AOI-CHAN ...
Kaoru-sama ...?
..Kaoru-sama...

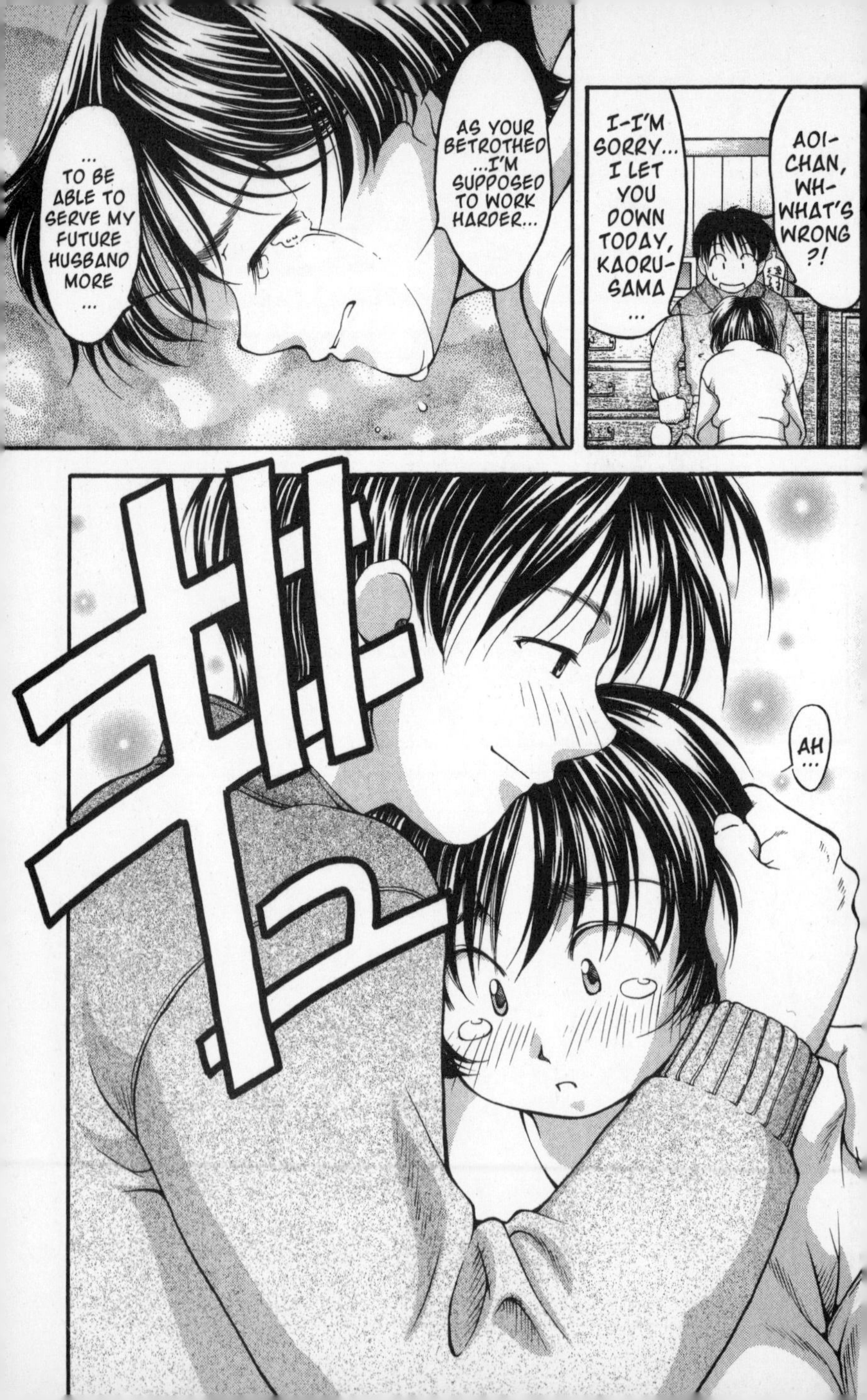
AOI-CHAN, WH-WHAT'S WRONG ?!
I-I'M SORRY... I LET YOU DOWN TODAY, KAORU-SAMA ...
AS YOUR BETROTHED ...I'M SUPPOSED TO WORK HARDER...
... TO BE ABLE TO SERVE MY FUTURE HUSBAND MORE ...
AH ...

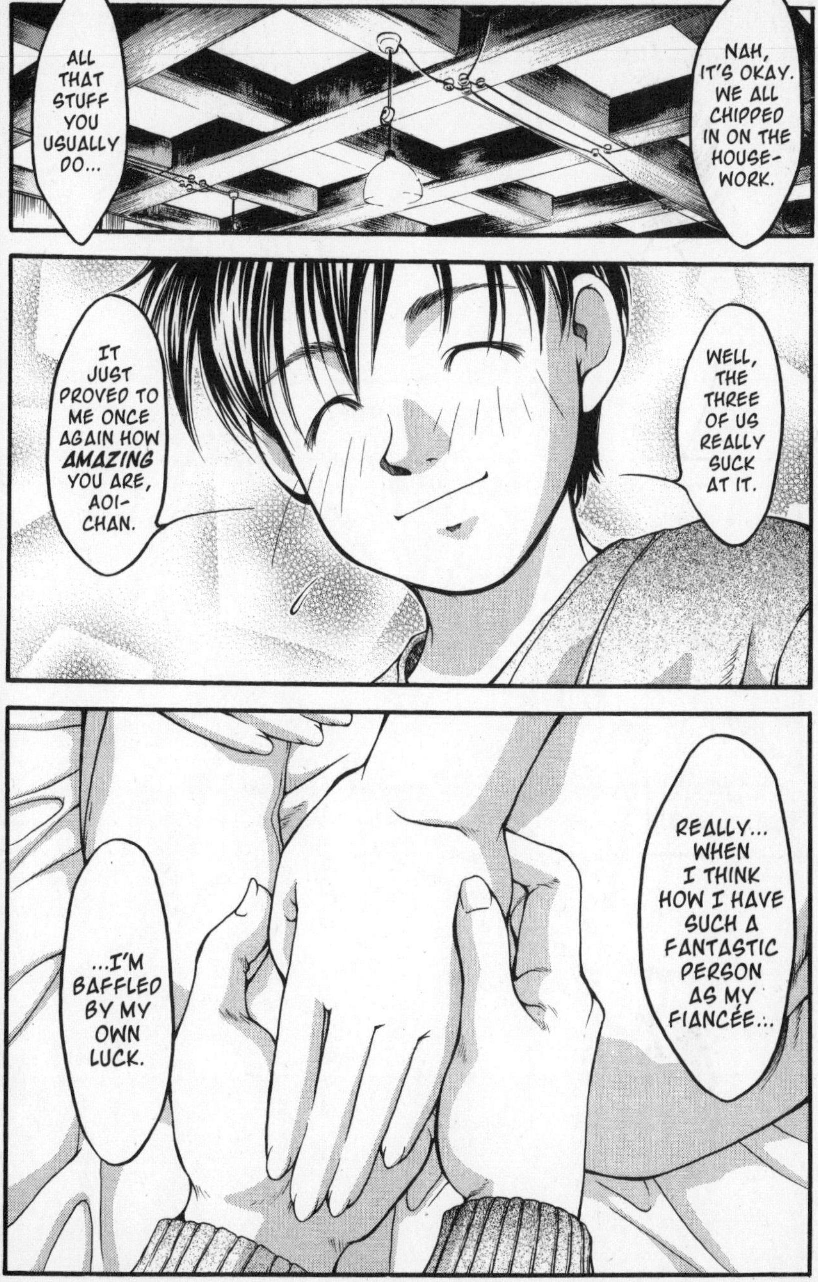
NAH, IT'S OKAY. WE ALL CHIPPED IN ON THE HOUSE-WORK.
ALL THAT STUFF YOU USUALLY DO...
WELL, THE THREE OF US REALLY SUCK AT IT.
IT JUST PROVED TO ME ONCE AGAIN HOW *AMAZING* YOU ARE, AOI-CHAN.
REALLY... WHEN I THINK HOW I HAVE SUCH A FANTASTIC PERSON AS MY FIANCÉE...
...I'M BAFFLED BY MY OWN LUCK.

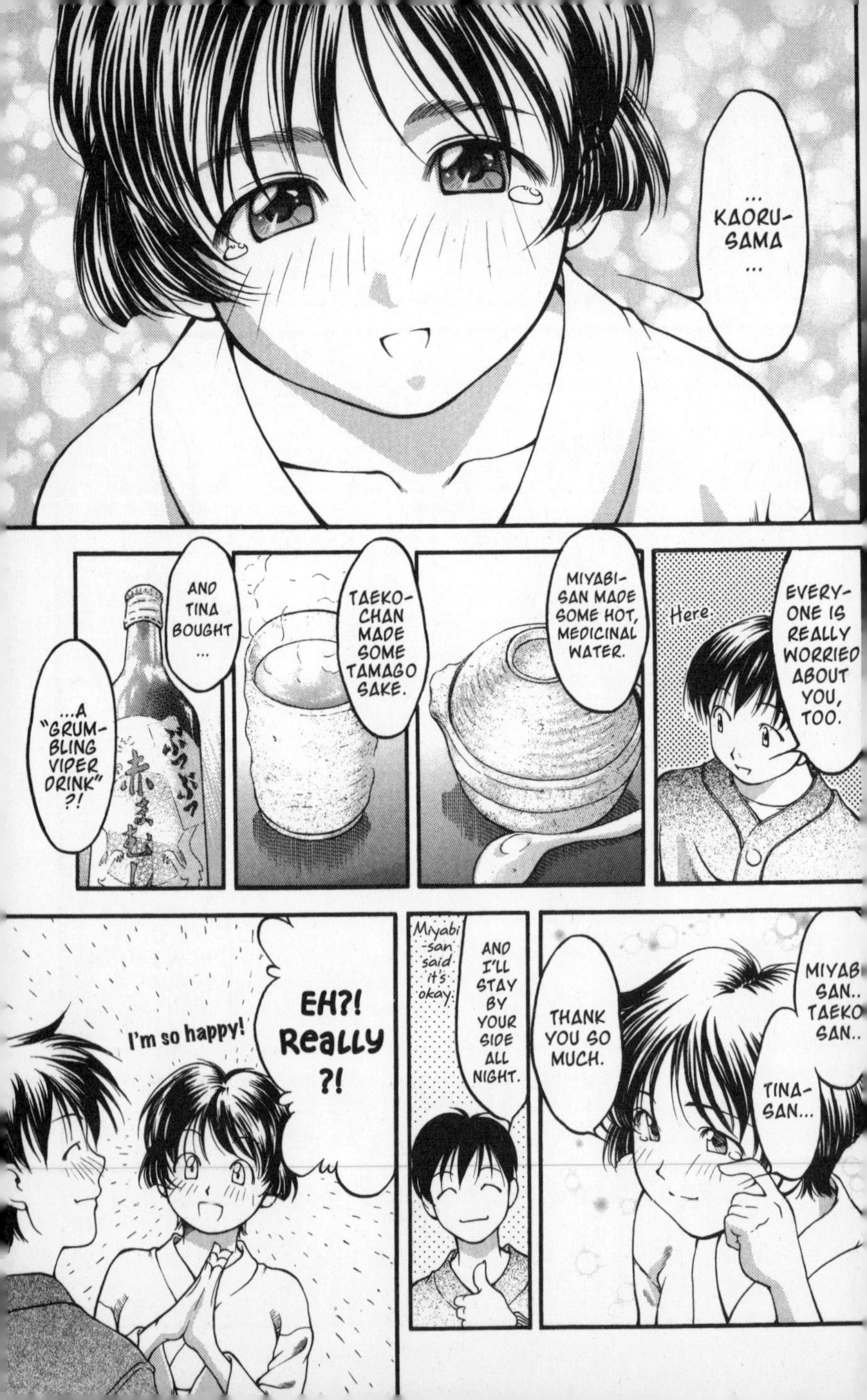
... KAORU-SAMA ...
EVERY-ONE IS REALLY WORRIED ABOUT YOU, TOO.
Here
MIYABI-SAN MADE SOME HOT, MEDICINAL WATER.
TAEKO-CHAN MADE SOME TAMAGO SAKE.
AND TINA BOUGHT ...
...A "GRUMBLING VIPER DRINK"?!
MIYAB SAN.. TAEKO SAN..
TINA-SAN...
THANK YOU SO MUCH.
AND I'LL STAY BY YOUR SIDE ALL NIGHT.
Miyabi-san said it's okay.
EH?! Really?!
I'm so happy!

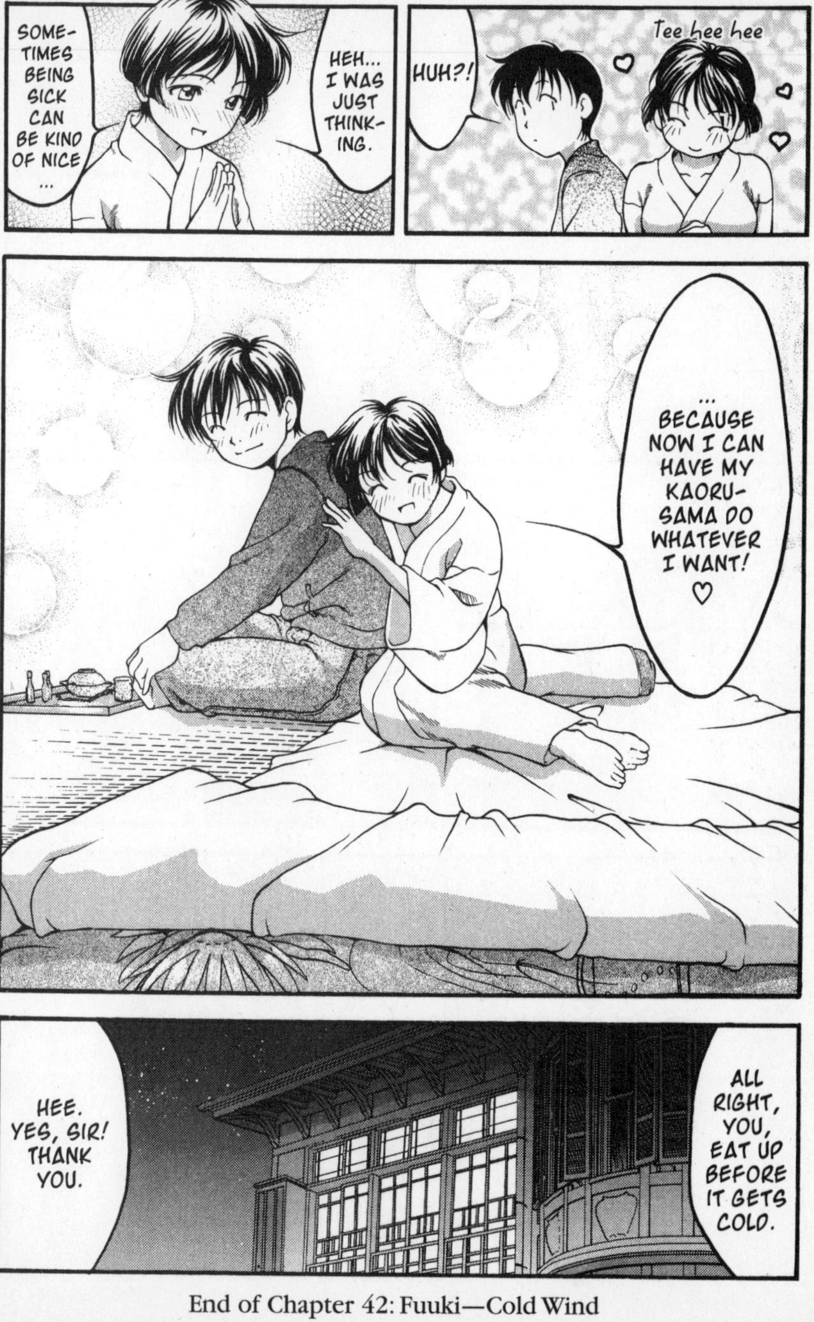
Tee hee hee
HUH?!
HEH... I WAS JUST THINKING.
SOMETIMES BEING SICK CAN BE KIND OF NICE ...
... BECAUSE NOW I CAN HAVE MY KAORU-SAMA DO WHATEVER I WANT! ♡
ALL RIGHT, YOU, EAT UP BEFORE IT GETS COLD.
HEE. YES, SIR! THANK YOU.

End of Chapter 42: Fuuki—Cold Wind

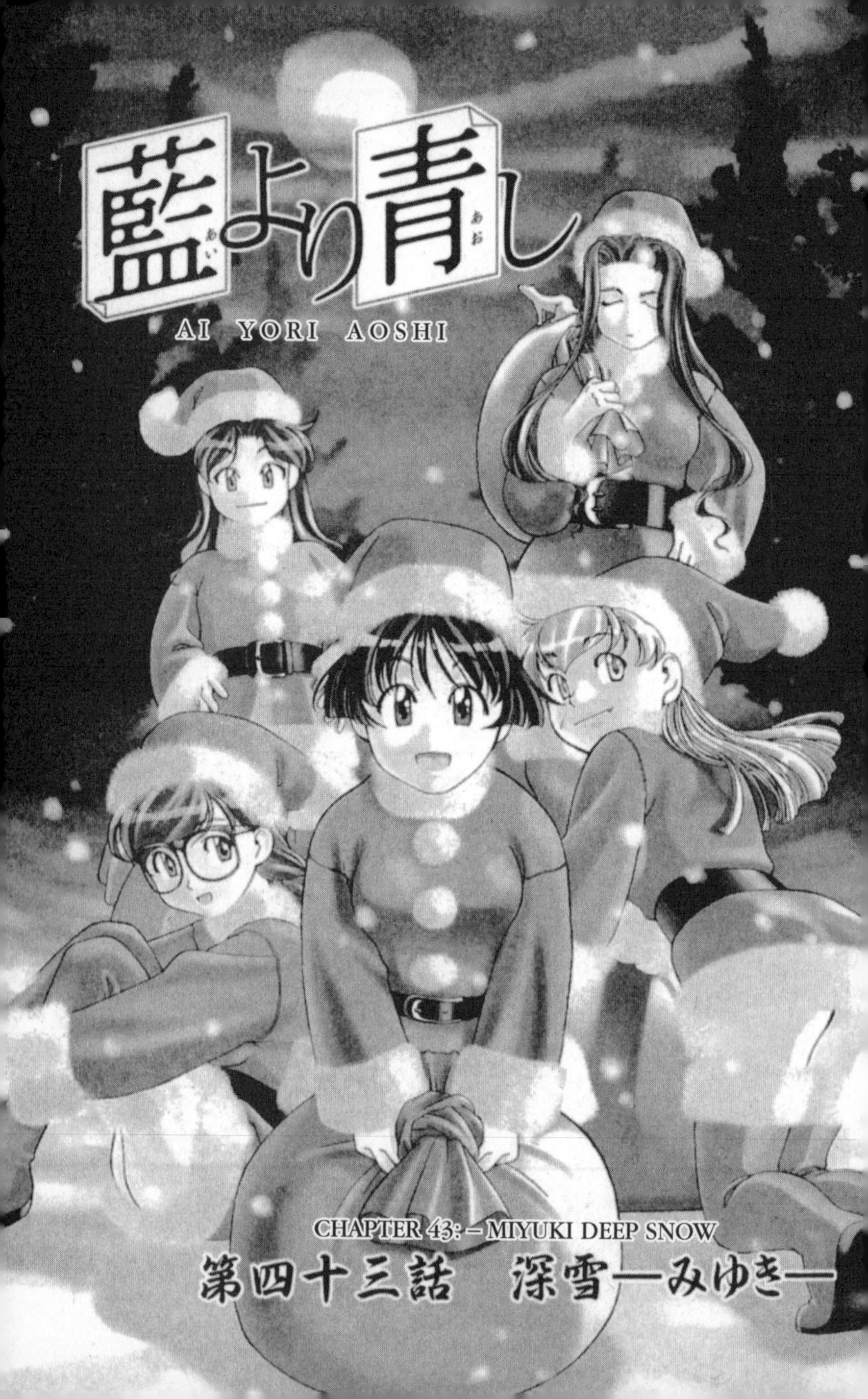
藍(あい)より青(あお)し
AI YORI AOSHI
CHAPTER 43: – MIYUKI DEEP SNOW
第四十三話　深雪—みゆき—

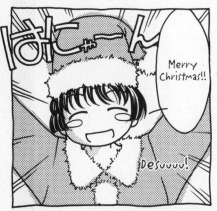

Ai-Ao Theatre, part 10

Fake Aoi

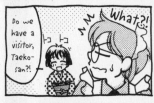

はにゃーん
Merry Christmas!!
Desuuuu!

Huh?! Why are you wearing that, Aoi-san ...?
It's still spring!
Nice to meet you! I'm Santa.
へこん
What?!
トコ トコ
Do we have a visitor, Taeko-san?!
はわわ
Th-there are two Aoi-sans ?!!
Don't be fooled!
That one is a fake!
Now, tell us your true identity !!
Huh?

To be continued...

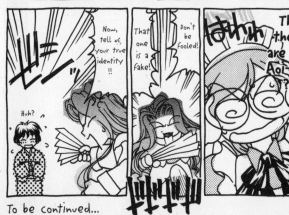

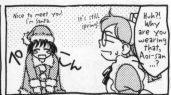

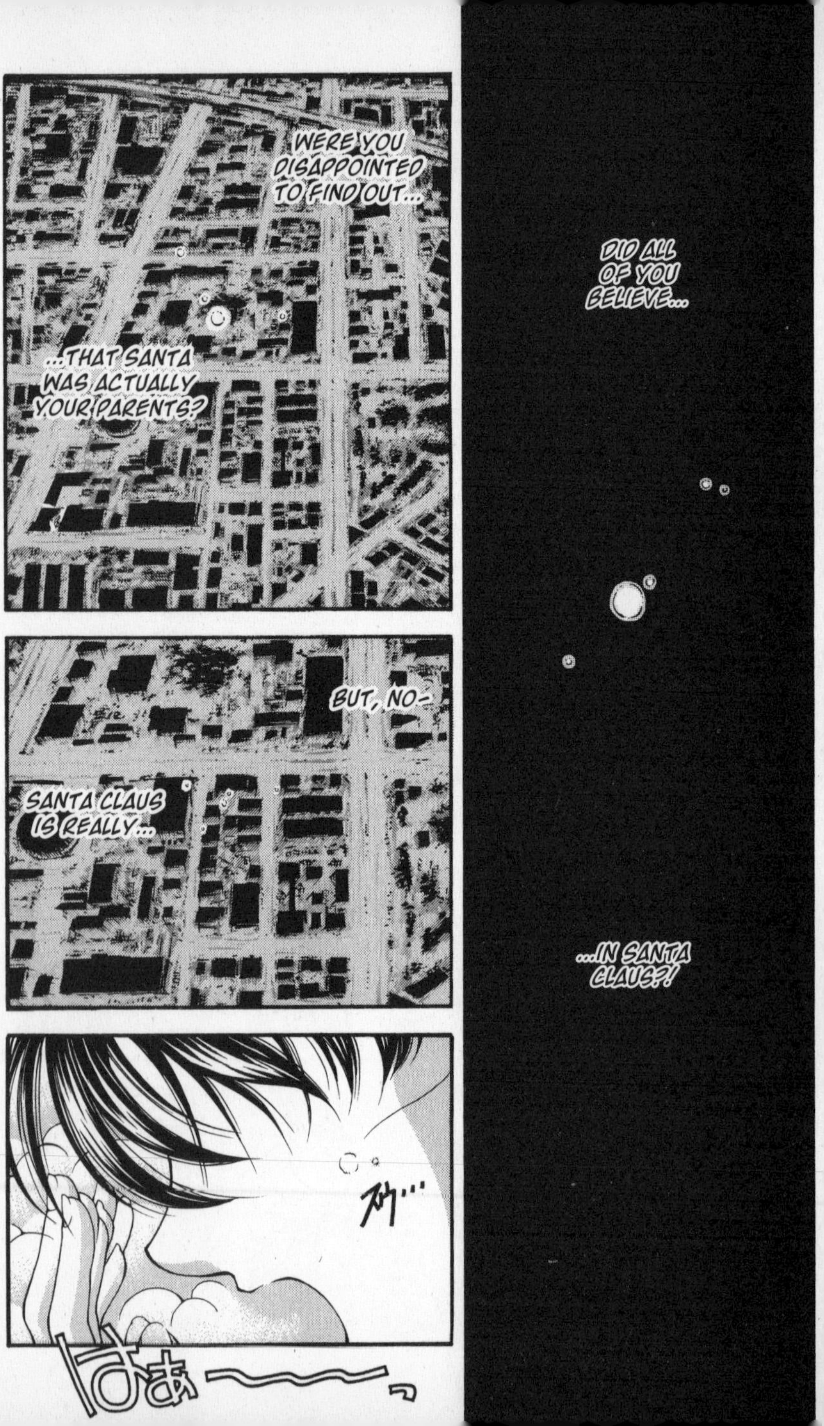
DID ALL OF YOU BELIEVE...
...IN SANTA CLAUS?!
WERE YOU DISAPPOINTED TO FIND OUT...
...THAT SANTA WAS ACTUALLY YOUR PARENTS?
BUT, NO-
SANTA CLAUS IS REALLY...
はあ〜〜〜っ

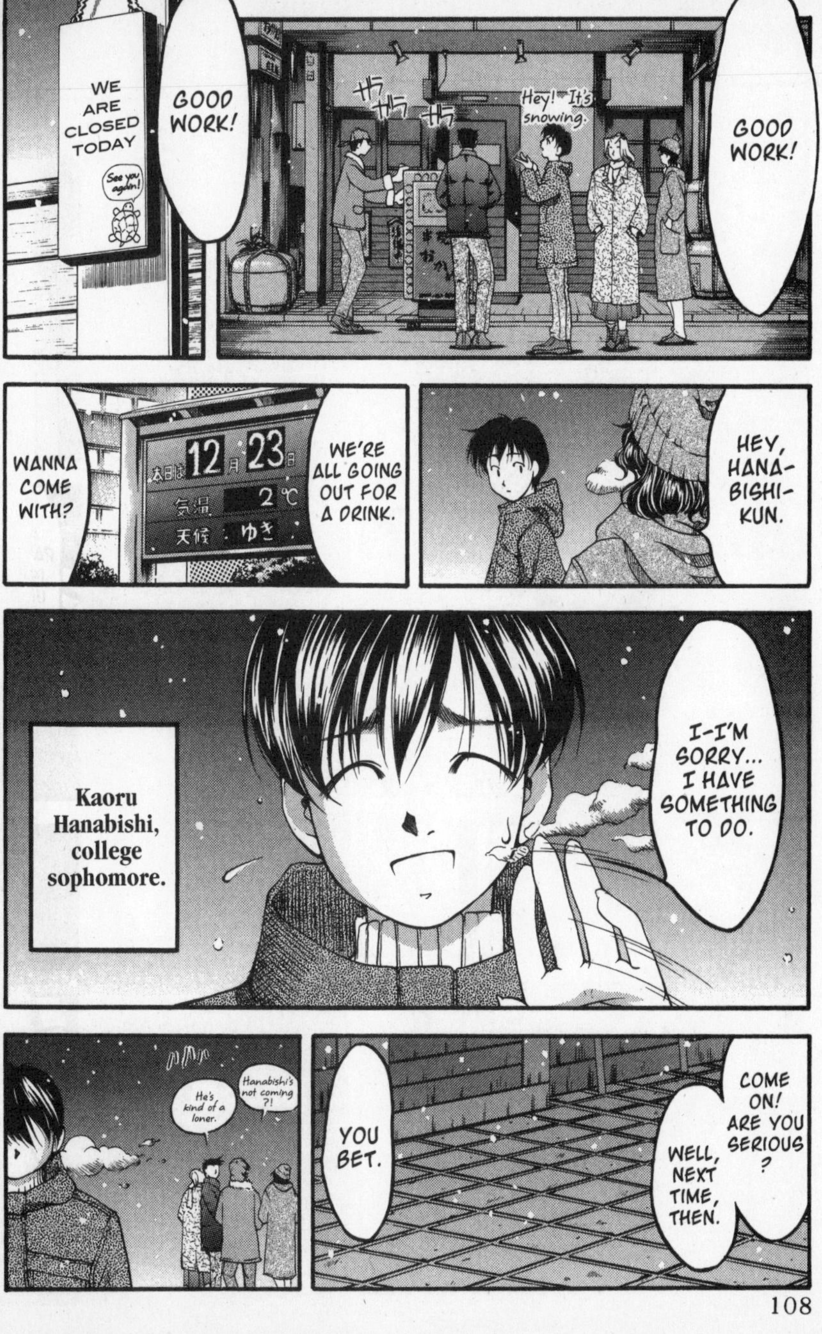
GOOD WORK!
ガラ ガラ ガラ
Hey! It's snowing.
GOOD WORK!
WE ARE CLOSED TODAY
See you again!
HEY, HANA-BISHI-KUN.
WE'RE ALL GOING OUT FOR A DRINK.
本日は 12 月 23 日
気温 2℃
天候 ゆき
WANNA COME WITH?
I-I'M SORRY... I HAVE SOMETHING TO DO.
Kaoru Hanabishi, college sophomore.
COME ON! ARE YOU SERIOUS?
WELL, NEXT TIME, THEN.
YOU BET.
Hanabishi's not coming?!
He's kind of a loner.

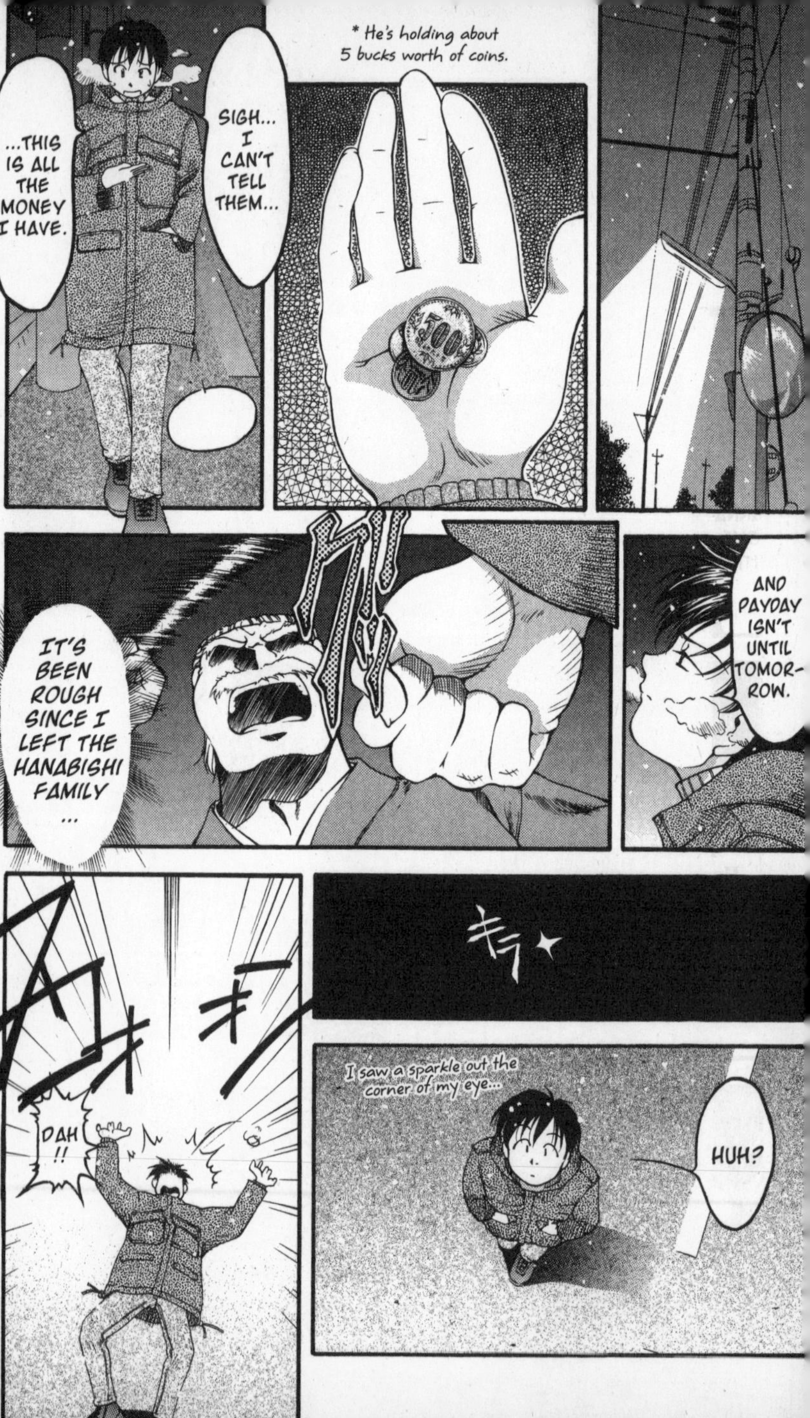
* He's holding about 5 bucks worth of coins.
SIGH... I CAN'T TELL THEM...
...THIS IS ALL THE MONEY I HAVE.
AND PAYDAY ISN'T UNTIL TOMORROW.
IT'S BEEN ROUGH SINCE I LEFT THE HANABISHI FAMILY ...
キラ
I saw a sparkle out the corner of my eye...
HUH?
DAH !!

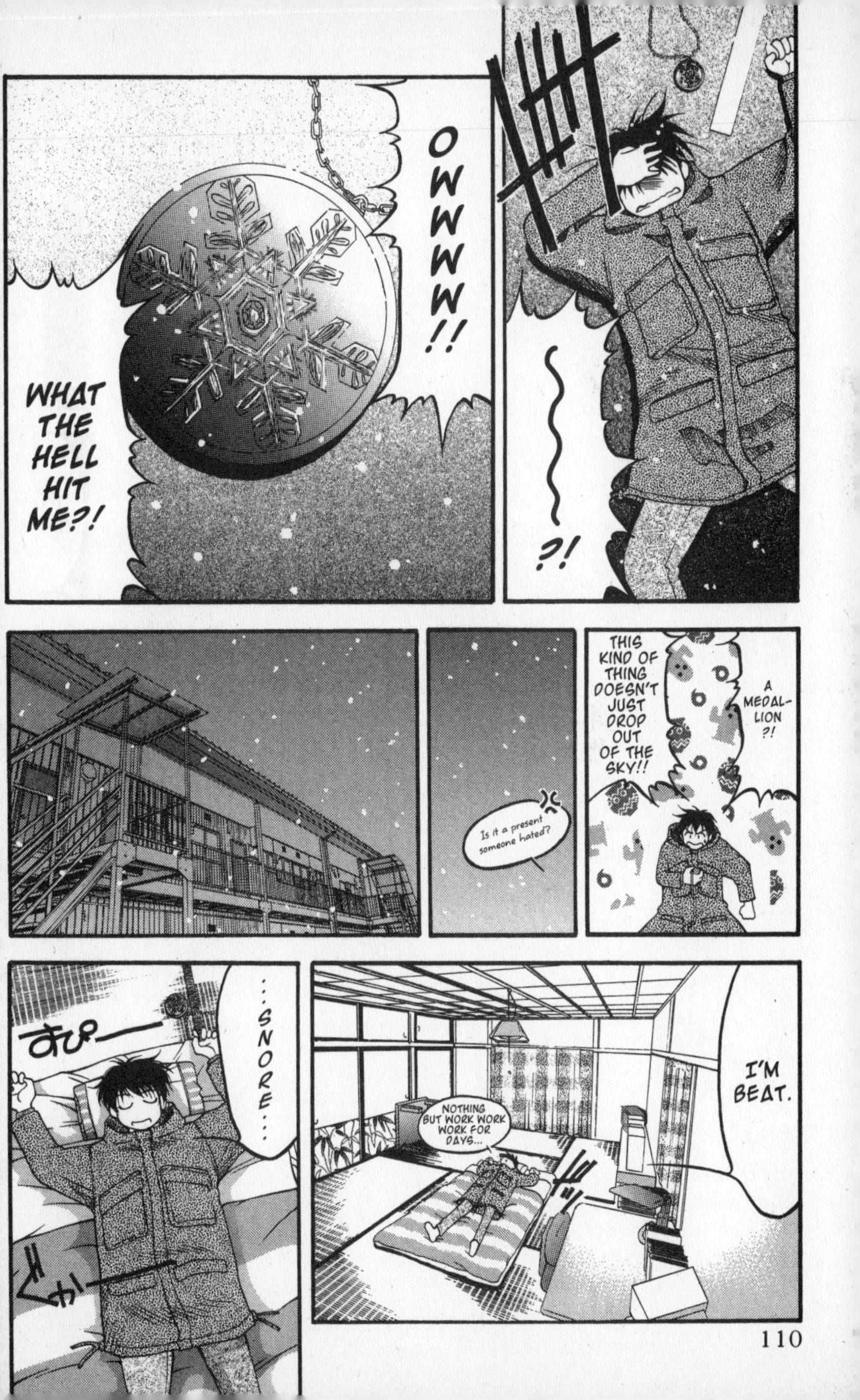

?!
OWWWWW!!
WHAT THE HELL HIT ME?!
A MEDALLION?!
THIS KIND OF THING DOESN'T JUST DROP OUT OF THE SKY!!
Is it a present someone hated?
I'M BEAT.
NOTHING BUT WORK WORK WORK FOR DAYS...
...SNORE...
すぴー

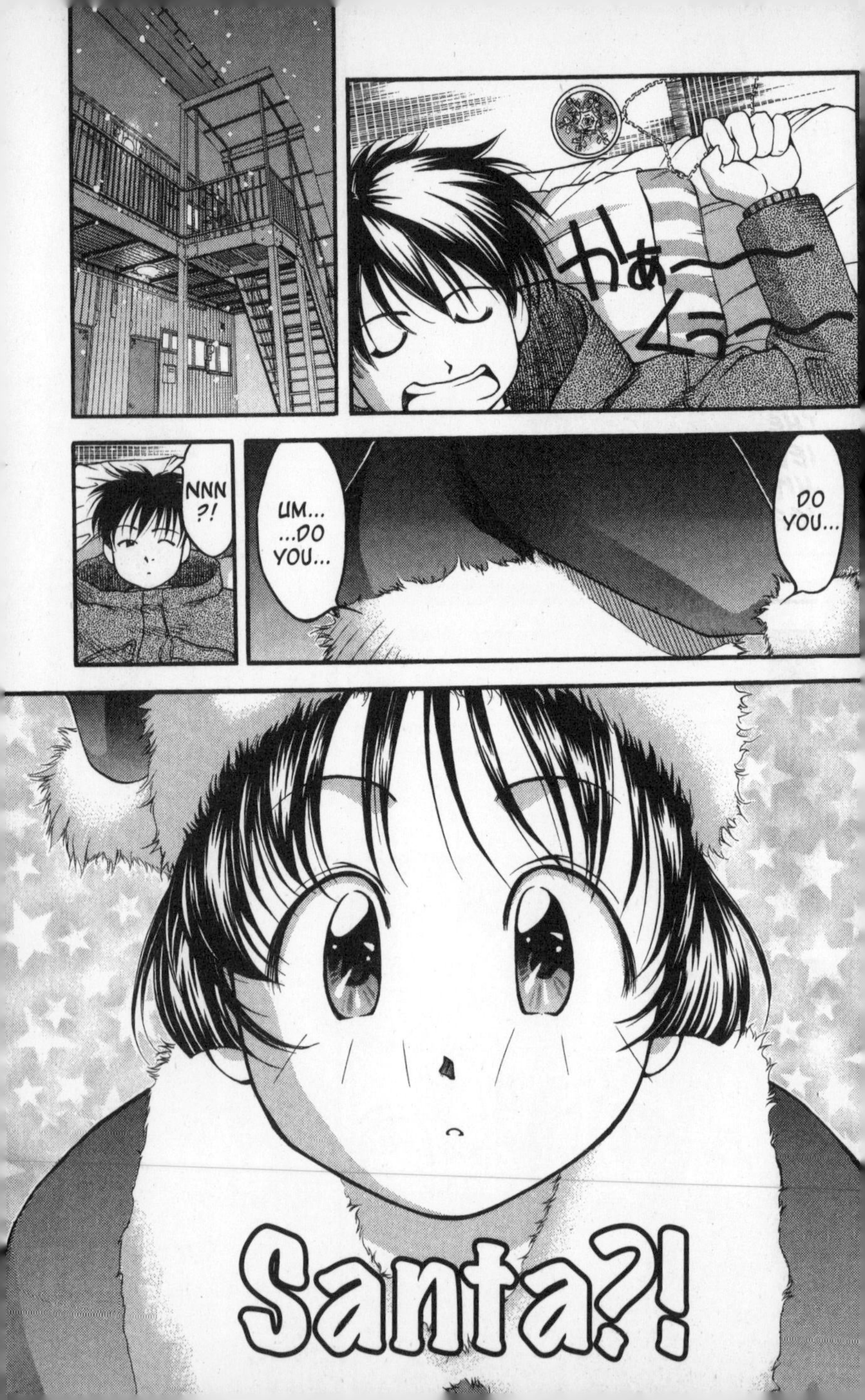
かぁ〜〜
くぅ〜〜
DO YOU...
UM... ...DO YOU...
NNN ?!
Santa?!

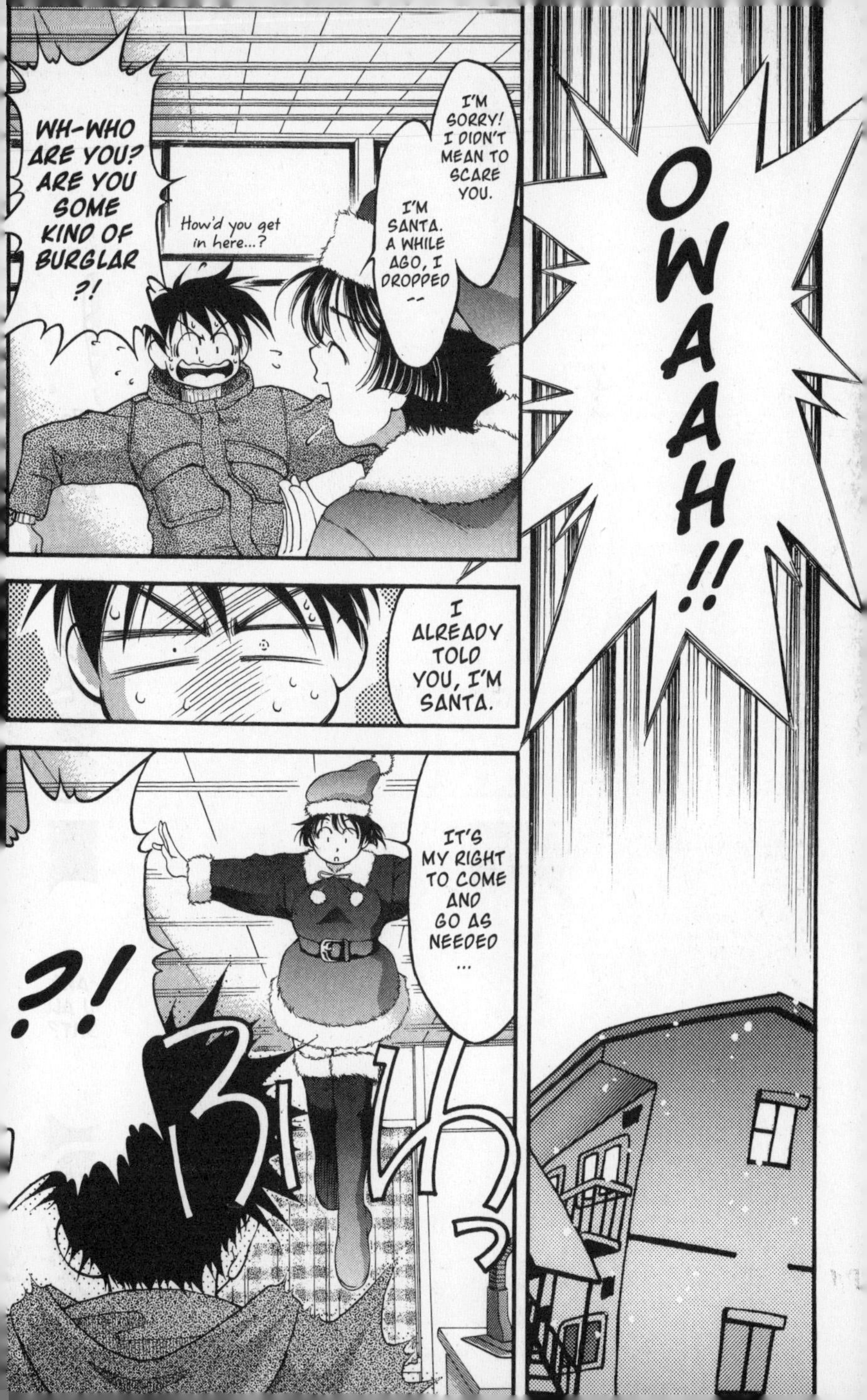
OWAAH!!
I'M SORRY! I DIDN'T MEAN TO SCARE YOU.
I'M SANTA. A WHILE AGO, I DROPPED --
WH-WHO ARE YOU? ARE YOU SOME KIND OF BURGLAR ?!
How'd you get in here...?
I ALREADY TOLD YOU, I'M SANTA.
IT'S MY RIGHT TO COME AND GO AS NEEDED ...
ふわっ
?!

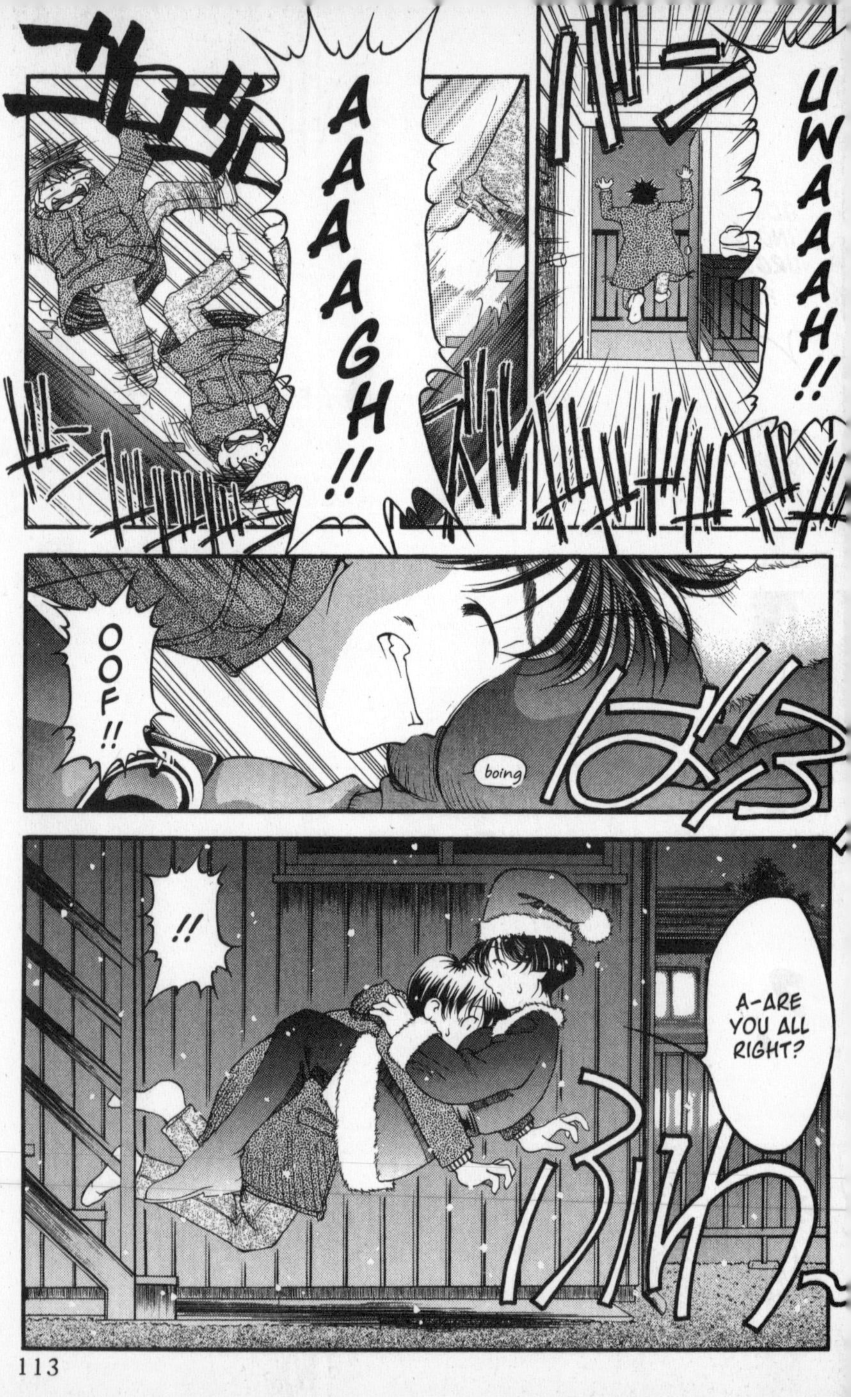
UWAAAAAH!!
AAAAAGH!!
OOF!!
boing
A-ARE YOU ALL RIGHT?
!!

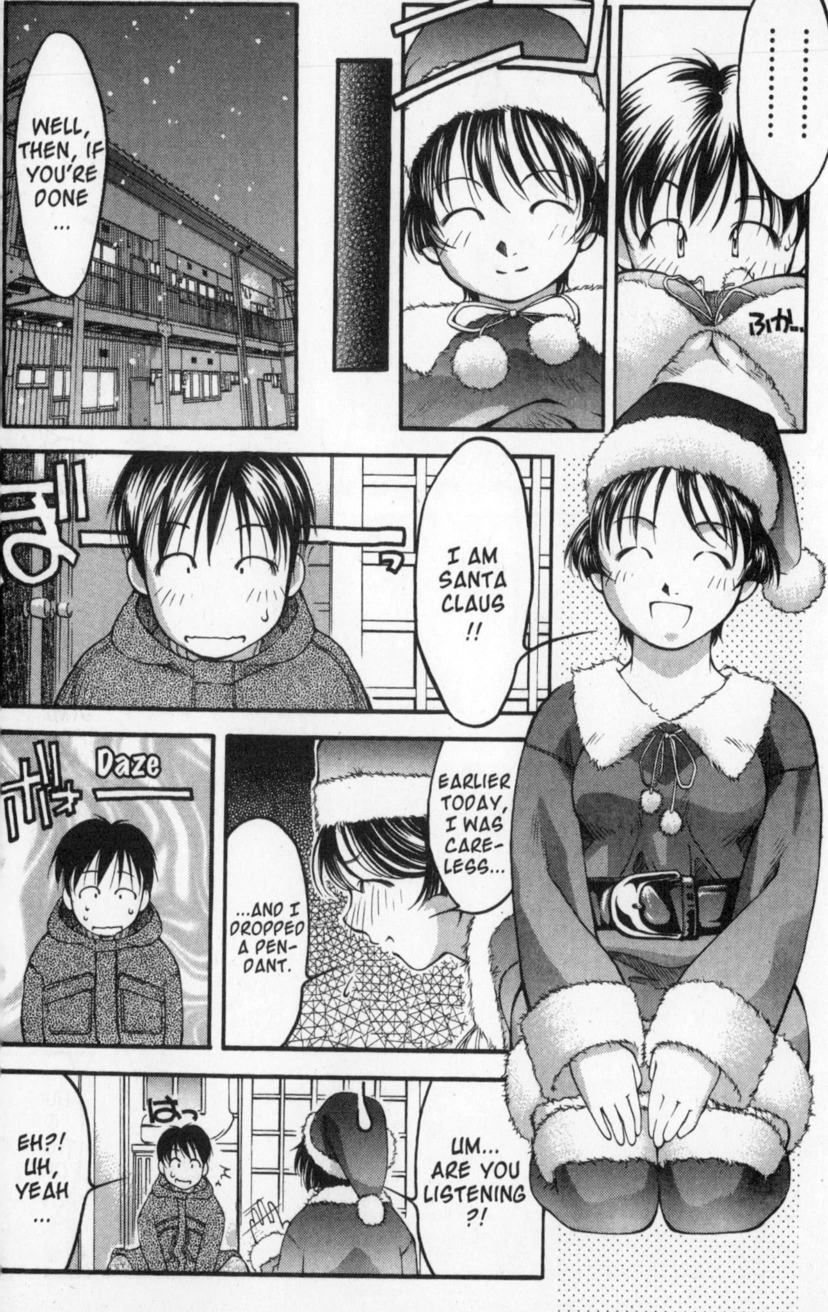

......
WELL, THEN, IF YOU'RE DONE ...
I AM SANTA CLAUS !!
EARLIER TODAY, I WAS CARELESS...
...AND I DROPPED A PENDANT.
Daze
UM... ARE YOU LISTENING ?!
はっ
EH?! UH, YEAH ...

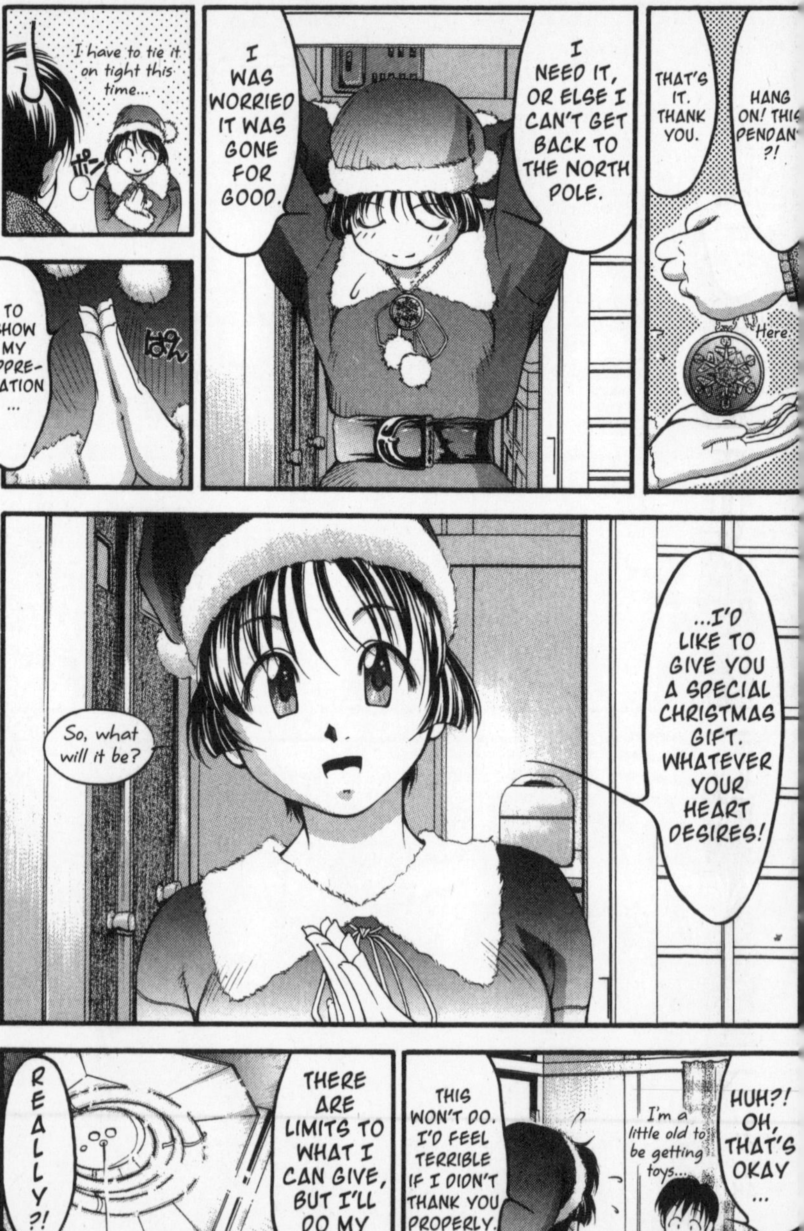
HANG ON! THIS PENDAN ?!
THAT'S IT. THANK YOU.
Here
I NEED IT, OR ELSE I CAN'T GET BACK TO THE NORTH POLE.
I WAS WORRIED IT WAS GONE FOR GOOD.
I have to tie it on tight this time...
ポン
TO SHOW MY APPRECIATION ...
ぱん
...I'D LIKE TO GIVE YOU A SPECIAL CHRISTMAS GIFT. WHATEVER YOUR HEART DESIRES!
So, what will it be?
HUH?! OH, THAT'S OKAY ...
I'm a little old to be getting toys...
THIS WON'T DO. I'D FEEL TERRIBLE IF I DIDN'T THANK YOU PROPERLY.
THERE ARE LIMITS TO WHAT I CAN GIVE, BUT I'LL DO MY BEST.
REALLY?!

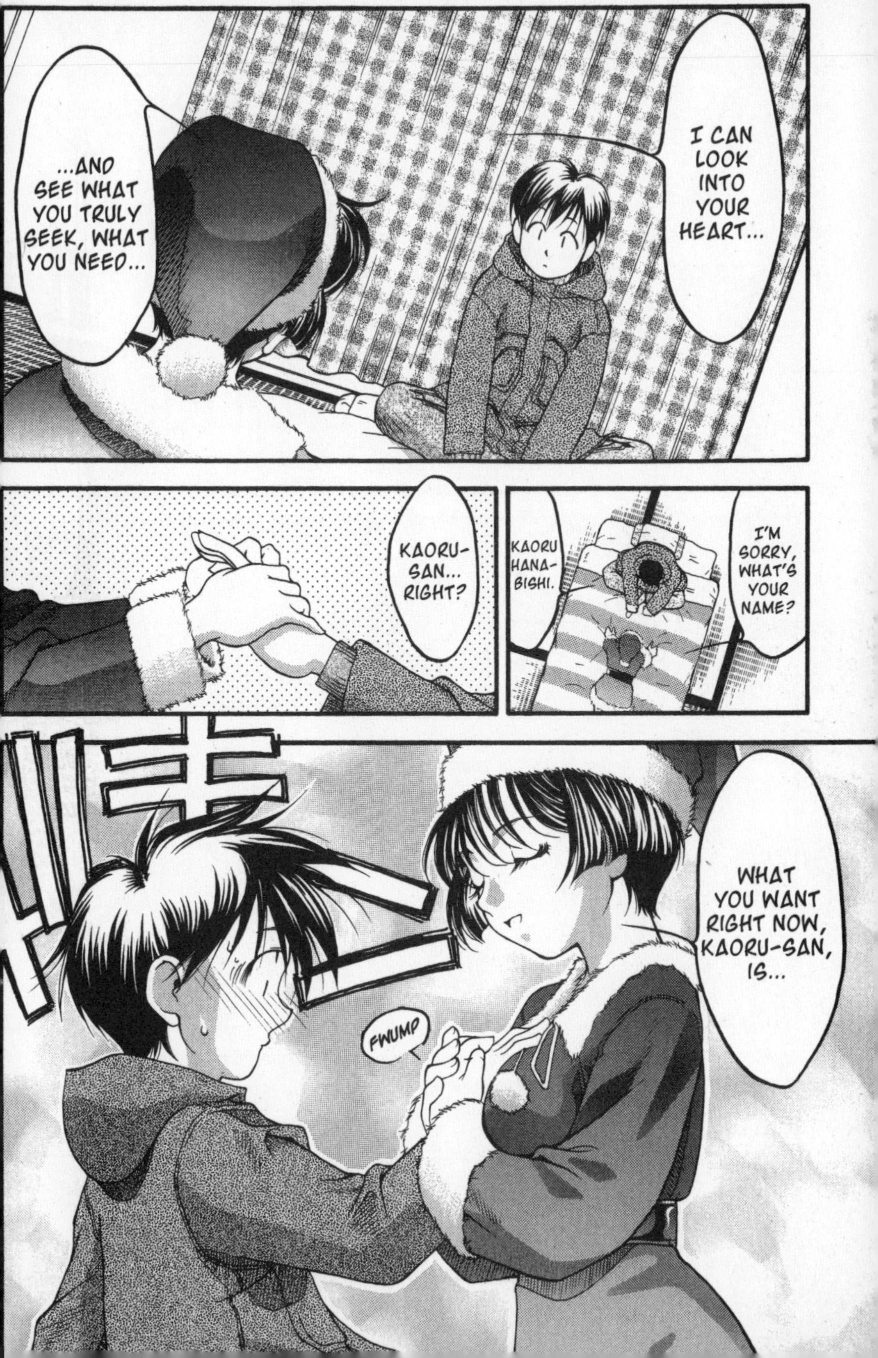
I CAN LOOK INTO YOUR HEART...
...AND SEE WHAT YOU TRULY SEEK, WHAT YOU NEED...
I'M SORRY, WHAT'S YOUR NAME?
KAORU HANABISHI.
KAORU-SAN... RIGHT?
WHAT YOU WANT RIGHT NOW, KAORU-SAN, IS...
FWUMP

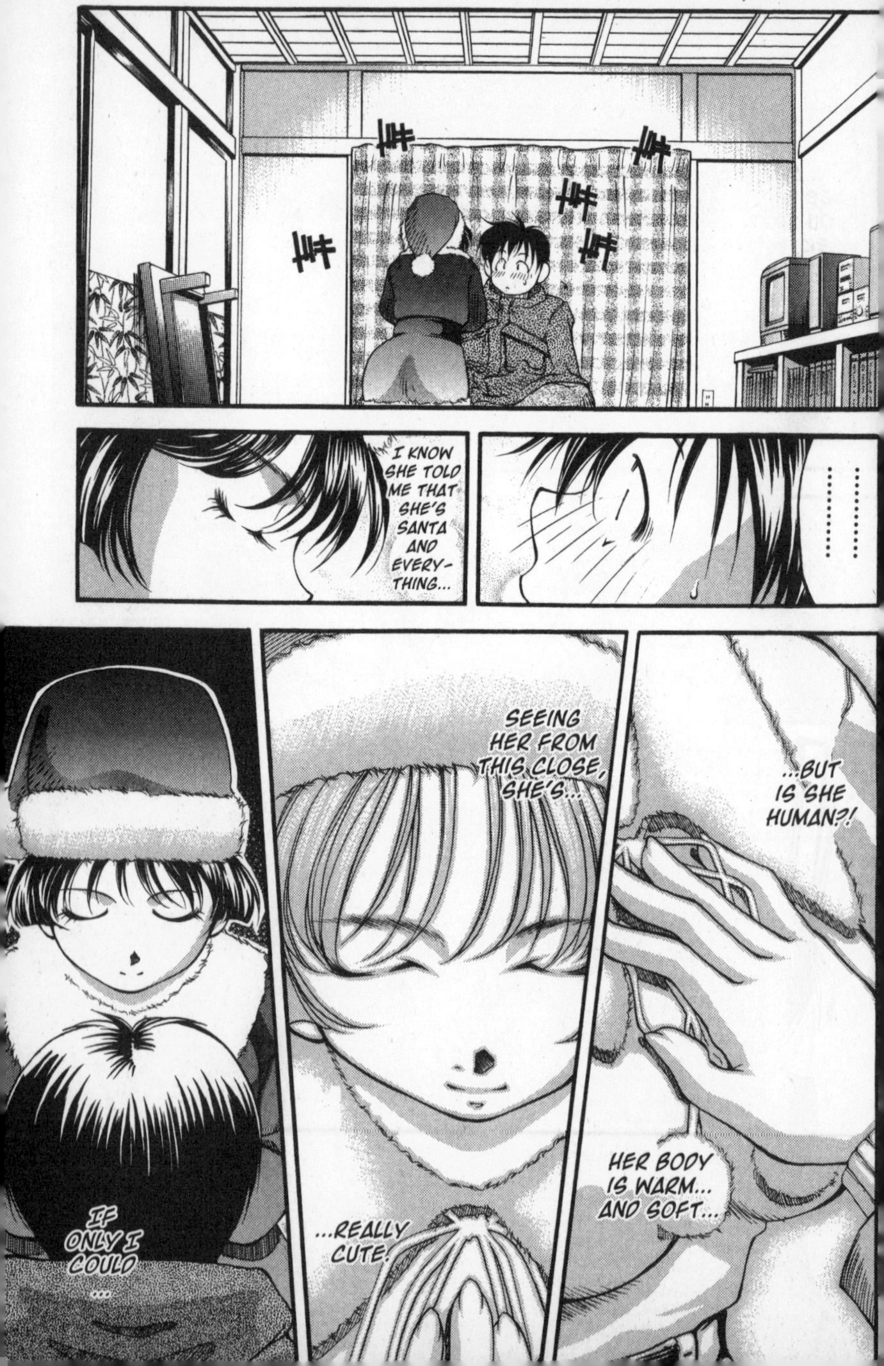
......
I KNOW SHE TOLD ME THAT SHE'S SANTA AND EVERYTHING...
...BUT IS SHE HUMAN?!
HER BODY IS WARM... AND SOFT...
SEEING HER FROM THIS CLOSE, SHE'S...
...REALLY CUTE.
IF ONLY I COULD ...

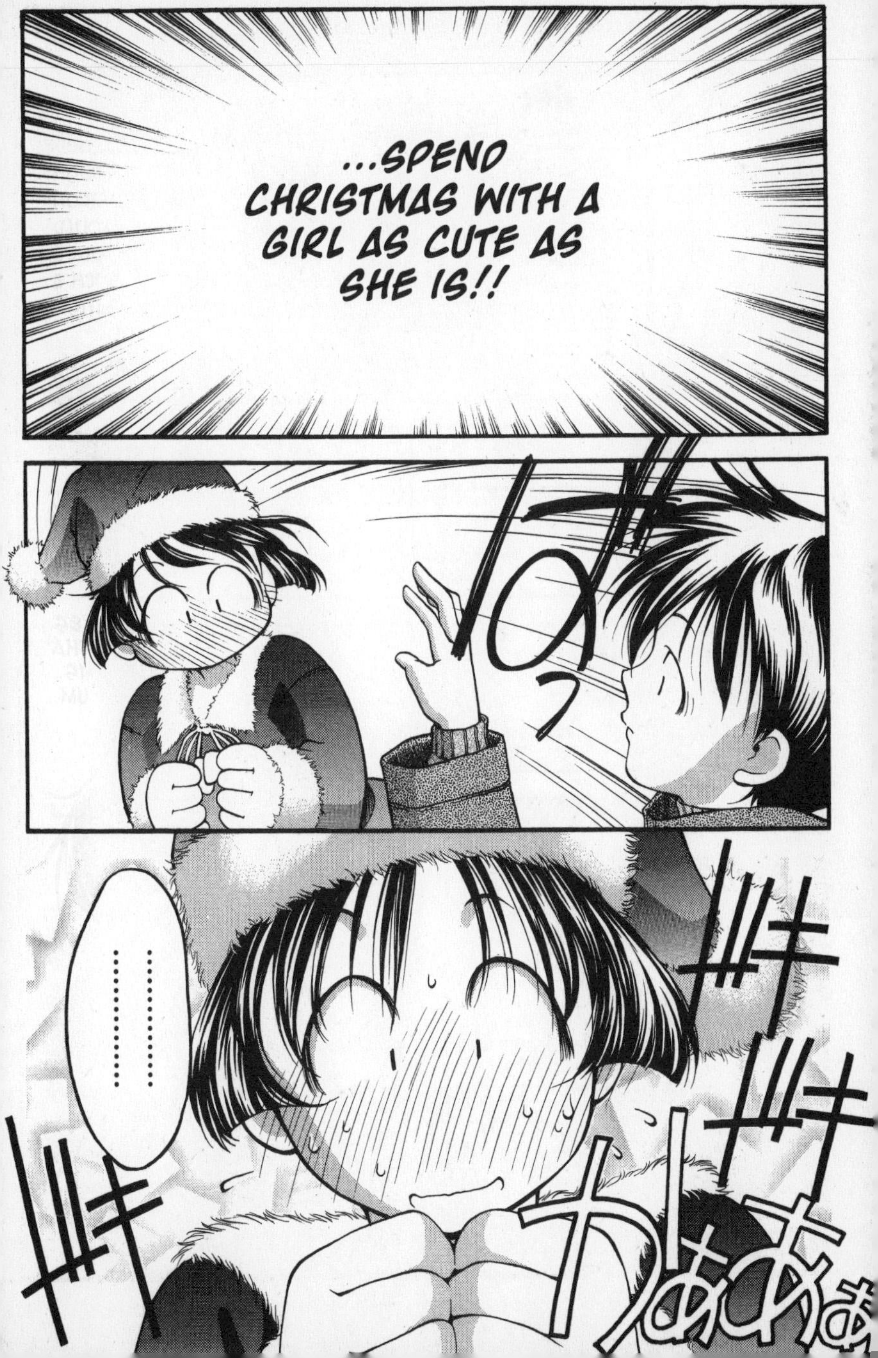
...SPEND CHRISTMAS WITH A GIRL AS CUTE AS SHE IS!!
……

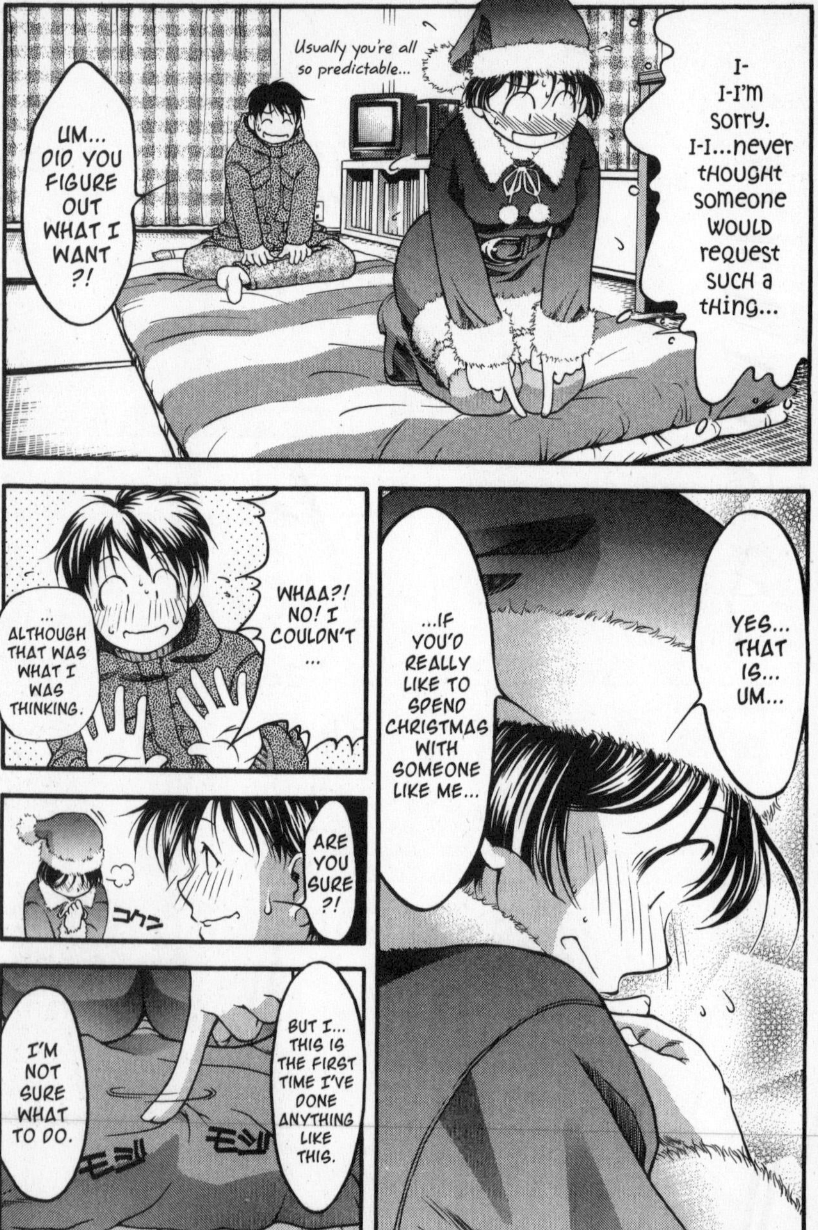
I- I-I'm sorry. I-I...never thought someone would request such a thing...
Usually you're all so predictable...
UM... DID YOU FIGURE OUT WHAT I WANT?!
YES... THAT IS... UM...
...IF YOU'D REALLY LIKE TO SPEND CHRISTMAS WITH SOMEONE LIKE ME...
WHAA?! NO! I COULDN'T ...
... ALTHOUGH THAT WAS WHAT I WAS THINKING.
ARE YOU SURE?!
コクン
BUT I... THIS IS THE FIRST TIME I'VE DONE ANYTHING LIKE THIS.
I'M NOT SURE WHAT TO DO.
モジ
モジ

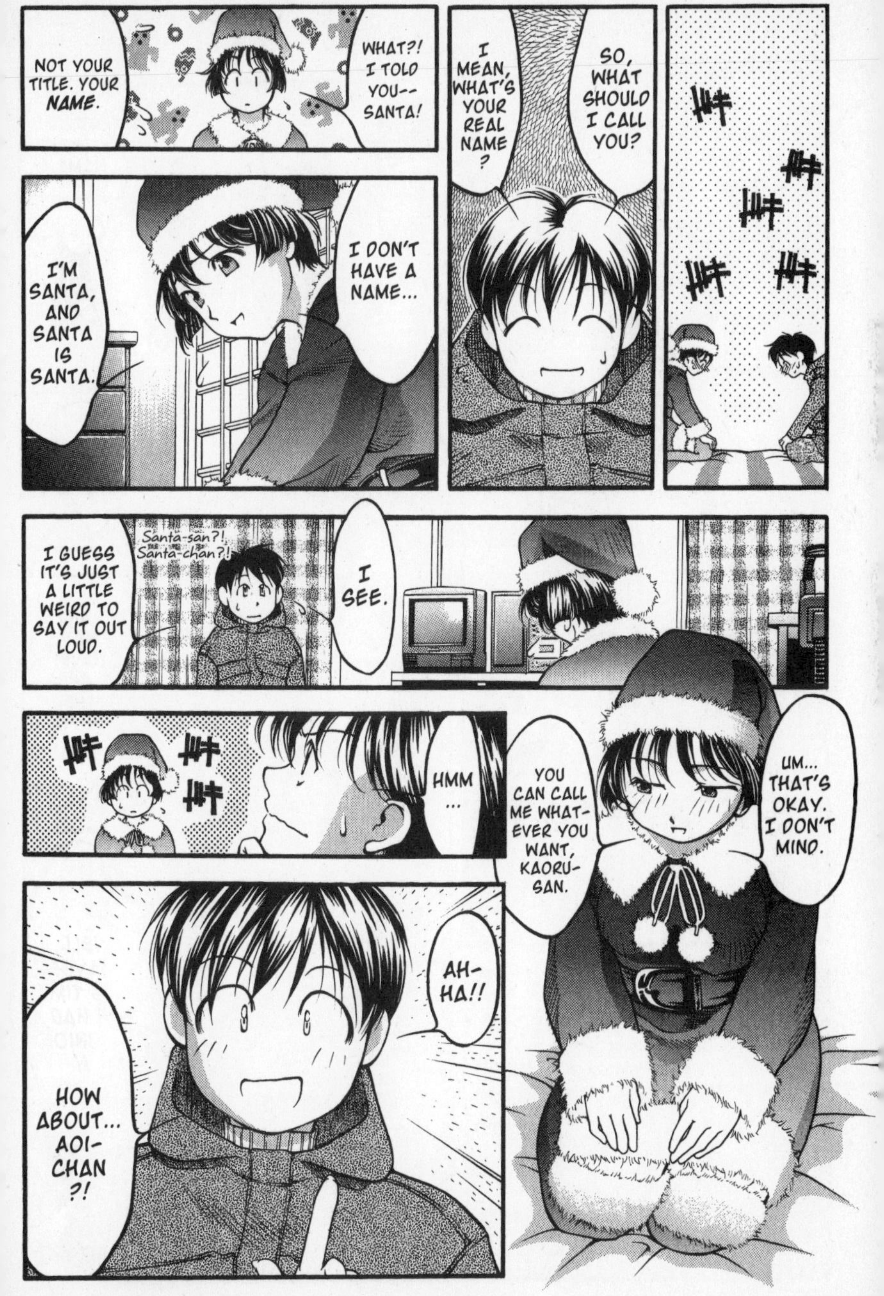
SO, WHAT SHOULD I CALL YOU?
I MEAN, WHAT'S YOUR REAL NAME?
WHAT?! I TOLD YOU-- SANTA!
NOT YOUR TITLE. YOUR NAME.
I DON'T HAVE A NAME...
I'M SANTA, AND SANTA IS SANTA.
I SEE.
Santa-san?! Santa-chan?!
I GUESS IT'S JUST A LITTLE WEIRD TO SAY IT OUT LOUD.
UM... THAT'S OKAY. I DON'T MIND.
YOU CAN CALL ME WHAT-EVER YOU WANT, KAORU-SAN.
HMM...
AH-HA!!
HOW ABOUT... AOI-CHAN?!

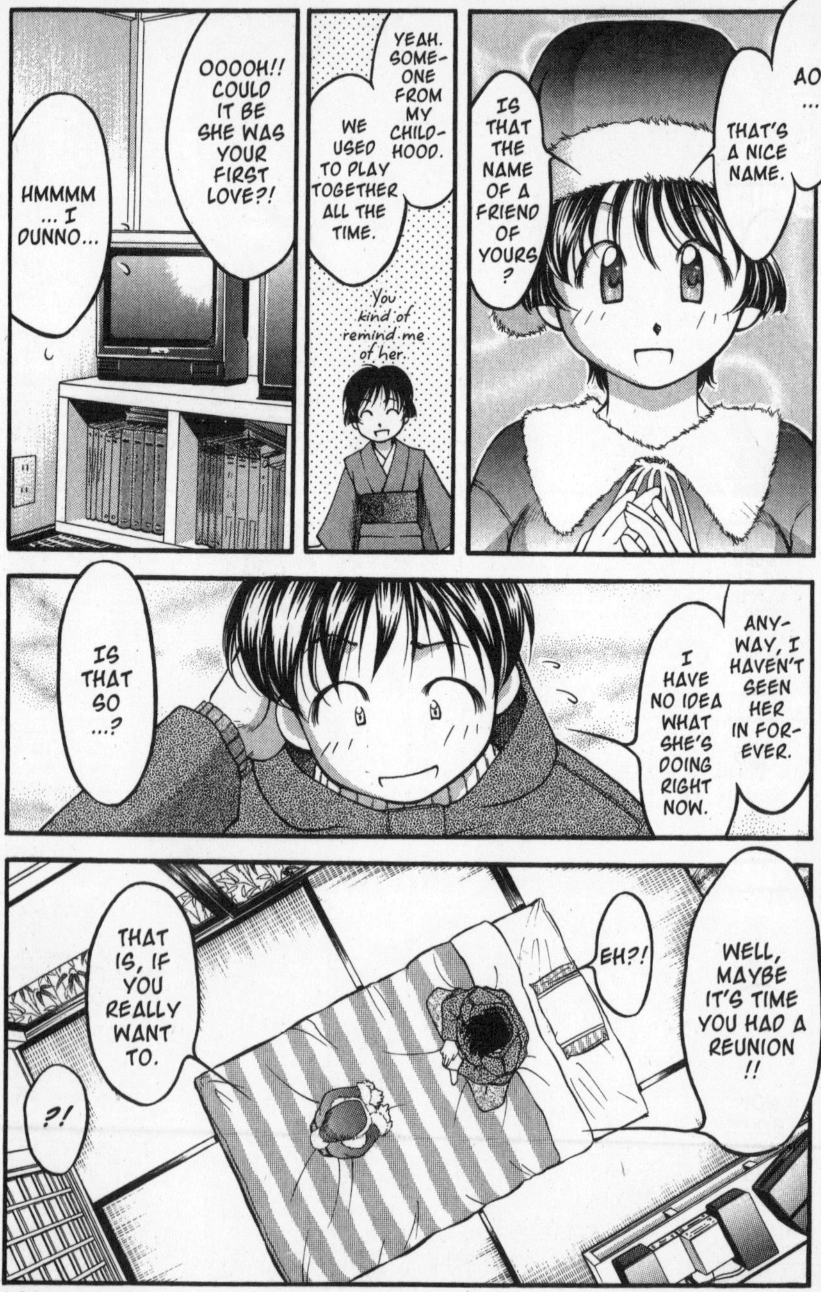
AOI ... THAT'S A NICE NAME.
IS THAT THE NAME OF A FRIEND OF YOURS?
YEAH. SOMEONE FROM MY CHILDHOOD.
WE USED TO PLAY TOGETHER ALL THE TIME.
You kind of remind me of her.
OOOOH!! COULD IT BE SHE WAS YOUR FIRST LOVE?!
HMMMM ... I DUNNO...
ANYWAY, I HAVEN'T SEEN HER IN FOREVER.
I HAVE NO IDEA WHAT SHE'S DOING RIGHT NOW.
IS THAT SO ...?
WELL, MAYBE IT'S TIME YOU HAD A REUNION !!
EH?!
THAT IS, IF YOU REALLY WANT TO.
?!

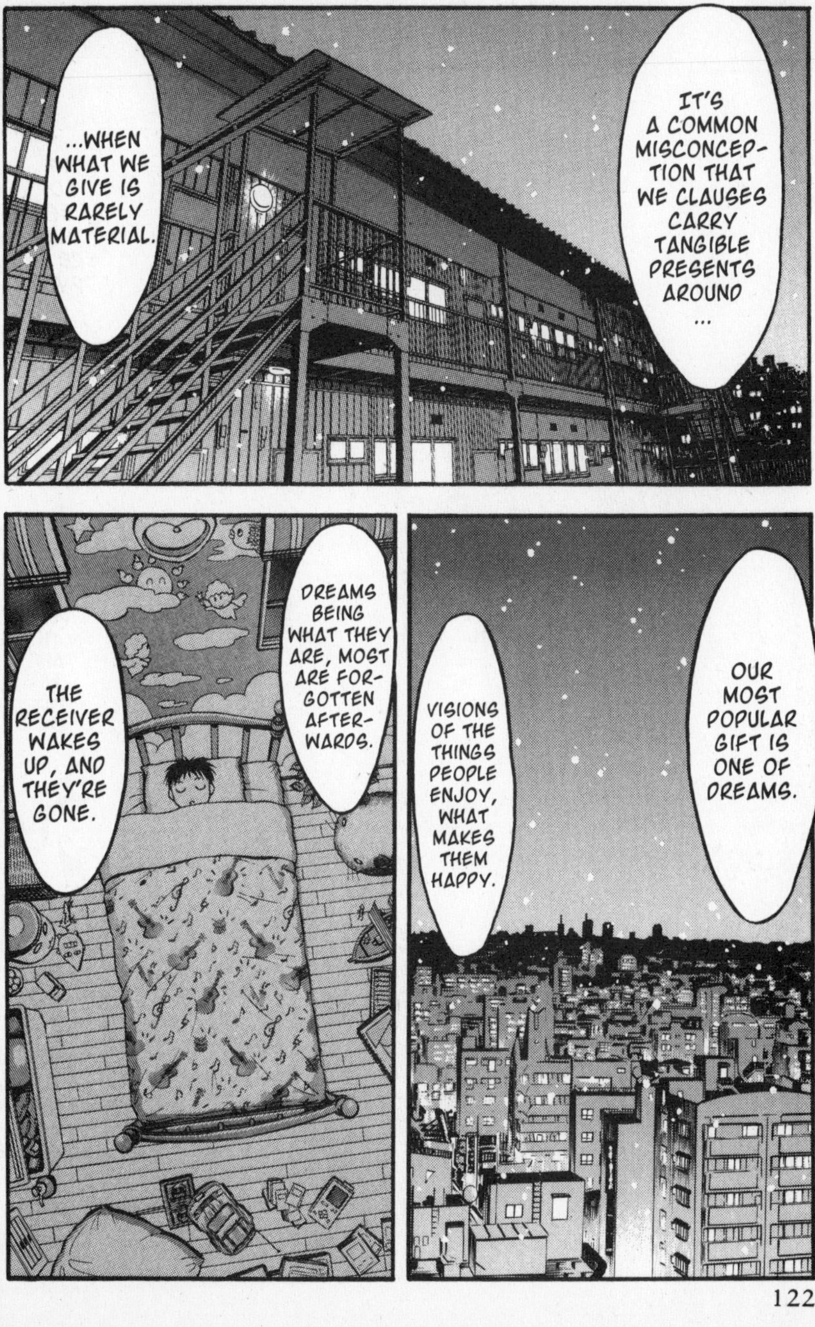
IT'S A COMMON MISCONCEPTION THAT WE CLAUSES CARRY TANGIBLE PRESENTS AROUND...
...WHEN WHAT WE GIVE IS RARELY MATERIAL.
OUR MOST POPULAR GIFT IS ONE OF DREAMS.
VISIONS OF THE THINGS PEOPLE ENJOY, WHAT MAKES THEM HAPPY.
DREAMS BEING WHAT THEY ARE, MOST ARE FORGOTTEN AFTERWARDS.
THE RECEIVER WAKES UP, AND THEY'RE GONE.

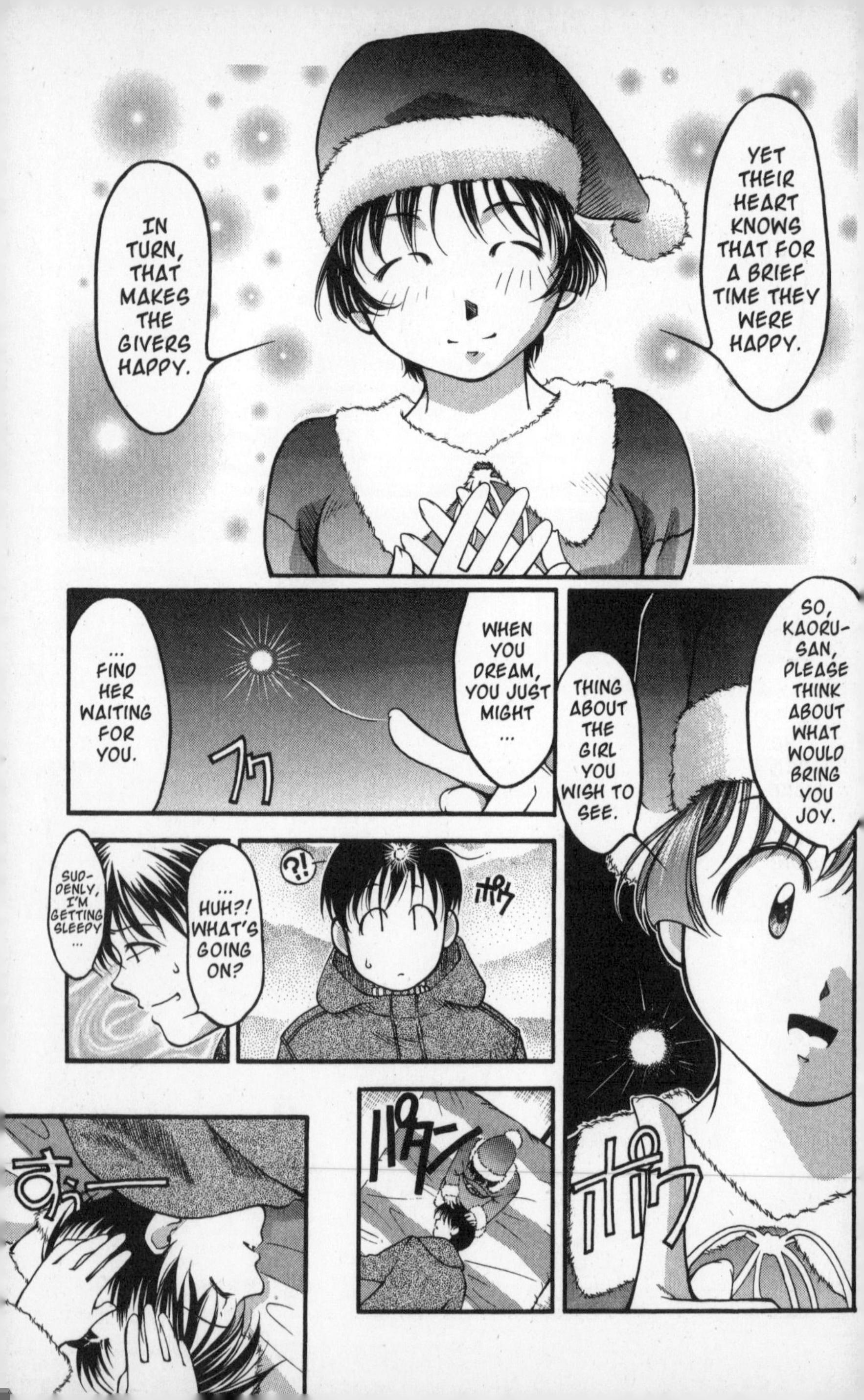
YET THEIR HEART KNOWS THAT FOR A BRIEF TIME THEY WERE HAPPY.
IN TURN, THAT MAKES THE GIVERS HAPPY.
SO, KAORU-SAN, PLEASE THINK ABOUT WHAT WOULD BRING YOU JOY.
ポウ
THING ABOUT THE GIRL YOU WISH TO SEE.
WHEN YOU DREAM, YOU JUST MIGHT ...
... FIND HER WAITING FOR YOU.
フッ
?!
ポウ
... HUH?! WHAT'S GOING ON?
SUD-DENLY, I'M GETTING SLEEPY ...
パタン
すぅーー

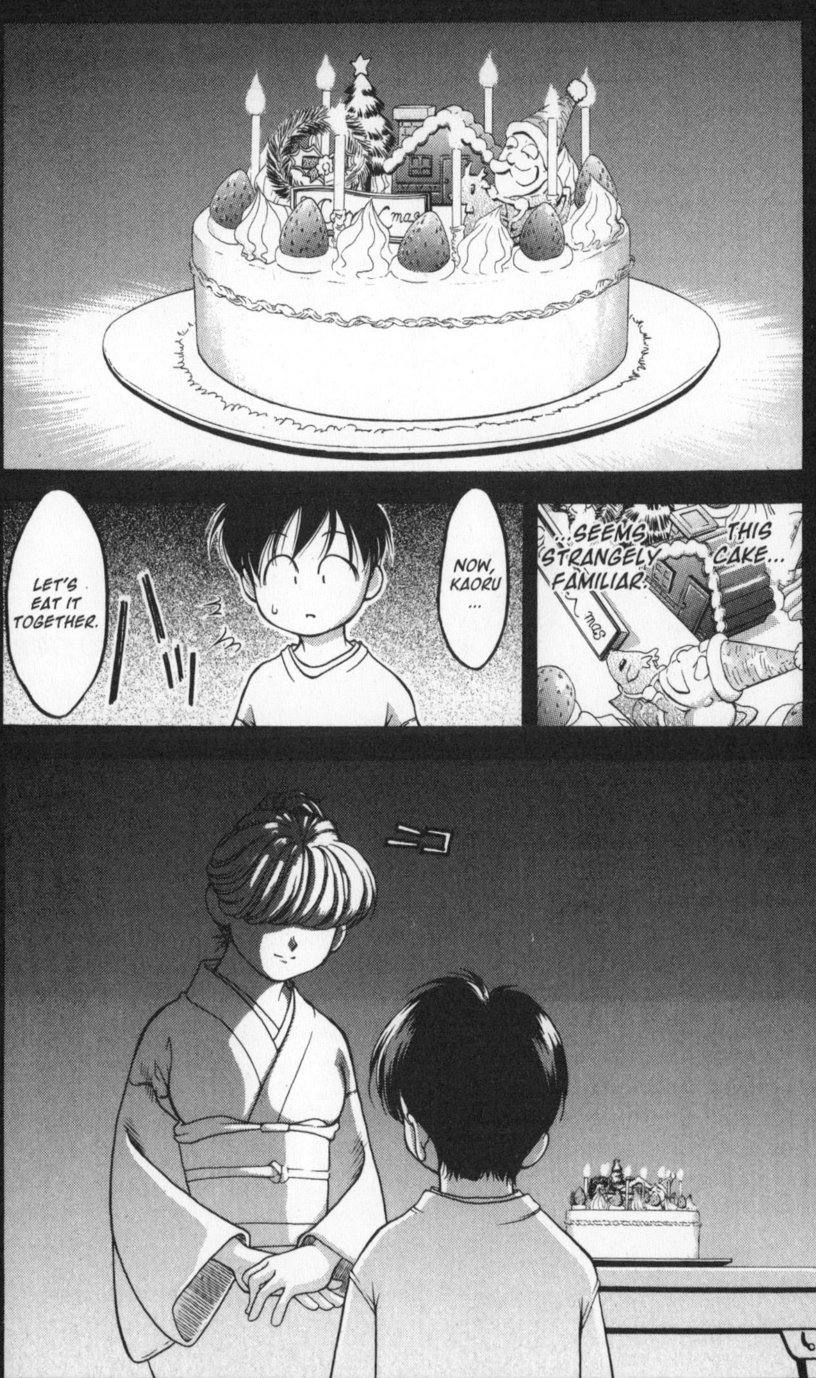
THIS CAKE...
...SEEMS STRANGELY FAMILIAR.
NOW, KAORU ...
LET'S EAT IT TOGETHER.

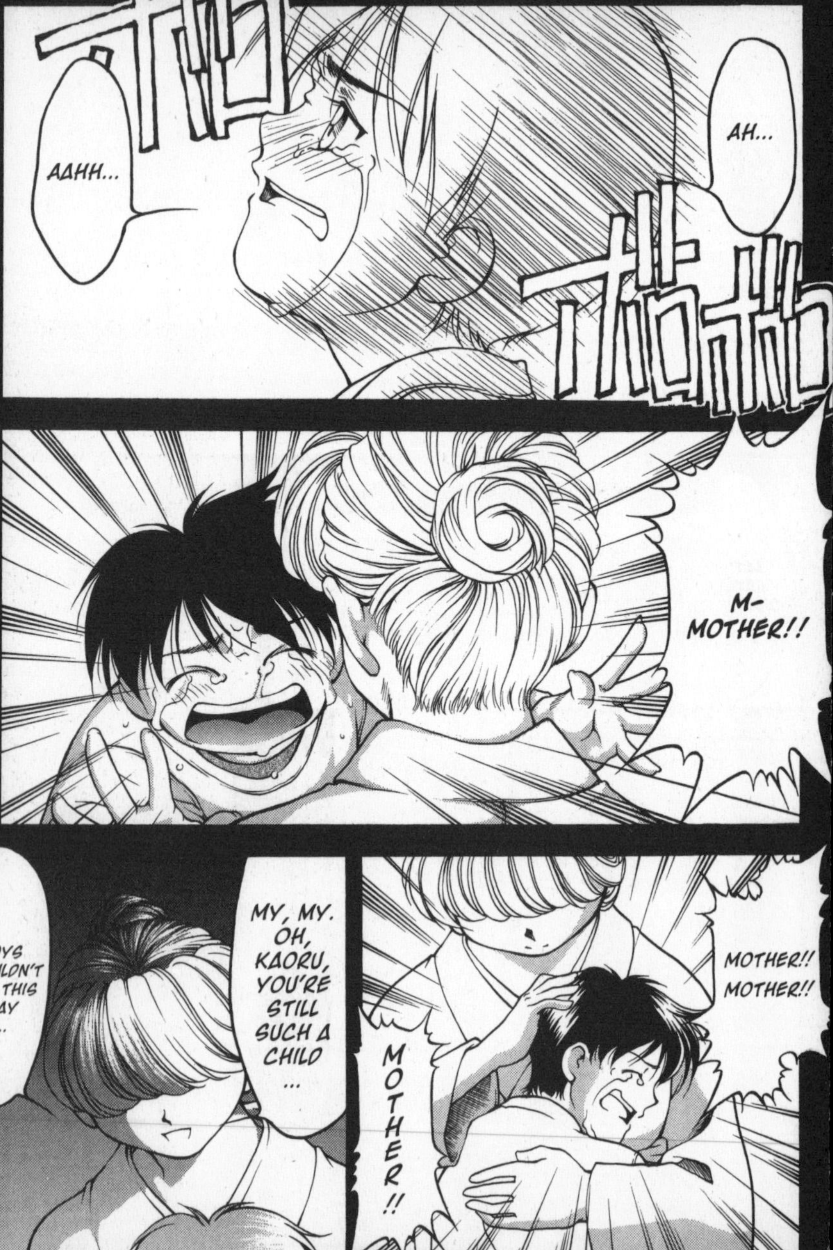
AH...
AAHH...
M-MOTHER!!
MOTHER!! MOTHER!!
MOTHER!!
MY, MY. OH, KAORU, YOU'RE STILL SUCH A CHILD ...
BOYS SHOULDN'T CRY THIS WAY ...

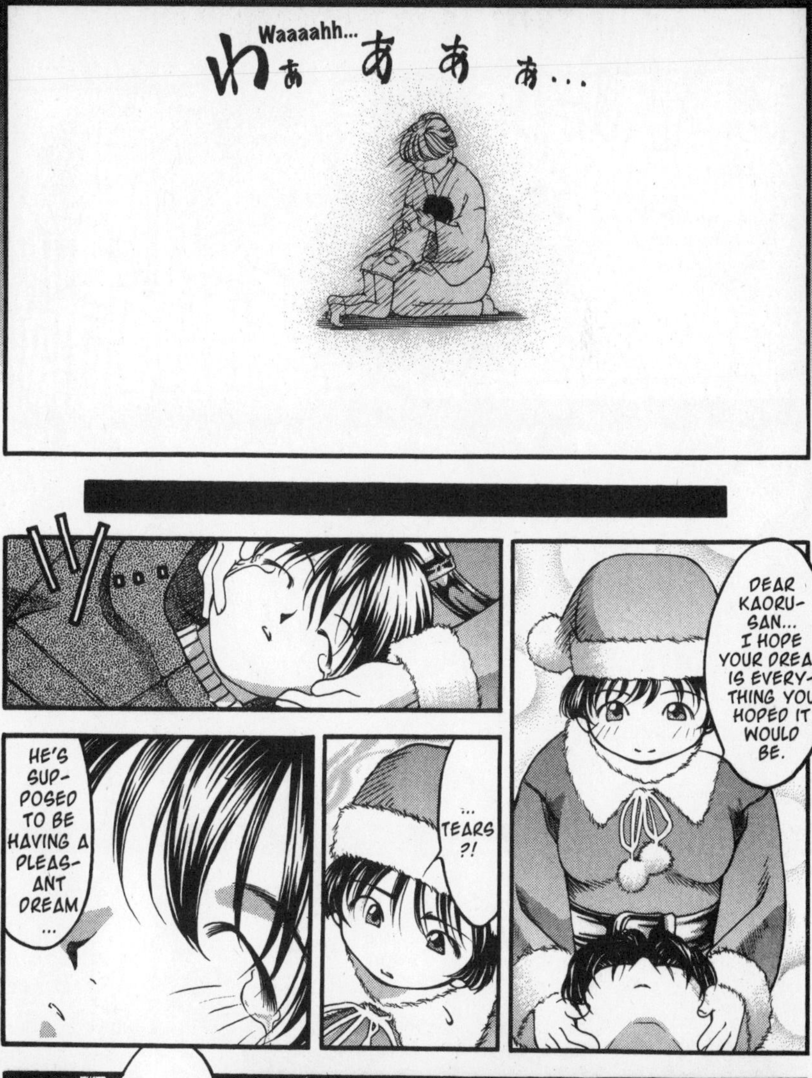
Waaaahh...
わぁぁぁぁ...
DEAR KAORU-SAN... I HOPE YOUR DREAM IS EVERYTHING YOU HOPED IT WOULD BE.
...
...TEARS?!
HE'S SUPPOSED TO BE HAVING A PLEASANT DREAM...
I WONDER WHY HE'S CRYING?

End of Chapter 43: Miyuki—Deep Snow

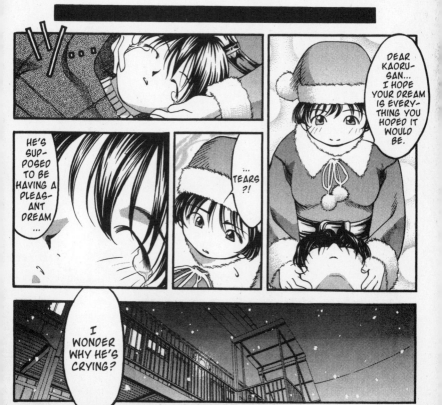

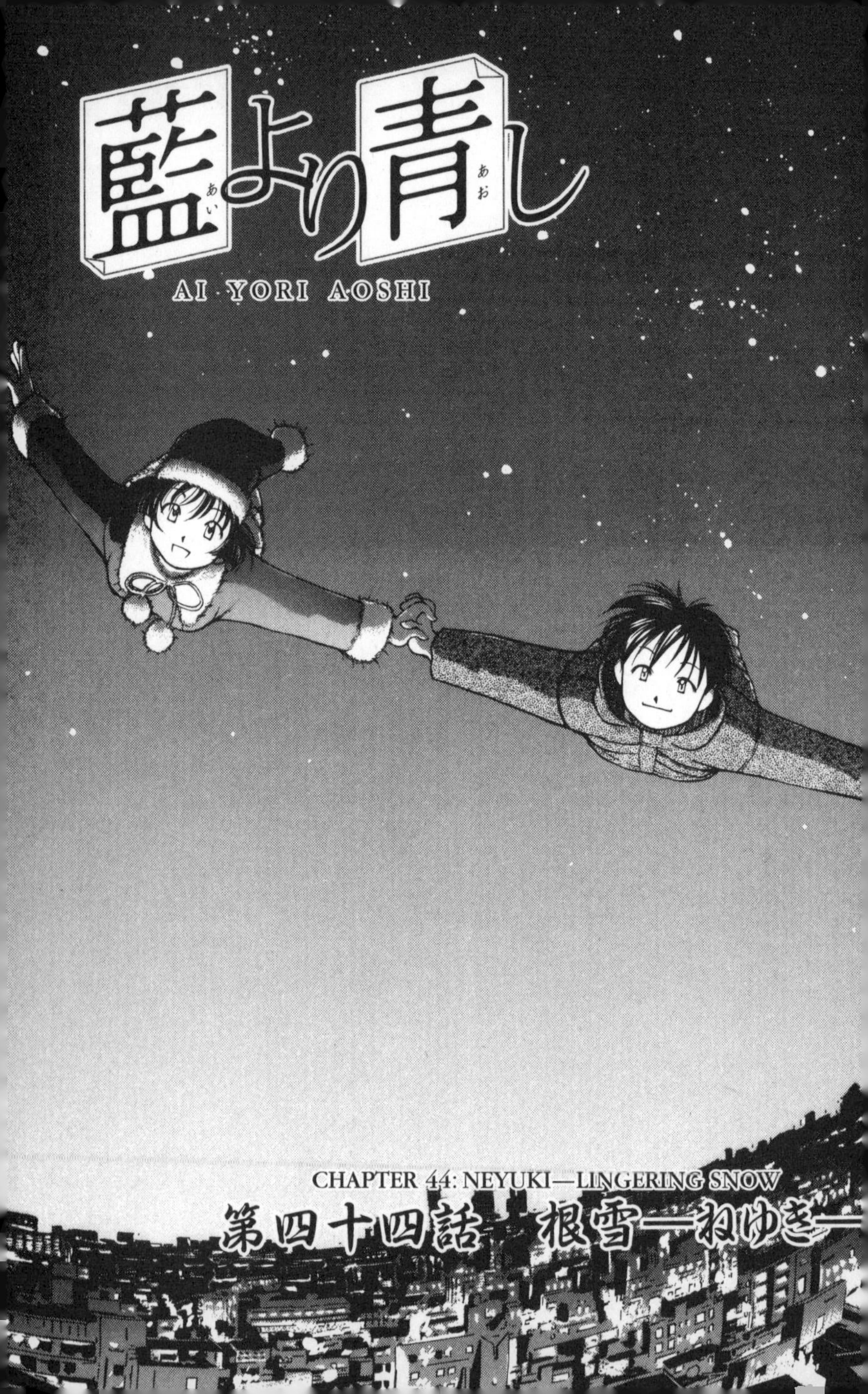
藍より青し
あい
あお
AI YORI AOSHI
CHAPTER 44: NEYUKI—LINGERING SNOW
第四十四話 根雪—ねゆき—

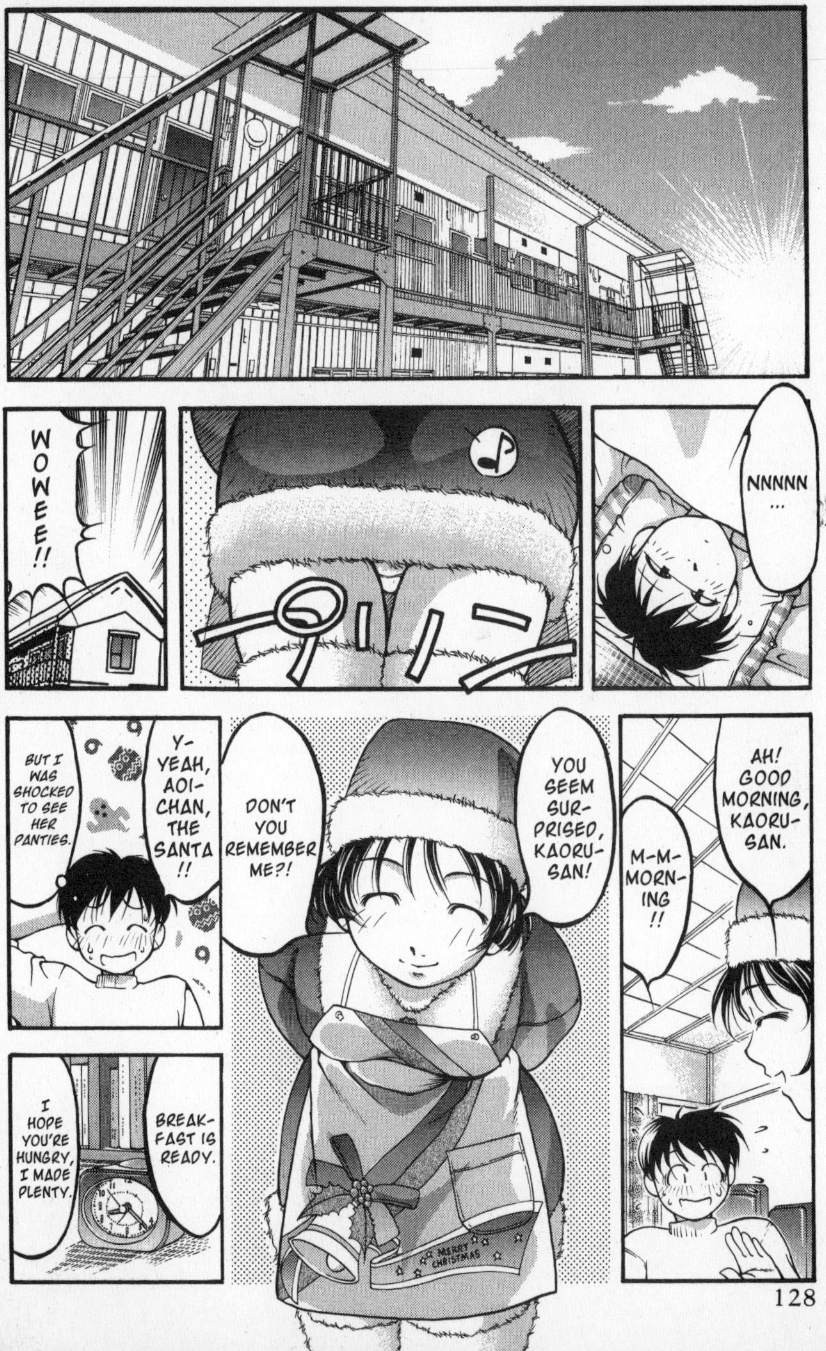
NNNNN ...
WOWEE!!
AH! GOOD MORNING, KAORU-SAN.
M-M-MORNING!!
YOU SEEM SURPRISED, KAORU-SAN!
DON'T YOU REMEMBER ME?!
MERRY CHRISTMAS
Y-YEAH, AOI-CHAN, THE SANTA!!
BUT I WAS SHOCKED TO SEE HER PANTIES.
BREAKFAST IS READY.
I HOPE YOU'RE HUNGRY, I MADE PLENTY.

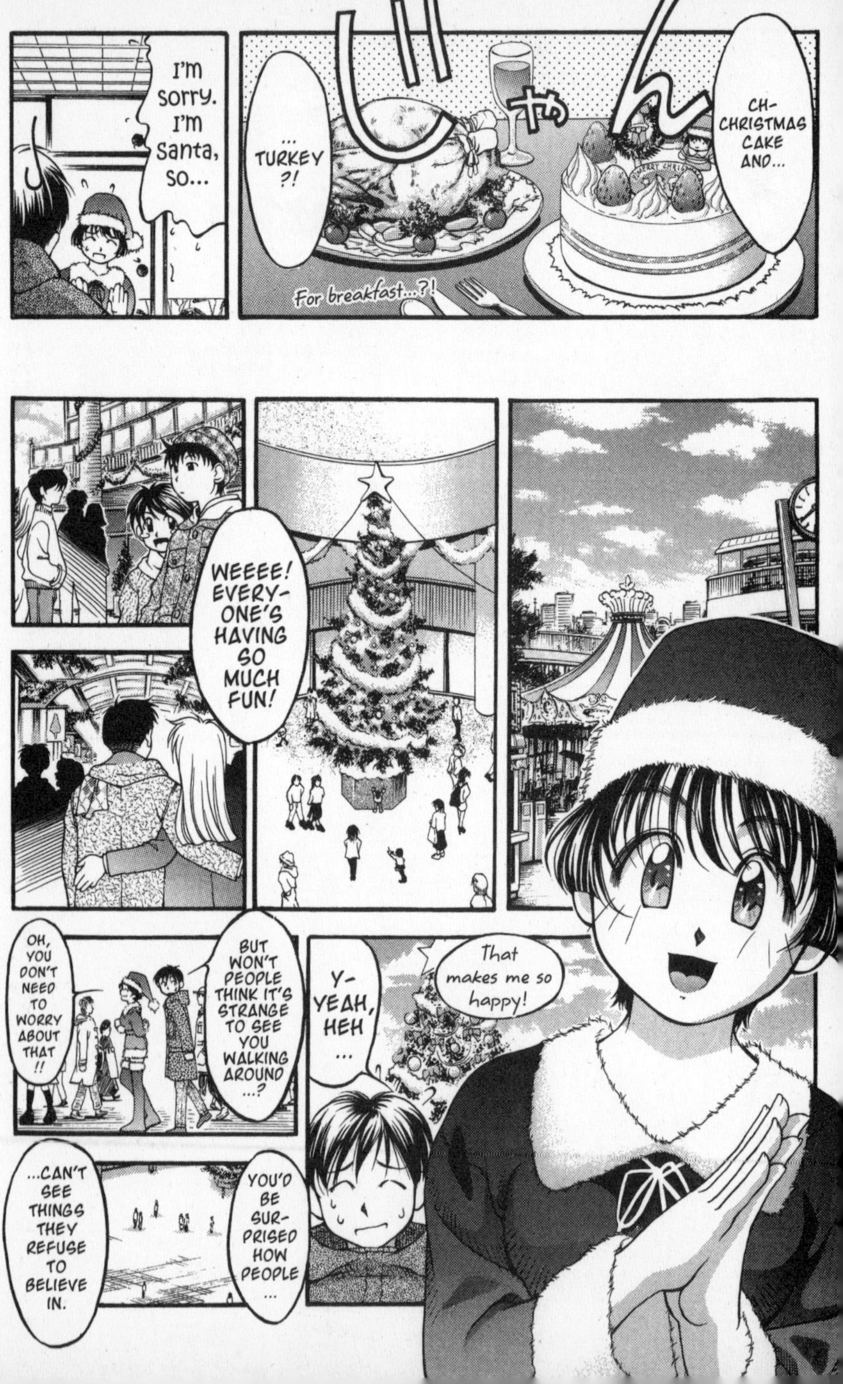
CH-CHRISTMAS CAKE AND...
...TURKEY?!
For breakfast...?!
I'm sorry. I'm Santa, so...
WEEEE! EVERYONE'S HAVING SO MUCH FUN!
That makes me so happy!
Y-YEAH, HEH...
BUT WON'T PEOPLE THINK IT'S STRANGE TO SEE YOU WALKING AROUND...?
OH, YOU DON'T NEED TO WORRY ABOUT THAT!!
YOU'D BE SURPRISED HOW PEOPLE...
...CAN'T SEE THINGS THEY REFUSE TO BELIEVE IN.

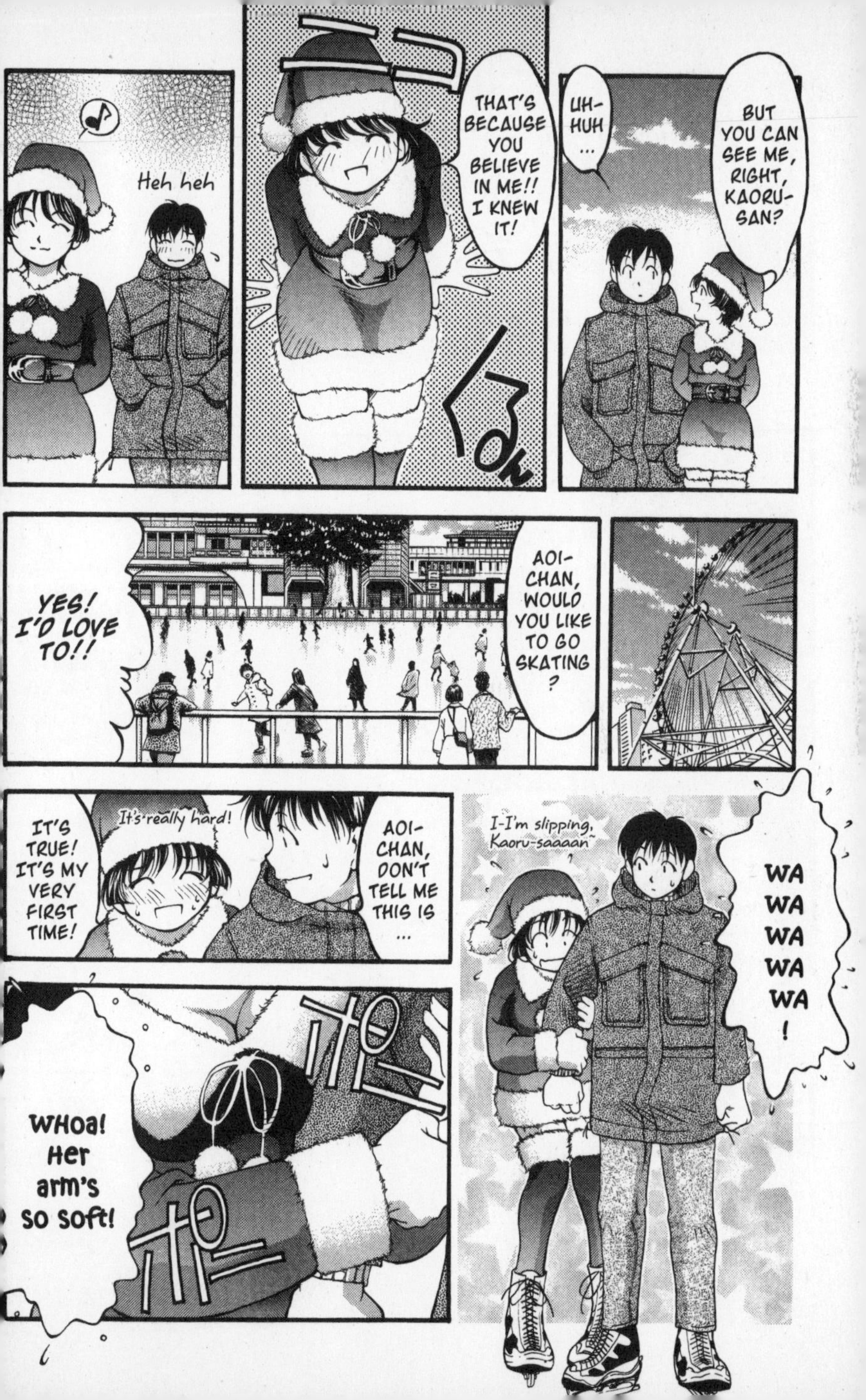

BUT YOU CAN SEE ME, RIGHT, KAORU-SAN?
UH-HUH ...
THAT'S BECAUSE YOU BELIEVE IN ME!! I KNEW IT!
Heh heh
AOI-CHAN, WOULD YOU LIKE TO GO SKATING?
YES! I'D LOVE TO!!
WA WA WA WA WA!
I-I'm slipping, Kaoru-saaaan~
AOI-CHAN, DON'T TELL ME THIS IS ...
IT'S TRUE! IT'S MY VERY FIRST TIME!
It's really hard!
Whoa! Her arm's so soft!

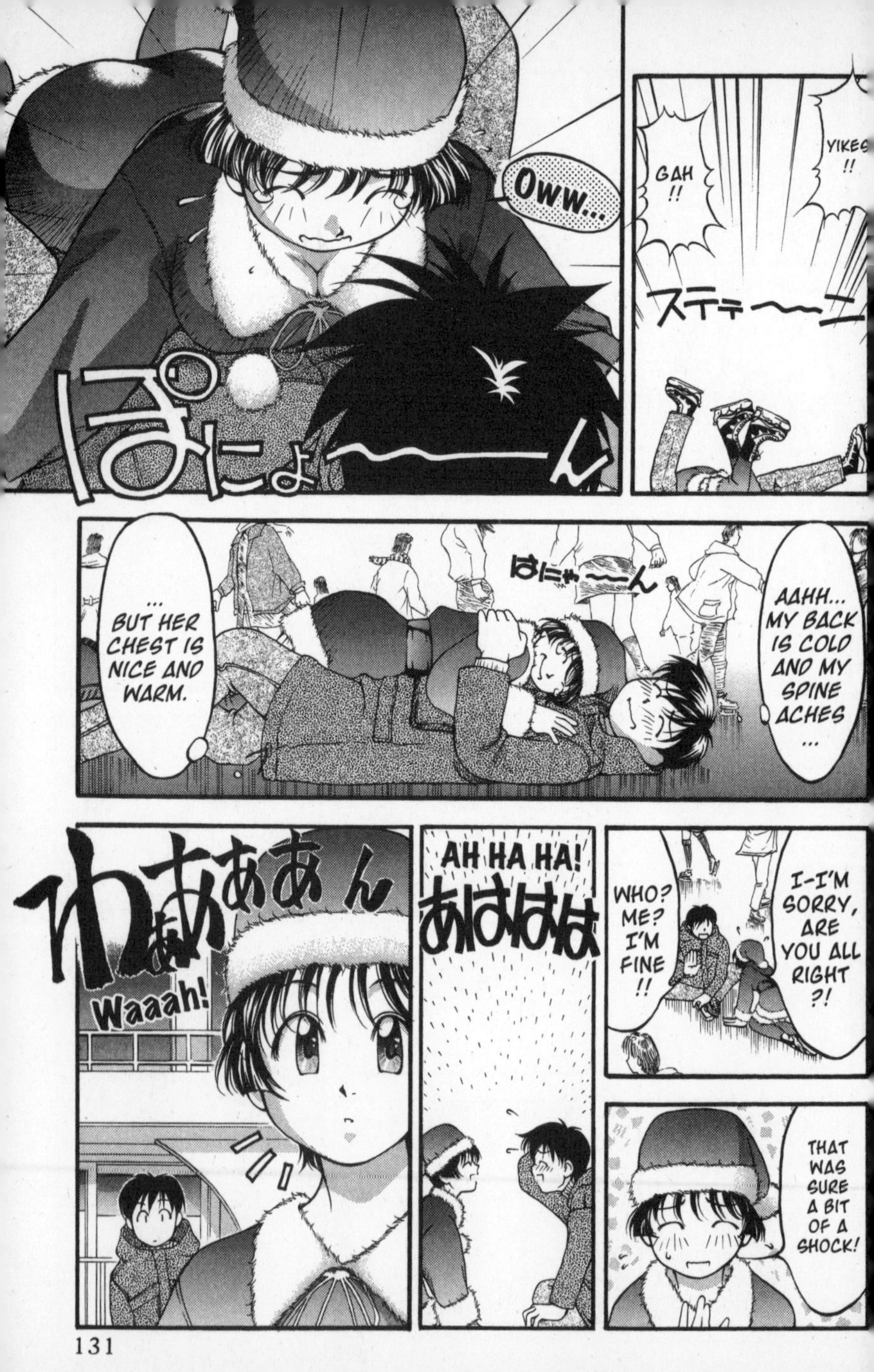
YIKES!!
GAH!!
ステテ〜〜ン
Oww...
ぽにょ〜〜〜ん
AAHH... MY BACK IS COLD AND MY SPINE ACHES...
はにゃ〜〜ん
... BUT HER CHEST IS NICE AND WARM.
I-I'M SORRY, ARE YOU ALL RIGHT?!
WHO? ME? I'M FINE!!
THAT WAS SURE A BIT OF A SHOCK!
AH HA HA!
あははは
わああああん
Waaah!

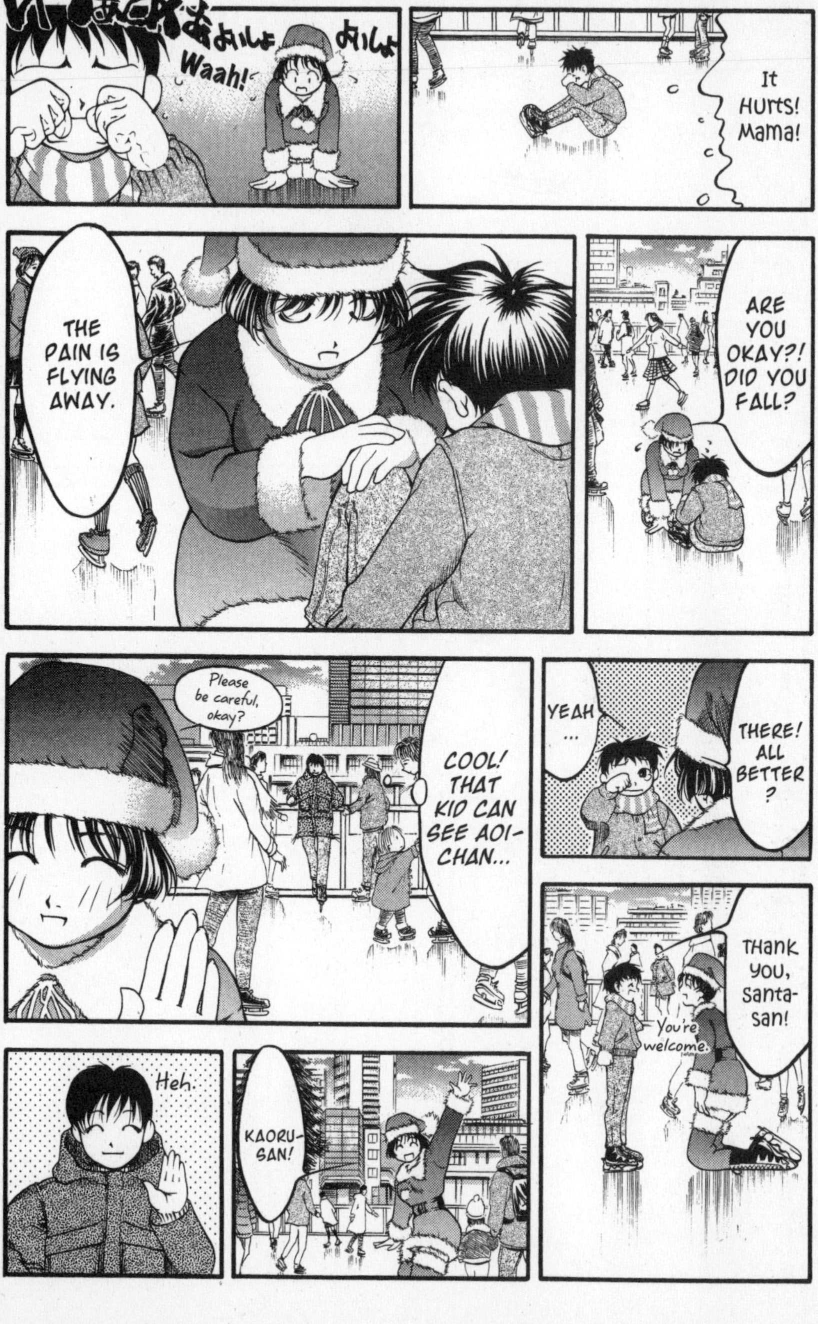
It Hurts! Mama!
よいしょ よいしょ
Waah!
ARE YOU OKAY?! DID YOU FALL?
THE PAIN IS FLYING AWAY.
THERE! ALL BETTER?
YEAH ...
COOL! THAT KID CAN SEE AOI-CHAN...
Please be careful, okay?
Thank you, Santa-san!
You're welcome.
KAORU-SAN!
Heh.

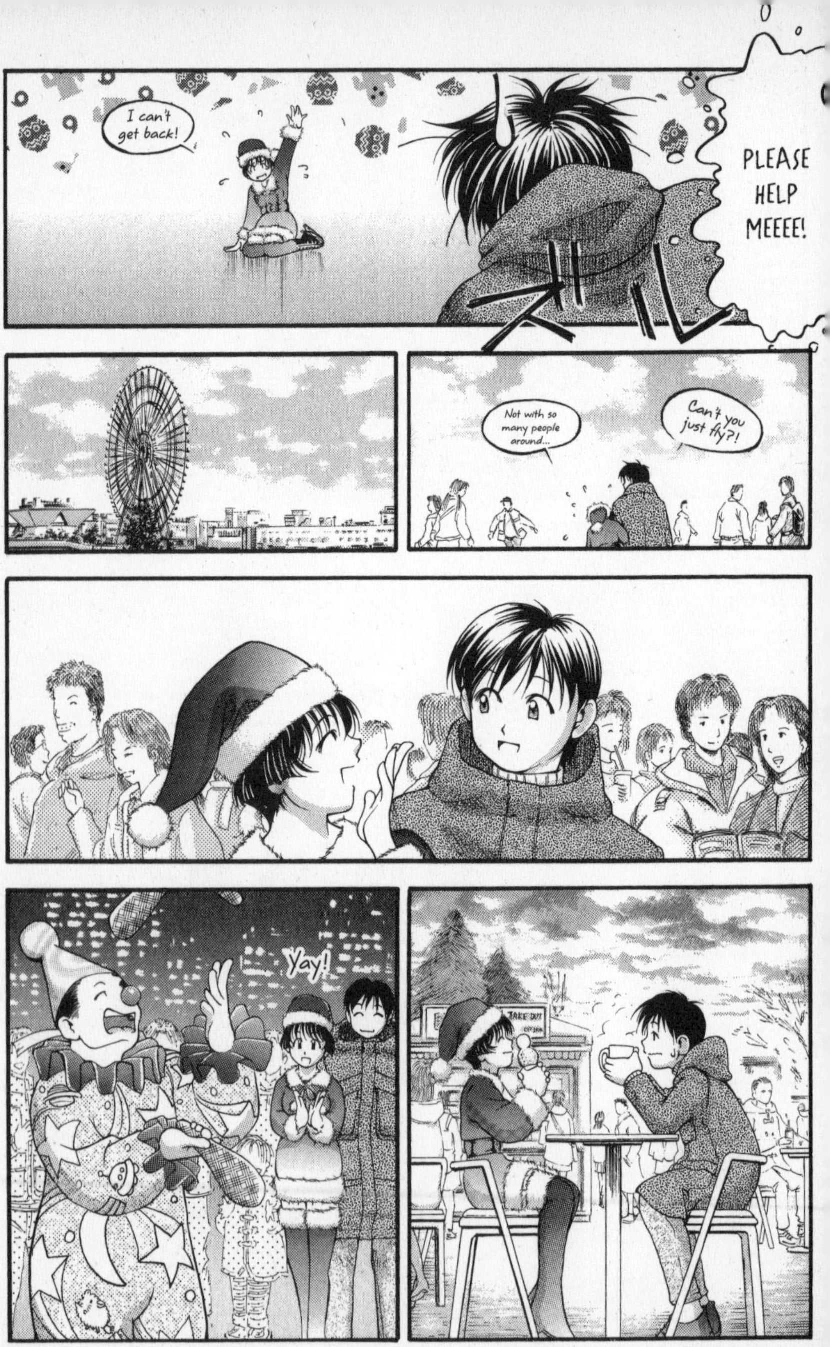
PLEASE HELP MEEEE!
I can't get back!
Can't you just fly?!
Not with so many people around...
Yay!

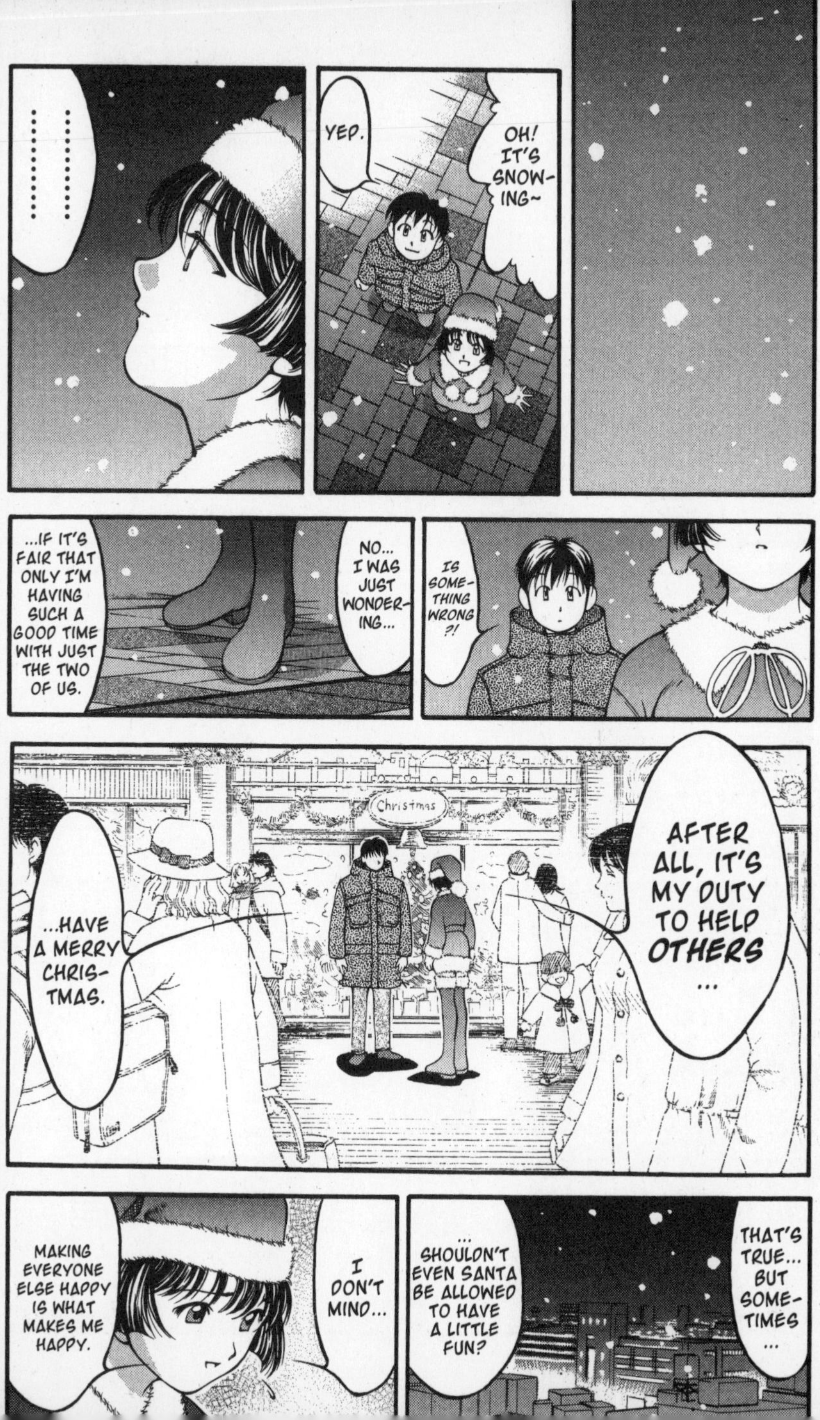
OH! IT'S SNOWING~
YEP.
......
IS SOMETHING WRONG?!
NO... I WAS JUST WONDERING...
...IF IT'S FAIR THAT ONLY I'M HAVING SUCH A GOOD TIME WITH JUST THE TWO OF US.
AFTER ALL, IT'S MY DUTY TO HELP **OTHERS**...
Christmas
...HAVE A MERRY CHRISTMAS.
THAT'S TRUE... BUT SOMETIMES...
...SHOULDN'T EVEN SANTA BE ALLOWED TO HAVE A LITTLE FUN?
I DON'T MIND...
MAKING EVERYONE ELSE HAPPY IS WHAT MAKES ME HAPPY.

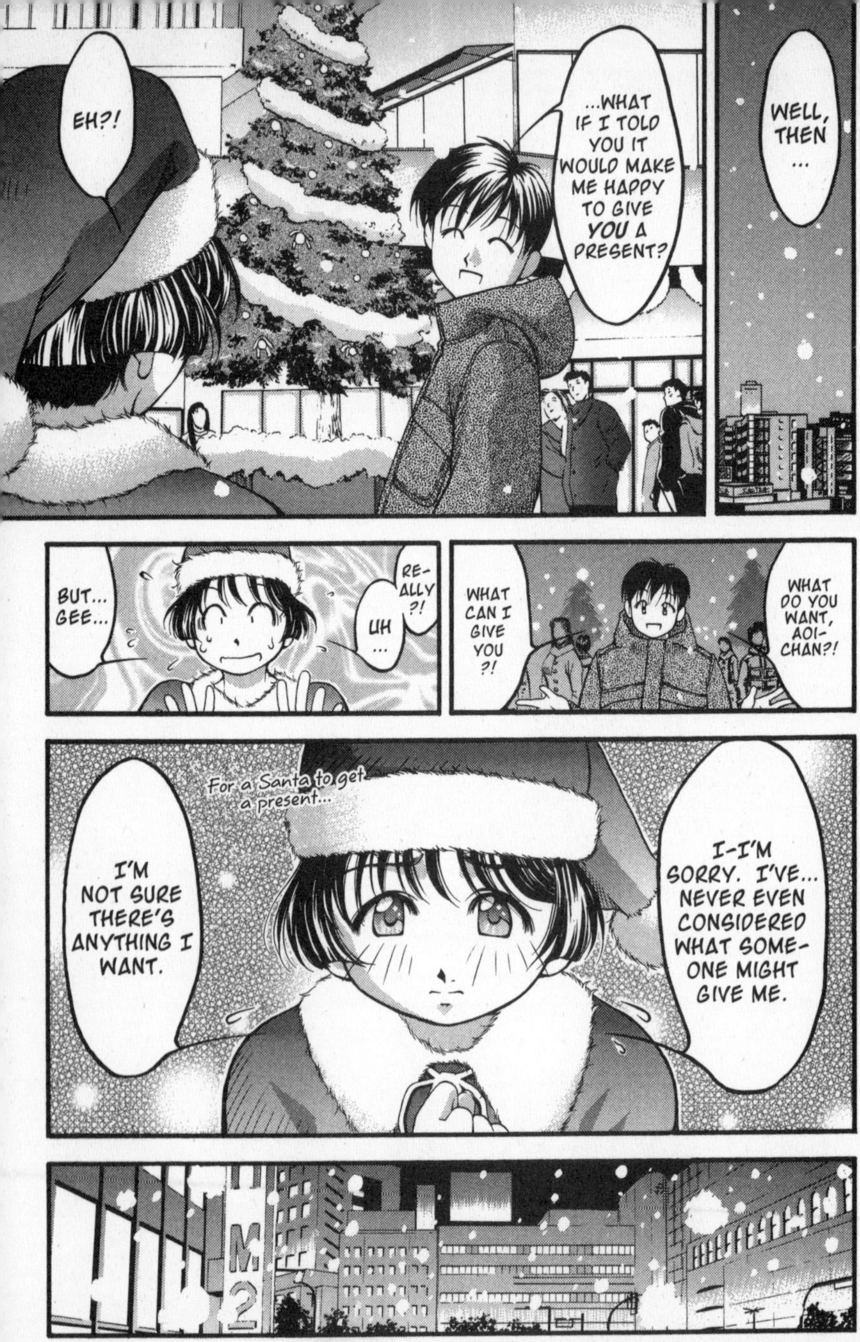

WELL, THEN ...
...WHAT IF I TOLD YOU IT WOULD MAKE ME HAPPY TO GIVE YOU A PRESENT?
EH?!
WHAT DO YOU WANT, AOI-CHAN?!
WHAT CAN I GIVE YOU ?!
RE-ALLY ?!
UH ...
BUT... GEE...
I-I'M SORRY. I'VE... NEVER EVEN CONSIDERED WHAT SOME-ONE MIGHT GIVE ME.
For a Santa to get a present...
I'M NOT SURE THERE'S ANYTHING I WANT.

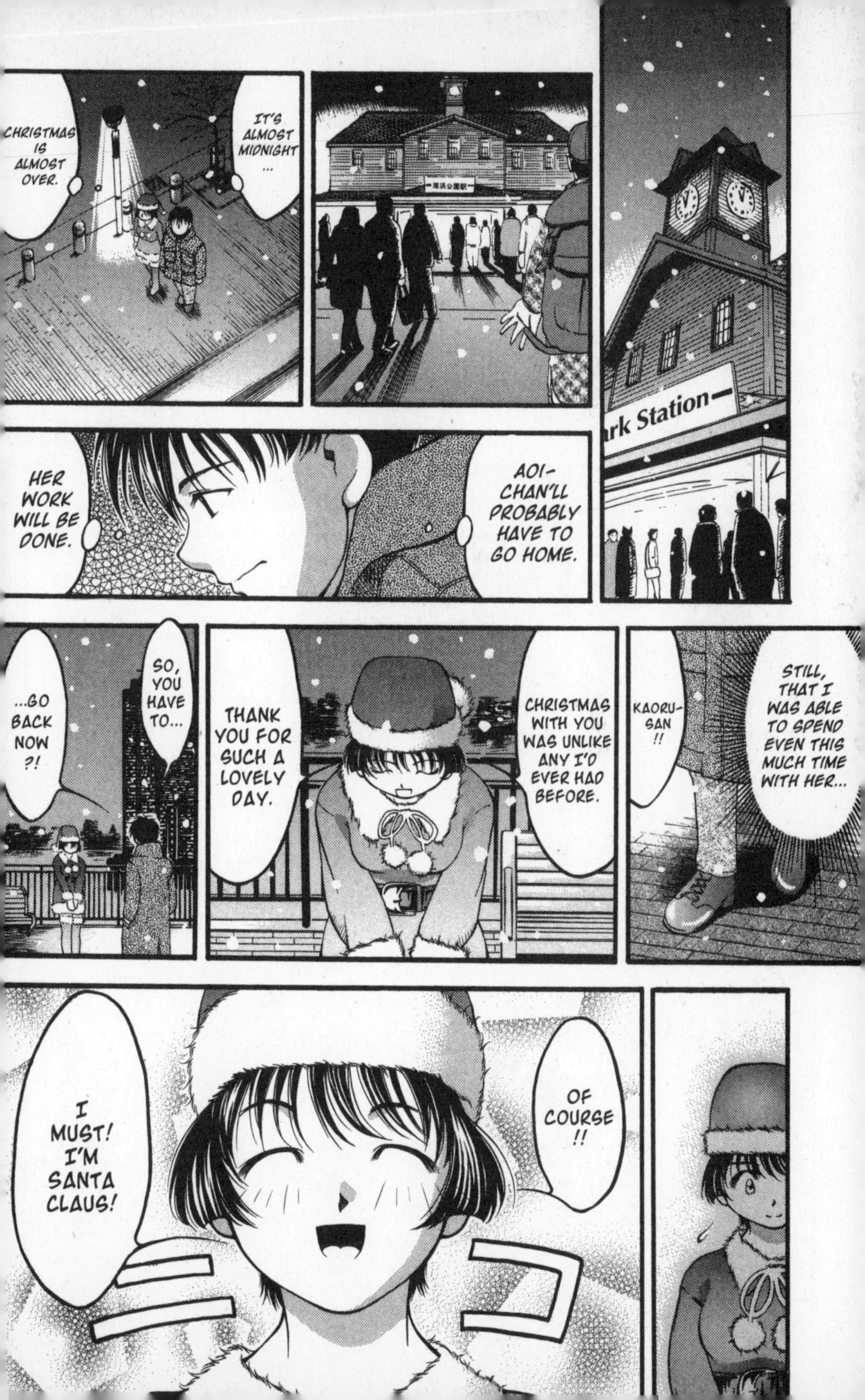
ark Station
IT'S ALMOST MIDNIGHT ...
CHRISTMAS IS ALMOST OVER.
AOI-CHAN'LL PROBABLY HAVE TO GO HOME.
HER WORK WILL BE DONE.
STILL, THAT I WAS ABLE TO SPEND EVEN THIS MUCH TIME WITH HER...
KAORU-SAN !!
CHRISTMAS WITH YOU WAS UNLIKE ANY I'D EVER HAD BEFORE.
THANK YOU FOR SUCH A LOVELY DAY.
SO, YOU HAVE TO...
...GO BACK NOW ?!
OF COURSE !!
I MUST! I'M SANTA CLAUS!

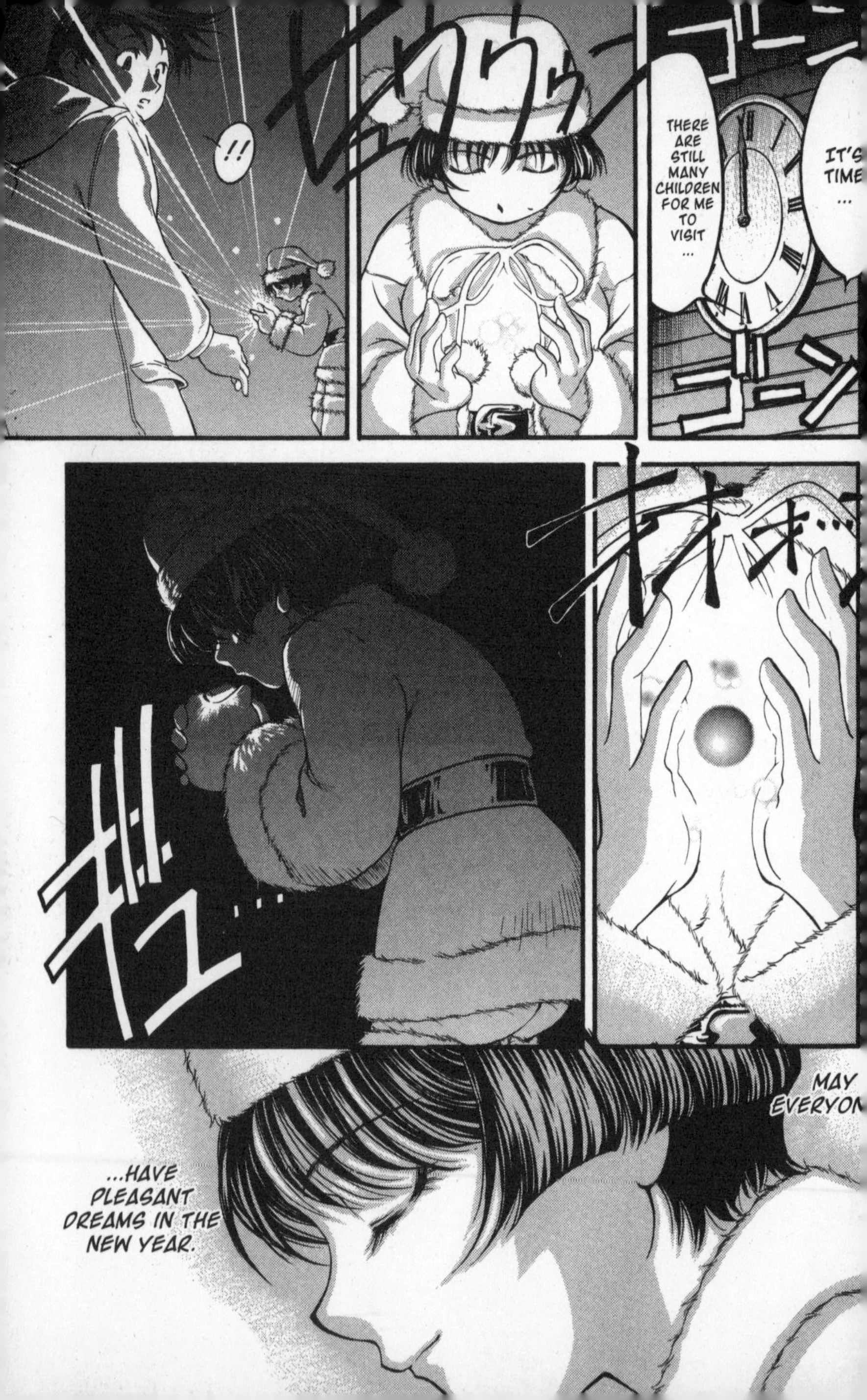
IT'S TIME ...
THERE ARE STILL MANY CHILDREN FOR ME TO VISIT ...
!!
MAY EVERYON
...HAVE PLEASANT DREAMS IN THE NEW YEAR.

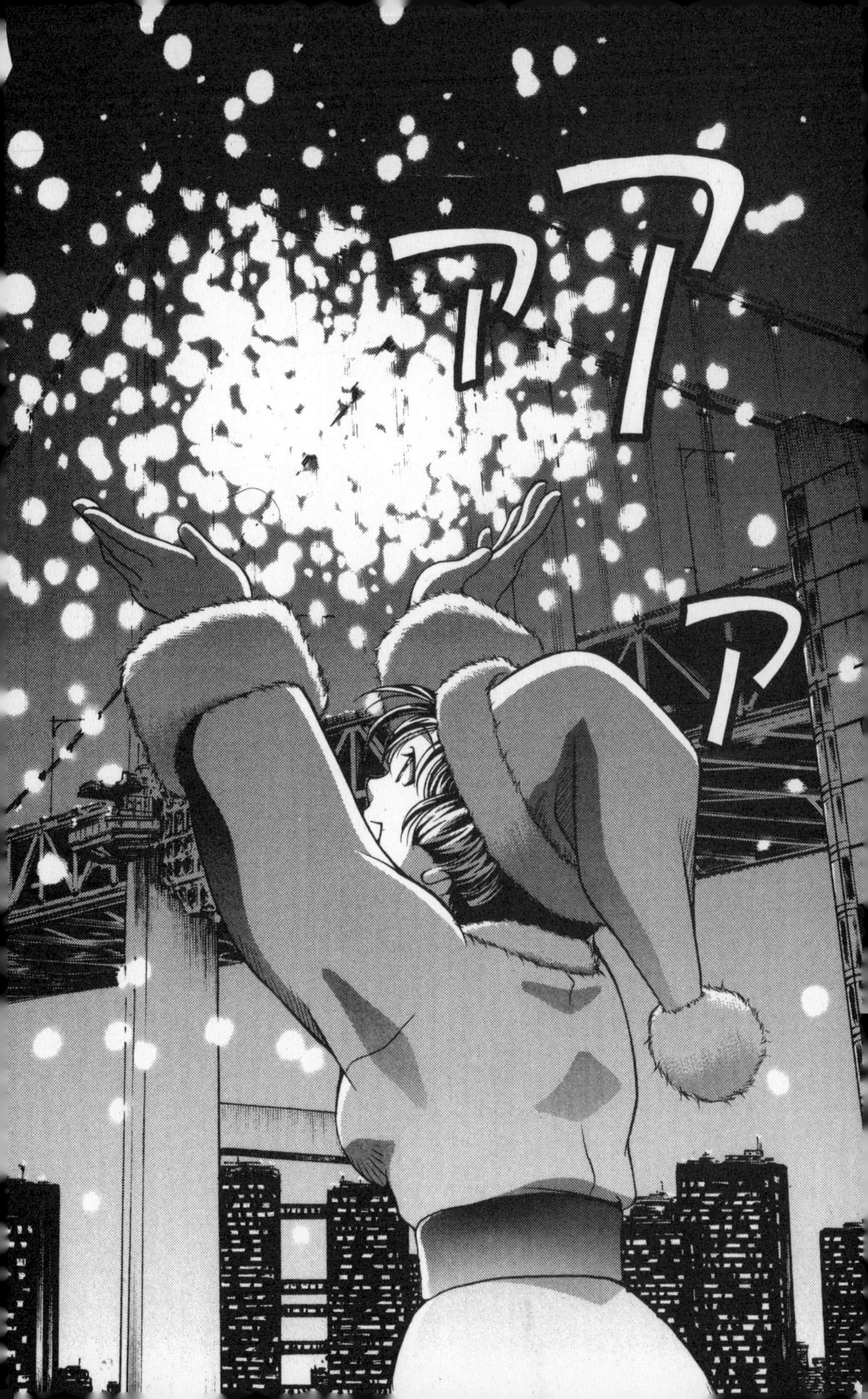
アアア

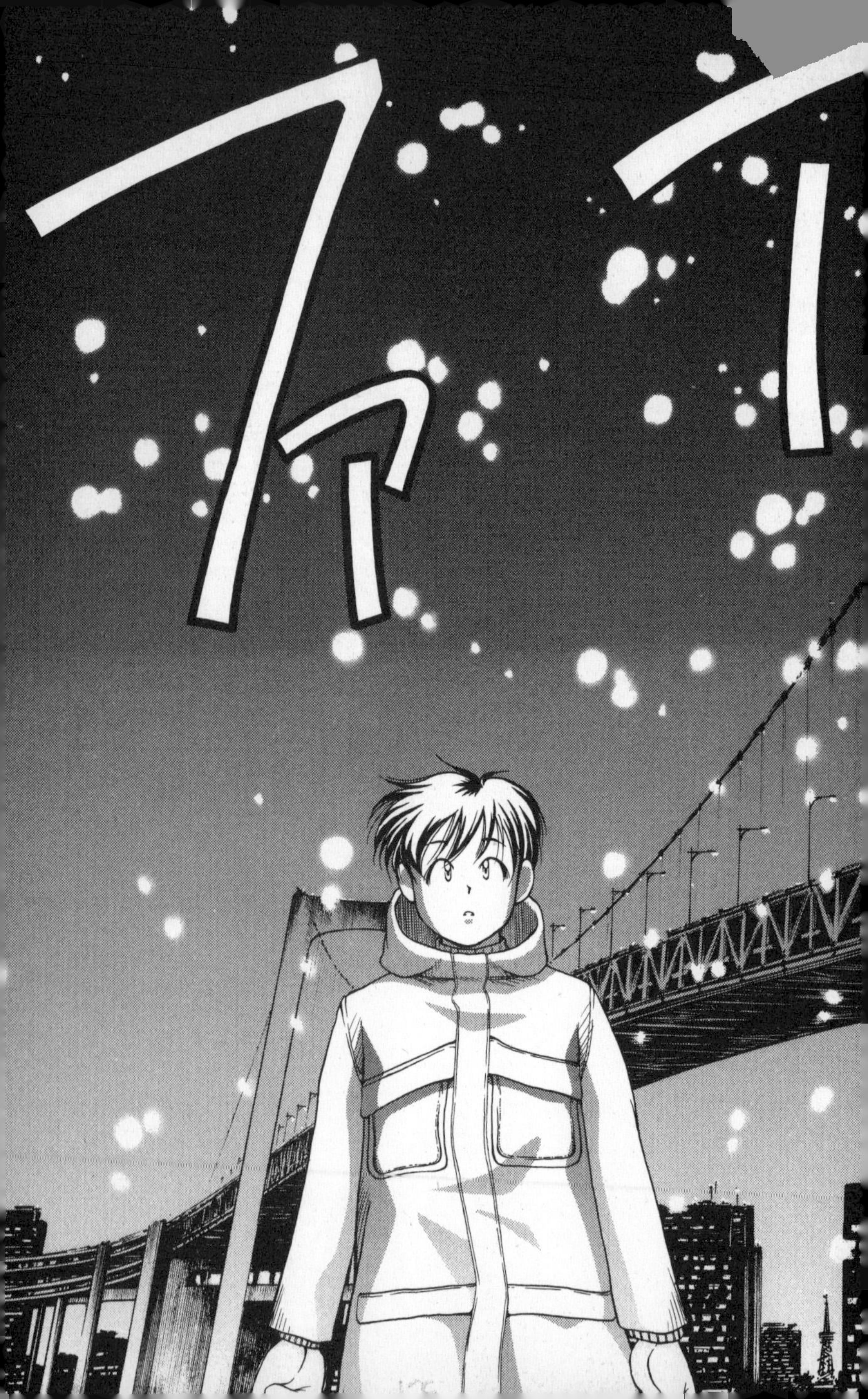
ファイ

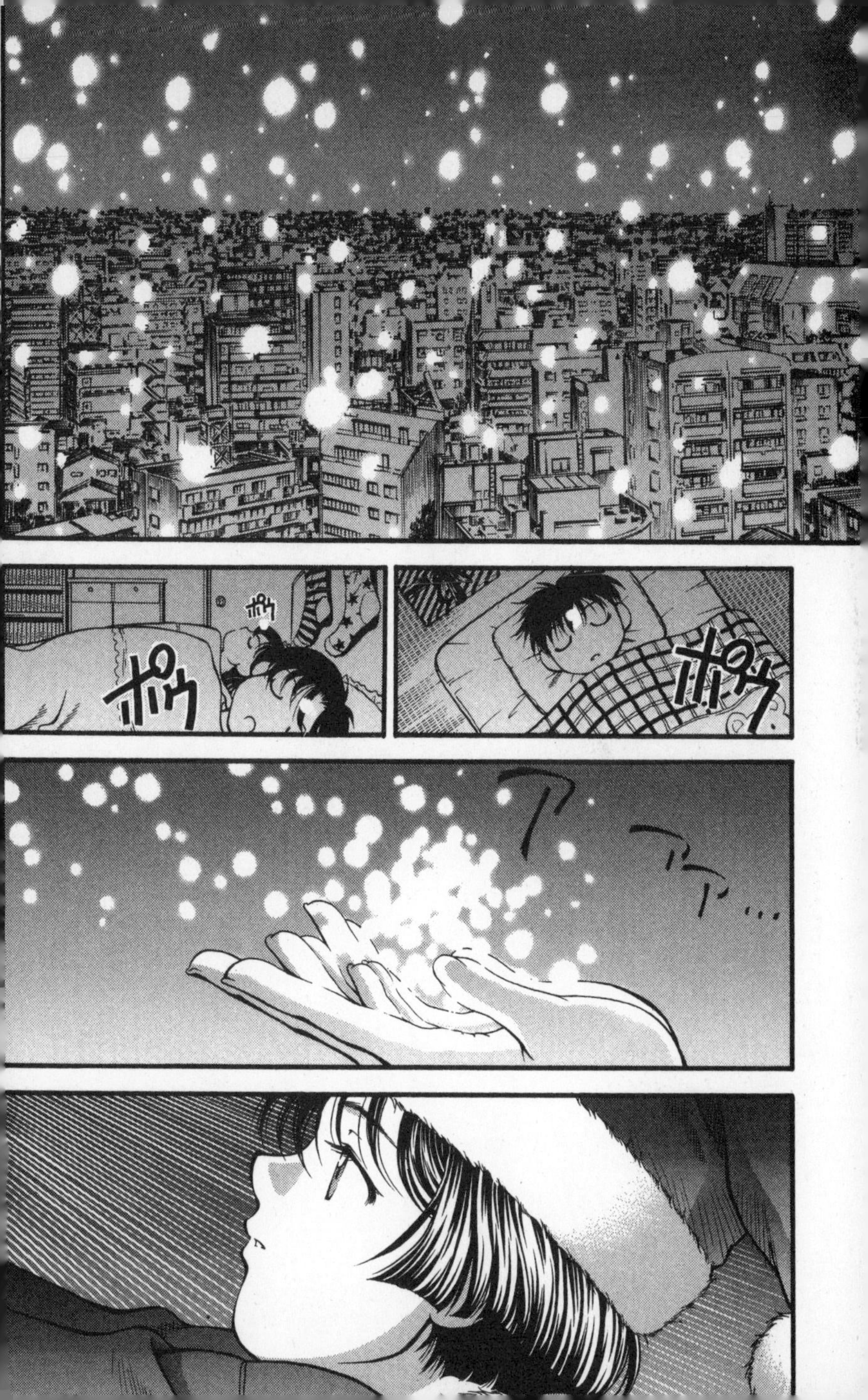
ポクッ
ポク
ポク
ア アア…

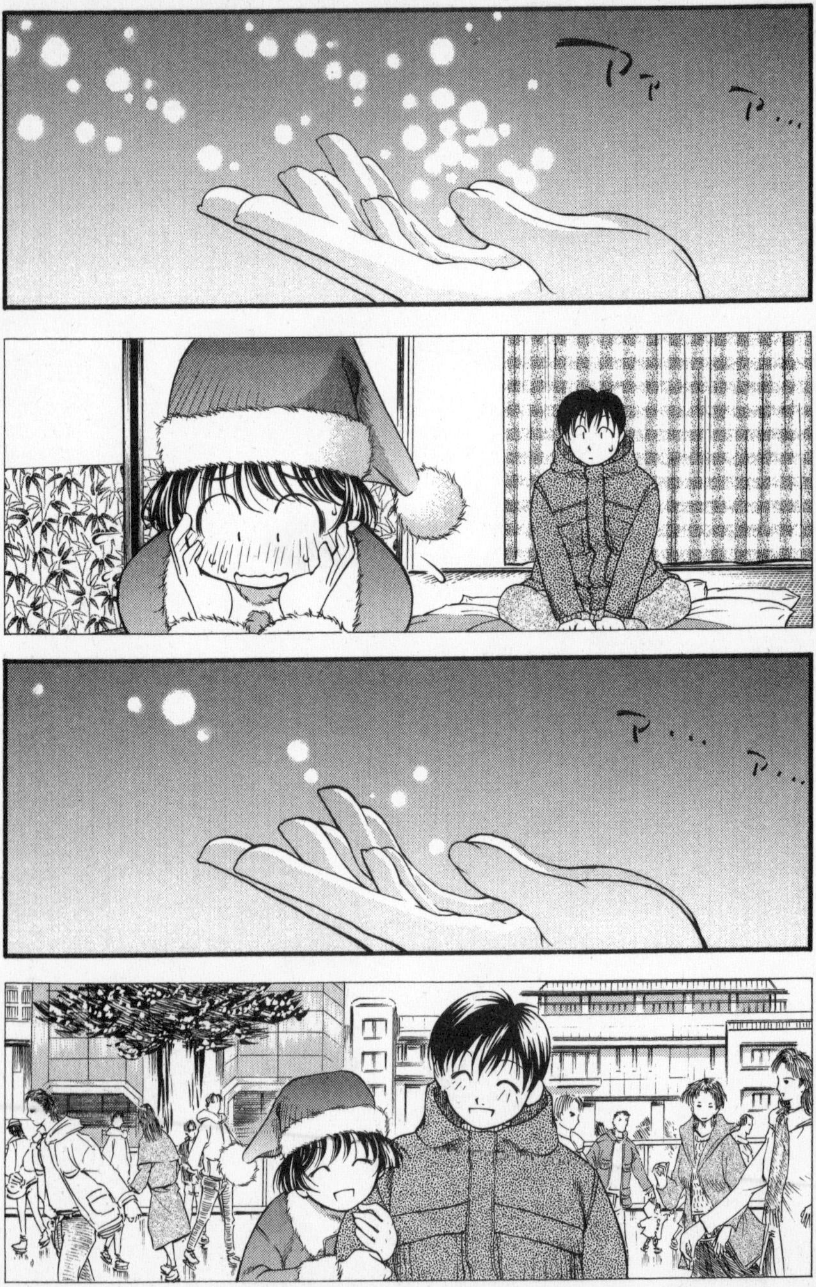
アァ
ア…
ア…
ア…

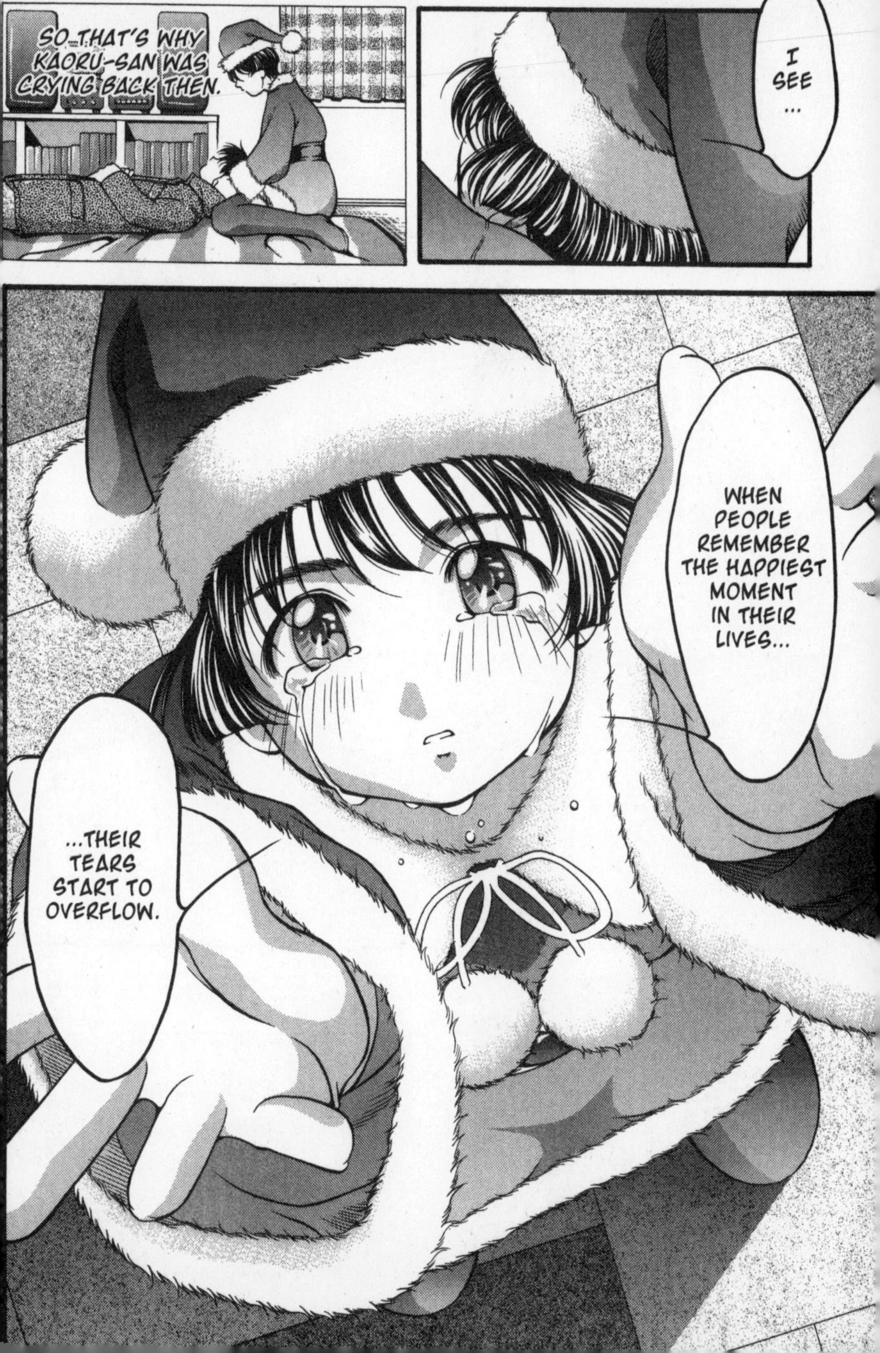
I SEE ...
SO THAT'S WHY KAORU-SAN WAS CRYING BACK THEN.
WHEN PEOPLE REMEMBER THE HAPPIEST MOMENT IN THEIR LIVES...
...THEIR TEARS START TO OVERFLOW.

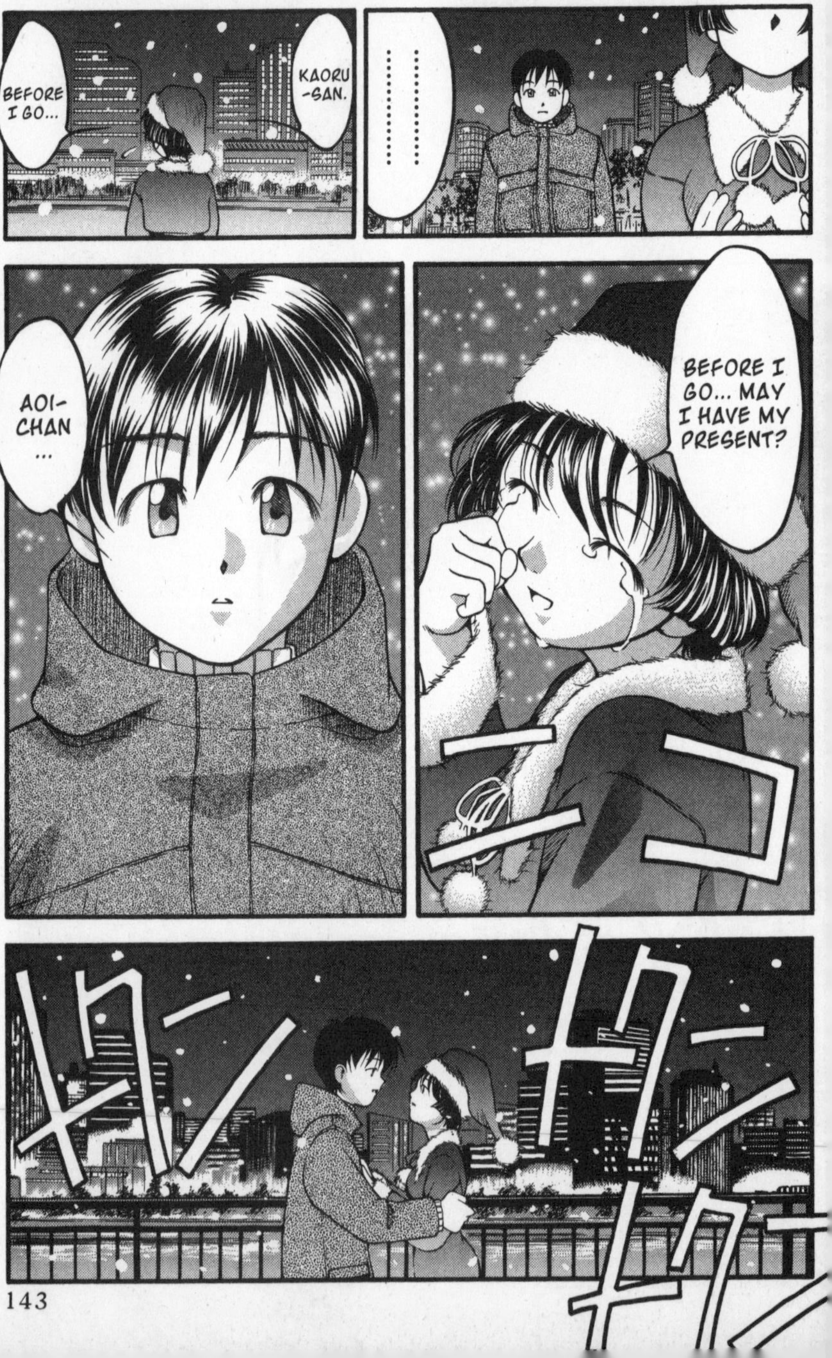

……
KAORU-SAN.
BEFORE I GO...
BEFORE I GO... MAY I HAVE MY PRESENT?
AOI-CHAN ...

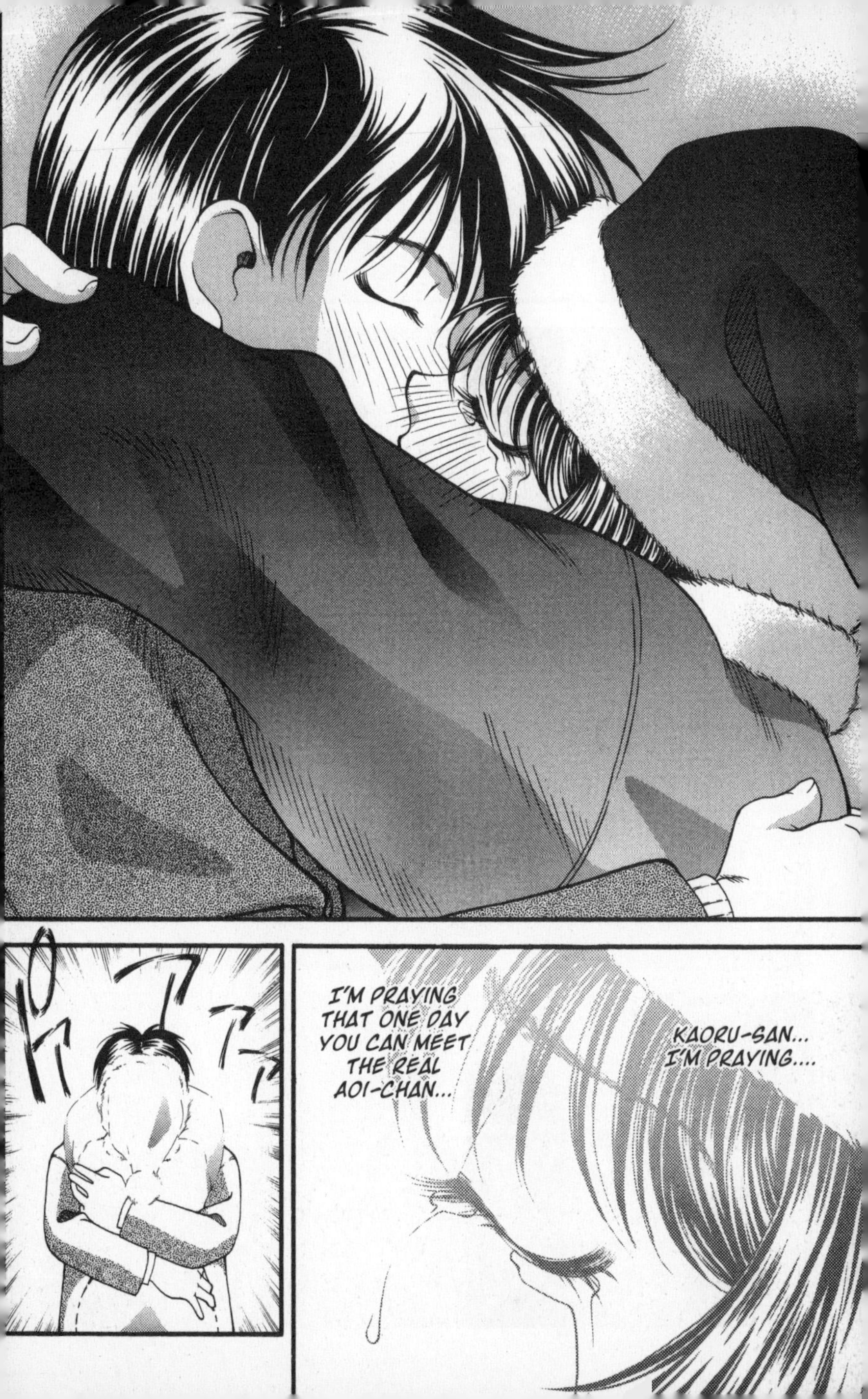
KAORU-SAN... I'M PRAYING....
I'M PRAYING THAT ONE DAY YOU CAN MEET THE REAL AOI-CHAN...

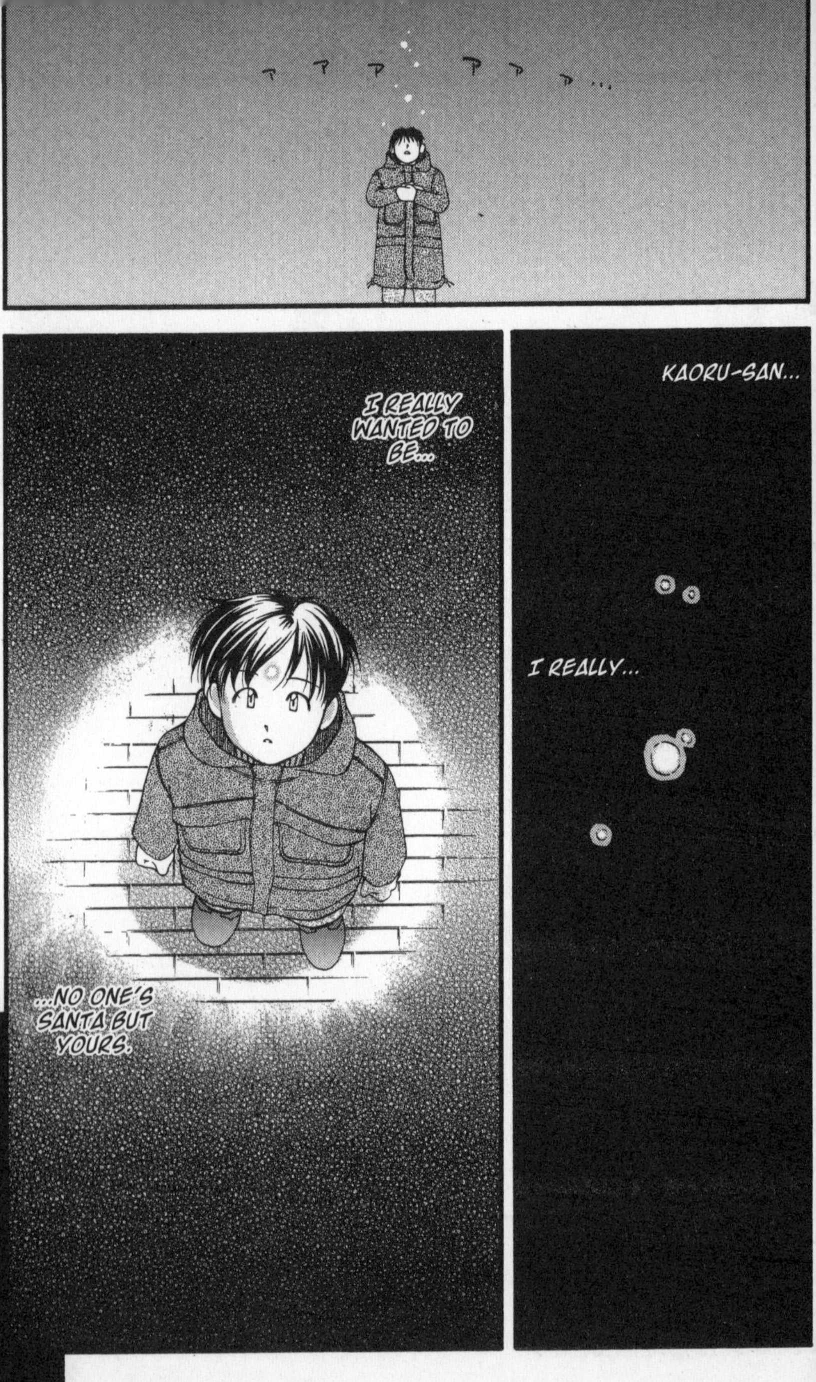
ァアア アアァ…
KAORU-SAN...
I REALLY...
I REALLY WANTED TO BE...
...NO ONE'S SANTA BUT YOURS.

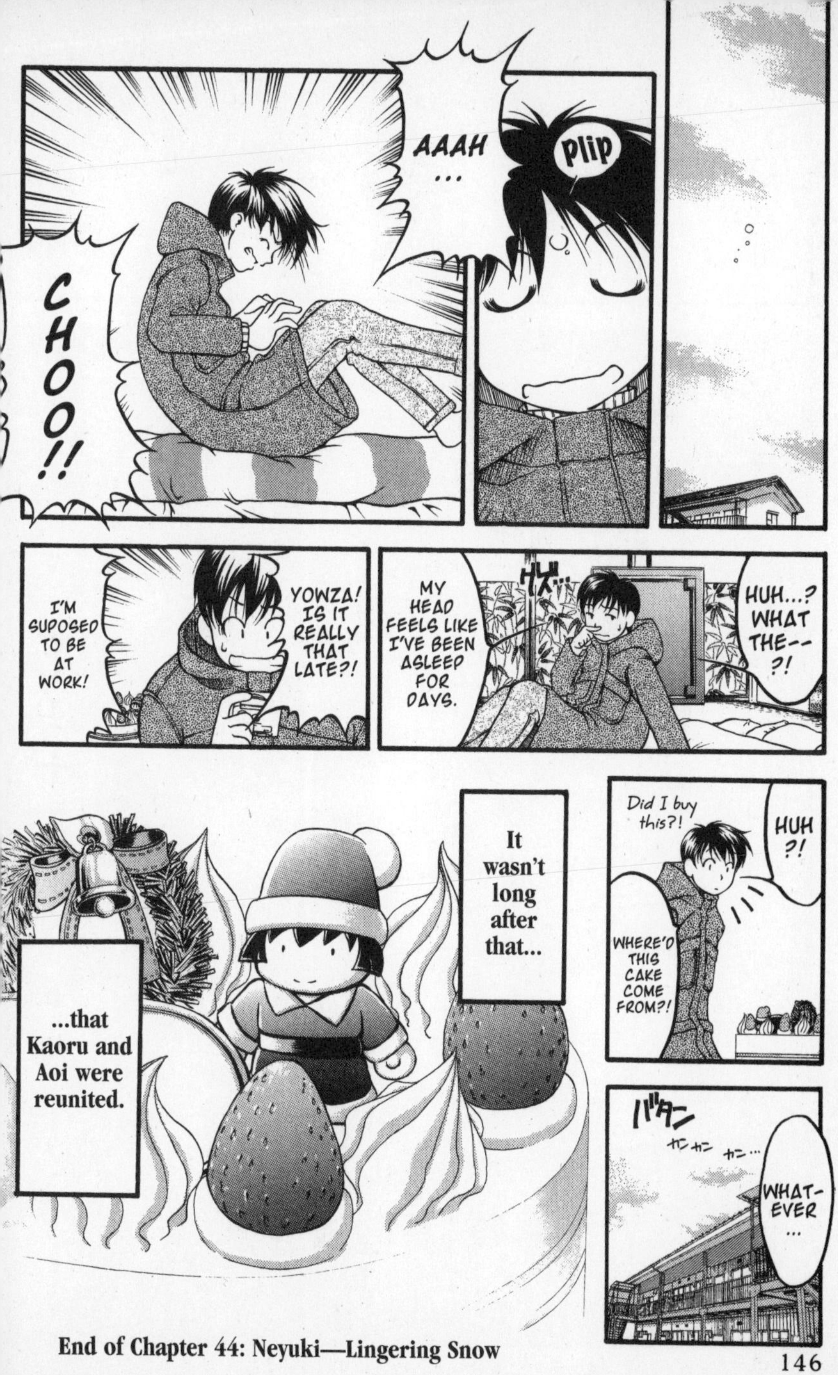
plip
AAAH ...
CHOOO!!
HUH...? WHAT THE--?!
MY HEAD FEELS LIKE I'VE BEEN ASLEEP FOR DAYS.
YOWZA! IS IT REALLY THAT LATE?!
I'M SUPOSED TO BE AT WORK!
HUH ?!
Did I buy this?!
WHERE'D THIS CAKE COME FROM?!
バタン
カンカン カン…
WHAT-EVER ...
It wasn't long after that...
...that Kaoru and Aoi were reunited.

End of Chapter 44: Neyuki—Lingering Snow

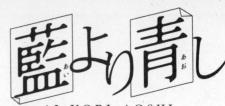

藍より青し

AI YORI AOSHI

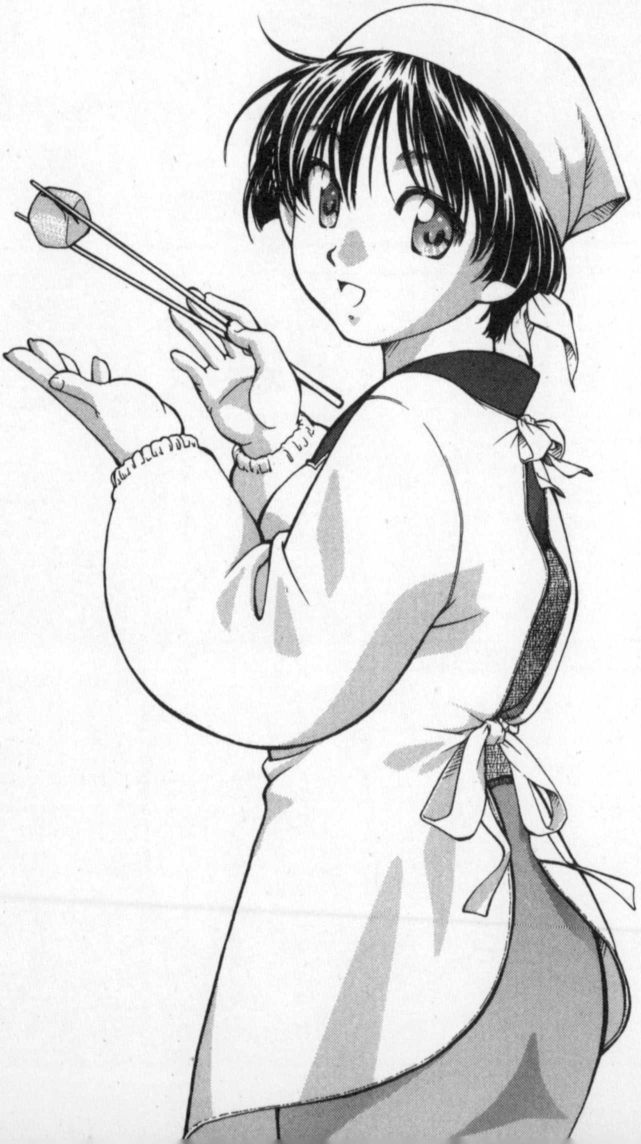

第四十五話　供御―くご―

CHAPTER 45 KUGO EMPEROR'S MEAL

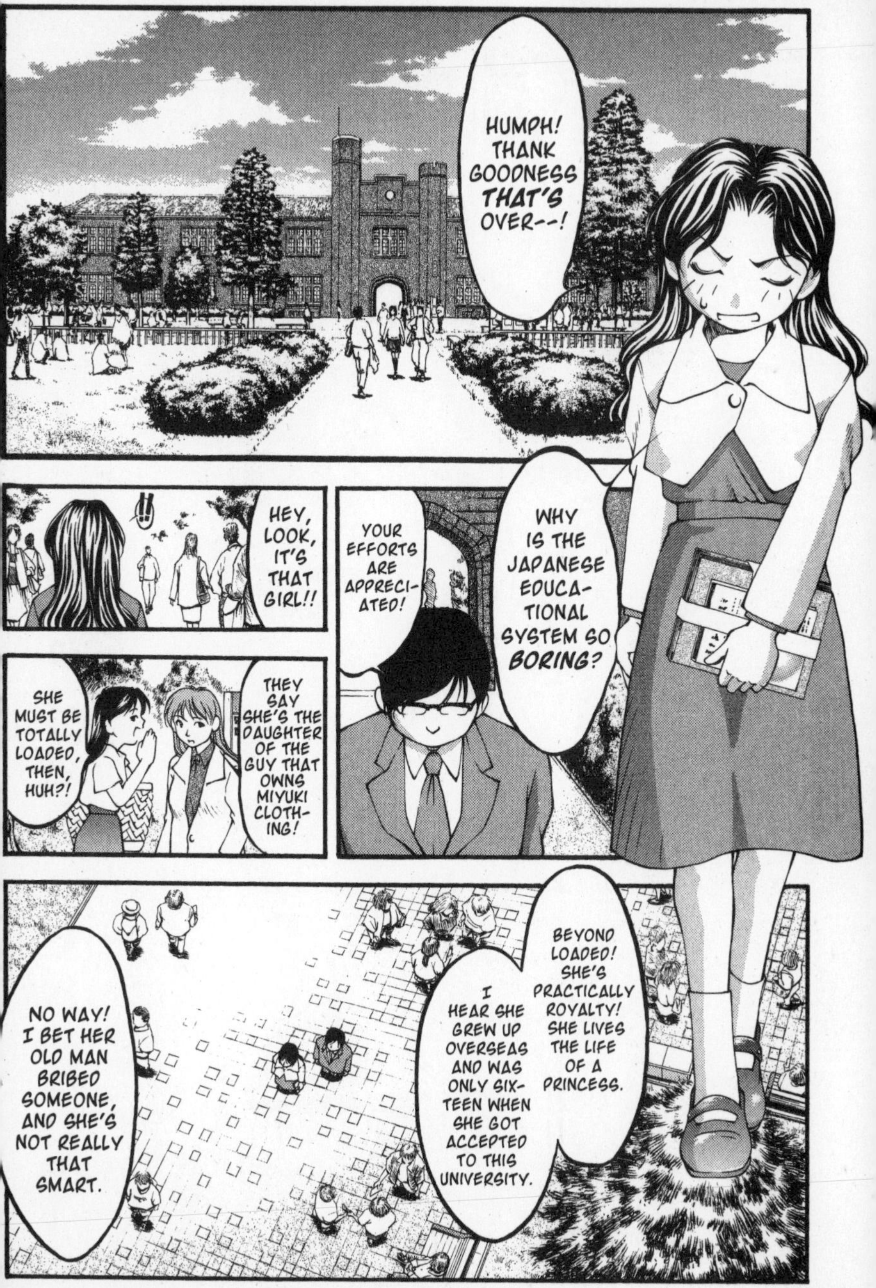
HUMPH! THANK GOODNESS *THAT'S* OVER--!
WHY IS THE JAPANESE EDUCATIONAL SYSTEM SO *BORING*?
YOUR EFFORTS ARE APPRECIATED!
HEY, LOOK, IT'S THAT GIRL!!
THEY SAY SHE'S THE DAUGHTER OF THE GUY THAT OWNS MIYUKI CLOTHING!
SHE MUST BE TOTALLY LOADED, THEN, HUH?!
BEYOND LOADED! SHE'S PRACTICALLY ROYALTY! SHE LIVES THE LIFE OF A PRINCESS.
I HEAR SHE GREW UP OVERSEAS AND WAS ONLY SIXTEEN WHEN SHE GOT ACCEPTED TO THIS UNIVERSITY.
NO WAY! I BET HER OLD MAN BRIBED SOMEONE, AND SHE'S NOT REALLY THAT SMART.

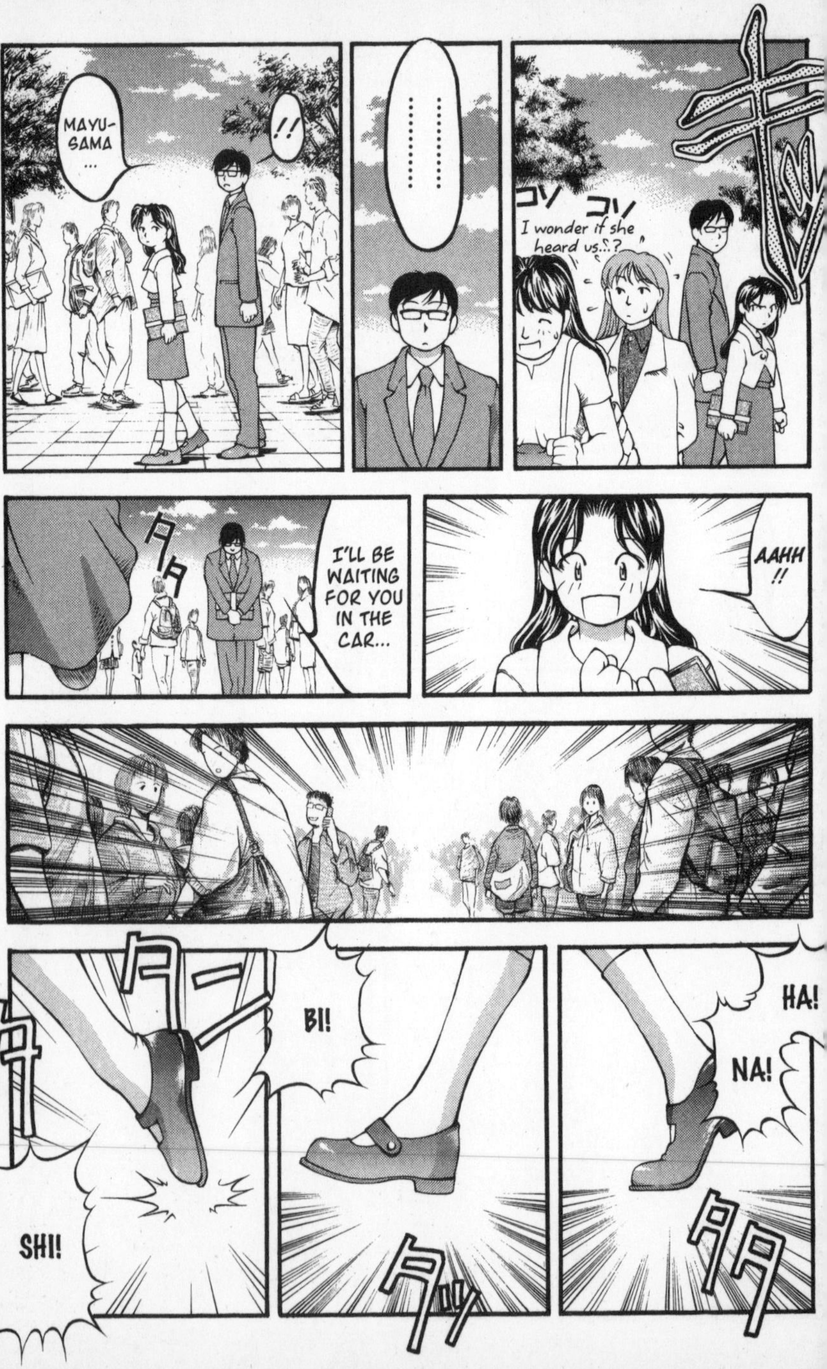
キッ
コソ コソ
I wonder if she heard us...?
......
!!
MAYU-SAMA ...
AAHH !!
タタ
I'LL BE WAITING FOR YOU IN THE CAR...
HA!
NA!
タタ
BI!
タッ
ター
タ
SHI!

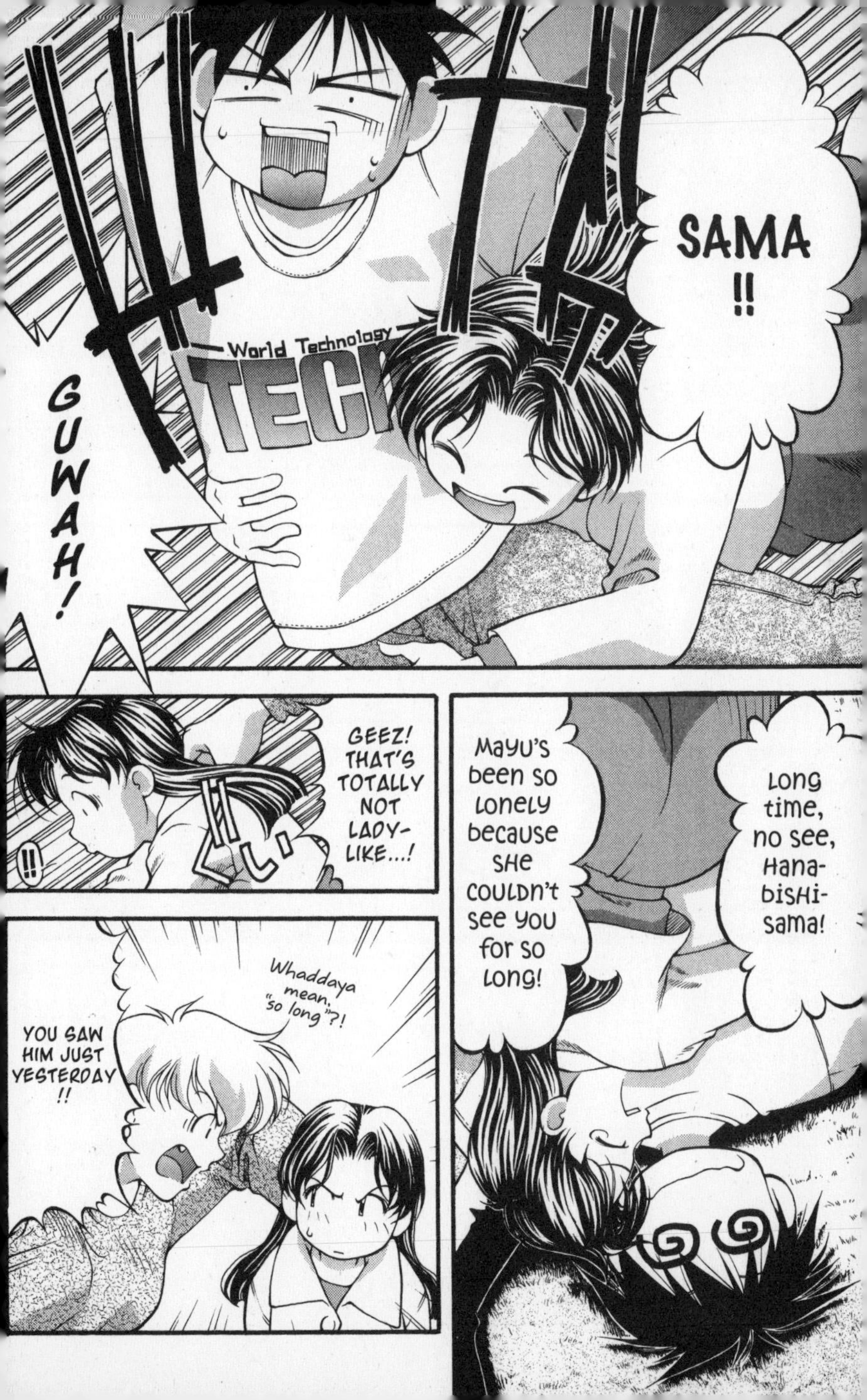
SAMA !!
GUWAH!
Long time, no see, Hana-bishi-sama!
Mayu's been so lonely because she couldn't see you for so long!
GEEZ! THAT'S TOTALLY NOT LADY-LIKE...!
!!
Whaddaya mean, "so long"?!
YOU SAW HIM JUST YESTERDAY !!

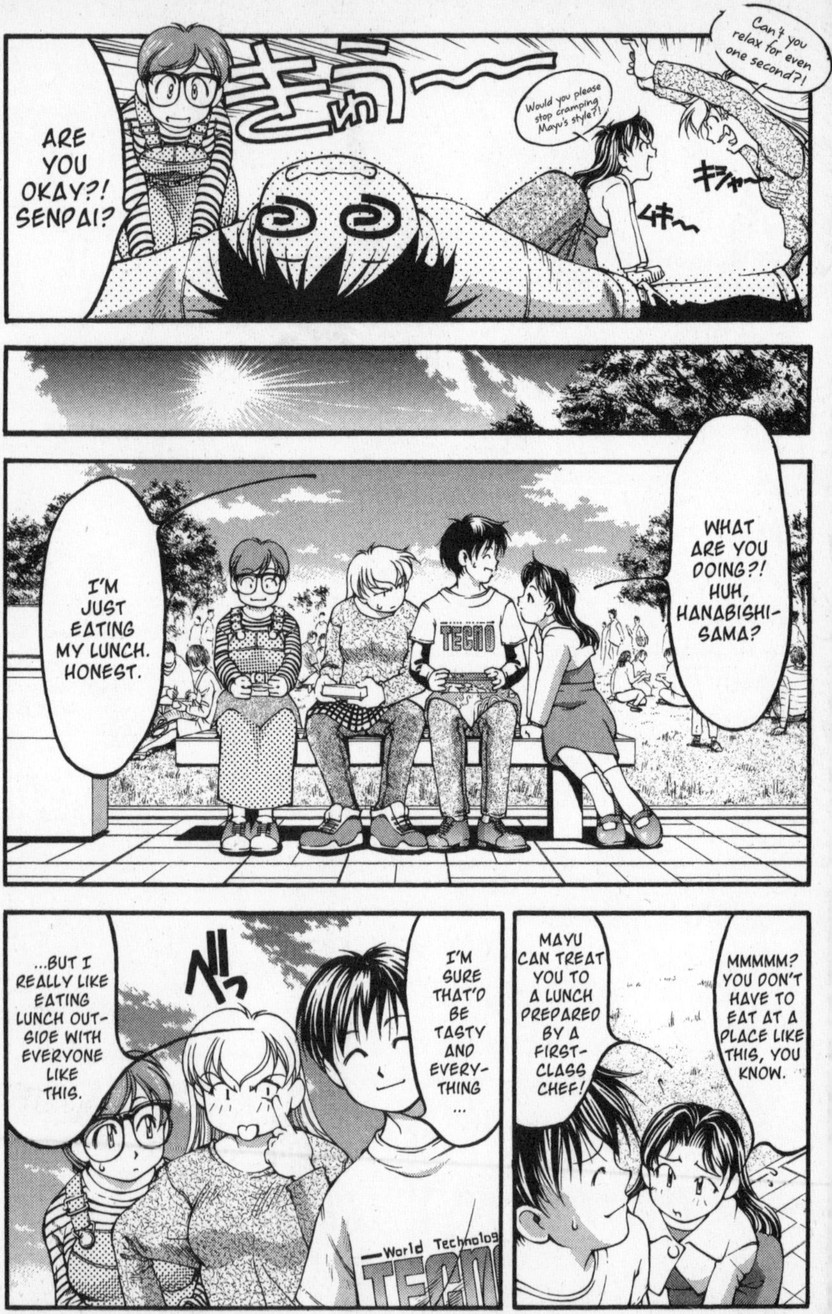
Can't you relax for even one second?!
キシャ〜
Would you please stop cramping Mayu's style?!
ムキ〜
きゅう〜〜
ARE YOU OKAY?! SENPAI?
WHAT ARE YOU DOING?! HUH, HANABISHI-SAMA?
TECNO
I'M JUST EATING MY LUNCH. HONEST.
MMMMM? YOU DON'T HAVE TO EAT AT A PLACE LIKE THIS, YOU KNOW.
MAYU CAN TREAT YOU TO A LUNCH PREPARED BY A FIRST-CLASS CHEF!
I'M SURE THAT'D BE TASTY AND EVERYTHING ...
べっ
...BUT I REALLY LIKE EATING LUNCH OUTSIDE WITH EVERYONE LIKE THIS.

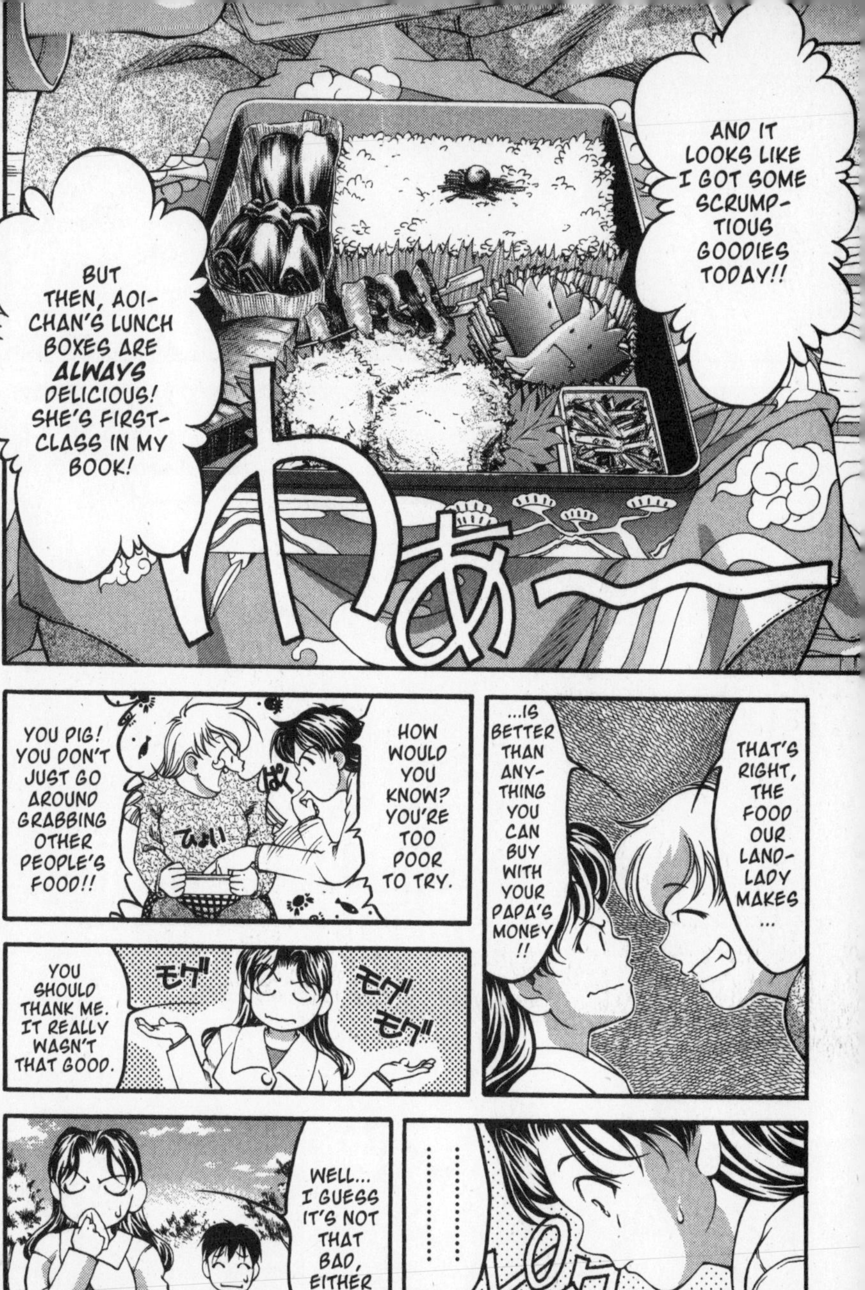
AND IT LOOKS LIKE I GOT SOME SCRUMPTIOUS GOODIES TODAY!!
BUT THEN, AOI-CHAN'S LUNCH BOXES ARE **ALWAYS** DELICIOUS! SHE'S FIRST-CLASS IN MY BOOK!
わあ～
THAT'S RIGHT, THE FOOD OUR LANDLADY MAKES...
...IS BETTER THAN ANYTHING YOU CAN BUY WITH YOUR PAPA'S MONEY!!
HOW WOULD YOU KNOW? YOU'RE TOO POOR TO TRY.
ぱく
ひょい
YOU PIG! YOU DON'T JUST GO AROUND GRABBING OTHER PEOPLE'S FOOD!!
モグ
モグ
モグ
YOU SHOULD THANK ME. IT REALLY WASN'T THAT GOOD.
......
WELL... I GUESS IT'S NOT THAT BAD, EITHER...

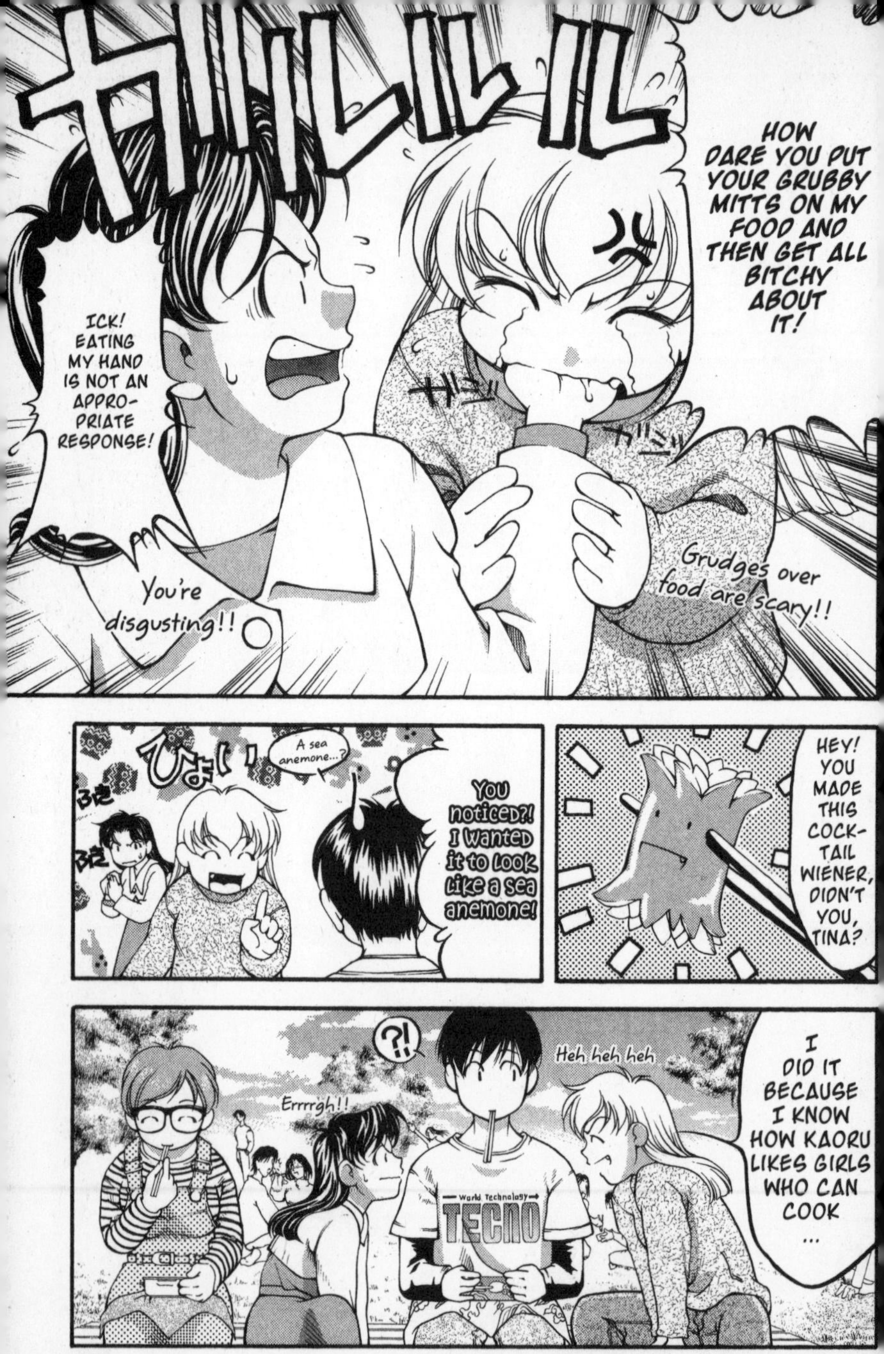
HOW DARE YOU PUT YOUR GRUBBY MITTS ON MY FOOD AND THEN GET ALL BITCHY ABOUT IT!
ICK! EATING MY HAND IS NOT AN APPRO-PRIATE RESPONSE!
Grudges over food are scary!!
You're disgusting!!
HEY! YOU MADE THIS COCK-TAIL WIENER, DIDN'T YOU, TINA?
You noticed?! I wanted it to look like a sea anemone!
A sea anemone...?
ひょい
I DID IT BECAUSE I KNOW HOW KAORU LIKES GIRLS WHO CAN COOK ...
Heh heh heh
?!
Errrgh!!
World Technology
TECNO

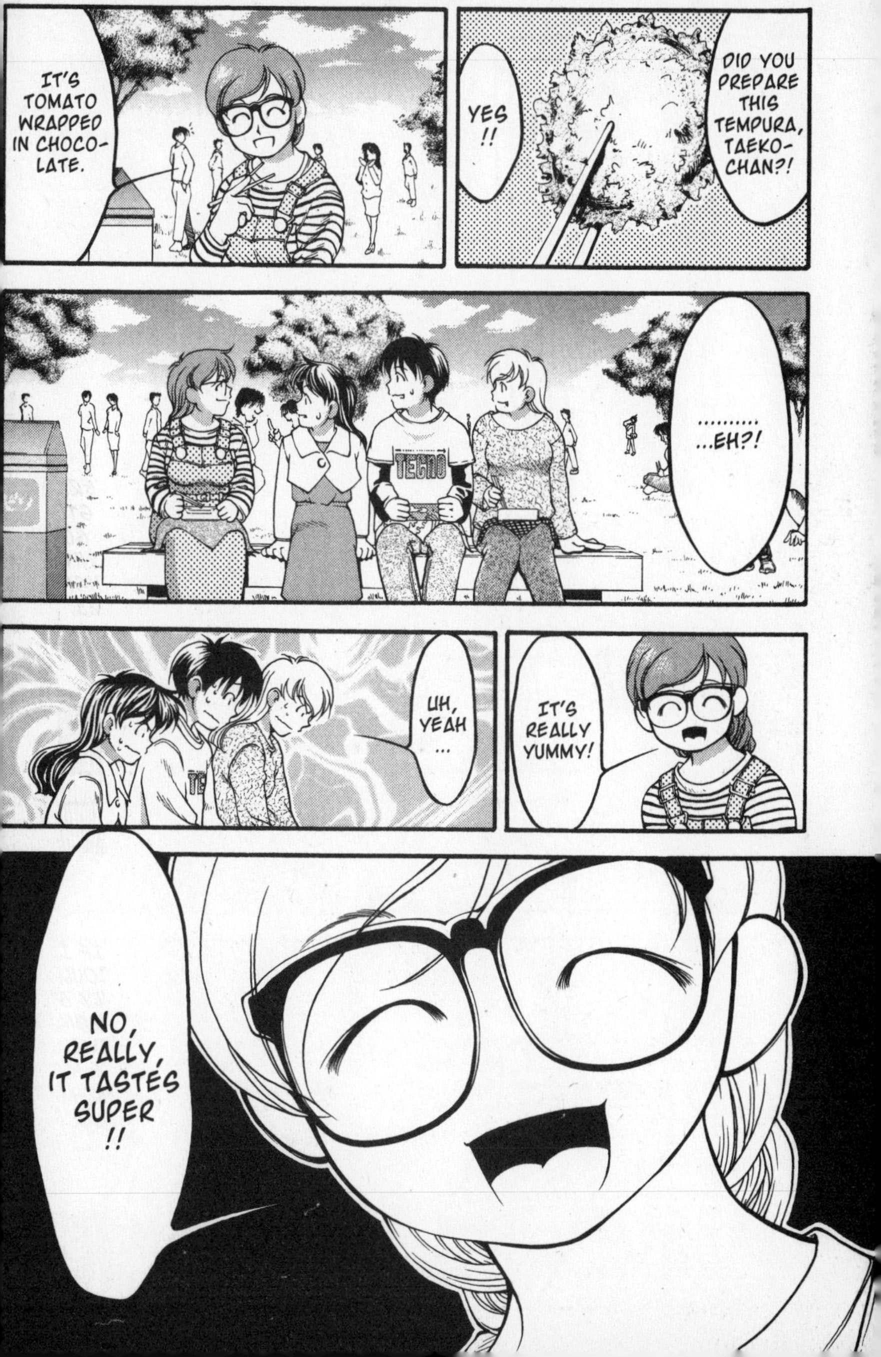
DID YOU PREPARE THIS TEMPURA, TAEKO-CHAN?!
YES !!
IT'S TOMATO WRAPPED IN CHOCO-LATE.
....EH?!
IT'S REALLY YUMMY!
UH, YEAH ...
NO, REALLY, IT TASTES SUPER !!

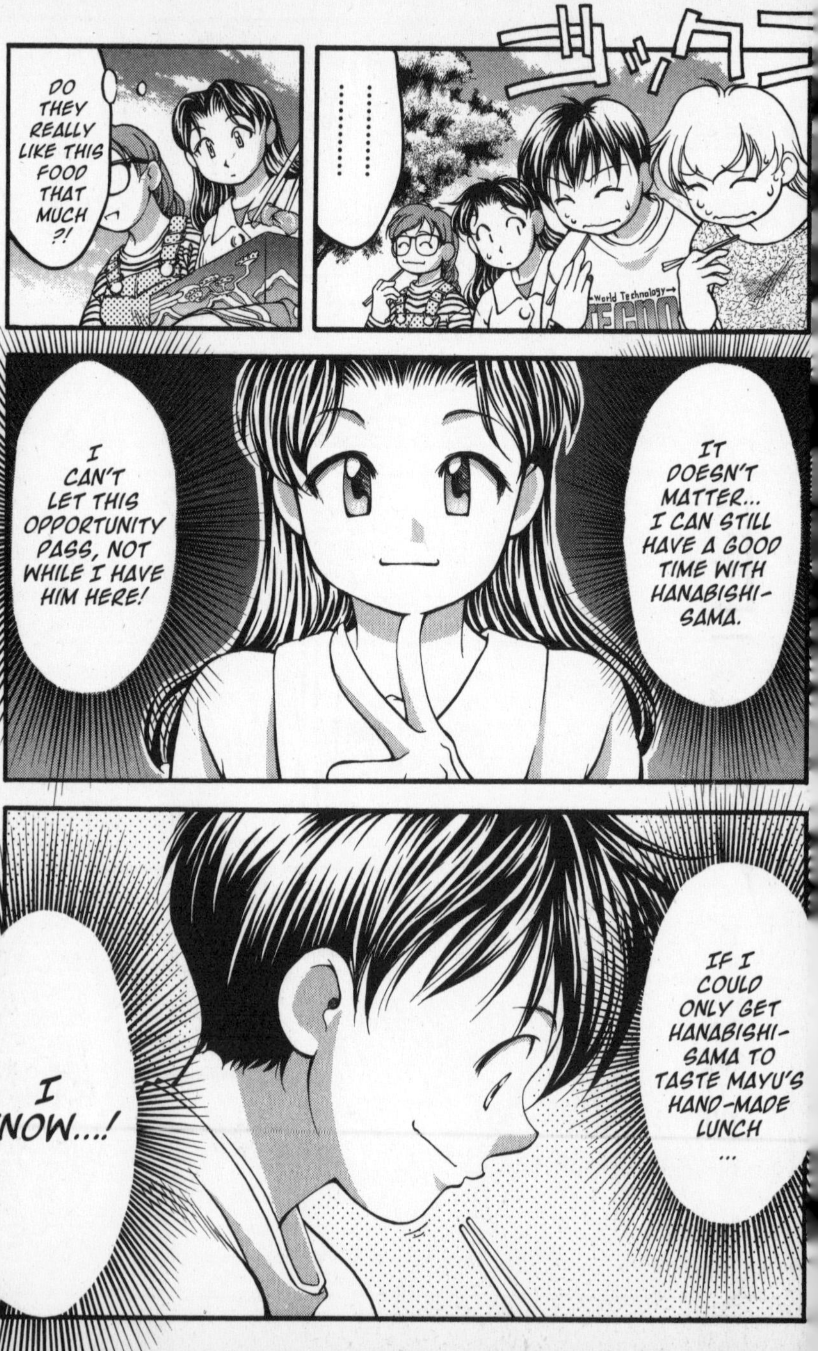
......
World Technology→
DO THEY REALLY LIKE THIS FOOD THAT MUCH?!
IT DOESN'T MATTER... I CAN STILL HAVE A GOOD TIME WITH HANABISHI-SAMA.
I CAN'T LET THIS OPPORTUNITY PASS, NOT WHILE I HAVE HIM HERE!
IF I COULD ONLY GET HANABISHI-SAMA TO TASTE MAYU'S HAND-MADE LUNCH...
I KNOW...!

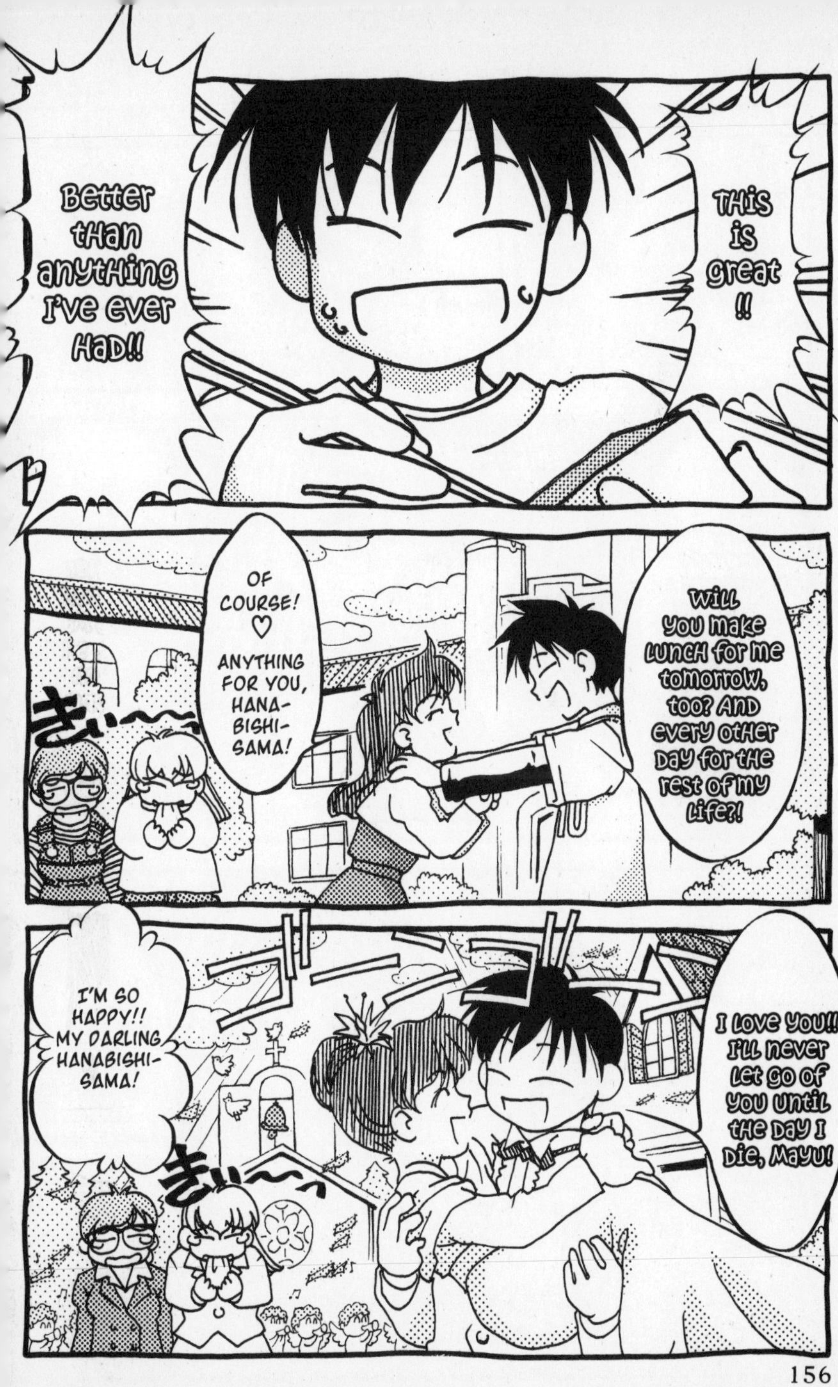
This is great!!
Better than anything I've ever had!!
Will you make lunch for me tomorrow, too? And every other day for the rest of my life?!
Of course! ♡ Anything for you, Hanabishi-sama!
I love you!! I'll never let go of you until the day I die, Mayu!
I'm so happy!! My darling Hanabishi-sama!

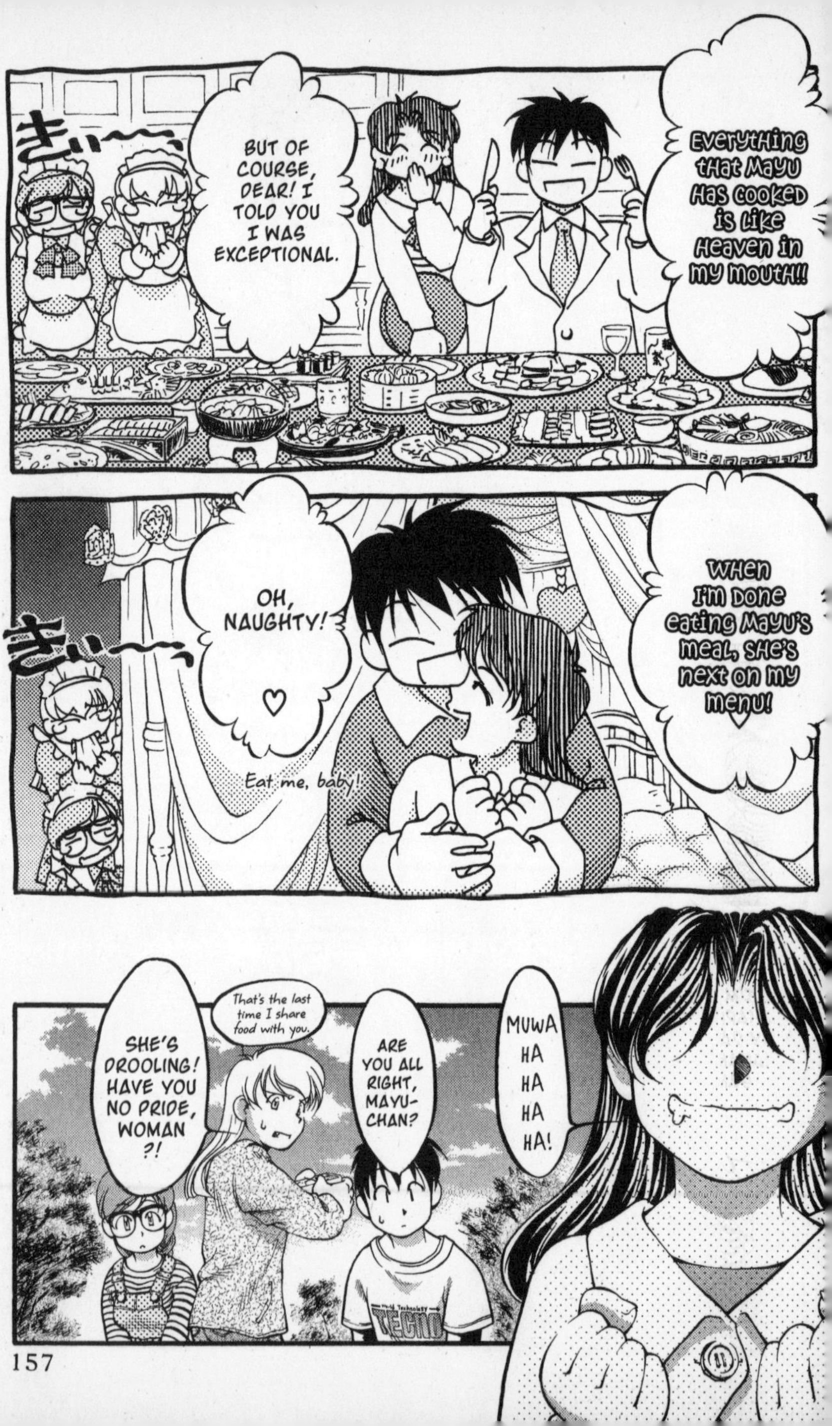
EVERYTHING THAT MAYU HAS COOKED IS LIKE HEAVEN IN MY MOUTH!!
BUT OF COURSE, DEAR! I TOLD YOU I WAS EXCEPTIONAL.
きぃ〜〜
WHEN I'M DONE EATING MAYU'S MEAL, SHE'S NEXT ON MY MENU!
OH, NAUGHTY! ♡
Eat me, baby!
きぃ〜〜
MUWA HA HA HA HA!
ARE YOU ALL RIGHT, MAYU-CHAN?
That's the last time I share food with you.
SHE'S DROOLING! HAVE YOU NO PRIDE, WOMAN?!
TECNO

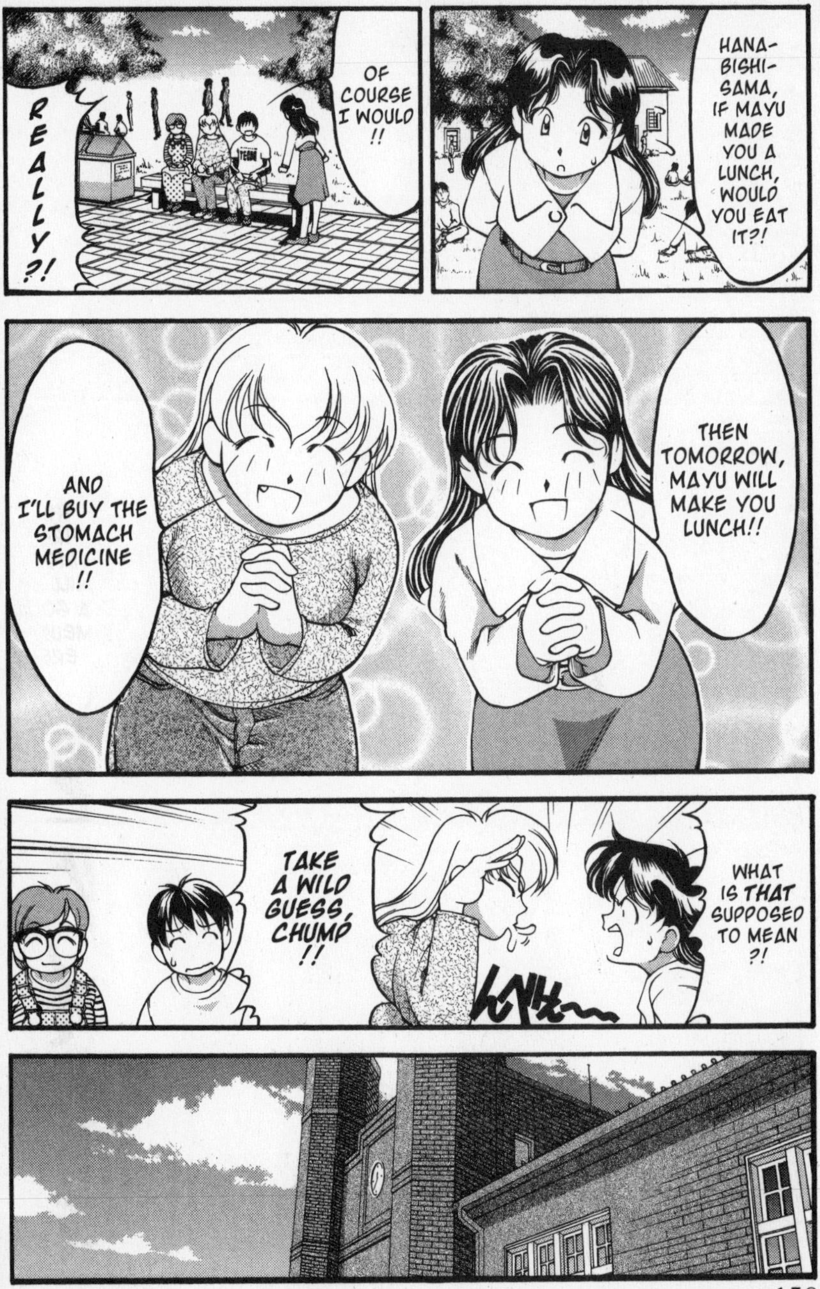
HANA-BISHI-SAMA, IF MAYU MADE YOU A LUNCH, WOULD YOU EAT IT?!
OF COURSE I WOULD!!
REALLY?!
THEN TOMORROW, MAYU WILL MAKE YOU LUNCH!!
AND I'LL BUY THE STOMACH MEDICINE!!
WHAT IS THAT SUPPOSED TO MEAN?!
TAKE A WILD GUESS, CHUMP!!

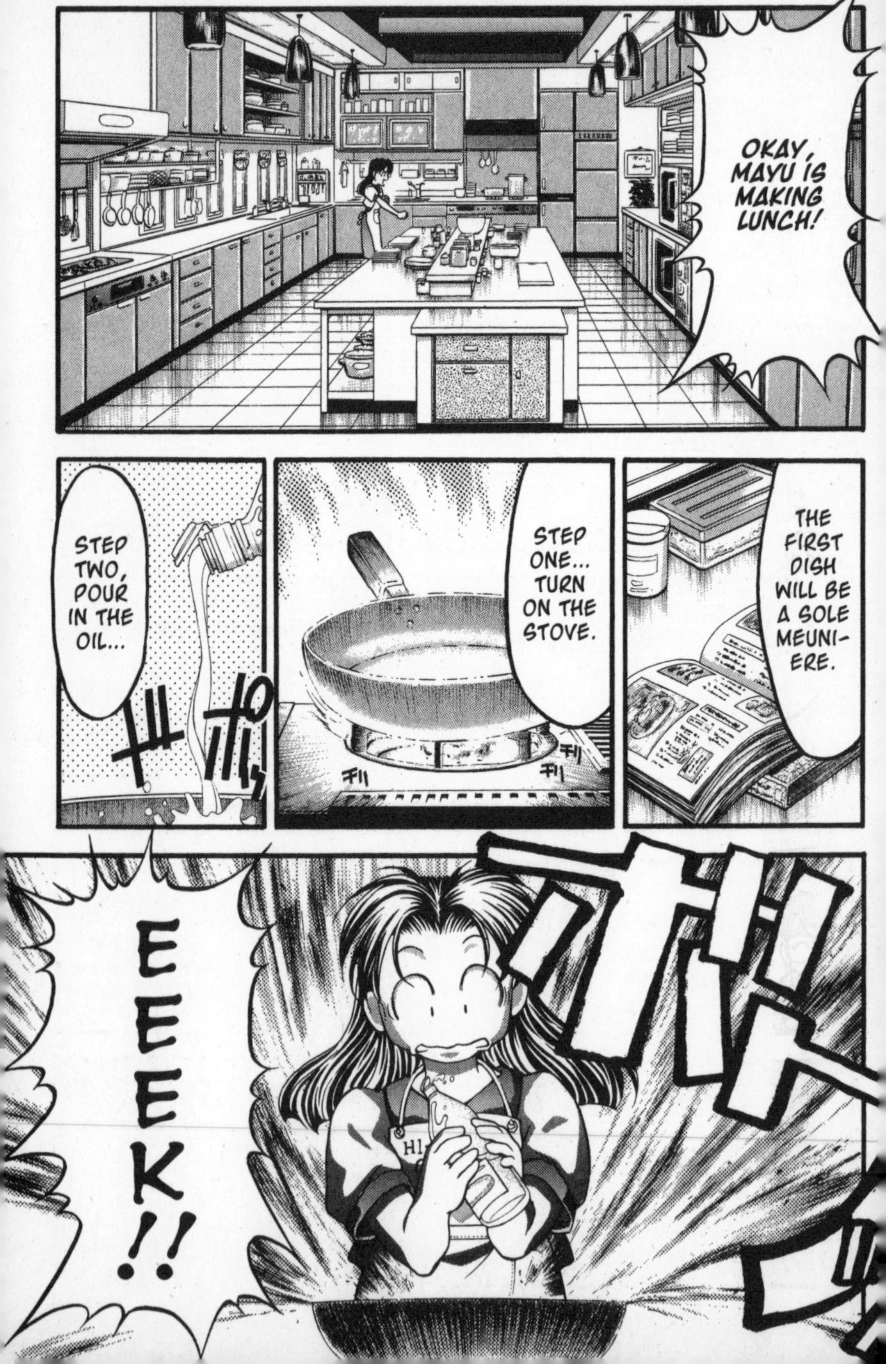
OKAY, MAYU IS MAKING LUNCH!
THE FIRST DISH WILL BE A SOLE MEUNI-ERE.
STEP ONE... TURN ON THE STOVE.
STEP TWO, POUR IN THE OIL...
EEEEK!!

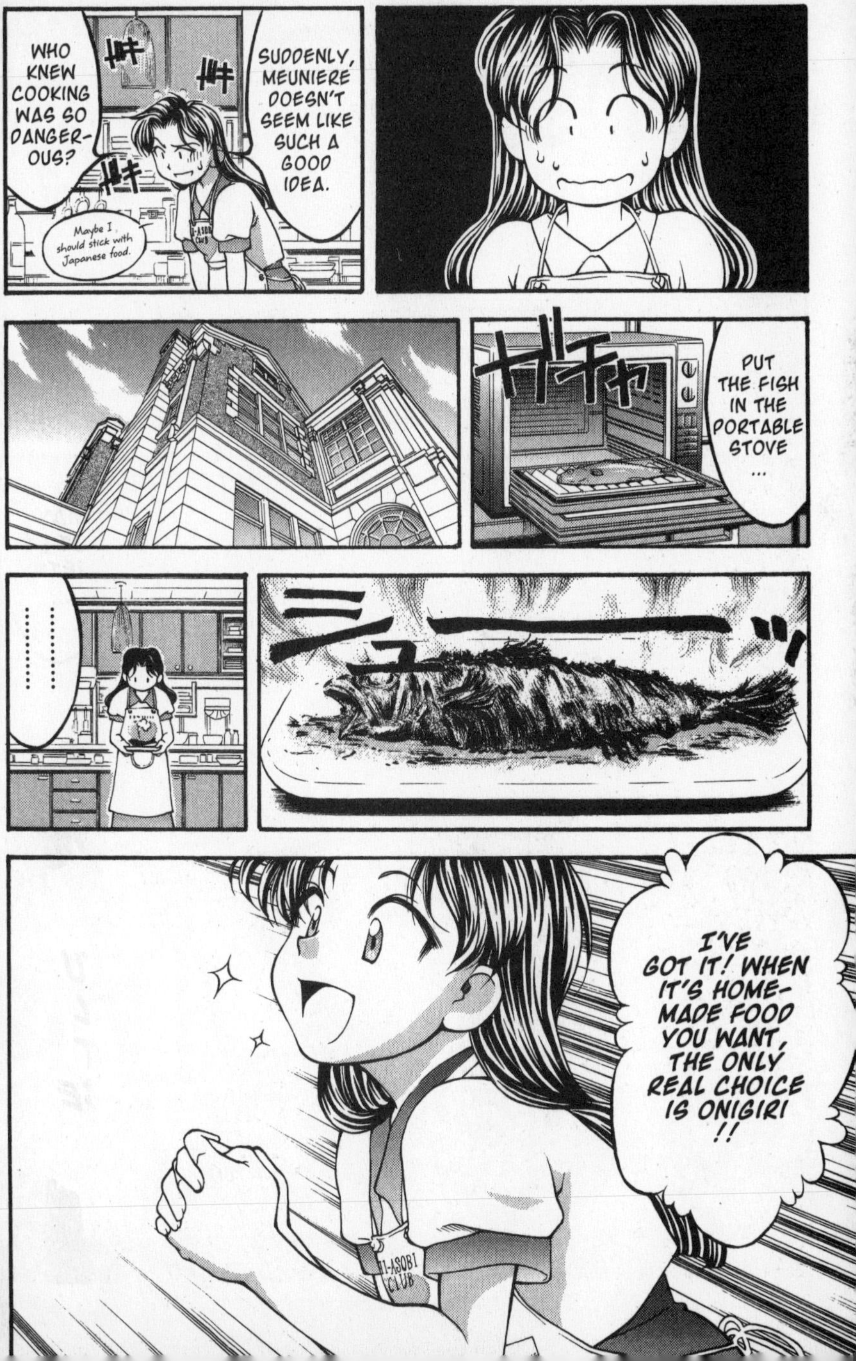
SUDDENLY, MEUNIERE DOESN'T SEEM LIKE SUCH A GOOD IDEA.
WHO KNEW COOKING WAS SO DANGER-OUS?
Maybe I should stick with Japanese food.
PUT THE FISH IN THE PORTABLE STOVE ...
ガチャ
シューーーッ
......
I'VE GOT IT! WHEN IT'S HOME-MADE FOOD YOU WANT, THE ONLY REAL CHOICE IS ONIGIRI !!

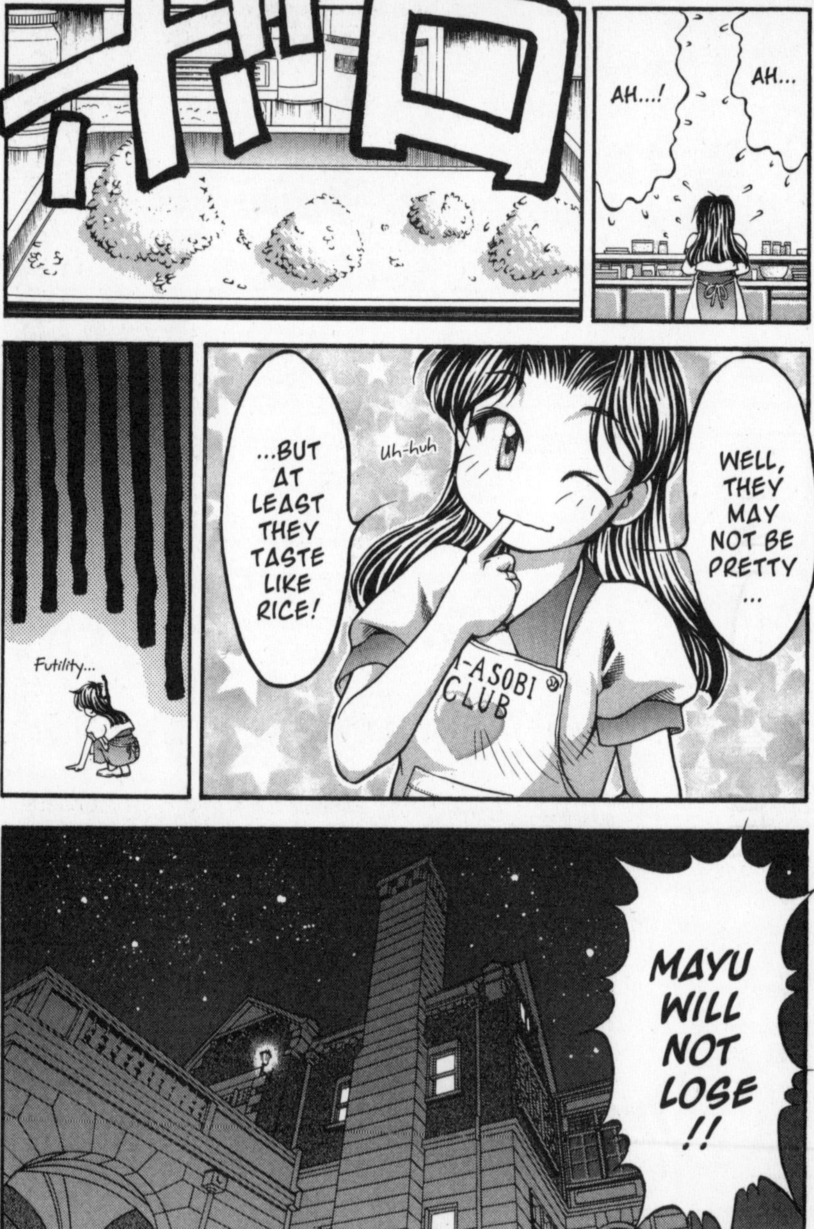
AH...
AH...!
ボロ
WELL, THEY MAY NOT BE PRETTY ...
Uh-huh
...BUT AT LEAST THEY TASTE LIKE RICE!
ASOBI CLUB
Futility...
MAYU WILL NOT LOSE !!

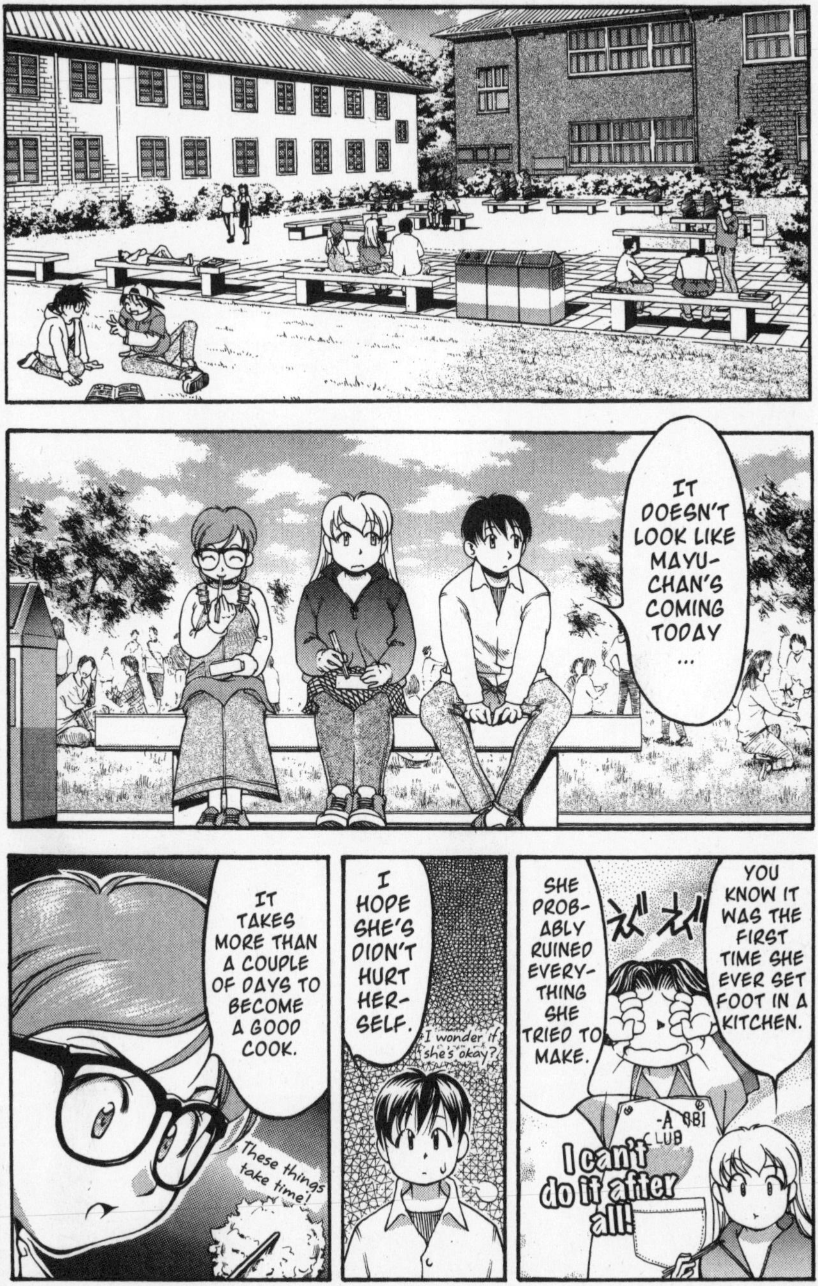
IT DOESN'T LOOK LIKE MAYU-CHAN'S COMING TODAY ...
YOU KNOW IT WAS THE FIRST TIME SHE EVER SET FOOT IN A KITCHEN.
SHE PROBABLY RUINED EVERYTHING SHE TRIED TO MAKE.
I can't do it after all!
I HOPE SHE'S DIDN'T HURT HERSELF.
I wonder if she's okay?
IT TAKES MORE THAN A COUPLE OF DAYS TO BECOME A GOOD COOK.
These things take time!

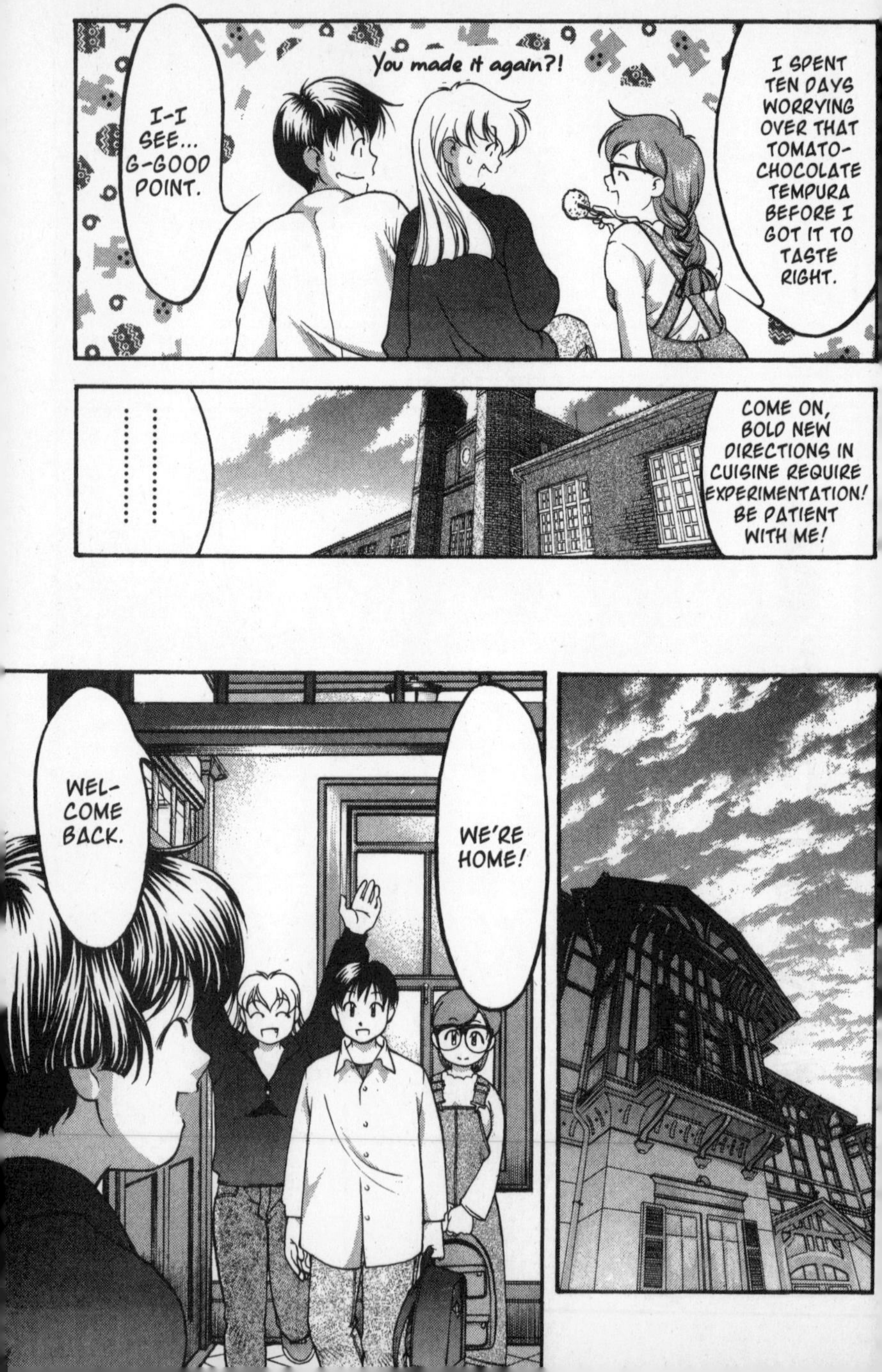
I SPENT TEN DAYS WORRYING OVER THAT TOMATO-CHOCOLATE TEMPURA BEFORE I GOT IT TO TASTE RIGHT.
You made it again?!
I-I SEE... G-GOOD POINT.
COME ON, BOLD NEW DIRECTIONS IN CUISINE REQUIRE EXPERIMENTATION! BE PATIENT WITH ME!
......
WE'RE HOME!
WEL-COME BACK.

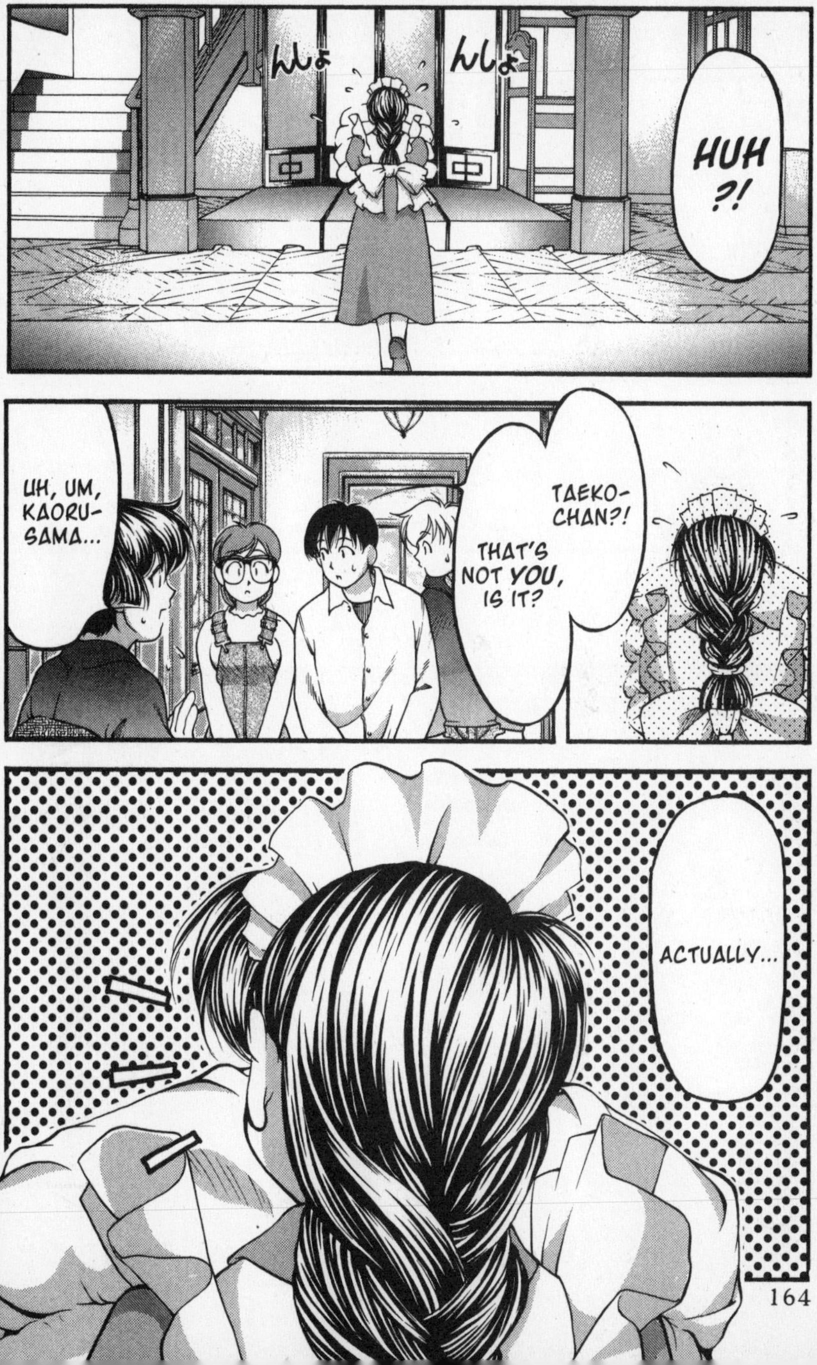
HUH?!
んしょ
んしょ
TAEKO-CHAN?!
THAT'S NOT YOU, IS IT?
UH, UM, KAORU-SAMA...
ACTUALLY...

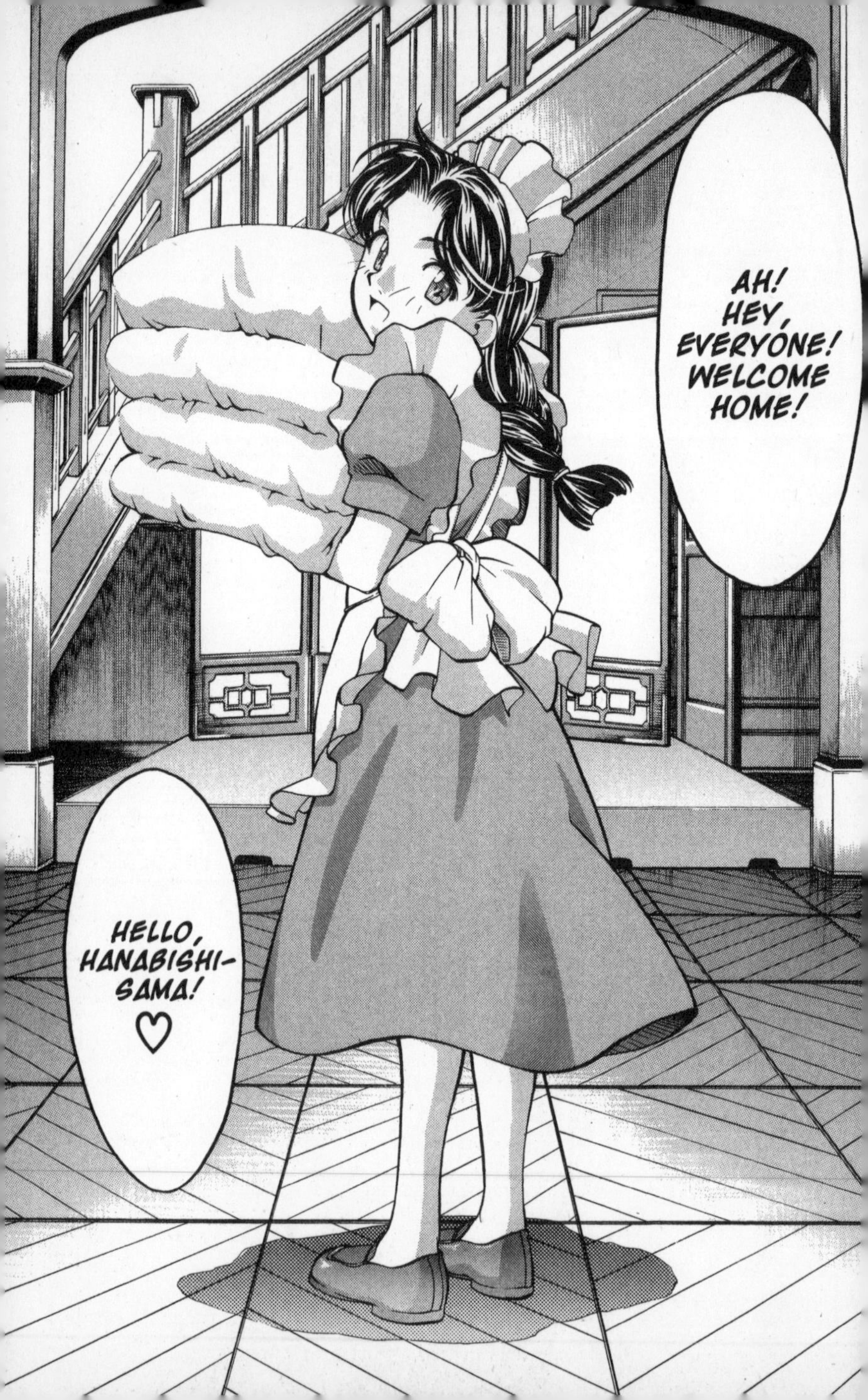
AH! HEY, EVERYONE! WELCOME HOME!
HELLO, HANABISHI-SAMA! ♡

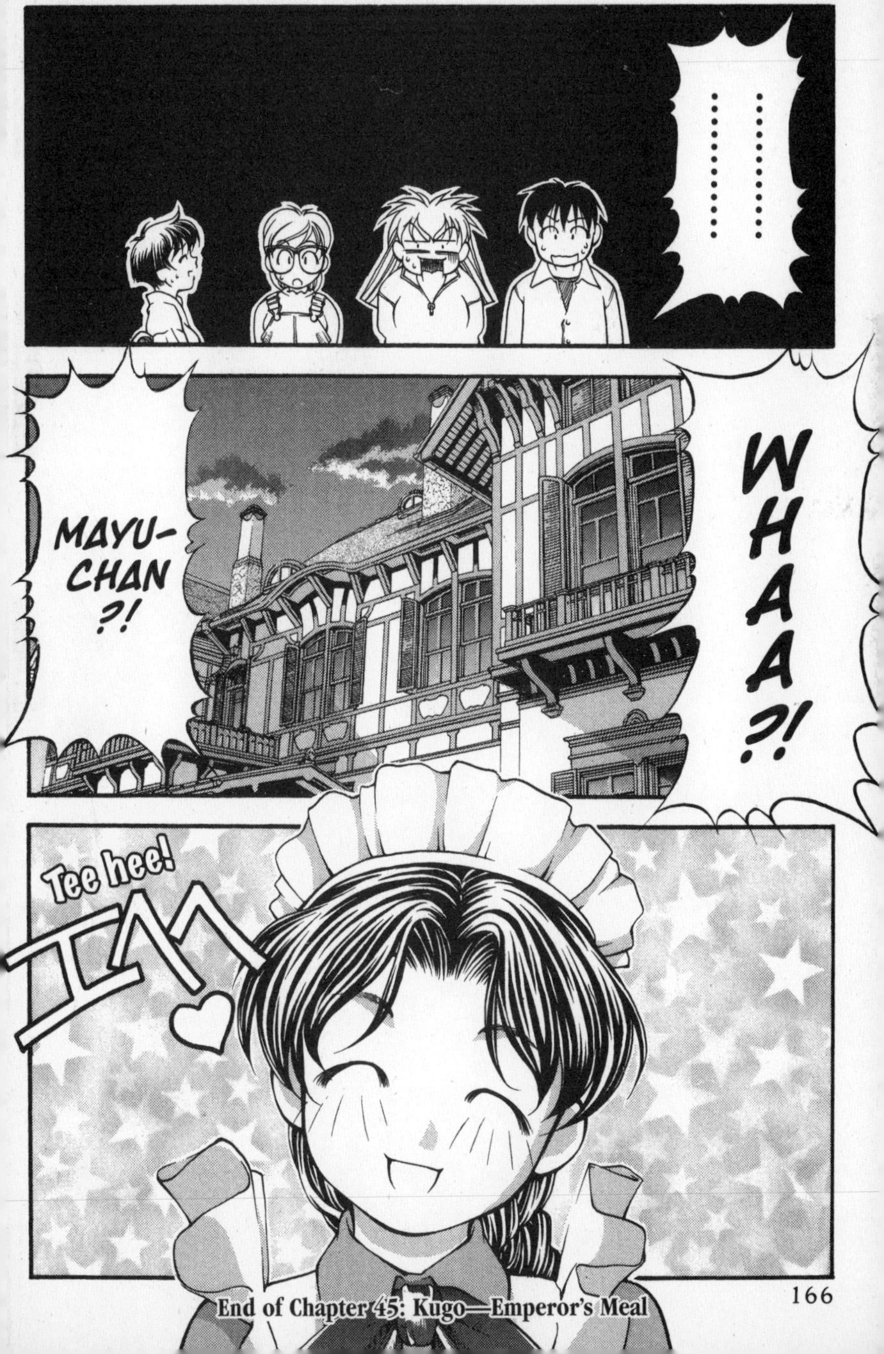
......
WHAA?!
MAYU-CHAN?!
Tee hee!
I'M ♥

End of Chapter 45: Kugo—Emperor's Meal

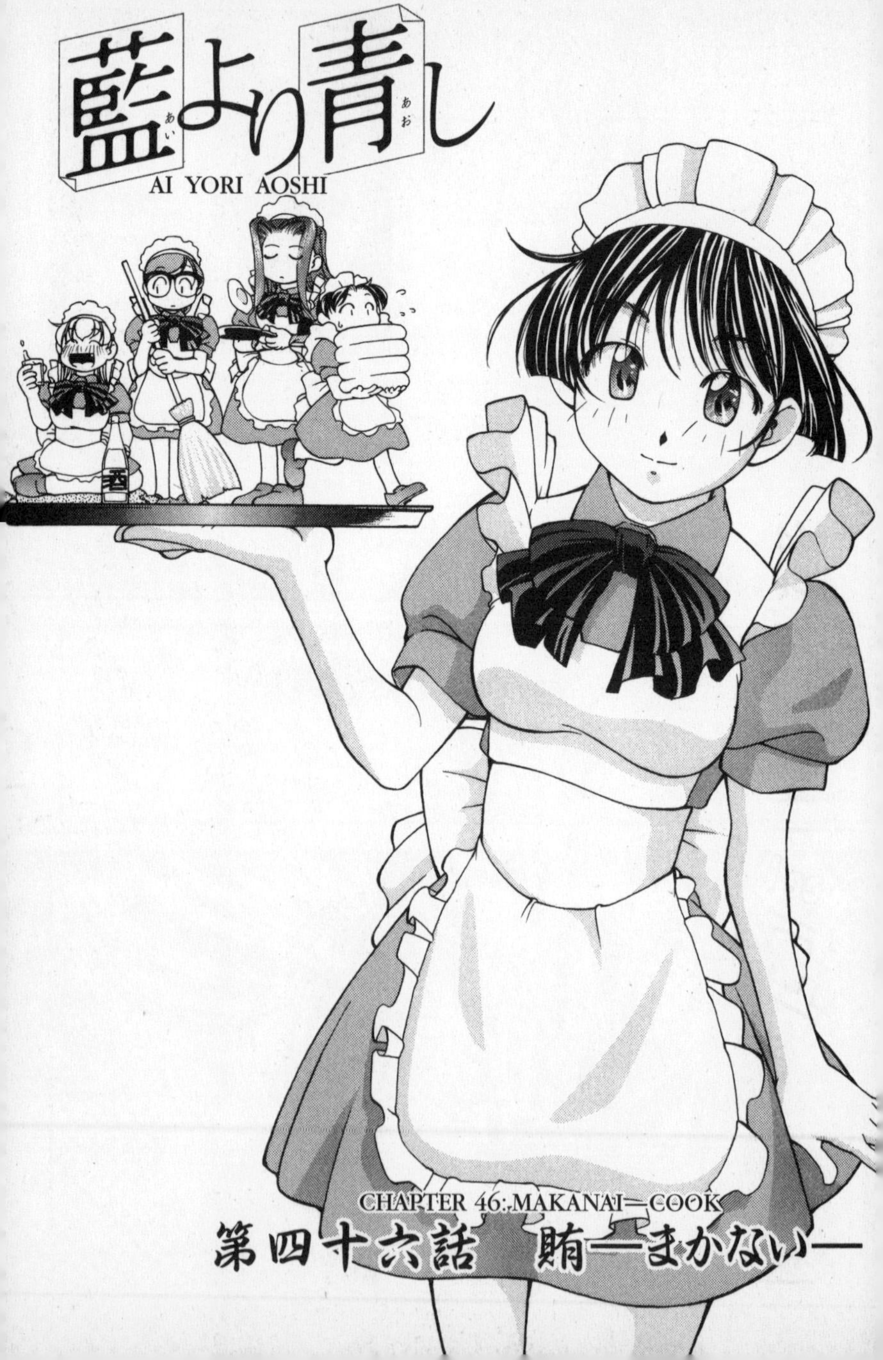
藍(あい)より青(あお)し
AI YORI AOSHI
酒
CHAPTER 46: MAKANAI—COOK
第四十六話　賄—まかない—

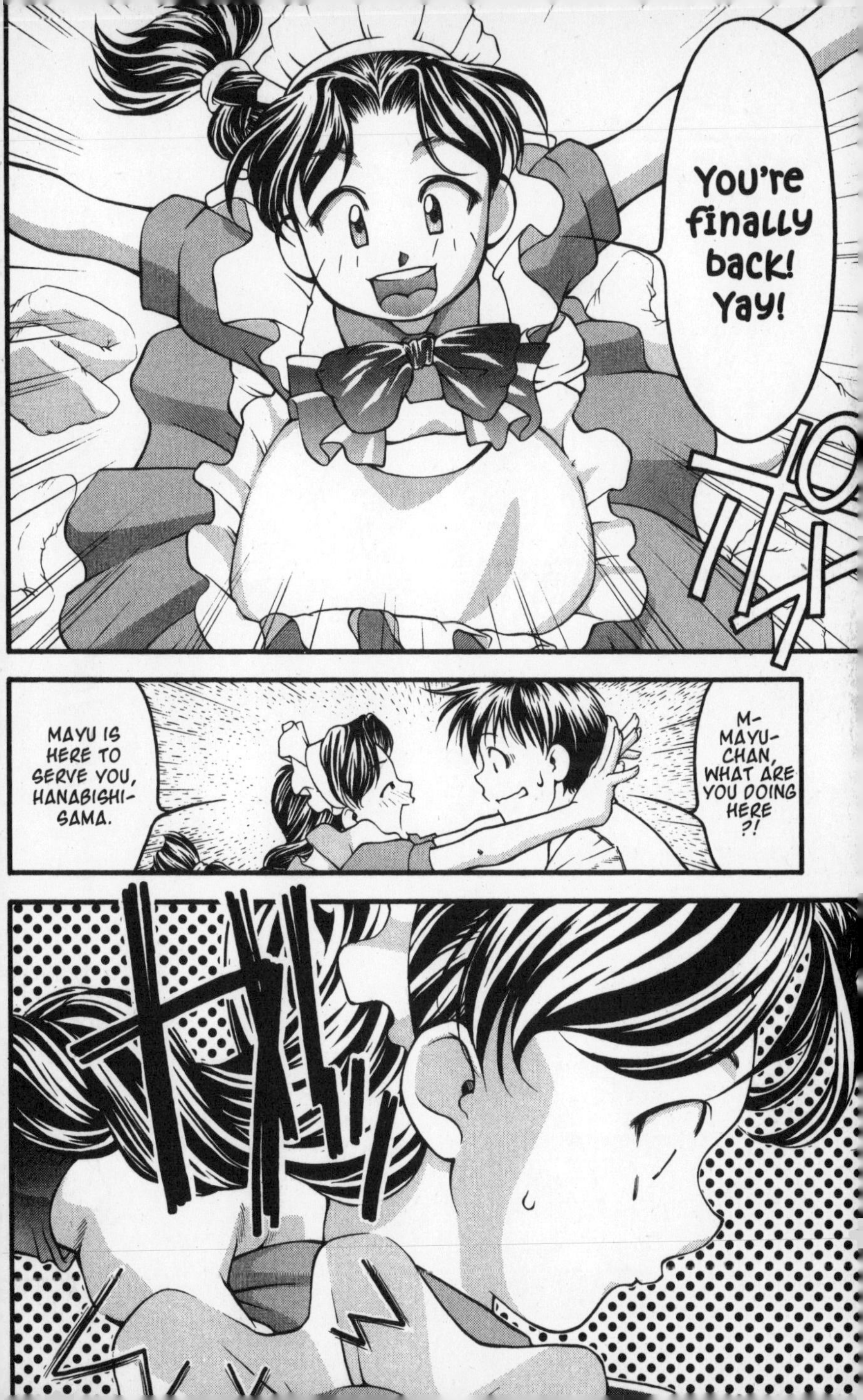
You're finally back! Yay!
M-Mayu-chan, what are you doing here ?!
Mayu is here to serve you, Hanabishi-sama.

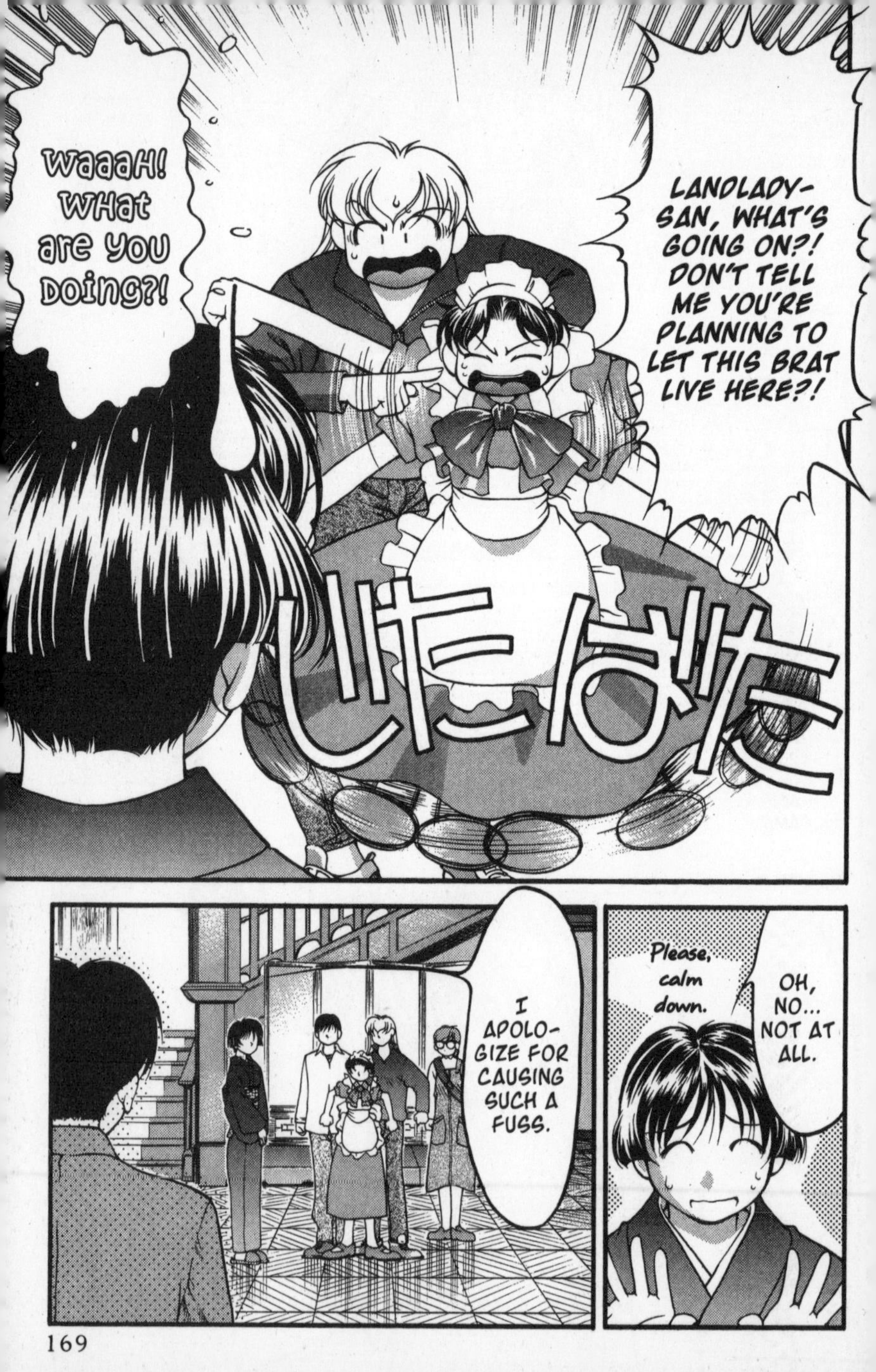
LANDLADY-SAN, WHAT'S GOING ON?! DON'T TELL ME YOU'RE PLANNING TO LET THIS BRAT LIVE HERE?!
WAAAH! WHAT ARE YOU DOING?!
じたばた
OH, NO... NOT AT ALL.
Please, calm down.
I APOLOGIZE FOR CAUSING SUCH A FUSS.

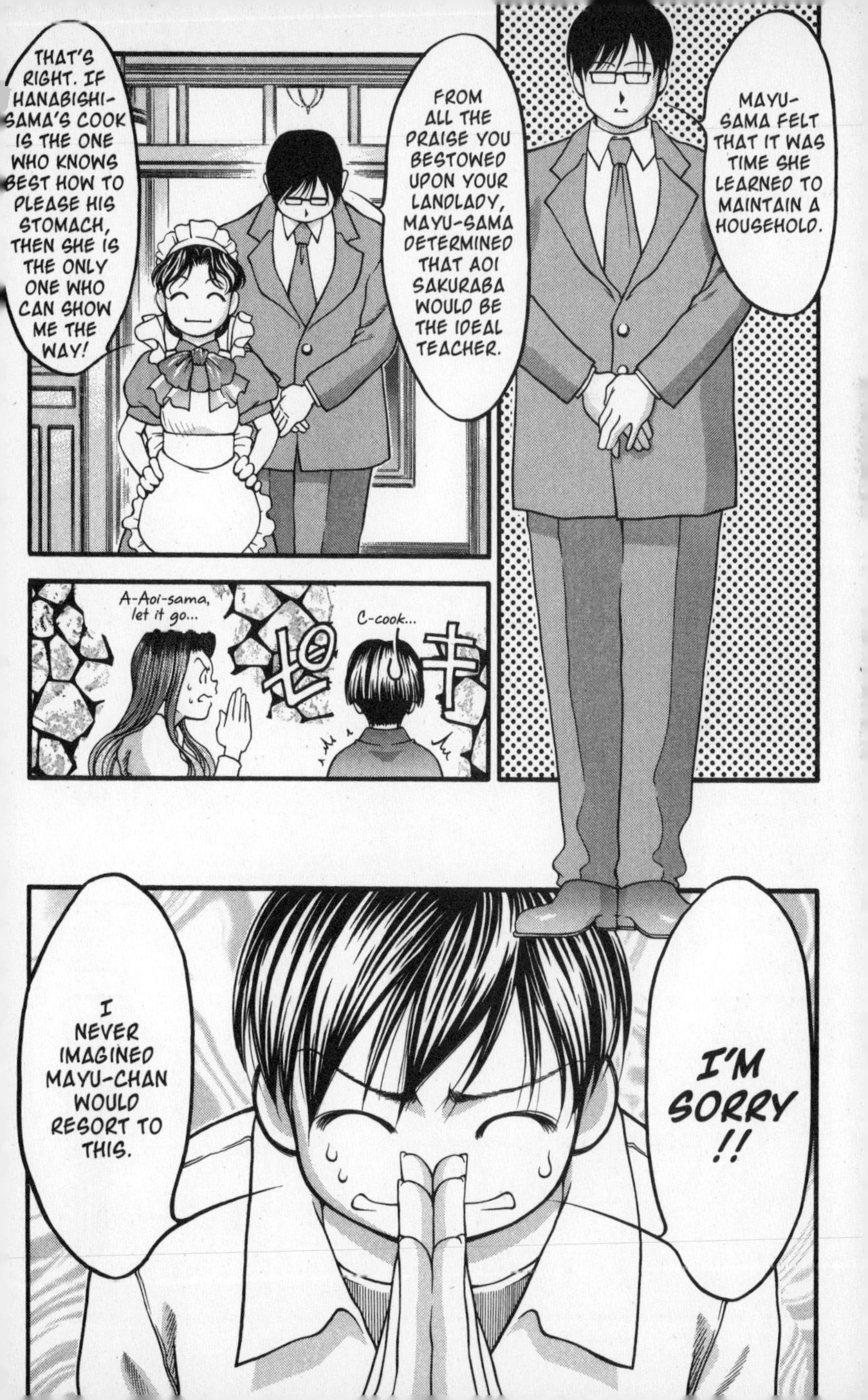
MAYU-SAMA FELT THAT IT WAS TIME SHE LEARNED TO MAINTAIN A HOUSEHOLD.
FROM ALL THE PRAISE YOU BESTOWED UPON YOUR LANDLADY, MAYU-SAMA DETERMINED THAT AOI SAKURABA WOULD BE THE IDEAL TEACHER.
THAT'S RIGHT. IF HANABISHI-SAMA'S COOK IS THE ONE WHO KNOWS BEST HOW TO PLEASE HIS STOMACH, THEN SHE IS THE ONLY ONE WHO CAN SHOW ME THE WAY!
C-cook...
A-Aoi-sama, let it go...
I'M SORRY!!
I NEVER IMAGINED MAYU-CHAN WOULD RESORT TO THIS.

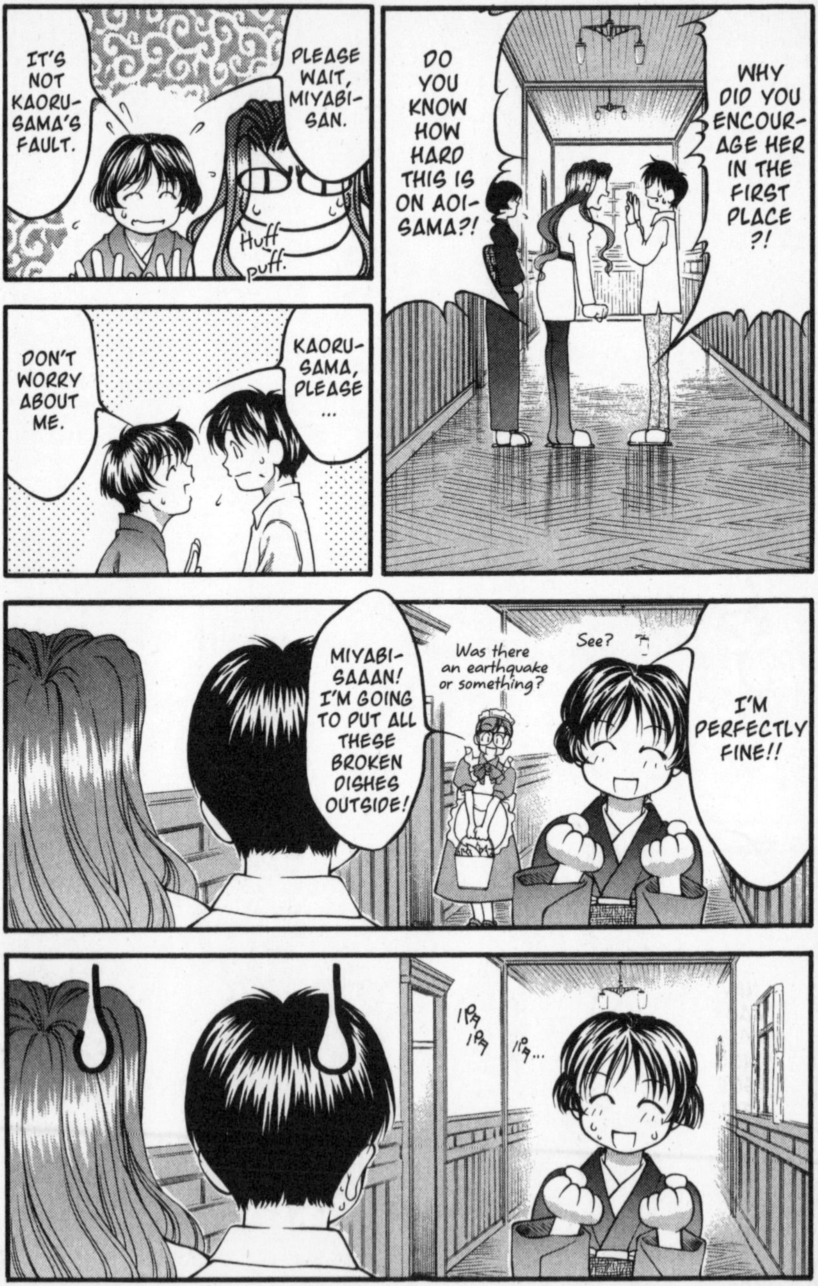
WHY DID YOU ENCOURAGE HER IN THE FIRST PLACE ?!
DO YOU KNOW HOW HARD THIS IS ON AOI-SAMA?!
PLEASE WAIT, MIYABI-SAN.
IT'S NOT KAORU-SAMA'S FAULT.
Huff puff.
KAORU-SAMA, PLEASE ...
DON'T WORRY ABOUT ME.
See?
I'M PERFECTLY FINE!!
Was there an earthquake or something?
MIYABI-SAAAN! I'M GOING TO PUT ALL THESE BROKEN DISHES OUTSIDE!
パタ
パタ
パタ…

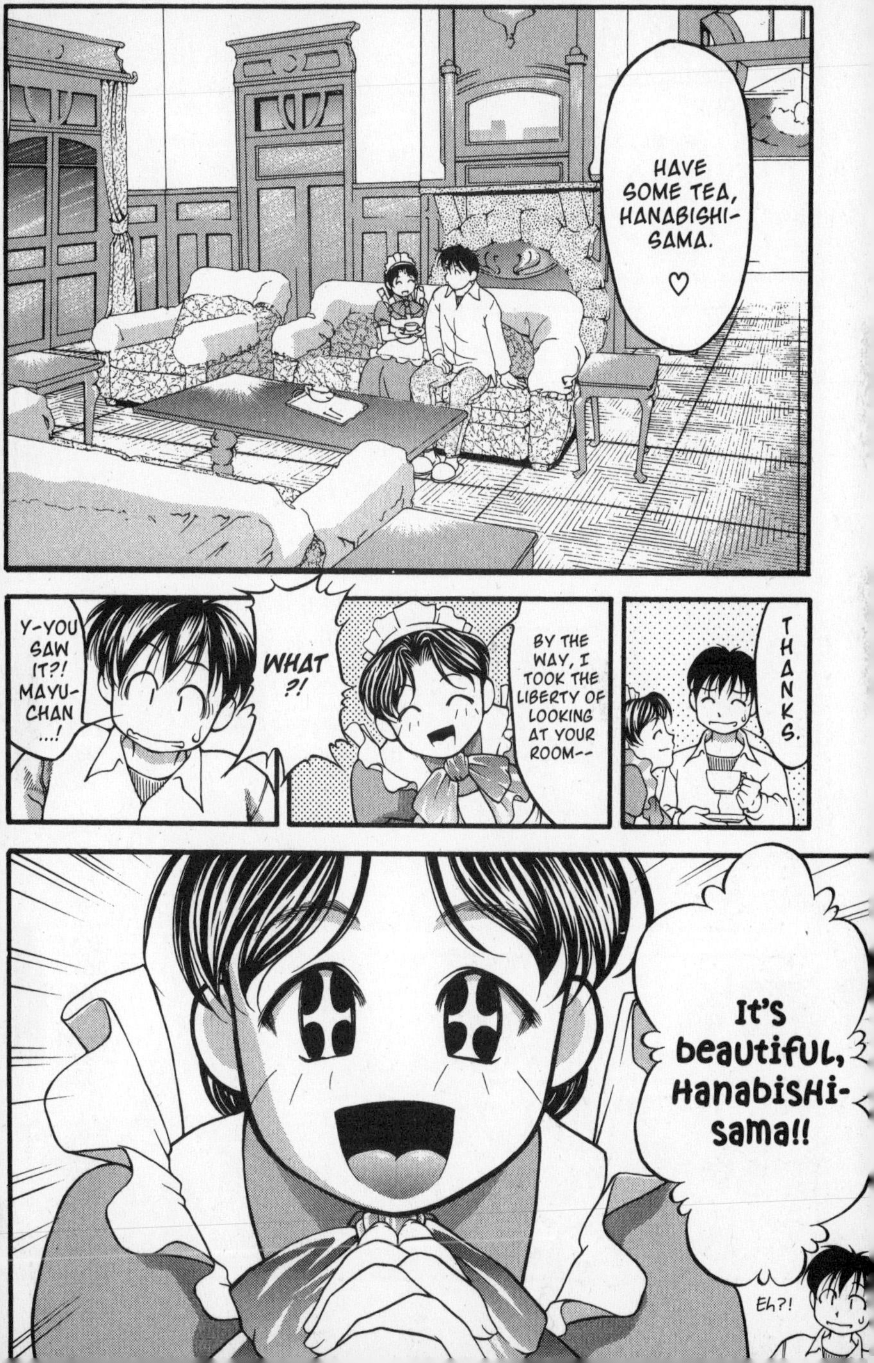
HAVE SOME TEA, HANABISHI-SAMA. ♡
THANKS.
BY THE WAY, I TOOK THE LIBERTY OF LOOKING AT YOUR ROOM--
WHAT ?!
Y-YOU SAW IT?! MAYU-CHAN ...!
It's beautiful, Hanabishi-sama!!
Eh?!

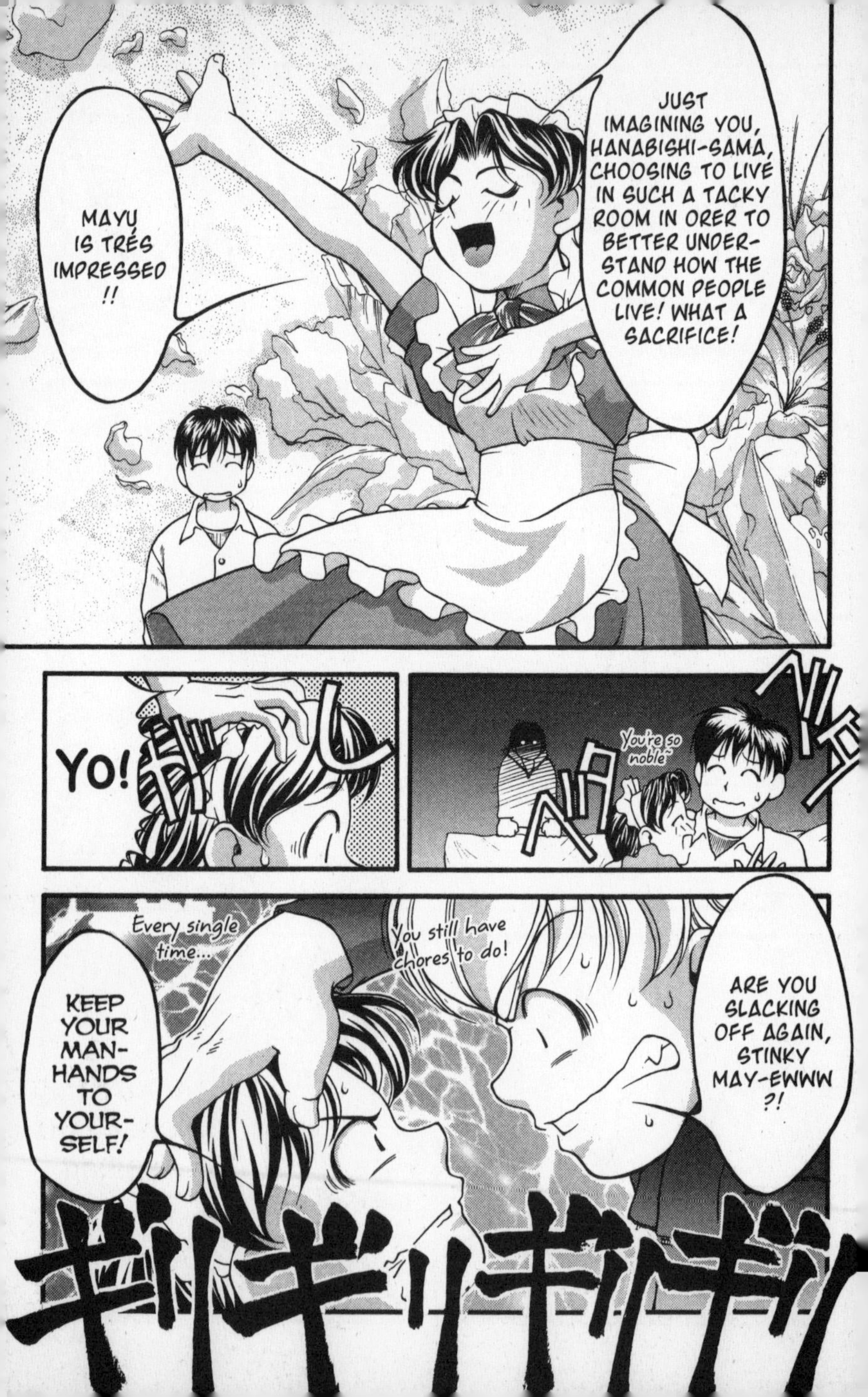
JUST IMAGINING YOU, HANABISHI-SAMA, CHOOSING TO LIVE IN SUCH A TACKY ROOM IN ORER TO BETTER UNDER-STAND HOW THE COMMON PEOPLE LIVE! WHAT A SACRIFICE!
MAYU IS TRÉS IMPRESSED !!
You're so noble~
YO!
ARE YOU SLACKING OFF AGAIN, STINKY MAY-EWWW ?!
You still have chores to do!
Every single time...
KEEP YOUR MAN-HANDS TO YOUR-SELF!

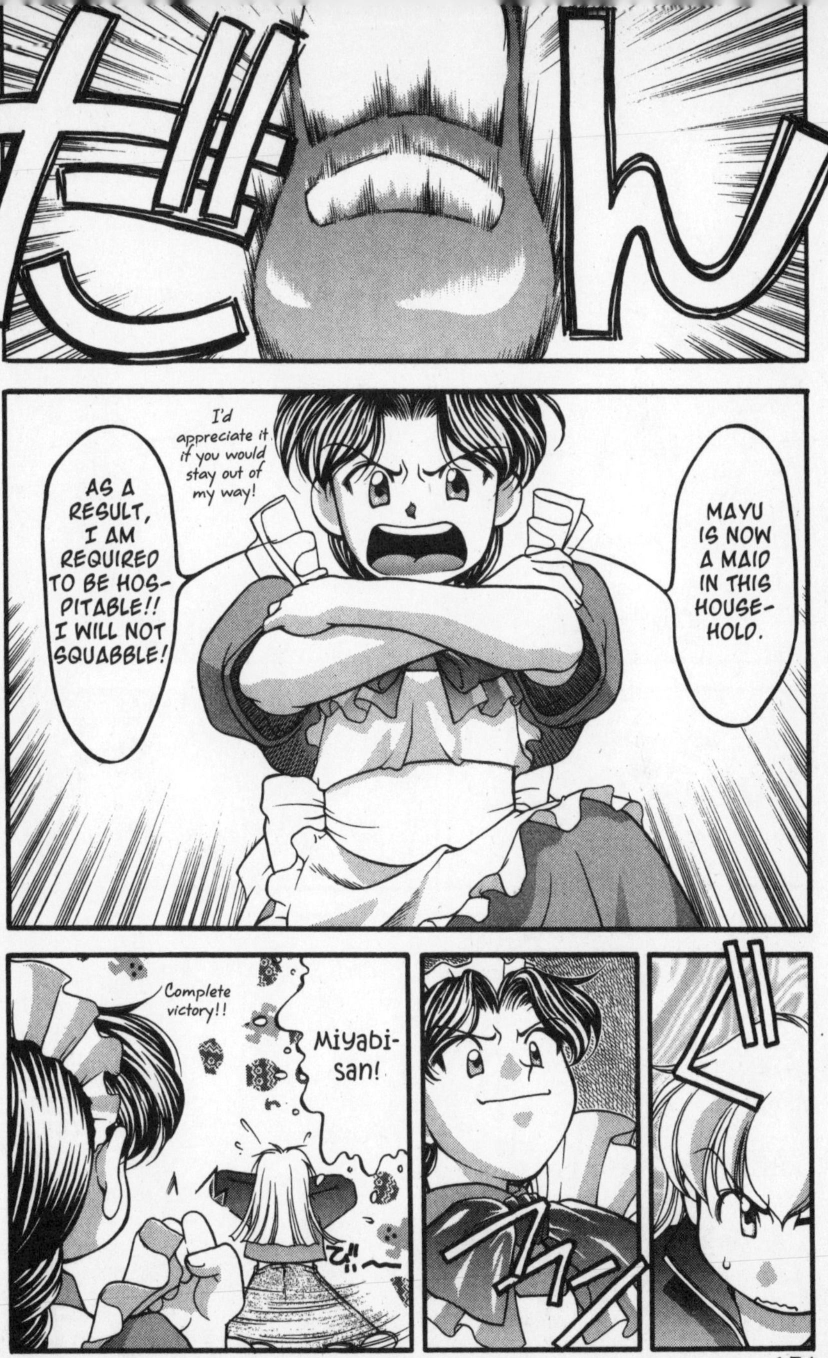

だん
MAYU IS NOW A MAID IN THIS HOUSE-HOLD.
AS A RESULT, I AM REQUIRED TO BE HOS-PITABLE!! I WILL NOT SQUABBLE!
I'd appreciate it if you would stay out of my way!
Miyabi-san!
Complete victory!!

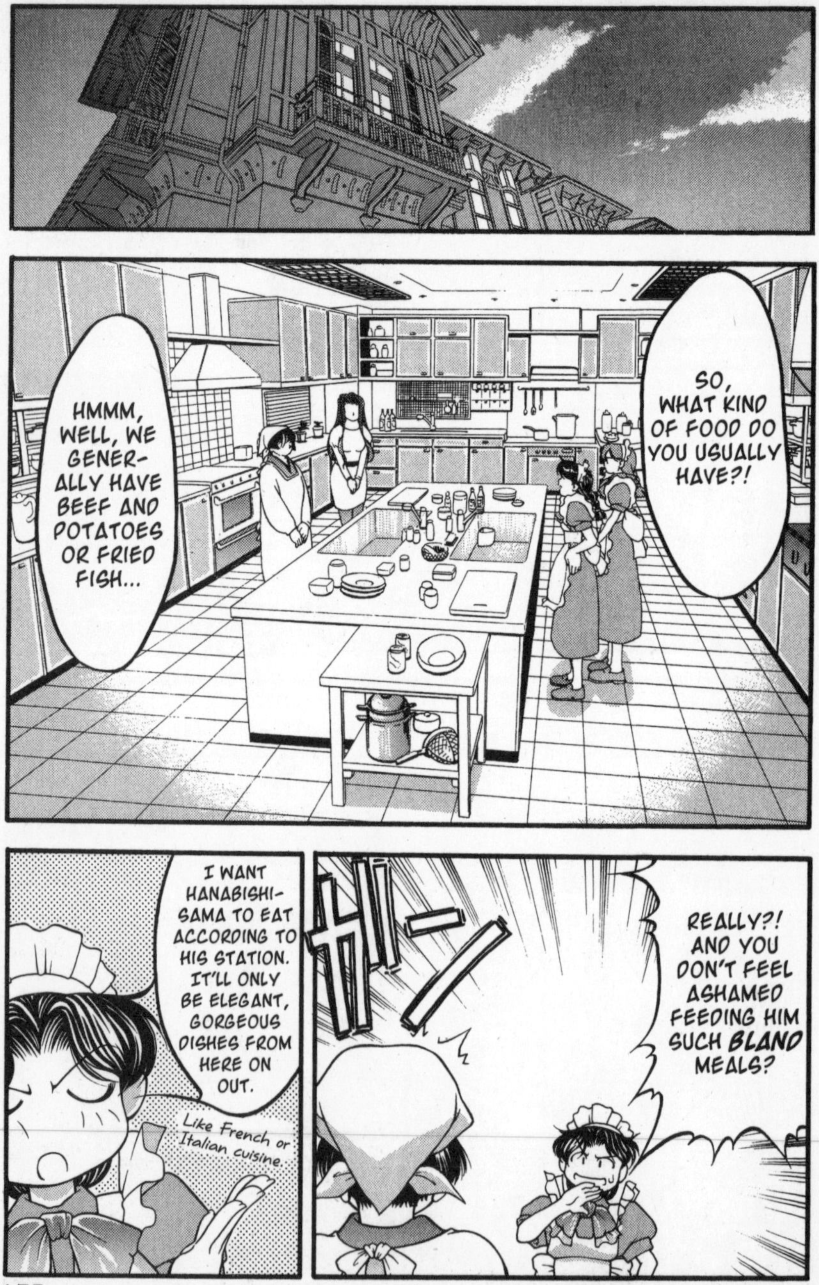
SO, WHAT KIND OF FOOD DO YOU USUALLY HAVE?!
HMMM, WELL, WE GENERALLY HAVE BEEF AND POTATOES OR FRIED FISH...
REALLY?! AND YOU DON'T FEEL ASHAMED FEEDING HIM SUCH *BLAND* MEALS?
ガーン
I WANT HANABISHI-SAMA TO EAT ACCORDING TO HIS STATION. IT'LL ONLY BE ELEGANT, GORGEOUS DISHES FROM HERE ON OUT.
Like French or Italian cuisine.

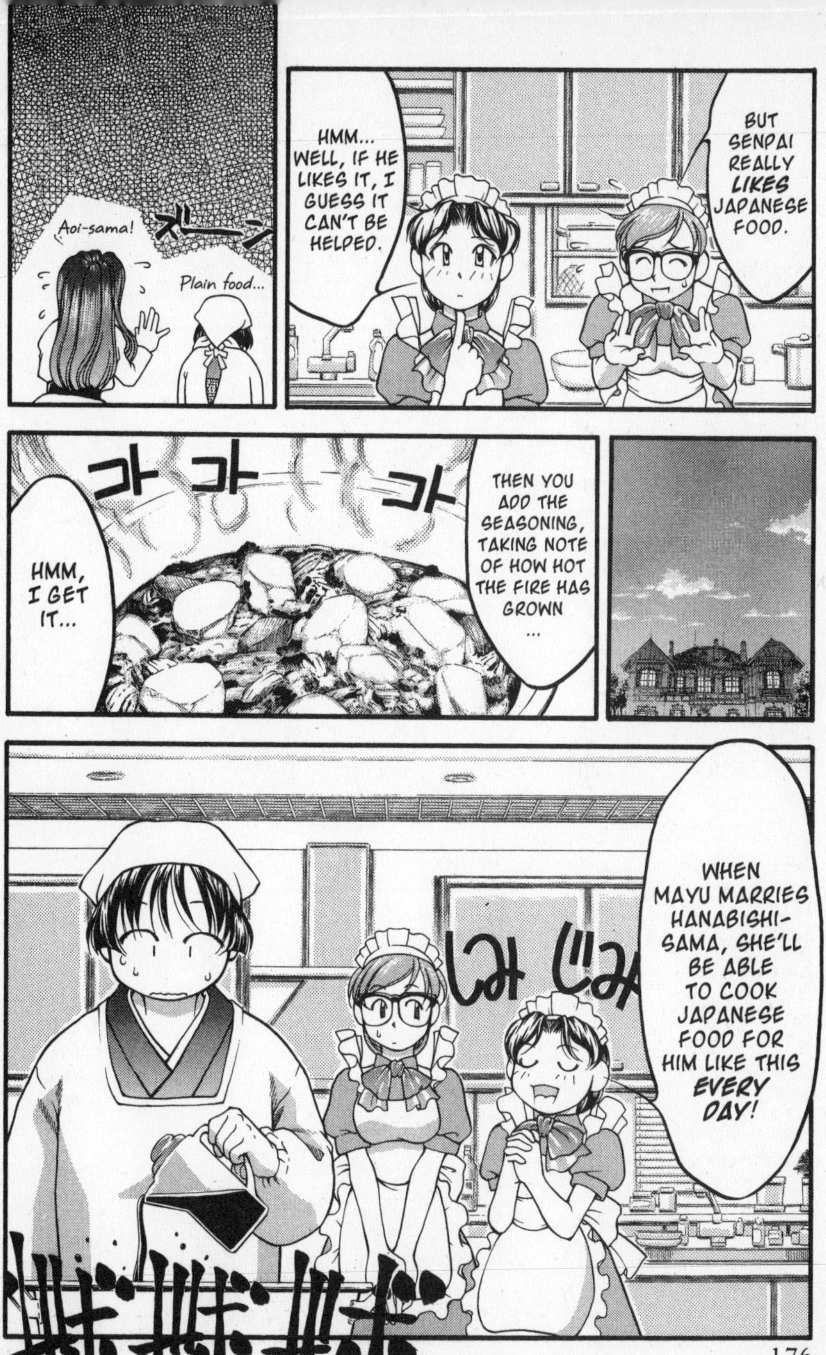
BUT SENPAI REALLY **LIKES** JAPANESE FOOD.
HMM... WELL, IF HE LIKES IT, I GUESS IT CAN'T BE HELPED.
Aoi-sama!
ズーン
Plain food...
コト コト コト
THEN YOU ADD THE SEASONING, TAKING NOTE OF HOW HOT THE FIRE HAS GROWN ...
HMM, I GET IT...
WHEN MAYU MARRIES HANABISHI-SAMA, SHE'LL BE ABLE TO COOK JAPANESE FOOD FOR HIM LIKE THIS **EVERY DAY**!
しみじみ

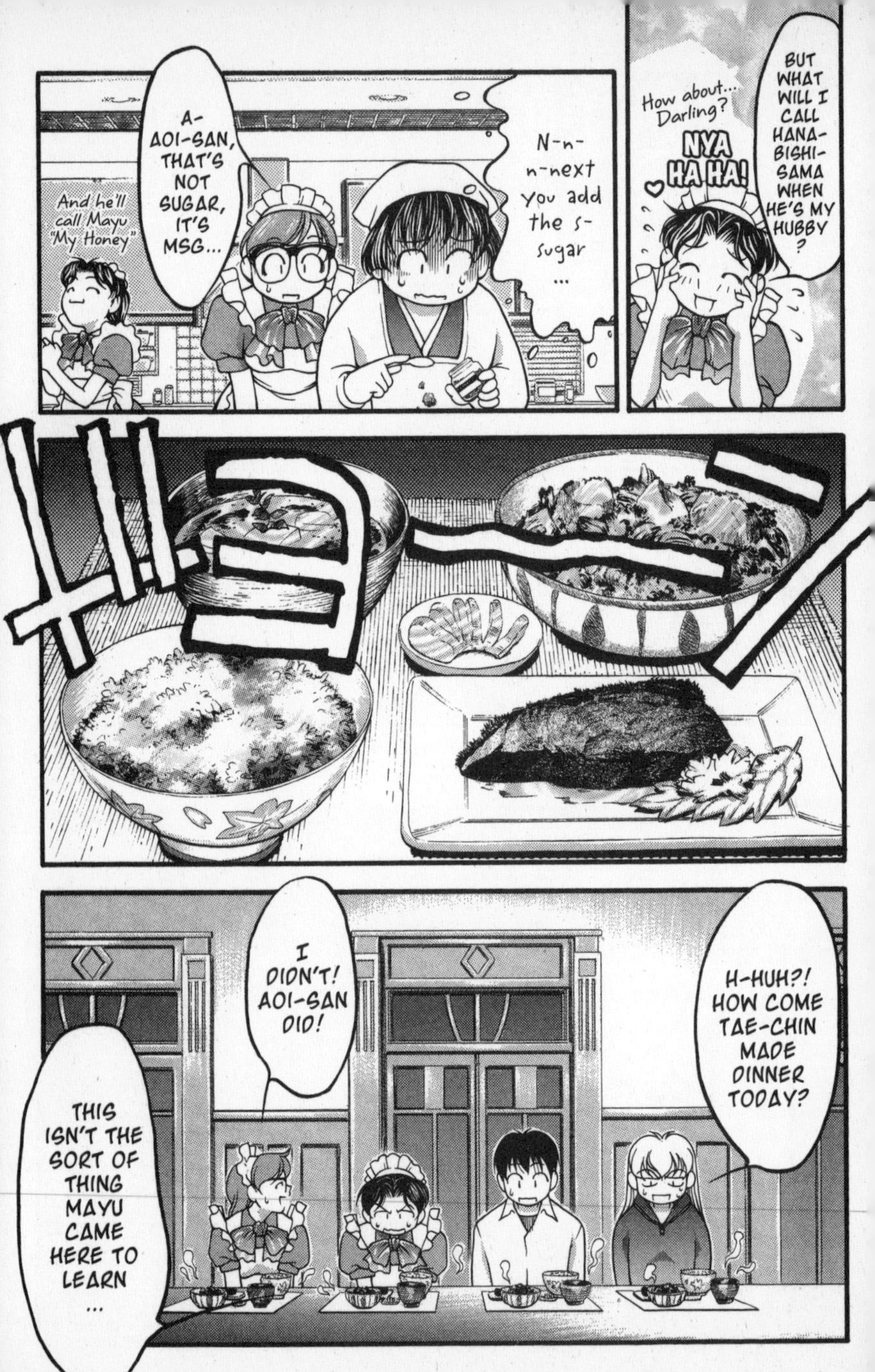
BUT WHAT WILL I CALL HANA-BISHI-SAMA WHEN HE'S MY HUBBY?
How about... Darling?
NYA HA HA!
N-n-n-next you add the s-sugar...
A-AOI-SAN, THAT'S NOT SUGAR, IT'S MSG...
And he'll call Mayu "My Honey"
H-HUH?! HOW COME TAE-CHIN MADE DINNER TODAY?
I DIDN'T! AOI-SAN DID!
THIS ISN'T THE SORT OF THING MAYU CAME HERE TO LEARN...

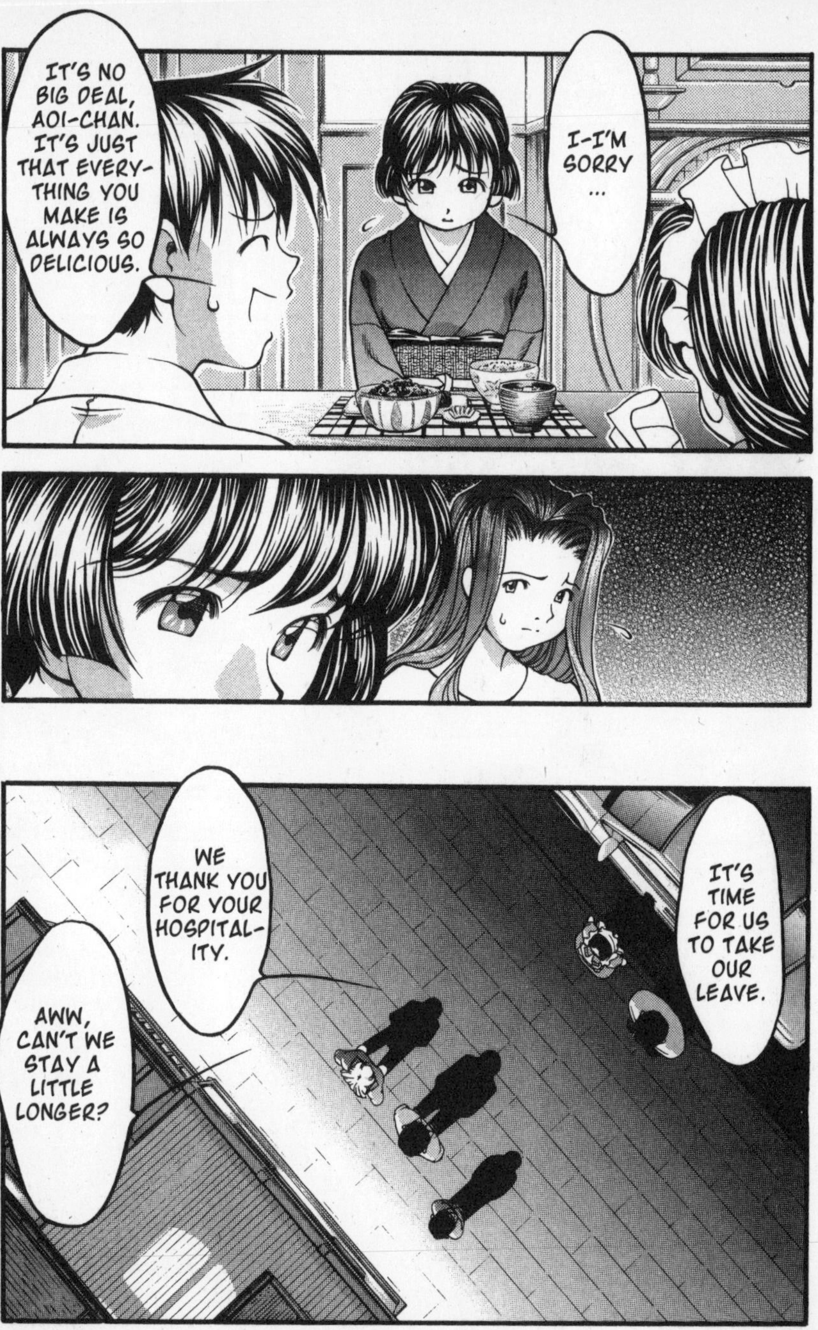
I-I'M SORRY ...
IT'S NO BIG DEAL, AOI-CHAN. IT'S JUST THAT EVERY-THING YOU MAKE IS ALWAYS SO DELICIOUS.
IT'S TIME FOR US TO TAKE OUR LEAVE.
WE THANK YOU FOR YOUR HOSPITAL-ITY.
AWW, CAN'T WE STAY A LITTLE LONGER?

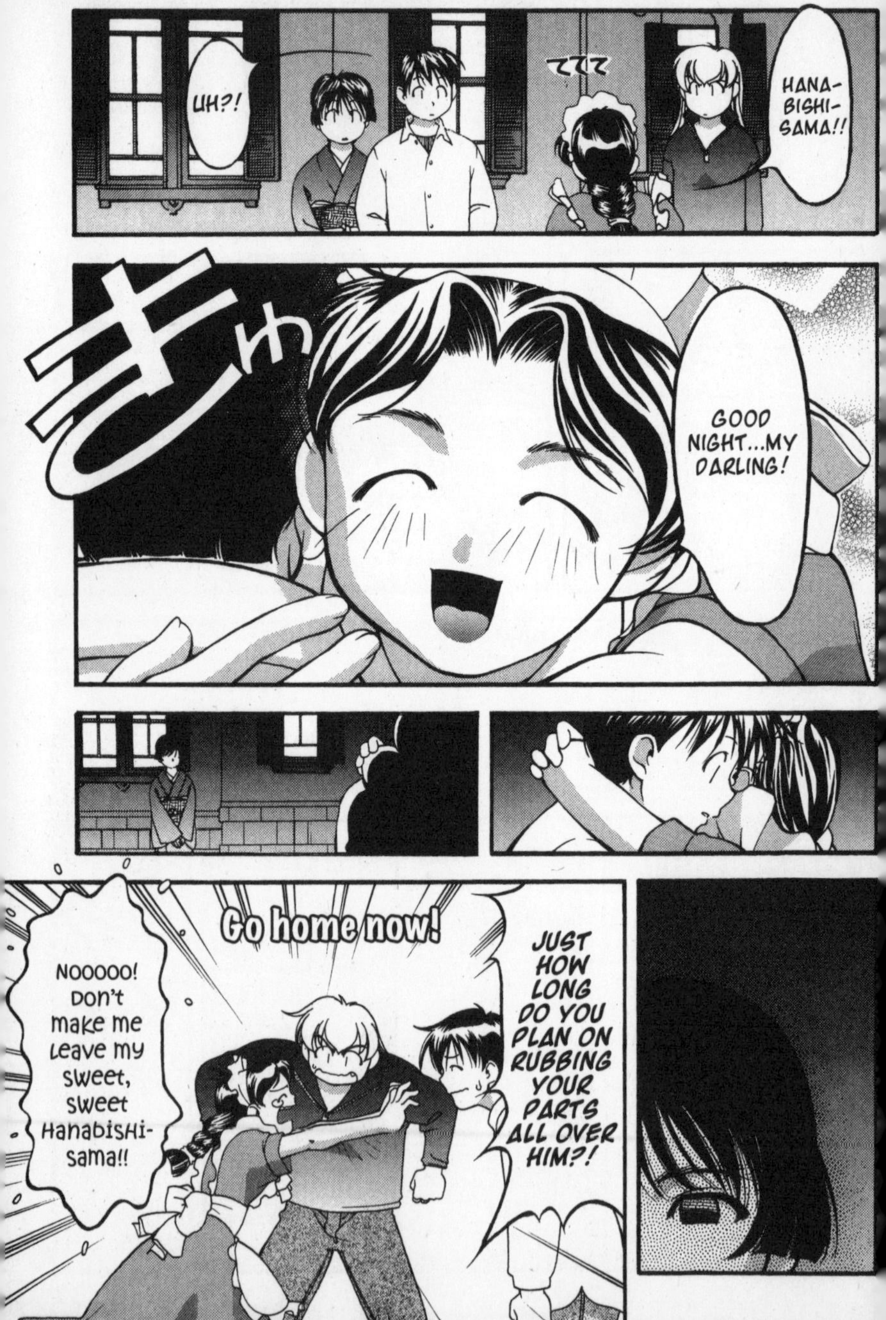
HANA-BISHI-SAMA!!
ててて
UH?!
GOOD NIGHT...MY DARLING!
きゅ
JUST HOW LONG DO YOU PLAN ON RUBBING YOUR PARTS ALL OVER HIM?!
Go home now!
NOOOOO! Don't make me leave my sweet, sweet Hanabishi-sama!!

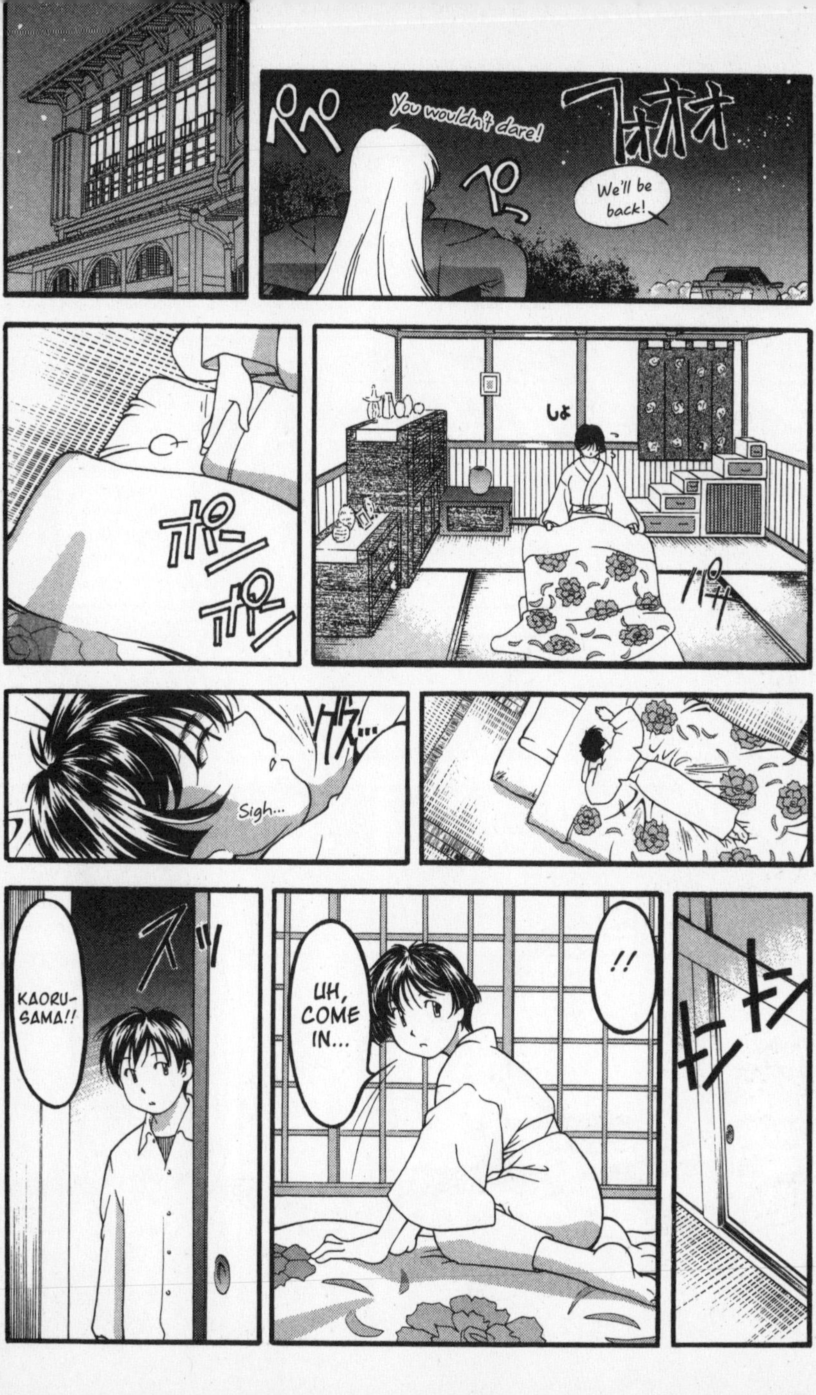
フォオオ
You wouldn't dare!
ペペ
We'll be back!
ペっ
しょ
パサ
ポーン
ポン
グズ…
Sigh...
トン
トン
!!
UH, COME IN...
スッ
KAORU-SAMA!!

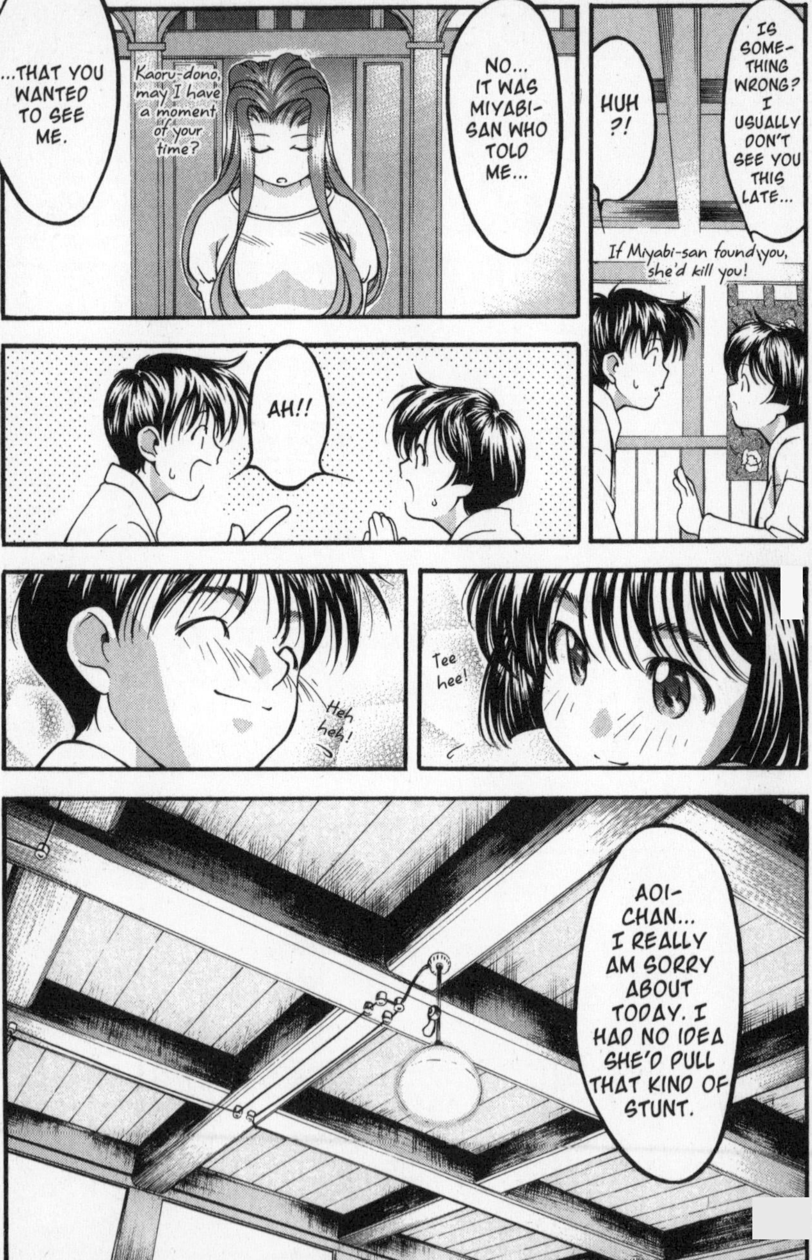
IS SOME-THING WRONG? I USUALLY DON'T SEE YOU THIS LATE...
HUH?!
If Miyabi-san found you, she'd kill you!
NO... IT WAS MIYABI-SAN WHO TOLD ME...
Kaoru-dono, may I have a moment of your time?
...THAT YOU WANTED TO SEE ME.
AH!!
Tee hee!
Heh heh!
AOI-CHAN... I REALLY AM SORRY ABOUT TODAY. I HAD NO IDEA SHE'D PULL THAT KIND OF STUNT.

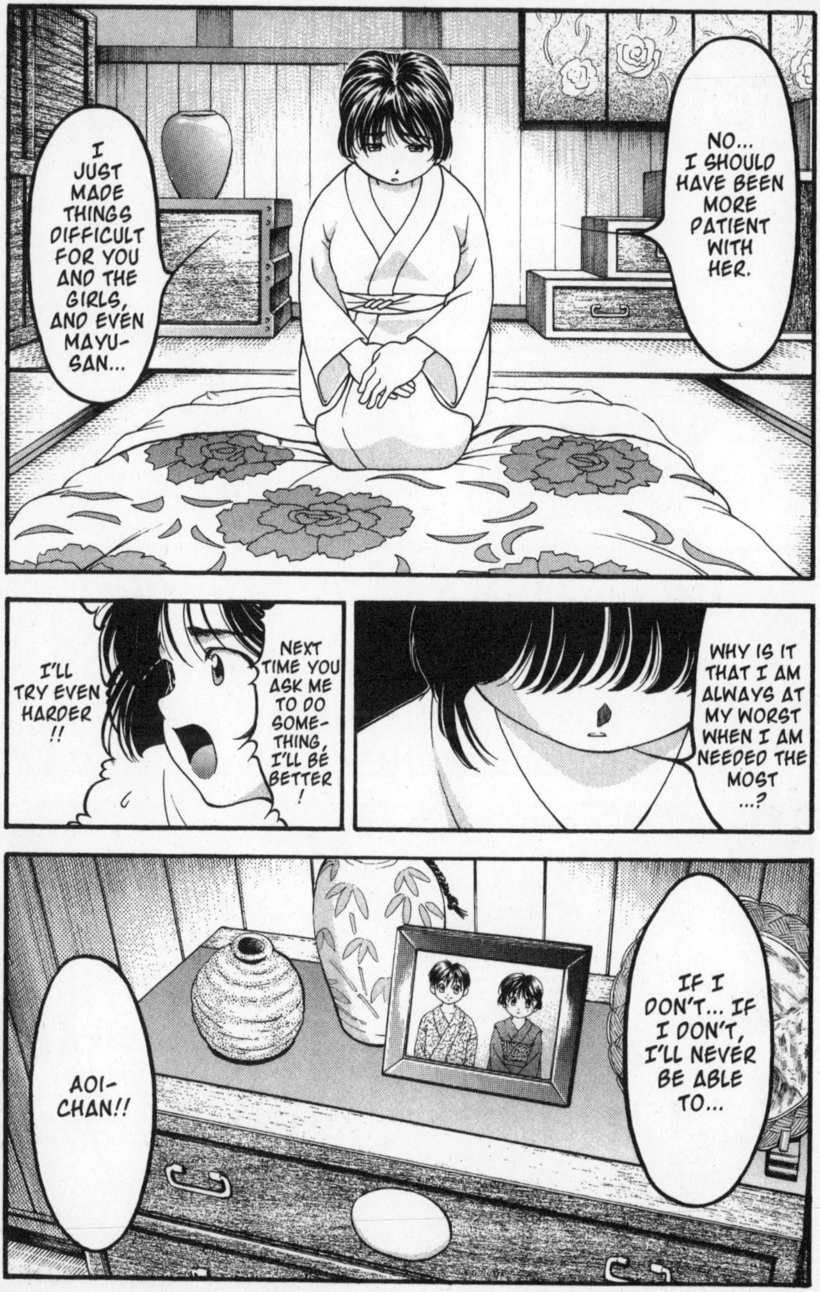
NO... I SHOULD HAVE BEEN MORE PATIENT WITH HER.
I JUST MADE THINGS DIFFICULT FOR YOU AND THE GIRLS, AND EVEN MAYU-SAN...
WHY IS IT THAT I AM ALWAYS AT MY WORST WHEN I AM NEEDED THE MOST ...?
NEXT TIME YOU ASK ME TO DO SOMETHING, I'LL BE BETTER!
I'LL TRY EVEN HARDER!!
IF I DON'T... IF I DON'T, I'LL NEVER BE ABLE TO...
AOI-CHAN!!

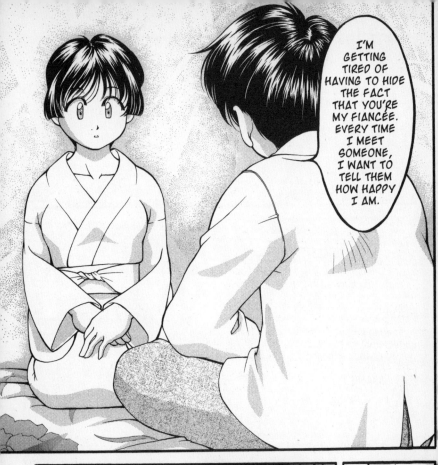

I'M GETTING TIRED OF HAVING TO HIDE THE FACT THAT YOU'RE MY FIANCÉE. EVERY TIME I MEET SOMEONE, I WANT TO TELL THEM HOW HAPPY I AM.

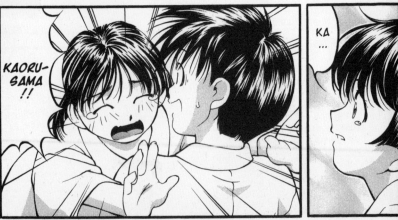

KAORU-SAMA!!

KA...

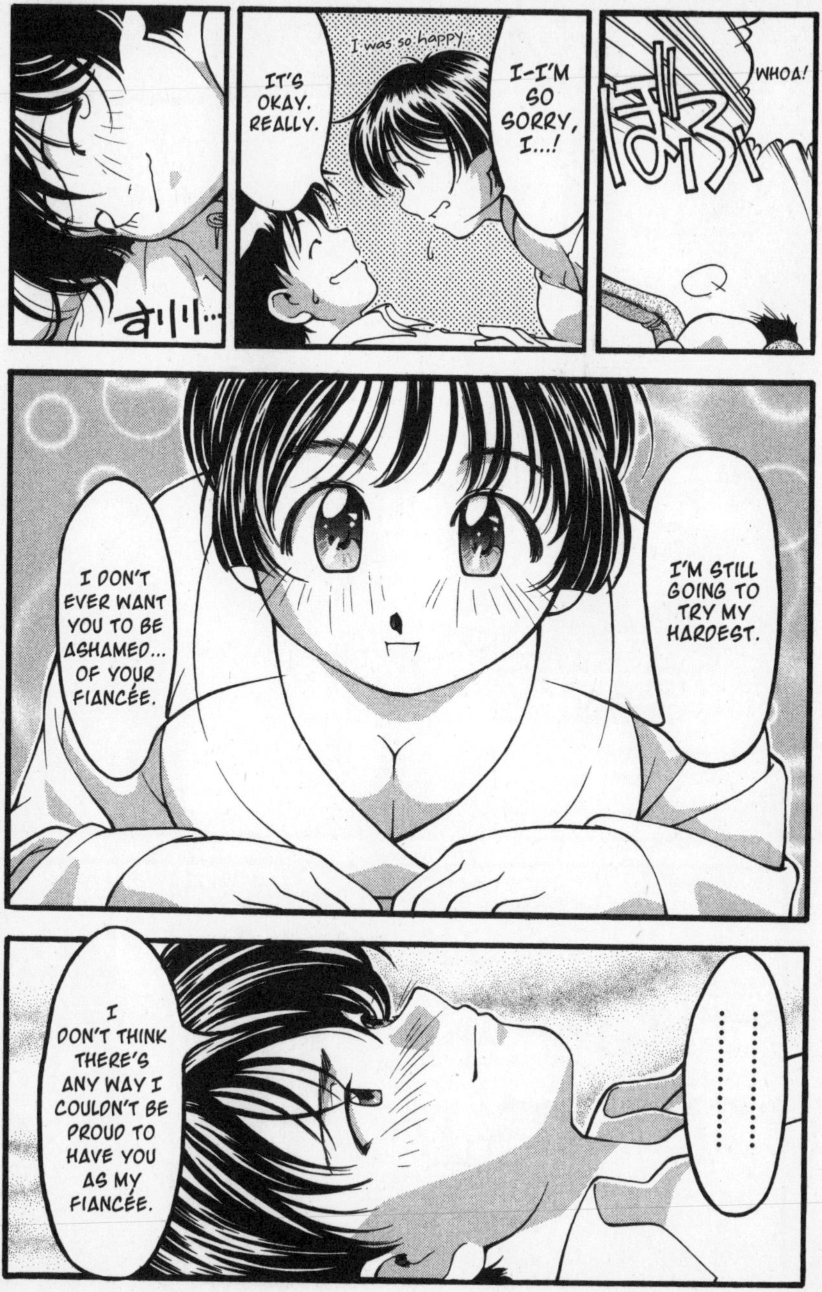
WHOA!
I-I'M SO SORRY, I...!
I was so happy...
IT'S OKAY. REALLY.
すりり…
I'M STILL GOING TO TRY MY HARDEST.
I DON'T EVER WANT YOU TO BE ASHAMED... OF YOUR FIANCÉE.
......
I DON'T THINK THERE'S ANY WAY I COULDN'T BE PROUD TO HAVE YOU AS MY FIANCÉE.

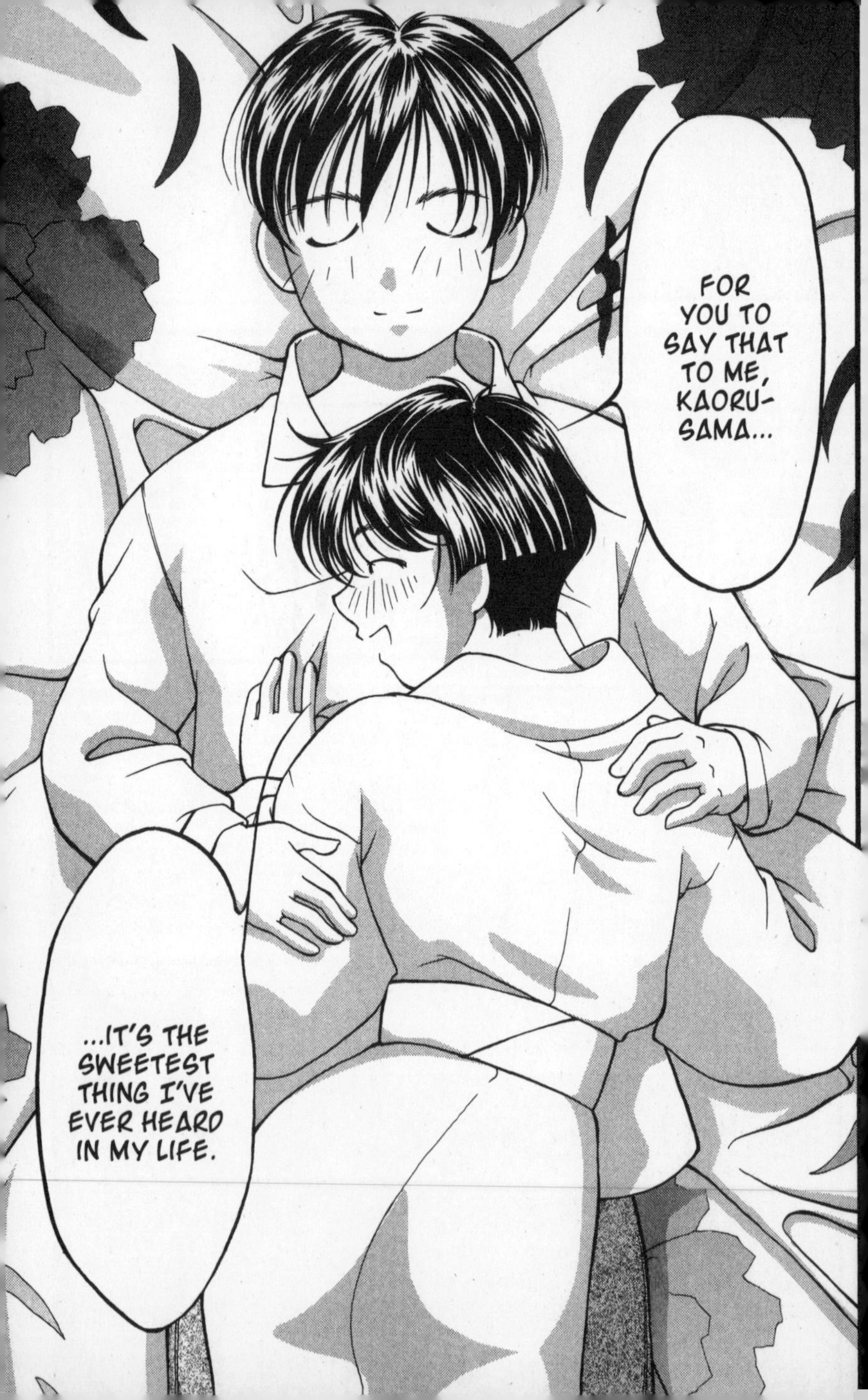
FOR YOU TO SAY THAT TO ME, KAORU-SAMA...
...IT'S THE SWEETEST THING I'VE EVER HEARD IN MY LIFE.

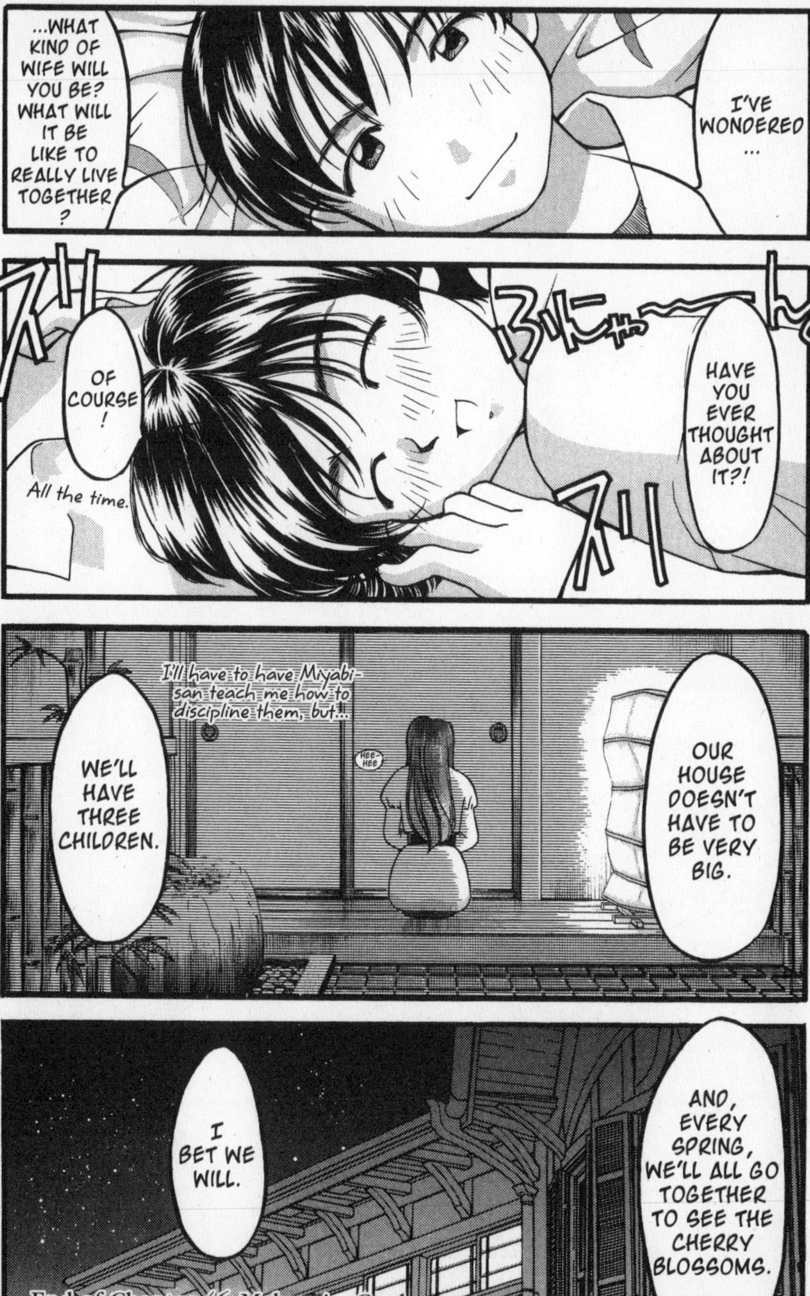
I'VE WONDERED ...
...WHAT KIND OF WIFE WILL YOU BE? WHAT WILL IT BE LIKE TO REALLY LIVE TOGETHER?
ふにゃ〜〜ん♡
HAVE YOU EVER THOUGHT ABOUT IT?!
スリ
スリ
OF COURSE!
All the time.
OUR HOUSE DOESN'T HAVE TO BE VERY BIG.
HEE-HEE
I'll have to have Miyabi-san teach me how to discipline them, but...
WE'LL HAVE THREE CHILDREN.
AND, EVERY SPRING, WE'LL ALL GO TOGETHER TO SEE THE CHERRY BLOSSOMS.
I BET WE WILL.
End of Chapter 46: Makanai—Cook

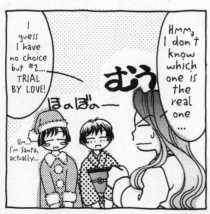

Ai-Ao Theatre, part 11

Big Hill Judgment

Hmm, I don't know which one is the real one...
むう
ほのぼのー
I guess I have no choice but #2... TRIAL BY LOVE!
Um... I'm Santa, actually...

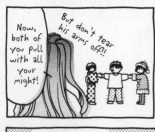

Now, both of you pull with all your might!
But don't tear his arms off!!
Oh, no! I'd feel too bad for Kaoru-sama. I can't tug on his arms like that!
Dang. No good, huh...?

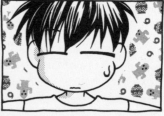

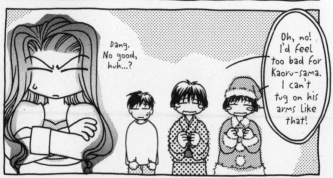

ASSIST

Etuko   Ichinohe
Hiroaki Satou

Hozumi

Kazuhiko Haru

THANKS

Mitukage Syoutengai

Miyuki   Nara

School Izumi

Tomohiro Horie

EDITOR

Syouichi Nakazawa
‹HAKUSENSHA›

PRODUCE

Kou Fumizuki
‹STUDIO LITTLE COTTON›

http://www.tim.hi-ho.ne.jp/fumifumi

NEXT TIME IN

藍(あい)より青(あお)し
AI YORI AOSHI™

The Sakuraba family has been against their engagement from the beginning, so when Aoi goes home to the family estate and doesn't come back, Kaoru fears the worst. Are Kaoru's nightmares coming true?

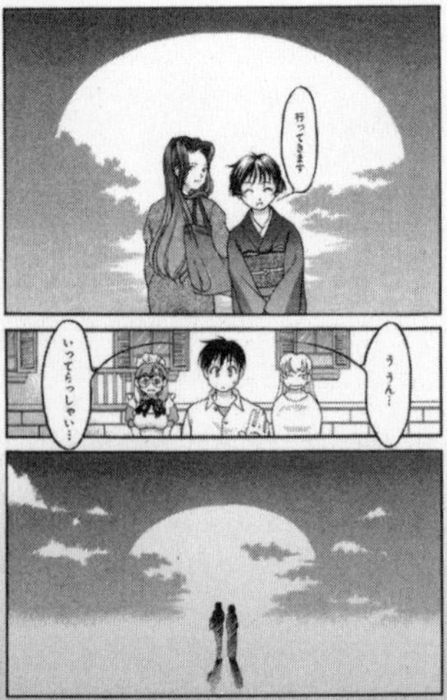

行ってきます
うん…
いってらっしゃい…

Ai Yori Aoshi Vol. 6—
Available November 2004

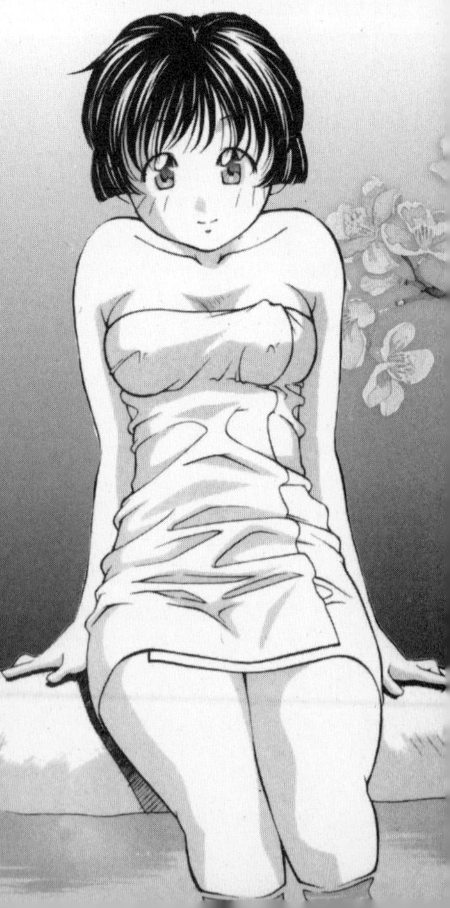

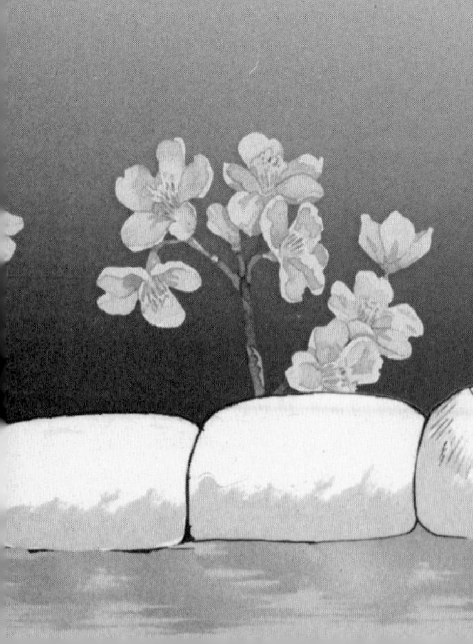

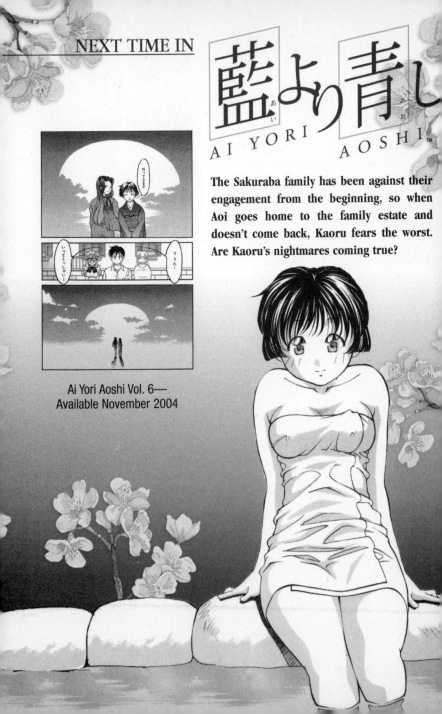

GLOSSARY

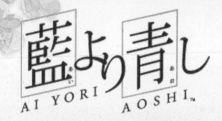

AI YORI AOSHI™

Love Hotels

In a country where space is hard to come by, with rice-paper walls and cramped living quarters, love hotels are an excellent source of escape for Japanese seeking private-time with their lover. And with 2 million patrons on any given day at Japan's 20,000 love hotels, the services these rooms offer are clearly in demand.

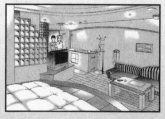

Though most love hotels are nothing more than a one-room apartment, some specialize in themes, ranging from a kid's playroom to Alcatraz prison. These themed hotels often feature showers resembling natural waterfalls or bath-tubs surrounded by underwater murals. These extra decorations help to build a romantic escapist feel for its lodgers, as well as a special treat. Sex-toy vending machines are also a common sight in love hotels, and when a television is available, porn channels are all that is shown.

Unlike other hotels, services are largely automated, allowing couples to choose the room of their liking from a colorful room menu complete with photo and prices, just like a vending machine. After pressing the button next to the photo, a key is handed over, with no awkward face-to-face time with a reception-ist, furthering the sense of privacy. Rooms are typically rented out for a short "rest" or a longer "stay."

Uzume

Uzume is the Shinto goddess of Joy, Happiness and Good Health. Her name means "whirling"—quite appropriate for a legendary dancer. The most famous legend surrounding Uzume is the one mentioned in this book. One day, the sun goddess Amaterasu became so disgusted by the behavior of her brother,

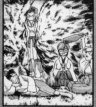

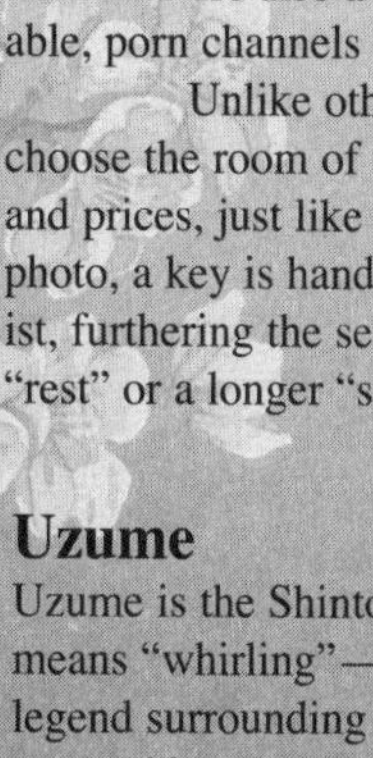

Susanoo-no-mikoto, that she hid herself in a cave, leaving the world in darkness. To lure her out, Uzume performed a dance outside the cave for the other gods, putting on such a wild and bawdy display that the other gods laughed uncon-trollably. Amaterasu came out to investigate the commotion, and with her emergence, light and life returned to the world. Uzume is the patron goddess of *Miko*, the priestesses who serve in Shinto temples to this day.

Koto

The Japanese Koto is a two-meter
long harp with 13 strings. When
playing it, a musician kneels on the
ground and plucks the strings with
ivory picks, or *tsume*. The koto is
incredibly difficult to play, requir-
ing years of study to even begin to
master it. In feudal Japan, the koto
was played by geisha or women of
the samurai class. Today, the koto

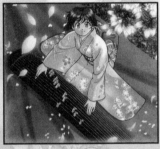

endures mostly as a relic of days past, and is commonly heard at
festivals or in traditional theater, although a few masters still breathe
new life into this ancient instrument.

Bento

Bento is the style of food preparation and presentation in which an
assortment of dishes is served in separate compartments of an elegant
box. Dishes typically include a combination of vegetable, meat and
rice items. As items are kept separate, tastes can range from vinegary
salads to salty fried items with no danger of mixing. Boxes are stackable for easy transport. Bento is most often served at lunch, so you can find

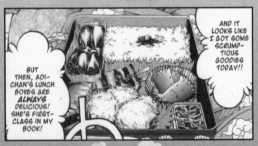

AND IT LOOKS LIKE I GOT SOME SCRUMPTIOUS GOODIES TODAY!!

BUT THEN, AOI-CHAN'S LUNCH BOXES ARE *ALWAYS* DELICIOUS! SHE'S FIRST-CLASS IN MY BOOK!

restaurants serving them near commuter trains and business districts
throughout Japan. And of course, they're great fun to make at home! If
you're interested in making your own bento, you can find bento boxes
at Asian restaurant supply stores and online. You don't have to make
traditional dishes—as Tina proves, even cocktail weenies can look
gourmet when served bento style!

RECOMMENDED READING

If you like Ai Yori Aoshi, check out these other hit manga from TOKYOPOP!

Chobits

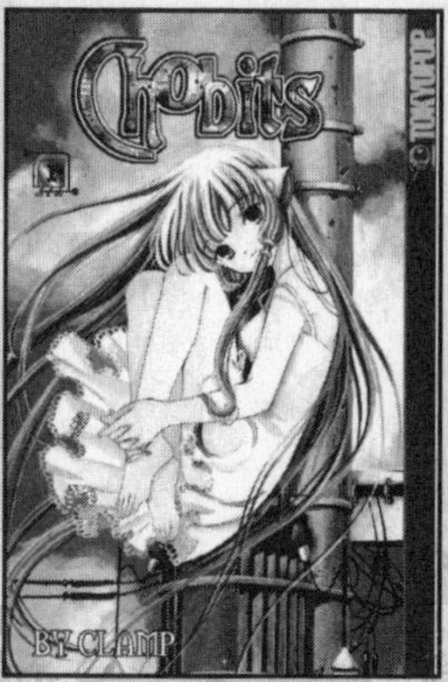
Chobits
BY CLAMP
TOKYOPOP
©2001 CLAMP, Kodansha

In the future boys will be boys and girls will be... robots? Well, technically they're persocoms—humanoid computers programmed to be the ultimate companions. 19-year-old Hideki never thought he could afford a persocom of his own, but one day he finds a strange (but cute!) model lying in the trash and takes her home. Her name is Chi, and her programming is different from any other 'coms out there—it's almost as if she has feelings! Created by CLAMP, the superstar studio that created *X*, *Cardcaptor Sakura* and *Rayearth*, Chobits quickly became the top-selling manga in the world. All eight volumes are now available in English, as is the complete anime series. Filled with equal parts comedy, romance, mystery and sex appeal, Chobits is series that will satisfy otaku of every ilk. If you haven't yet checked out this modern-day classic, now's the time to collect them all!

Samurai Deeper Kyo

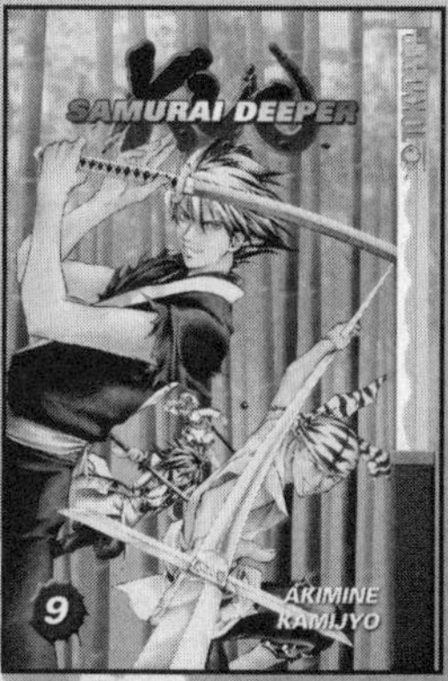
SAMURAI DEEPER
9
AKIMINE
KAMIJYO
TOKYOPOP
©2001 Akimine Kamijo

If intense action with larger-than-life heroes is your thing, you can't go wrong with *Samurai Deeper Kyo*. Set against the backdrop of Japan's Edo Era, Samurai Deeper is the story of two legendary swordsmen trapped in one body. At first, peaceful Kyoshiro keeps the savage Demon Eyes Kyo suppressed...at least until he draws his sword. But when the tables are turned and Kyo's spirit takes control, he sets forth on a quest to reclaim his body and kill Kyoshiro. History and legend collide as Kyo and his band of allies fight ninjas, demons and the shogun himself in the ultimate quest for power.

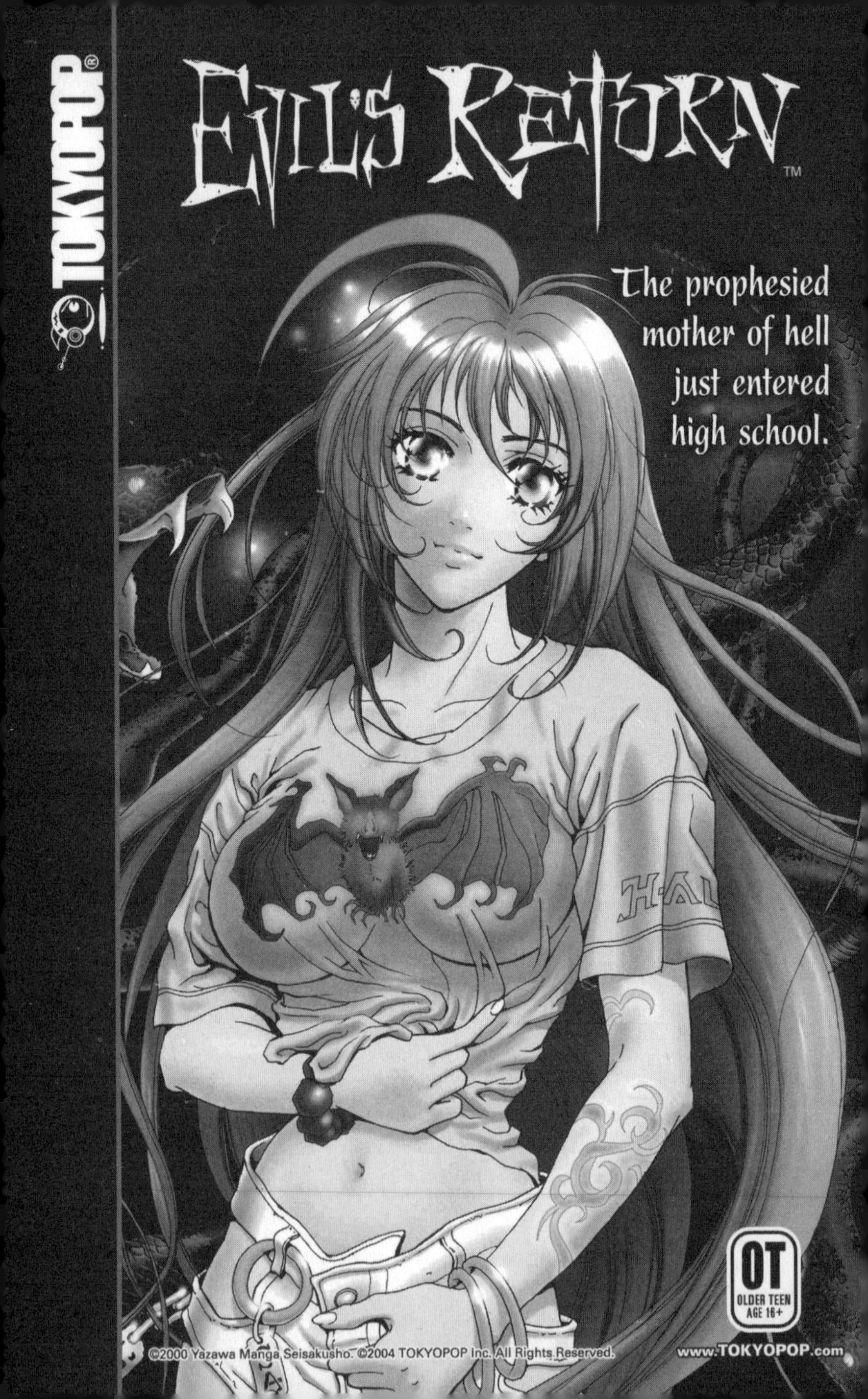
TOKYOPOP®
EVIL'S RETURN™
The prophesied mother of hell just entered high school.
OT OLDER TEEN AGE 16+
©2000 Yazawa Manga Seisakusho. ©2004 TOKYOPOP Inc. All Rights Reserved.
www.TOKYOPOP.com

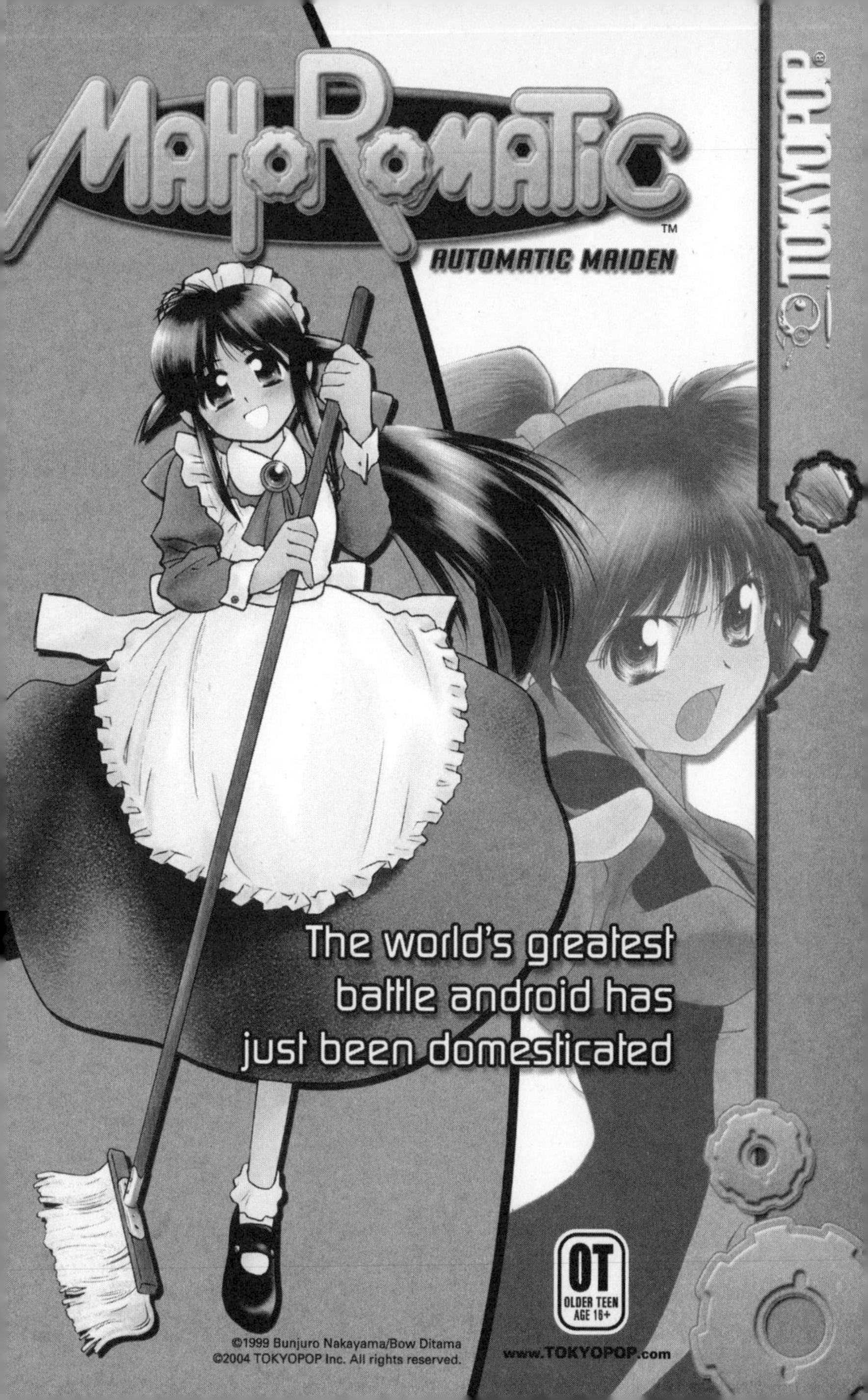
MAHOROMATIC™
AUTOMATIC MAIDEN
TOKYOPOP®
The world's greatest battle android has just been domesticated
OT OLDER TEEN AGE 16+
©1999 Bunjuro Nakayama/Bow Ditama
©2004 TOKYOPOP Inc. All rights reserved.
www.TOKYOPOP.com

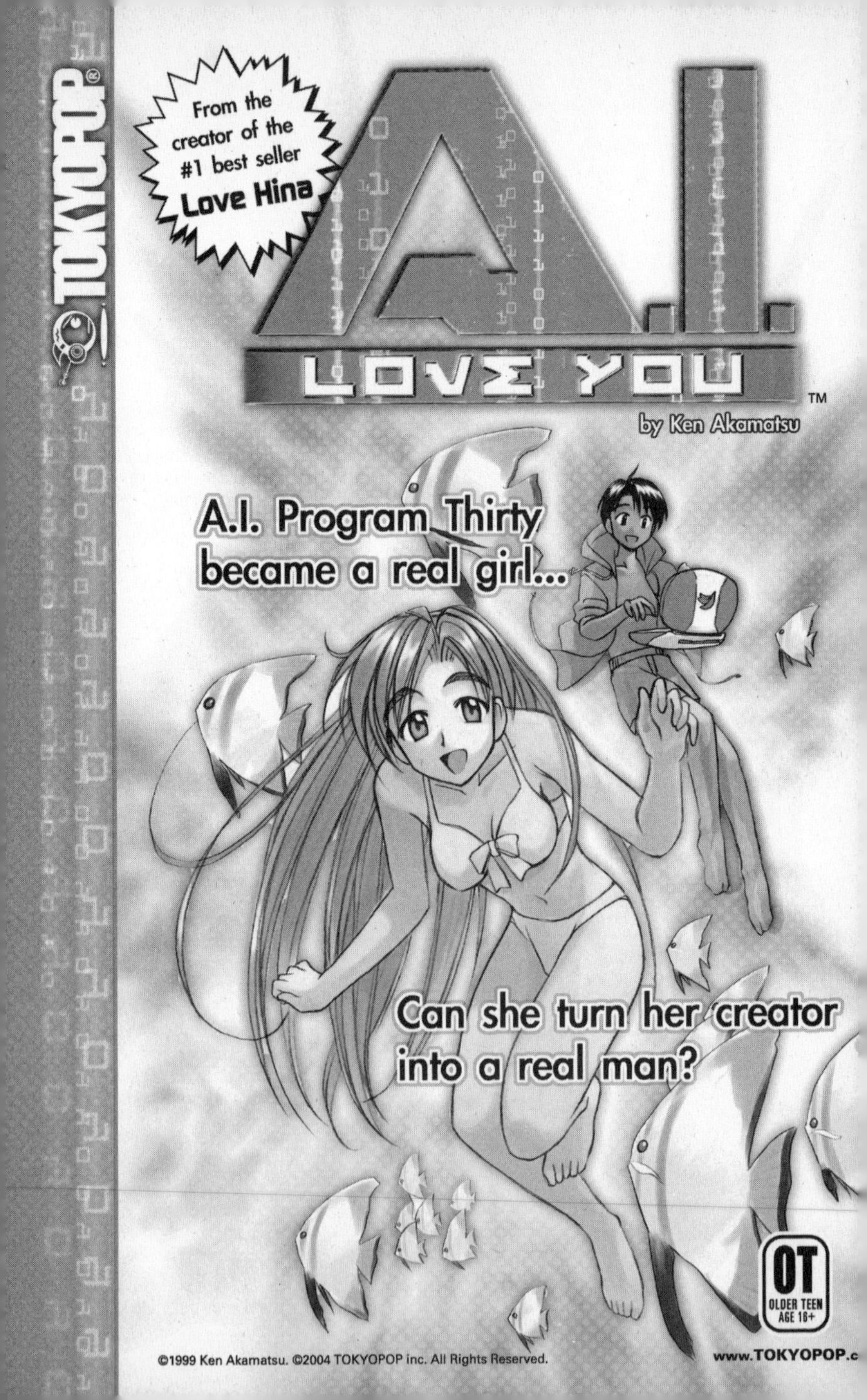
TOKYOPOP®
From the creator of the #1 best seller Love Hina
A.I. LOVE YOU™
by Ken Akamatsu
A.I. Program Thirty became a real girl...
Can she turn her creator into a real man?
OT OLDER TEEN AGE 16+
©1999 Ken Akamatsu. ©2004 TOKYOPOP inc. All Rights Reserved.
www.TOKYOPOP.c

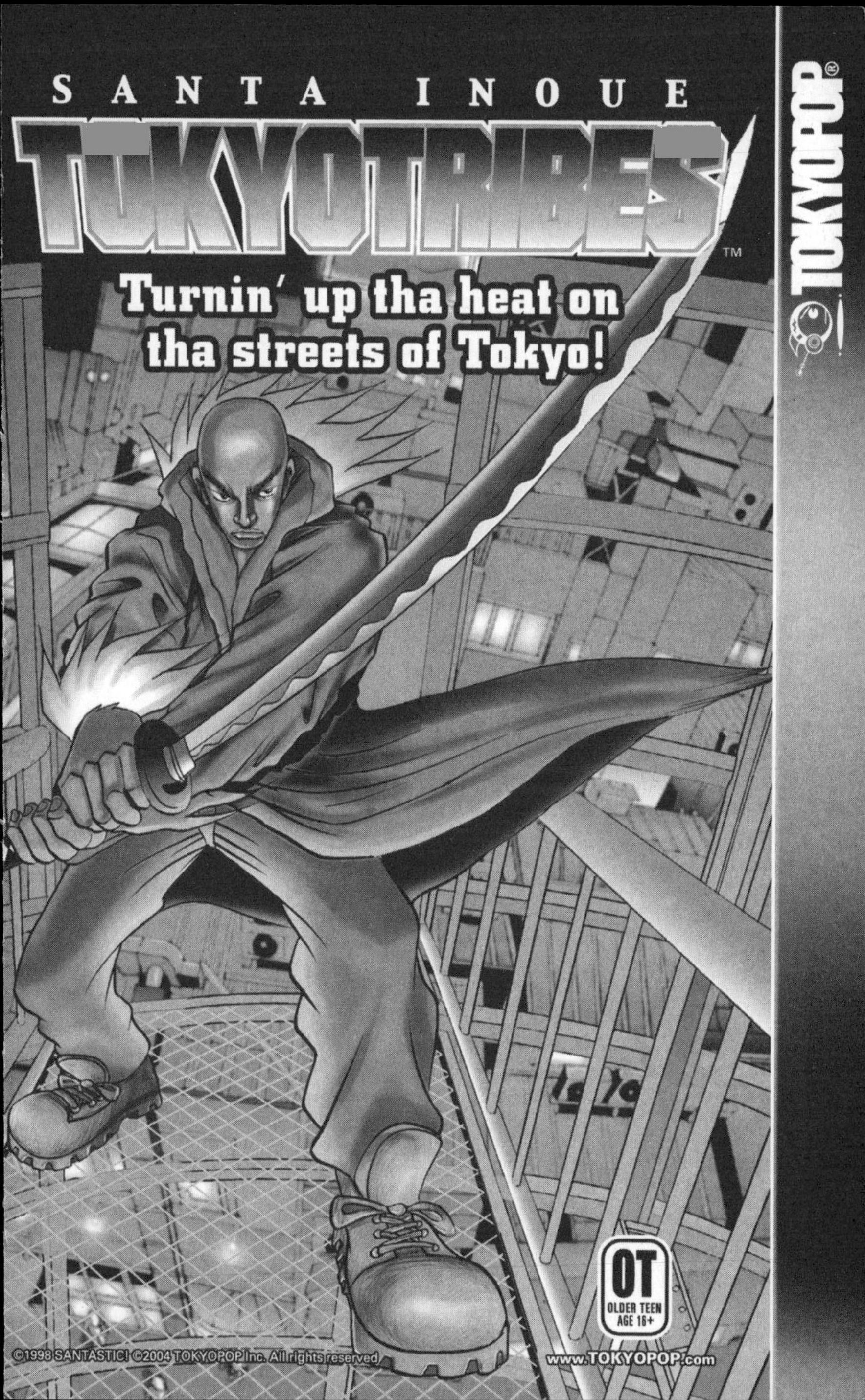
SANTA INOUE
TOKYO TRIBES
TM
Turnin' up tha heat on tha streets of Tokyo!
OT
OLDER TEEN
AGE 16+
©1998 SANTASTIC! ©2004 TOKYOPOP Inc. All rights reserved
www.TOKYOPOP.com
TOKYOPOP®

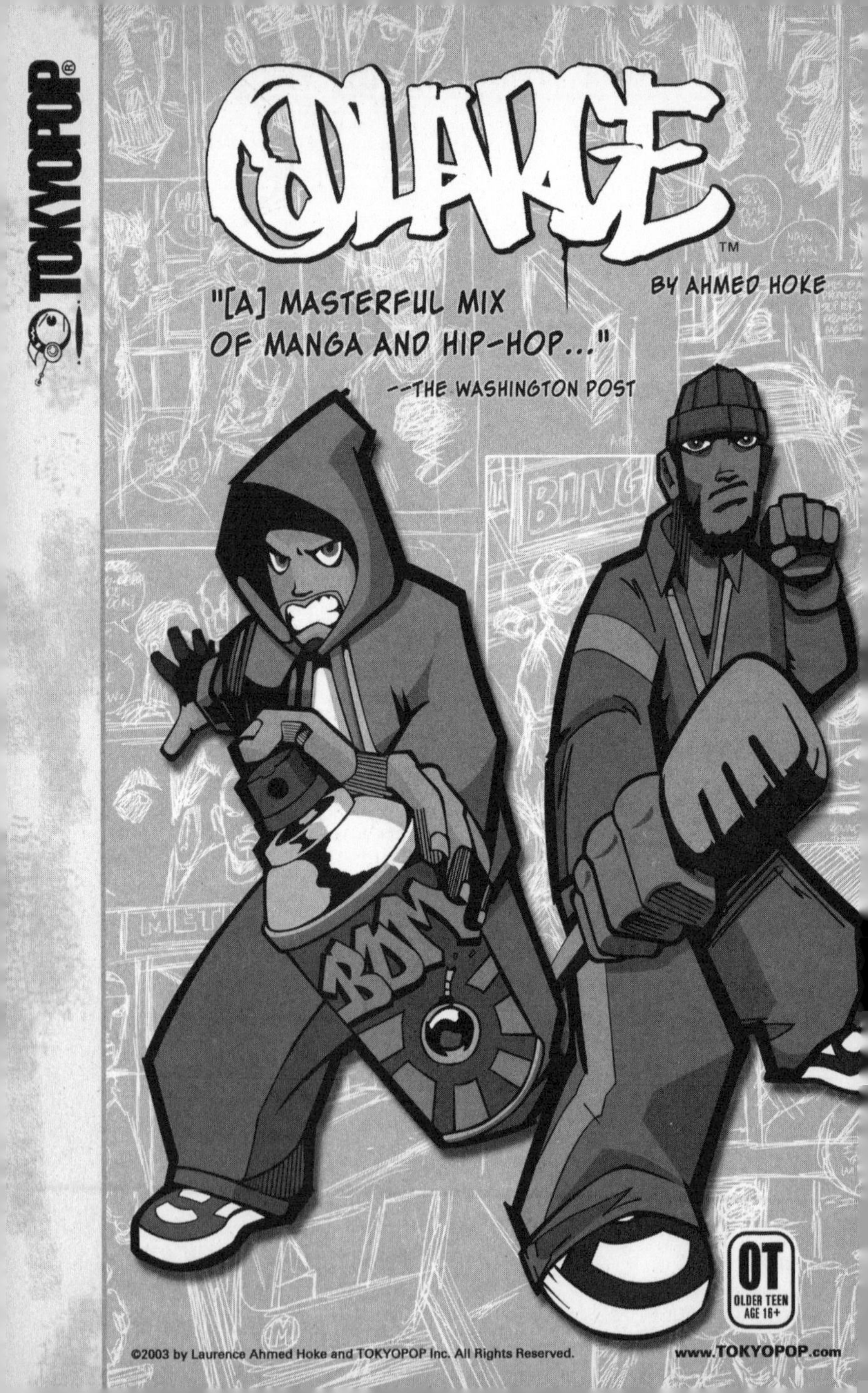
TOKYOPOP®
@LARGE™
BY AHMED HOKE
"[A] MASTERFUL MIX
OF MANGA AND HIP-HOP..."
--THE WASHINGTON POST
BING
OT
OLDER TEEN
AGE 16+
©2003 by Laurence Ahmed Hoke and TOKYOPOP Inc. All Rights Reserved.
www.TOKYOPOP.com

ALSO AVAILABLE FROM TOKYOPOP®

PET SHOP OF HORRORS
PITA-TEN
PLANET LADDER
PLANETES
PRIEST
PRINCESS AI
PSYCHIC ACADEMY
QUEEN'S KNIGHT, THE
RAGNAROK
RAVE MASTER
REALITY CHECK
REBIRTH
REBOUND
REMOTE
RISING STARS OF MANGA
SABER MARIONETTE J
SAILOR MOON
SAINT TAIL
SAIYUKI
SAMURAI DEEPER KYO
SAMURAI GIRL REAL BOUT HIGH SCHOOL
SCRYED
SEIKAI TRILOGY, THE
SGT. FROG
SHAOLIN SISTERS
SHIRAHIME-SYO: SNOW GODDESS TALES
SHUTTERBOX
SKULL MAN, THE
SNOW DROP
SORCERER HUNTERS
STONE
SUIKODEN III
SUKI
THREADS OF TIME
TOKYO BABYLON
TOKYO MEW MEW
TOKYO TRIBES
TRAMPS LIKE US
UNDER THE GLASS MOON
VAMPIRE GAME
VISION OF ESCAFLOWNE, THE
WARRIORS OF TAO
WILD ACT
WISH
WORLD OF HARTZ
X-DAY
ZODIAC P.I.

NOVELS

CLAMP SCHOOL PARANORMAL INVESTIGATORS
KARMA CLUB
SAILOR MOON
SLAYERS

ART BOOKS

ART OF CARDCAPTOR SAKURA
ART OF MAGIC KNIGHT RAYEARTH, THE
PEACH: MIWA UEDA ILLUSTRATIONS

ANIME GUIDES

COWBOY BEBOP
GUNDAM TECHNICAL MANUALS
SAILOR MOON SCOUT GUIDES

TOKYOPOP KIDS

STRAY SHEEP

CINE-MANGA™

ALADDIN
CARDCAPTORS
DUEL MASTERS
FAIRLY ODDPARENTS, THE
FAMILY GUY
FINDING NEMO
G.I. JOE SPY TROOPS
GREATEST STARS OF THE NBA
JACKIE CHAN ADVENTURES
JIMMY NEUTRON: BOY GENIUS, THE ADVENTURES OF
KIM POSSIBLE
LILO & STITCH: THE SERIES
LIZZIE MCGUIRE
LIZZIE MCGUIRE MOVIE, THE
MALCOLM IN THE MIDDLE
POWER RANGERS: DINO THUNDER
POWER RANGERS: NINJA STORM
PRINCESS DIARIES 2
RAVE MASTER
SHREK 2
SIMPLE LIFE, THE
SPONGEBOB SQUAREPANTS
SPY KIDS 2
SPY KIDS 3-D: GAME OVER
THAT'S SO RAVEN
TOTALLY SPIES
TRANSFORMERS: ARMADA
TRANSFORMERS: ENERGON
VAN HELSING

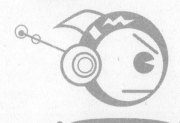

You want it? We got it!
A full range of TOKYOPOP
products are available now at:
www.TOKYOPOP.com/shop

05.26.04T

ALSO AVAILABLE FROM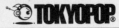

MANGA

.HACK//LEGEND OF THE TWILIGHT
@LARGE
ABENOBASHI: MAGICAL SHOPPING ARCADE
A.I. LOVE YOU
AI YORI AOSHI
ANGELIC LAYER
ARM OF KANNON
BABY BIRTH
BATTLE ROYALE
BATTLE VIXENS
BRAIN POWERED
BRIGADOON
B'TX
CANDIDATE FOR GODDESS, THE
CARDCAPTOR SAKURA
CARDCAPTOR SAKURA - MASTER OF THE CLOW
CHOBITS
CHRONICLES OF THE CURSED SWORD
CLAMP SCHOOL DETECTIVES
CLOVER
COMIC PARTY
CONFIDENTIAL CONFESSIONS
CORRECTOR YUI
COWBOY BEBOP
COWBOY BEBOP: SHOOTING STAR
CRAZY LOVE STORY
CRESCENT MOON
CROSS
CULDCEPT
CYBORG 009
D•N•ANGEL
DEMON DIARY
DEMON ORORON, THE
DEUS VITAE
DIABOLO
DIGIMON
DIGIMON TAMERS
DIGIMON ZERO TWO
DOLL
DRAGON HUNTER
DRAGON KNIGHTS
DRAGON VOICE
DREAM SAGA
DUKLYON: CLAMP SCHOOL DEFENDERS
EERIE QUEERIE!
ERICA SAKURAZAWA: COLLECTED WORKS
ET CETERA
ETERNITY
EVIL'S RETURN
FAERIES' LANDING
FAKE
FLCL
FLOWER OF THE DEEP SLEEP
FORBIDDEN DANCE
FRUITS BASKET
G GUNDAM

GATEKEEPERS
GETBACKERS
GIRL GOT GAME
GIRLS EDUCATIONAL CHARTER
GRAVITATION
GTO
GUNDAM BLUE DESTINY
GUNDAM SEED ASTRAY
GUNDAM WING
GUNDAM WING: BATTLEFIELD OF PACIFISTS
GUNDAM WING: ENDLESS WALTZ
GUNDAM WING: THE LAST OUTPOST (G-UNIT)
GUYS' GUIDE TO GIRLS
HANDS OFF!
HAPPY MANIA
HARLEM BEAT
HYPER RUNE
I.N.V.U.
IMMORTAL RAIN
INITIAL D
INSTANT TEEN: JUST ADD NUTS
ISLAND
JING: KING OF BANDITS
JING: KING OF BANDITS - TWILIGHT TALES
JULINE
KARE KANO
KILL ME, KISS ME
KINDAICHI CASE FILES, THE
KING OF HELL
KODOCHA: SANA'S STAGE
LAMENT OF THE LAMB
LEGAL DRUG
LEGEND OF CHUN HYANG, THE
LES BIJOUX
LOVE HINA
LUPIN III
LUPIN III: WORLD'S MOST WANTED
MAGIC KNIGHT RAYEARTH I
MAGIC KNIGHT RAYEARTH II
MAHOROMATIC: AUTOMATIC MAIDEN
MAN OF MANY FACES
MARMALADE BOY
MARS
MARS: HORSE WITH NO NAME
MINK
MIRACLE GIRLS
MIYUKI-CHAN IN WONDERLAND
MODEL
MOURYOU KIDEN
MY LOVE
NECK AND NECK
ONE
ONE I LOVE, THE
PARADISE KISS
PARASYTE
PASSION FRUIT
PEACH GIRL
PEACH GIRL: CHANGE OF HEART

05.26.04T

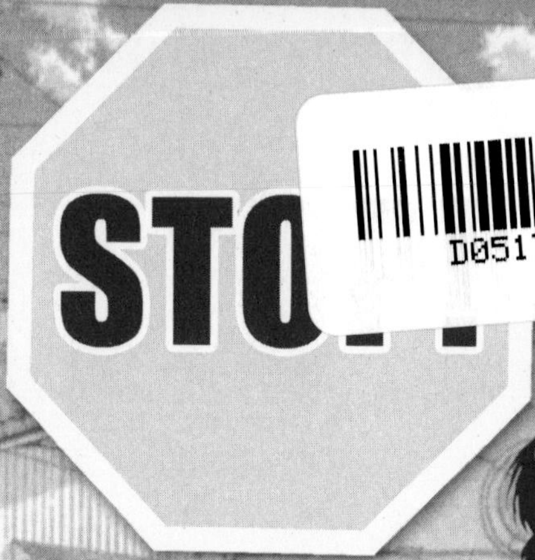
STO

Sumimasen! In your haste, you have opened to the back of the book. It would be most unfortunate if you were to start reading from this point. Perhaps you are new to TOKYOPOP's 100% authentic format? You see, in Japan, pages and panels read from right-to-left, and in respect for the manga-ka, TOKYOPOP keeps this format intact in its translated manga. At first it might feel bizarre reading like this, but we assure you that it will be second nature in no time! Please, so that you may properly enjoy this manga, turn the book over and begin reading from the other side. Arigatou gozaimasu!

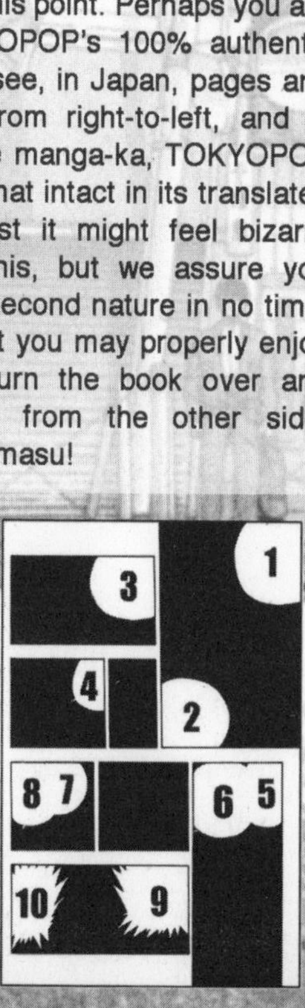
1
3
2
4
5
6
7
8
9
10

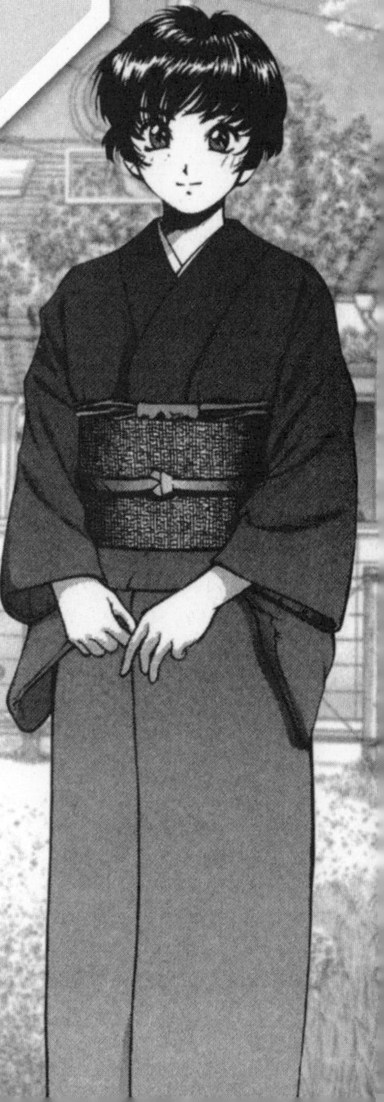

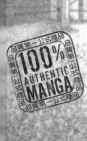